MID-VICTORIAN STUDIES

Geoffrey Tillotson and
Kathleen Tillotson

BLOOMSBURY ACADEMIC COLLECTIONS
English Literary Criticism – 18th–19th Centuries

BLOOMSBURY
NEW DELHI • LONDON • OXFORD • NEW YORK • SYDNEY

BLOOMSBURY INDIA
Bloomsbury Publishing India Pvt. Ltd
Second Floor, Building No. 4
DDA Complex LSC, Pocket C – 6 & 7
Vasant Kunj, New Delhi 110070
www.bloomsbury.com

BLOOMSBURY, Bloomsbury Academic India and the Diana logo are trademarks of Bloomsbury Publishing Plc

First published in India 2021
First published in 1965
This edition published in 2013 by Bloomsbury Publishing plc

This edition published with permission from Bloomsbury Publishing Plc, 50 Bedford Square, London, WC1B3DP, UK

British Library Cataloguing-in-Publication Data
A catalogue record for this book is available from the British Library.

Library of Congress Cataloging-in-Publication Data
A catalog record for this book is available from the Library of Congress

ISBN: 978-93-54351-86-0

For sale in the Indian subcontinent only

Digitally Printed and bound in India by Replika Press Pvt. Ltd.

MID-VICTORIAN STUDIES

Bloomsbury Academic Collections: English Literary Criticism

This carefully chosen selection of 56 classic works of literary criticism comes from the archives of Athlone Press, one of the most distinguished publishers of English criticism in the period 1950–2000.

The volumes in the collection cover all periods and styles of literary criticism, from Beowulf to Pinter, and include works of literary theory as well as studies of specific periods, writers or works. Authors include Herbert Grierson, Barbara Hardy, Christopher Norris, George Kane, EMW Tillyard, Patricia Ball, Geoffrey Tillotson, David Holbrook, and John Sutherland.

All titles are issued in cased bindings as complete facsimile editions; ebook versions are also available.

Titles in English Literary Criticism are available in the following subsets:

English Literary Criticism: General Theory and History
English Literary Criticism: Pre-1700
English Literary Criticism: 18th-19th Centuries
English Literary Criticism: 20th Century

Other titles available in English Literary Criticism: 18th–19th Centuries include:

Augustan Poetic Diction, Geoffrey Tillotson
Augustan Studies, Geoffrey Tillotson
Blake's Innocence and Experience Retraced, Stanley Gardner
Boswell and Johnson: Their Companions and Contemporaries, John Francis Waller
Criticism and the Nineteenth Century, Geoffrey Tillotson
Dickens and the City, F.S. Schwarzbach
Frail Vessels: Woman's Role in Women's Novels from Fanny Burney to George Eliot, Hazel Mews
Jane Austen and her Works, Sarah Tytler
Love, Mystery and Misery: Feeling in Gothic Fiction, Coral Ann Howells
Middlemarch: Critical Approaches to the Novel, Barbara Nathan Hardy
Protean Shape: A Study in Eighteenth-century Vocabulary and Usage, Susie L. Tucker
Sir Walter Scott: Landscape and Locality, James Reed
Thackeray at Work, John Sutherland
The Active Universe: Pantheism and the Concept of Imagination in the English Romantic Poets, H.W. Piper
The Book Beautiful: Walter Pater and the House of Macmillan, Edited by Robert M. Seiler
The Central Self: A Study in Romantic and Victorian Imagination, Patricia M. Ball
The Heart's Events: The Victorian Poetry of Relationships, Patricia M. Ball
The Novels of Thomas Hardy, Penelope Vigar
The Science of Aspects, Patricia M. Ball
Victorian Novelists and Publishers, John Sutherland

MID-VICTORIAN
STUDIES

Mid-Victorian Studies

by

GEOFFREY and KATHLEEN TILLOTSON

UNIVERSITY OF LONDON
THE ATHLONE PRESS
1965

Published by
THE ATHLONE PRESS
UNIVERSITY OF LONDON
at 2 Gower Street London WC1
Distributed by Constable & Co Ltd
12 Orange Street London WC2

Canada
Oxford University Press
Toronto

U.S.A.
Oxford University Press Inc
New York

Printed in Great Britain by
THE ALDEN PRESS LTD
OXFORD

To

GORDON HAIGHT

PREFACE

Our separate shares in this joint volume are easily discriminated. Though many of the pieces had the benefit of mutual advice and criticism, they were all written independently, and the responsibility is as indicated in the table of contents. There is a grain of truth, but no more, in the view of Middlemarch, which credited Fred Vincy and Mary with the authorship of each other's publications: 'Middlemarch had never been deceived, and there was no need to praise anyone for writing a book since it was always done by somebody else.'

The collection is various in origin, a few public lectures, broadcasts, and reviews being included as well as articles; but though the approach of both contributors is modified by the different occasions, it is essentially the same throughout, and can be defined by the words of Thackeray quoted on the final page. This was 'counsel' addressed to 'young hearers', but it is doubtless more congenial to middle age than to youth.

Another common concern of the authors is a related 'work in progress', the writing of the mid-nineteenth-century volume of the *Oxford History of English Literature*. The pieces in the present volume are in no sense samples of that history, but rather milestones, or halting-places, in the several ways that lead towards it.

This collection is representative of our published writings on the period (other than books and introductions to editions) in the last fifteen years, with one exception: articles on Dickens have been deliberately omitted as being connected with other projects and in any case not strictly 'mid-Victorian'. Harriett Mozley too is just outside that period, but her links with her brother John Henry Newman and her disciple Charlotte Yonge justify her inclusion.

Revision has been slight and has not often taken account of subsequently published criticism of the Victorians; but primary material since made available has been noted. This indeed has been the great contribution of the last decade or so to Victorian studies: the publication of great new editions, especially of letters—the letters of George Eliot, Clough,

Swinburne, and Newman. That contribution is recognized here by the inclusion of several reviews, and underlined in the case of George Eliot's letters, by the inclusion of more than one.

A word about our index of names. It does not include names occurring in quotations, nor in general names of editors, nor names used allusively.

Five items are printed here for the first time: 'Tennyson's Serial Poem' (the James Bryce Memorial Lecture delivered at Somerville College in May 1963), 'Writers and Readers in 1851' (a lecture in a series instituted by Bedford College in the centenary year of the Great Exhibition), 'Clough's *Bothie*', '*The Heir of Redclyffe*' (broadcast as a centenary tribute), 'The George Eliot Letters III' (broadcast on the completion of the edition in question).

For the rest, the following are the particulars of their earlier printing: 'The Tale and the Teller' (Rupert Hart-Davis, 1959), 'Novelists and Near-Novelists' (*Sewanee Review*, Autumn 1956), 'Harriett Mozley' (*Listener*, 31 July 1952), 'Trollope's Style' (*Forum*, Ball State Teachers College, Muncie, Indiana, Winter 1961–2), 'The George Eliot Letters I' (*Spectator*, 26 November 1954), 'The George Eliot Letters II' (*Sewanee Review*, Summer 1955), 'A Word for Browning' (*Sewanee Review*, Summer 1964), 'Clough: Thought and Action' (*Times Literary Supplement*, 6 December 1957), 'Matthew Arnold in Our Time' (*Spectator*, 2 April 1954), 'Yes: in the Sea of Life' (*Review of English Studies*, October 1952), 'Rugby 1850: Arnold, Clough, Walrond and *In Memoriam*' (*Review of English Studies*, April 1953), 'Arnold: The Lecturer and Journalist' (*Times Literary Supplement*, 16 September 1960), 'Swinburne' (*Times Literary Supplement*, 3 June 1960), 'Matthew Arnold and Carlyle' (Warton Lecture of the British Academy, 1956), 'Newman the Writer' (the Introduction to the Reynard Library *Newman*, 1957), 'Newman: Thought and Action' (*Times Literary Supplement*, 7 September 1956), 'Newman in his Letters' (*Times Literary Supplement*, 26 January 1962), 'Donne's Poetry in the Nineteenth Century' (contributed to *Elizabethan and Jacobean Studies presented to Frank Percy Wilson*, Clarendon Press, 1959),

'The Victorian Frame of Mind' (*Victorian Studies*, December 1957).

We are grateful to the editors and publishers who have kindly allowed the reprinting of these pieces.

London,
April 1965

G.T.
K.T.

CONTENTS

ABBREVIATIONS

Arnold, *Letters*	*Letters of Matthew Arnold 1844–88*, ed. G. W. E. Russell, 2 vols., 1895
Arnold, *Letters to Clough*	*Letters of Matthew Arnold to Arthur Hugh Clough*, ed. H. F. Lowry, 1932
Clough, *Correspondence*	*The Corrrespondence of Arthur Hugh Clough*, ed. Frederick L. Mulhauser, 2 vols., 1957
George Eliot Letters	*The George Eliot Letters 1836–1880*, ed. Gordon S. Haight, 7 vols., 1954–6
Newman, *Letters*	*Letters and Correspondence of John Henry Newman during his Life in the English Church*, ed. Anne Mozley, 2 vols., 1891
Tennyson, *Memoir*	*Alfred Lord Tennyson, a Memoir by his son*, 2 vols., 1897
Tinker and Lowry, *Commentary*	C. B. Tinker and H. F. Lowry, *The Poetry of Matthew Arnold: a Commentary*, 1940

I

THE TALE AND THE TELLER[1]

THE CHAIR to which I have the honour of being appointed was established recently enough for me to have known, in some measure, all four of its previous occupants—Caroline Spurgeon, Lascelles Abercrombie, F. P. Wilson, and Una Ellis-Fermor. Their names are known wherever English literature is studied, for each has given us a body of published writings, books that we all constantly recur to, indispensable, original, exhilarating. To define our debt to these distinguished teachers, I cannot do better than use borrowed words:

> The highest teaching can never be that of him whose chief business is to teach. Socrates, Plato, and Aristotle were resorted to, not because they had made teaching their business, but because they were believed to make philosophy their business. . . . He who learns from one occupied in learning, drinks of a running stream. He who learns from one who has learnt all he is to teach, drinks 'the green mantle of the stagnant pool'. To catch information is something; to catch the life and spirit of the pursuit and contemplation of truth, is infinitely more. . . . The existence of such men is communicative. Their manner of being leavens that which is around them.

It is pleasant to think that these were the words of the very first Professor of English who lectured at this College, the Rev. A. J. Scott—though he addressed them not to the Ladies' College in 1849 but to Owens College, Manchester, in 1851, when he became the first Principal; and incidentally also became Professor of English Literature, Professor of Comparative Grammar, and Professor of Logic and Mental Philosophy, simultaneously. Motives of economy doubtless operated, but there were giants in those days, and Professors of English in this College before there were University Chairs. To one or two of these early professors I propose to devote a few pages.

A. J. Scott was the first, and the first of our many helpers from University College. His inaugural lecture here in October

[1] An inaugural lecture given at Bedford College, University of London, 29 January 1959.

1849 survives, published in a little pamphlet called *Some Suggestions for Female Education*. Now, at that time, English Literature as a university study was a novelty, at least south of the Tweed (and unknown to Oxford and Cambridge, except of course for Anglo-Saxon, for nearly half a century more). This new study needed defence. Scott had already defended it in his inaugural address at University College in the previous year, called *On the Academical Study of a Vernacular Literature*. In addressing the Ladies' College, he wished especially to allay a natural alarm that the treasured relaxation of reading for pleasure might be encroached upon:

> Is the schoolmaster or the professor to hunt us boys and girls into the bedroom; take *Guy Mannering* or *David Copperfield* from under our own bolster, spread it open and transmute it, by a fearful alchemy, into a sermon . . . ? From such awful prospects may we be delivered!

One of his instances is very up to date: in October 1849, only six serial instalments of *David Copperfield* had as yet appeared. Perhaps too Professor Scott was answering Charles Kingsley, who in lecturing to Queen's College, Harley Street, the year before had said: 'I cannot see why we are to teach the young about the past and not about the present.' But Scott thought these were 'awful prospects'.

What then was the duty of the teacher of English? It was, he said, to reveal the underlying principles of literature; and to ensure that the language is understood. (He quotes Dr Johnson, who said he had met many ladies who knew Latin but very few who knew English.) These are still, I hope, among our endeavours: though we are not now so diffident about taking the book from under the bolster as our material—thankful indeed if it is anything as good as *Guy Mannering* or *David Copperfield*. (Scott did not foresee 'Modern Literature' as a special subject.) With the understanding of the language we are increasingly concerned, and our apparatus is far more elaborate; but I am interested to find that Scott's chosen example of unsuspected difficulty is the famous line about Chaucer's knight—'And though that he were worthy, he was wise'—which must have been taken hundreds of times since 1849 to make that very point.

A. J. Scott left us in 1851; we then had seven professors in as many years—but not from University College, where we were perhaps less popular after dismissing a Professor of Geography whose religious doctrine was thought unsound. The Ladies' College had not much to offer its teachers in the fifties, and was therefore fortunate in 1859 in being able to appoint a writer already becoming known for his poetry and fairy tales—George Macdonald. A. J. Scott had introduced him to old Crabb Robinson, who bustled about recommending him, and was soon writing in his diary, 'Mr Macdonald is actually elected . . . at the Ladies' College, a very poorly remunerated office, but he thinks it may lead to something better.' So thinking, Macdonald applied a few years later for the Chair at Edinburgh, with testimonials from Charles Kingsley, F. D. Maurice, and John Ruskin—which may have alarmed the electors, who appointed David Masson of University College. Macdonald resigned from the Ladies' College two years after, in protest against having his pupils tested by an outside examiner. But he must have found his eight years here quite stimulating, for in that time he wrote the first five of his many novels. From these novels we may learn something of his teaching, for he is fond of having a teacher among his characters. Here is one, from *Annals of a Quiet Neighbourhood.* The hero has undertaken to teach a village boy:

When Tom came, I asked him if he had read any of Wordsworth. For I always give people what I like myself, because that must be wherein I can best help them. He said he had not. I therefore chose one of Wordsworth's sonnets. . . . He did not understand it at first. . . . But I was delighted that Tom at least knew that he did not know. For that is the very next step to knowing. Indeed, it may be said to be a more valuable gift than the other, being of general application . . . I had always had an impulse to teach; not for the teaching's sake, for that, regarded as the attempt to fill skulls with knowledge, had always been to me a desolate dreariness; but the moment I saw a sign of hunger, an indication of readiness to receive, I was invariably seized with a kind of passion for giving. I now proceeded to explain the sonnet . . . Tom said: 'It is very strange, sir; but now that I have heard you say what the poem means, I feel as if I had known it all the time, though I could not say it.'

Here at least was no common mind. . . .

The methods of David Masson were less gentle. He had no inhibitions about filling skulls with knowledge; and one of his lectures at University College is alarmingly military in its imagery: what was wanted in the teaching of English, he said, was a kind of 'intellectual generalship', that will 'muster youth in front of the masses of literature' and 'drill them' and 'lead them on according to a plan, in regular order and column'. This, in his view, is what colleges are for: youths are 'detained' there 'for their own good' and 'obliged to be present so many hours a day . . . and hear lectures on various subjects deliberately read to them, whether they will or not'. That is how it was at University College and Edinburgh University. Long after, two of Masson's old students meeting by chance, one a man of thirty and one nearly seventy, compared notes of the lectures they had heard, some forty years apart; they found that these 'bore a striking resemblance'. So, as one of them has observed, 'by having a course of lectures that wore well . . . Masson had time for his work on Milton'. (But I do not, of course, hold that up as an example: nor yet Masson's other time-saving habit, noted by R. W. Chambers, of setting the same examination questions every year.)

Some sympathy, however, with that note of fierceness in Masson's attitude I do admit to—as well as with the gentle persuasiveness of George Macdonald. Such fierceness is not uncommon in the nineteenth century; we catch it also in Matthew Arnold: 'With the young reader . . . our great endeavour should be to bring him face to face with masterpieces and to hold him there . . .'; or again: 'Those who cannot read Greek should read only Milton and parts of Wordsworth: the state should see to it.'

That comes from a letter of Arnold's to Arthur Hugh Clough, who followed Scott and preceded Masson as Professor of English at University College—how nearly, then, we might have had him here; and we may gauge our loss, for though none of Clough's lectures survives, we know from Walter Bagehot the kind of tutor he was:

> Several survivors may think they owe much to Mr Clough's quiet question, 'Ah, then you think—?' Many pretending creeds, and many wonderful demonstrations, passed away before that calm

inquiry. He had a habit of putting your own doctrine concisely before you, so that you might see what it came to, and that you did not like it.

And from Clough's poems too we know something of his lifelong 'pursuit and contemplation of truth':

It fortifies my soul to know
That, though I perish, Truth is so.

Let us seek Knowledge;—the rest may come and go as it happens.

Knowledge is hard to seek, and harder yet to adhere to.
Knowledge is painful often; and yet when we know we are happy.

In mentioning Arnold and Clough I have passed from actual to potential Professors of English; Arnold indeed is a 'near-miss', for he was Professor of Poetry at Oxford, and the first to lecture in English (instead of in Latin), and occasionally even to talk about English and not only about classical or Hebrew poetry. Another whom we might claim is Carlyle, who did lecture on literature—English as well as German—and who even at one time wished to be a Professor of something, somewhere; he applied for Chairs at different universities in Moral Philosophy and Astronomy. (But it was perhaps a joke when Francis Jeffrey proposed that he should become Professor of Mysticism at the newly founded King's College.) Later, in 1841, he was offered the Chair of History at Edinburgh, but declined, and the only time he ever addressed a university audience was as Rector at Edinburgh in 1867. He would really have been best fitted as 'Professor of Things-in-General', like his own Teufelsdröckh.

But the great nineteenth-century writer who would surely have had most to give to a Department of English is Ruskin; who is responsible, for instance, for one of the best examples of what is now called 'practical criticism'—not, as commonly supposed, invented in 1928. Addressing an audience of young women in 1865, in the lectures we know as *Sesame and Lilies*, Ruskin quoted some twenty lines from 'Lycidas'—'let us think over this passage and examine its words'. For five pages, he does just that, and concludes (this again is rather fierce in tone):

We have got something out of the lines, I think, and much more is yet to be found in them; but we have done enough by way of example of the kind of word-by-word examination of your author which is rightly called 'reading'; watching every accent and expression, and putting ourselves always in the author's place, annihilating our own personality, and seeking to enter into his, so as to be able assuredly to say, 'Thus Milton thought', not 'Thus *I* thought, in mis-reading Milton'. And by this process you will gradually come to attach less weight to your own 'Thus I thought' at other times. You will begin to perceive that what *you* thought was a matter of no serious importance;—that your thoughts on any subject are not perhaps the clearest and wisest that could be arrived at thereupon: —in fact, that unless you are a very singular person, you cannot be said to have any 'thoughts' at all; that you have no materials for them, in any serious matters;—no right to 'think', but only to learn more of the facts.

I need not labour the relevance of these words for us all.

But perhaps the most salutary reminder for the teacher of English is a remark of Henry Sidgwick, the Cambridge philosopher: 'One great advantage of literature as an instrument of education is that it supplements a teacher's defects so much.' From this I draw some encouragement as I turn to my main theme.

I have called this lecture 'The Tale and the Teller'; what I am going to consider is a certain mode of narrative which has in this century fallen out of use. It belongs to narrative generally, but my illustrations will be taken mainly from nineteenth-century novels (on George Macdonald's principle, 'I always give people what I like myself'). You will see that this justifies the imputation of A. J. Scott—'Is the schoolmaster or the professor to take *Guy Mannering* or *David Copperfield* from under our own bolster?' That *is* rather the general idea.

The mode I speak of has, I say, fallen out of use, as I can quickly show by noting something that is lacking in nearly all modern novels. One character is missing: the narrator in person. There is no one there who stands outside the story and says 'I', who explains how he knows what he is telling us, who addresses the reader, who discourses, confides, cajoles, and exhorts. We are unbidden guests, there is no welcome, no hospitality—the social context embracing us as readers has gone. I speak in terms of the loss; the average reader is probably not aware of it, for behind this rejection of the teller there lies, I believe, the unconscious assumption of our time that drama is the dominant form, other modes aspiring towards its condition, whereby narrative as such loses its status. When the critic objects that the author's voice 'destroys the illusion', it is surely dramatic rather than narrative illusion that he has in mind; in narrative illusion, the teller has a rightful place. We have forgotten this place, because we have forgotten or lost the oral tradition that accompanied story-telling for so many centuries—the tradition of bard and minstrel, of Chaucer reciting his poems to the court; of reading novels aloud, to groups or individuals.

As I said, I am speaking in terms of loss; but most readers who are in a position to compare present novels with past seem to feel the change a clear gain. E. M. Forster expressed a common view when he said twenty years ago that for an author to take the reader into his confidence about the characters 'is devastating, it is bar-parlour chattiness, and nothing has been more harmful to the novels of the past.' There have been few apologists for the practice, since the American critic W. C. Brownell asked the pointed question, *à propos* of Thackeray: 'Can the reader do all this for himself? If he can, and can do it as well as Thackeray does for him, he may consider it surplusage.' That challenge has not been met.

Nowadays, the narrator who confides in his readers is referred to as the 'intrusive author'—at least he is regarded as intrusive in novels; we seem to allow more latitude to narrative poets, and no one has been purist enough to call Byron 'intrusive' in *Don Juan*. But in novels, we say that we prefer to be left alone, not 'told what to think'. This is very simple-minded; we are being directed all the while, by selection and emphasis and tone. Technically 'invisible', the author remains as a subliminal advertiser, a hidden persuader.

Often, of course, the author has set so individual a stamp upon every sentence of his work—like Carlyle's letters, they have 'the writer's signature in every word, not only at the end'—that his visible presence would be superfluous. A novel by, say, the later Henry James, or Virginia Woolf, or Ivy Compton-Burnett, or Elizabeth Bowen, is as completely that author's and no other's as any of Thackeray's or George Eliot's, and is in no way impoverished by the lack of explicit commentary. But in other novels the loss is patent; and in some lesser ones we can clearly see the first-person narrator misused, or the ejected author-narrator returning in disguise as a character transparently representative of the author (usually a clever young man or a wise old woman, sometimes a psychiatrist), who observes and reflects upon the action: the semi-omniscience and mock modesty of such personages are irritating, and they would do better if allowed to be frankly author-narrators. And, what here concerns me more, the modern disuse of this method obstructs our appreciation and understanding of earlier novels; as Forster's comment shows: 'nothing has been more harmful to the novels of the past'. Most novel-criticism now takes its criteria from the later Henry James, applying what might be called late Jacobean standards to Victorian and eighteenth-century novelists. We need to try and discern more clearly just what has been rejected—not a primitive, inartistic, clumsy device which the novel has outgrown; not an overflow of egoism and self-revelation, not 'bar-parlour chattiness', but a *method*, calling for great skill; one of the more delicate tools of narrative art.

To illustrate its possibilities I shall begin with a novelist whose use of it is sparing and discriminating, and whose novels have never been stigmatized as 'large loose baggy monsters' or 'fluid puddings' (as the later Henry James called the novels of Thackeray, Dostoievsky, and Tolstoy), but which have, on the contrary, been described as 'unlike most English novels in resembling the vase rather than the washtub'—I mean Jane Austen. She seldom speaks at large in her own person, preferring the *nuance* of an epithet ('poor Catherine') or a half-playful, half-pitying comment ('And lucky may she think herself, if she get another good night's rest in the course of the next three months'); though even this is much more than a modern novelist is allowed. So, when she does openly 'intrude' we tend either to pass over it indulgently, or else to give the statement the kind of weight it might have in a preface. A leading example is the opening of the final chapter of *Mansfield Park*:

> Let other pens dwell on guilt and misery. I quit such odious subjects as soon as I can, impatient to restore everybody not greatly in fault themselves to tolerable comfort, and to have done with all the rest.

This is sometimes taken as a kind of manifesto, a declaration of the limits within which Jane Austen chooses to move. But as such, in that context, it is simply not true. She *has* been dwelling on 'guilt and misery' and will do so again in this very chapter. Fanny, exiled at Portsmouth, had heard the news of the elopement of Henry Crawford and Mrs Rushworth with 'stupefaction' and 'horror', and had lain awake all night shuddering, thinking of the betrayal—

> the whole family, both families connected as they were, tie upon tie, all friends, all intimate together! it was too horrible a confusion of guilt, too gross a complication of evil. . . .

Two further chapters have dwelt upon the 'misery' brought to all at Mansfield Park by the 'guilt' of Maria; offstage though the catastrophe may be, it comes home to all the main characters. Moreover its 'guilt and misery' have been visibly forming under Fanny's helpless eyes through over half the novel. The narrator's words are no renunciation; they are rather a part of her moral judgment—the sin is 'odious'; but it has been in no way blinked; it has been dwelt upon, but not from the sensational or salacious motives that might have urged 'other pens'. It is also a bridge passage. She is gently preparing us for the expected happy ending, for the reassertion of the moral order so violently disturbed; but it comes gradually; before we have done with 'guilt and misery' we are to learn of the divorce, the refusal of marriage, the 'mutual wretchedness' of the lovers, her 'selfish passion', and his 'cold-blooded vanity', and of their punishment (the man's, as the author firmly observes, being 'a penalty less equal than could be wished'). Only when they are 'done with', can the consequent felicity of Edmund and Fanny be put in train: and with what artful 'intrusion' that is done:

> I purposely abstain from dates on this occasion, that everyone may be at liberty to fix their own, aware that the cure of unconquerable

passions, and the transfer of unchanging attachments, must vary much as to time in different people. I only entreat everybody to believe that exactly at the time when it was quite natural that it should be so, and not a week earlier, Edmund did cease to care about Miss Crawford, and became as anxious to marry Fanny as Fanny herself could desire.

'I purposely abstain.' She is using a device with a long history—one known to the mediaeval rhetoricians as 'dubitatio' and memorably used by Chaucer towards the end of *Troilus and Criseyde*:

> But trewely, how long it was bitwene
> That she forsook him for this Diomede
> There is noon auctour telleth it, I wene. . . .

Like Jane Austen, like Thackeray, Chaucer visibly hovers in irony and compassion over his characters and story:

> Swich is this world! whoso it can biholde
> In eche estat is litel hertes reste. . . .

Her happiness at this time was very much *à la* mortal, finely checkered. . . .

Ah, *Vanitas Vanitatum*! which of us is happy in the world? . . .

Surely these great narratives, *Troilus and Criseyde, Mansfield Park*, and *Vanity Fair*, would lose something if we were to be deprived of such comment in the name of 'objectivity'?

It has been finely said of Jane Austen by Miss Lascelles that she 'regarded her writing as an act of hospitality', and by Virginia Woolf that 'she wrote, as ladies talk, to give pleasure'; and her pleasure in doing so is part of our own. In an earlier and lighter novel, *Northanger Abbey*, she announces the imminent happy ending by remarking that the anxiety of Henry and Catherine, her hero and heroine,

can hardly extend, I fear, to the bosom of my readers, who will see in the tell-tale compression of the pages before them, that we are all hastening together to perfect felicity.

'All hastening together' is a key phrase; writer, characters, and readers are all within the same charmed circle. For a modern reader, it seems, such comments destroy the illusion of the novel's autonomous reality; but without them we miss, as I have already suggested, the writer's traditional role as host, welcoming us at a party and saying good-bye at the close—'Come, children, let us shut up the box and the puppets, for the play is played out.'

But Thackeray's 'hospitality' has a wry twist. His variant on 'all hastening together to perfect felicity' in *Vanity Fair* is:

> Here it is—the summit, the end—the last page of the third volume. Goodbye, Colonel . . . Farewell, dear Amelia. . . .

This is a sop to the conventionally minded reader, though with a concealed drop of acid in the concluding apostrophe—

> Grow green again, tender little parasite, round the rugged old oak to which you cling.

And it is not in fact the 'last page'; the actual last page casts doubt on the 'perfect felicity' of Dobbin and Amelia and makes its incompleteness illustrate the text of 'all is vanity'.

My instances from Jane Austen have shown the teller openly preparing readers for what is to come; this power to guide, and particularly to warn (or to promise under the guise of warning), is an important part of the author's freedom. My examples shall be drawn from works widely separated in type and time; the first, the opening sentence of a story deeply engrained in the early memories of many of us:

> I have made many stories about well-behaved people. Now, for a change, I am going to make a story about two disagreeable people, called Tommy Brock and Mr Tod.

The next is from Chaucer's Prologue to his Miller's Tale, which comes just after the Knight's Tale; he says that the next two tales are coarse—the Miller was a churl; so was the Reeve, 'and harlotrie they tolden bothe two'; in fact, a story about disagreeable people. The reader has been warned; if he does not care for this kind of thing, he may 'turn over the leef, and chese another tale'—and that gives Chaucer a convenient excuse to advertise the variety of choice in the *Canterbury Tales*. Even so does a novelist four centuries later remark that his heroine has 'all the virtues save one':

> but the virtue she lacked was such that I have found it impossible

so to tell her history as to make it quite fit and proper reading for the ubiquitous young person so dear to us all. Most deeply to my regret. For I had fondly hoped it might one day be said of me that ... I had at least never penned a line which a pure-minded young British mother might not read aloud to her little blue-eyed babe as it lies sucking its little bottle in its little bassinette.

Fate has willed it otherwise.

Obviously, such warnings as Chaucer's and Du Maurier's are not to be taken quite at their face value; the reader's eyes are meant to widen in pleased if shocked expectation, as the child's do at the *Tale of Mr Tod.* Consider also this, from the opening of Charlotte Bronte's *Shirley*:

If you think ... that anything like a romance is preparing for you, reader, you never were more mistaken. Do you anticipate sentiment, and poetry, and reverie? Do you expect passion, and stimulus, and melodrama? Calm your expectations; reduce them to a lowly standard. Something real, cool, and solid lies before you; something unromantic as Monday morning. ...

Her tone is unconciliating, triumphant rather than apologetic, but not without humour: satirizing a hypothetical reader, and making us, the intelligent ones, feel superior in sharing her own preference.

My final example is serious, and more subtle. It is from Henry James's *Portrait of a Lady*, at the close of the chapter in which Osmond, the least promising of Isabel's suitors, has declared his love:

The working of this young lady's spirit was strange, and I can only give it to you as I see it, not hoping to make it seem altogether natural. Her imagination stopped, as I say; there was a last vague space it could not cross—a dusky, uncertain tract which looked ambiguous, and even slightly treacherous, like a moorland seen in the winter twilight. But she was to cross it yet.

James wrote nothing more powerful than that last brief menacing sentence in an early novel, which his later method would not have permitted.

I have already incidentally suggested a particular aspect of the teller in the tale—the writer in process of writing the book. In a recent article on 'The Self-Conscious Narrator in

Comic Fiction', an American scholar[1] has traced this particular tradition from Cervantes to Sterne; he stops with Sterne, but we can easily recognize its continuance in the nineteenth century, and observe Thackeray's debt to these writers. Major examples of 'self-conscious narrators' are Swift (in *A Tale of A Tub*) and Fielding (who says that *Joseph Andrews* was 'written in the manner of Cervantes'); and in one minor eighteenth-century novel the narrator even introduces an imaginary reader in person, protesting against his proposed ending:

Oh Pox! says Widow Lackit, sure you won't give over without marrying her? . . . it's contrary to all Rule to end a History of this kind, without marrying the Hero and Heroine.

The author accordingly capitulates, with pretended reluctance; the device enabling him to have it both ways—to please, but under protest; an attitude very like Thackeray's in the passage I have already quoted from the end of *Vanity Fair*. There is another parallel in the sixth chapter of that novel, where Thackeray pretends to hesitate between different methods of writing; this chapter, he says, might have been written in the genteel, or the romantic, or the facetious manner; and gives examples of each (much fuller in the first edition) before reverting to his chosen method of realistic presentation. He wishes us to appreciate his choice by envisaging the rejected alternatives; we are not to overlook his conscious divergence from the conventions of current fiction.

But between Sterne and Thackeray stands a more remarkable instance of the self-conscious narrator, employed as a structural principle, far-reaching in its effects—in a work not usually associated with this tradition nor indeed with fiction at all, Carlyle's *Sartor Resartus*, first published as a serial in *Fraser's Magazine* in 1833–4. Its subtitle announces its affiliations with *Tristram Shandy*—'The Life and Opinions of Herr Teufelsdröckh'; and Carlyle's letters leave no doubt of his intentions; his real concern was to put across his 'clothes-philosophy' (he had begun by writing 'a strange piece on clothes'), but it was 'put together', he says, 'in the fashion of a kind of Didactic Novel'. His motive was partly caution, partly sheer love of

[1] Wayne C. Booth, in *PMLA* lxvii (1952), p. 163.

mischief and partly a genuine humility (*Humilitate* was the family motto). Besides Sterne, he had another precedent in his favourite writer Jean-Paul Richter, whose 'every work', as Caryle himself puts it,

> be it fiction or serious treatise, is embaled in some fantastic wrappage, some mad narrative accounting for its appearance, and connecting it with the author, who generally becomes a person in the drama himself, before all is over.

This could well describe *Sartor*, whose 'wrappage' is indeed 'fantastic'. Appropriately for appearance in a magazine, the narrator poses as a mere reviewer, confronted with 'a new Book from Professor Teufelsdröckh', published by 'Stillschweigen'. He finds the book itself baffling, from its 'almost total want of arrangement'; but he hopes also to have the assistance of 'biographic documents'. While waiting for these to arrive, he throws in a few personal reminiscences, and samples the book. Commenting on the extracts he gives, our 'self-conscious narrator' emerges as a puzzled, simple-minded man, easily shocked (as by the idea of a naked House of Lords) but occasionally impressed: his comments have the effect of shelving responsibility, forestalling criticism, and tacitly inviting the intelligent reader to see more in the book than he does. Now Book I of *Sartor* is complete; the 'documents' arrive—six paper bags, containing masses of 'sheets, shreds, and snips'—'a perfect chaos' (paper bags, by the way, were Carlyle's own method of filing—with his wife's clothes-pegs for paper clips). The prospects of searching through them are formidable; but 'what work nobler than transplanting foreign Thought into the barren domestic soil . . . ?' And so 'forward with us, courageous reader!' Throughout Book II, he works patiently through the paper bags, presenting fitful glimpses of the Professor's origins and history and his inner development from Everlasting No to Everlasting Yea. But suddenly, after ten chapters of this, a lurking suspicion is confirmed: one paper admits that the documents are not genuine, not factual at all. 'Somewhat exasperated and indeed exhausted', the editor shuts up the paper bags, and returns, in Book III, to the work under review, extracting and summarizing its philosophy; and finally takes leave of the Professor with mingled 'astonishment, gratitude and disapproval'. It is, he says, his duty as critic to warn against such a work, and prevent its ideas from spreading; and also, its style:

> What a result, should this piebald, entangled, hypermetaphorical style of writing, not to say of thinking, become general among our Literary Men! As it might so easily do.

It might, and did.

But, as an American reviewer somewhat laboriously pointed out, there was in fact no such person as Professor Teufelsdröckh —which reminds one of the clergyman's comment on *Gulliver's Travels*, that he didn't believe a word of it. Such disclaimers suggest some suspension of disbelief while reading; and certainly the stratagem works. The narrator is not Carlyle, but ourselves, the reader— inside the book; it is Teufelsdröckh who is Carlyle; if not in the facts of his history, in their 'mythic truth'. But by this fictitious framework our natural defences against propaganda and direct confession have been disarmed, so that we have accepted Carlyle's clothes-philosophy. Moreover, we have had the additional pleasure of being taken behind the scenes, and shown a book in the making—as in *Tristram Shandy*.

The 'narrator', here as elsewhere, is a method rather than a person; indeed the 'narrator' never is the author as man; much confusion has arisen from the identification, and much conscious art has been overlooked. Writing on George Eliot in 1877, Dowden said that the form that most persists in the mind after reading her novels is not any of the characters, but 'one who, if not the real George Eliot, is that second self who writes her books, and lives and speaks through them'. The 'second self', he goes on, is 'more substantial than any mere human personality', and has 'fewer reserves'; while 'behind it, lurks well pleased the veritable historical self secure from impertinent observation and criticism'.

There was no lack of 'impertinent observation' of authors: Thackeray was rumoured to be the original of Charlotte Brontë's Mr Rochester, Tennyson was identified with the heroes of 'Locksley Hall' and *Maud*, and was said, by an even less literate gossip writer, to have 'returned to his native Lakes and given up opium'. Thackeray for many years guarded his 'historical self' by pseudonyms; and we learn to distinguish Michael Angelo Titmarsh from William Makepeace Thackeray as surely as Elia from Lamb. He disguised himself, in later novels, behind Pendennis, who is the narrator of *The Newcomes*; but even when undisguised, he cheated curiosity and disclaimed 'autobiography' by being deliberately inconsistent—to take a simple point, about the narrator's age: 'Fifty years ago, when the present writer, being an interesting little boy . . .'; but Thackeray, when he wrote *Vanity Fair*, was thirty-seven. The speaker is an invented author, a 'second self' with a longer memory than is humanly possible; as is at once apparent if we take an instance not merely exaggerated but fantastic—'At the close, let us say, of Queen Anne's reign, when I was a boy at a preparatory school'. But it still has 'mythic truth'; the 'second self' is as old as that, and can step into other people's memories. The 'second self' is freer than the 'historical self'; of different ages; now married, now a bachelor; even perhaps varying in sex—Charles Reade in one of his novels says 'when I was a girl; or a boy; I forget which—it is so long ago'. And he is equally free to vary his opinions, his attitude to his material, his means of access to it. Is he a reporter, or an inventor? Does he know everything about his characters, or only guess? Either or both, according to the particular point in the story. Thackeray's favourite attitude is expressed in his characteristic phrase 'very likely'. 'Was she guilty or not?' he asks about Becky Sharp, at a crucial moment, and does not stay for an answer. This again is an old tradition. Did Chaucer's Criseyde know that Troilus was in love with her, before Pandarus told her? That also is crucial, and Chaucer leaves it in doubt:

> But how it was, certein, I can not seye;
> If that his lady understood not this
> Or feyned her she niste, oon of the tweye.

Or take a lighter example, from Trollope's *The Warden*: 'Did the archdeacon wink, or did he not? I am inclined to think he did not quite wink.' It was evidently a near thing; and the conflict between the cleric and the man could not be more neatly indicated. Here as before, the responsibility is shifted to the reader: in all these examples, far from being directly 'told what to think', we are invited to think for ourselves.

One special function of the teller is perhaps peculiar to nineteenth-century novels. Such novels, as I have said elsewhere, were very often about the past—the rememberable past of say thirty or sixty years before; and unless the hero or heroine is the narrator (as in *Jane Eyre* or *Villette*) this means that the author must be there to bridge past and present, to recall and compare and reflect upon the passage of time. His is now the poet's voice, adding a new perspective, a new dimension, to the novel. We are here no longer looking at a technical method, but something much more important—an enlargement of the novel's whole horizon. Such comments as these not only relate the past action to the author's present; they suggest that the present is as fleeting as the past:

> (there is always such a lady in a coach. Alas! was; for the coaches, where are they?) . . . To those great geniuses now in petticoats who shall write novels for the beloved reader's children, these men and things will be as much legend and history as Nineveh, or Coeur de Lion, or Jack Sheppard . . . Alas! we shall never hear the horn sing at mid-night, or see the pike-gates fly open any more.
>
> We are speaking of old times . . . when people were young—when most people were young. Other people are young now; but we no more. . . .

These of course are quotations from Thackeray—who said 'let us have middle-aged novels', and whose novels have been truly called 'novels of memory'. That is an equally apt description of most of George Eliot's novels, whose action is set either in the period of her own childhood, or like *Adam Bede*, a generation before that. To keep us aware of it the author constantly meditates over past and present; as in the well-known apostrophe to 'Fine old Leisure': 'gone where the spinning-wheels are gone, and the pack-horses, and the slow waggons . . .'; or even compares past, present and an imagined future, curiously recognizable as our present:

> Five-and-thirty years ago the glory had not yet departed from the old coach-roads . . . In those days there were pocket boroughs . . . unrepealed corn-laws, three-and-six penny letters, a brawny and many-breeding pauperism, and other departed evils; but there

were some pleasant things too, which have also departed . . . you have not the best of it in all things, O youngsters! the elderly man has his enviable memories . . . Posterity may be shot like a bullet through a tube . . . from Winchester to Newcastle . . . but the slow old-fashioned way of getting from one end of our country to the other is the better thing to have in the memory. The tube-journey can never lend much to picture and narrative. . . .

And so we are introduced to the setting of *Felix Holt*, by a picture seen from the vanished stage-coach. Or, travelling further backwards in time into the far past history of St Ogg's, in *The Mill on the Floss*, George Eliot recalls its patron saint 'of whose history I possess several manuscript versions', and the floods of old (in preparation of course for the novel's catastrophe); and then slowly tracks towards the recent past, the period of the main action, about 1830:

Ah! even Mrs Glegg's day seems far back in the past now, separated from us by changes that widen the years . . . Russia was only the place where the linseed came from [She was writing in 1860] . . . The Catholics, bad harvests, and the mysterious fluctuations of trade were the three evils mankind had to fear. . . .

In such meditations, the author almost stands for Time itself; and it is that sense of mutability that gives George Eliot's novels their peculiar pathos. At times the contrast lends itself to satiric observations: 'old Leisure . . . never went to Exeter Hall . . or read *Tracts for the Times* or *Sartor Resartus*'; the old-fashioned Tullivers, with their 'narrow notions about debt', 'may perhaps excite a smile . . . in these days of wide commercial views and wide philosophy, according to which everything rights itself without any trouble of ours'. This use of historic irony dignifies the characters and is in accord with George Eliot's view that 'there is no private life that is not determined by a wider public life'.

But in this novel, *The Mill on the Floss*, memory is also more personal: its prologue is not a piece of social history as in *Felix Holt*; here the author sees a vision of the river, the mill, and the child, enfolded in a trance of reverie—the rush of the water is 'a great curtain of sound, shutting one out from the world around'; she wakes in her armchair only to say 'Before I dozed off I was going to tell you what Mr and Mrs Tulliver were talking about on that very afternoon I have been dreaming of', and the other curtain goes up, on the mill-parlour and the dialogue about Tom's education. But the prologue is our preparation for the tone of brooding memory that haunts the whole book, directing our view of all the characters. Looking back from middle age, 'when memory is still half passionate and not merely contemplative', she appeals to her readers' memories of their own childhood ('when it was so long from one Midsummer to another') as a means to understanding and pity:

> There is no hopelessness so sad as that of early youth, when the soul is made up of wants, and has no long memories, no superadded life in the life of others; though we who look on, think lightly of such premature despair, as if our vision of the future lightened the blind sufferer's present.
>
> Maggie in her brown frock, with her eyes reddened and her heavy hair pushed back. . . .

The transition is immediate and effective; the author's reflections are there for Maggie's sake, not as an independent moral essay.

Much more could be said of George Eliot as the teller, and I should have liked to emphasize the further special value of her 'second self' in giving a voice to characters who are themselves almost inarticulate; without her voice, how could a Silas Marner, or even a Mr Tulliver, be realized to us? (The 'stream of consciousness' could do nothing for them, for they are unconscious.) But I have said the less of George Eliot, since her novels are now receiving much attention; they are in good hands, in this University and elsewhere, hands that I think will not brush aside 'the intrusive author'.

The break in this tradition begins to appear, I believe, soon after George Eliot's death in 1880; or even a little before. Critics of her last novels, *Middlemarch* and *Daniel Deronda*, already occasionally protested against the presence of the 'second self'; and the casual observation of a character in a slightly later novel is a straw in the wind. The clever sister in W. D. Howells's *The Rise of Silas Lapham* (1885) is reading

Middlemarch, and says 'I wish she would let you find out a little about the people for yourself'. It was to be said again.

There had always been isolated protests; as early as 1800, Lamb wrote to Wordsworth:

> An intelligent reader finds a sort of insult in being told, I will teach you how to think upon this subject. This fault, if I am right, is in ten thousandth worse degree to be found in Sterne and many many novelists and modern poets, who continually put a sign post up to shew where you are to feel. They set out with assuming their readers to be stupid.

Trollope was often criticized by contemporaries for his omnipresence; one reviewer in 1860 compared him to a 'talkative old guide', and said that his last story (*Framley Parsonage*) 'reads almost like an essay from the pen of Mrs Nickleby'. (Even Henry James never said anything harsher about Trollope than that.) To trace the change thoroughly, one would need to take account of the authors who encouraged fiction to approximate to documents, or to drama; 'believing', like Wilkie Collins, 'that the Novel and the Play are twin-sisters; that the one is a drama narrated, as the other is a drama acted'. Dickens himself practically abandoned the personal narrator and commentator after his early novels, except, and it is an interesting exception, in the *Christmas Books*. He even cancelled some such passages in revision; a confidence about 'my long-considered plans concerning this prose-epic' disappears from *Oliver Twist* after the first edition. He preferred to speak, as Ruskin said, 'within a circle of stage fire'; it was an instinctive preference in him; but it became a conscious choice. 'I don't want you, in a novel', he wrote in advising a contributor to *Household Words*, 'to present *yourself* to tell such things, but I want the things to be there.' 'My notion always is that when I have made the people to play out the play, it is, as it were, their business to do it and not mine.'

By the end of the century other influences were at work. An American critic of 1910, collecting some examples of 'soothing or explanatory remarks' from authors of the past, dismisses them with the exclamation 'Imagine Turgénev or Flaubert scribbling [such] interpolations!' The influence of

Flaubert penetrated increasingly into English fiction from the 1880's, and worked against all direct authorial intervention as destructive of 'reality'; and a still more decisive influence on the modern novel and modern novel-criticism is, as I have said, the later Henry James, who found Trollope's admission that he was inventing his story 'suicidal', 'a betrayal of his sacred office', and 'a terrible crime'. But James, as I have already suggested, himself began in the older tradition. In *Washington Square*, published serially in the *Cornhill* in 1881, the first chapter closes with these words about Catherine Sloper and her father:

Such as she was, he at least need have no fear of losing her. I say 'such as she was', because, to tell the truth— But this is a truth of which I will defer the telling.

(Like Chaucer again—'that shall I seyen when I see my time'.) Or he prepares us for a change in pace:

Our story has hitherto moved with very short steps, but as it approaches its termination it must take a long stride.

The change in James's method comes in the 1890's, when we find him, for example, delighting in the approximation of the separate books of *The Awkward Age* to 'the successive Acts of a Play', of which the 'divine distinction' is 'its special, its guarded objectivity'. He could not know how restricting that guard was to become.

But the older tradition did survive into our own century, and in one novelist, William De Morgan, is seen flowering so luxuriantly as to deserve much fuller treatment than I have time for here. It is appropriate that he should be my closing instance; with the name of De Morgan I have come full circle, back to the early days of our College and University. For his father was Professor Augustus De Morgan of University College, who lectured on Mathematics 'gratuitously' to the Ladies' College in the first two terms of its existence; and his mother was Sophia De Morgan, a friend of the College and closely connected with its founding. Augustus, always given to brandishing his resignation at University College, did finally resign after forty years or so, when he thought the College untrue to its ideals of toleration; and Sophia became doubtful about the wisdom of higher education for girls—hard work and examinations might bring on attacks of brain fever. I don't think this is among the terrors of my term of office: the female brain has, perhaps, been strengthened by use.

William De Morgan, their son, became a novelist of surely outstanding importance, though at present neglected in syllabuses on 'Modern Literature'; but he came to novel-writing late in life, after a long career as a craftsman and designer, emerging on the literary scene only in 1906, at the age of sixty-seven. He was a kind of Rip Van Winkle, who had read no novels since the deaths of Thackeray and Dickens, and followed Thackeray in being an omnipresent narrator. That he was instantly and deservedly successful shows that there was as yet, in the early twentieth century, no general prejudice against the older fashion: even critics who theoretically disapproved conceded that when the narrator was so interesting 'we cannot have too much of him'. So De Morgan remained unrepentant, though teasing his critical readers by saying in a postscript: 'I know that gossiping with one's readers is a disreputable Early Victorian practice and far from Modern, which everything ought to be.' Most of his novels were, like Thackeray's, 'novels of memory'; their time, as he says, is 'post-Johnsonian; but . . . older than the readers'; and this assists what is his usual pose, in his talk with the reader, of being a mere historian, an artless recorder. When he says 'my lack of skill is spoiling what might be a good story', we are reminded of Chaucer's 'my wit is shorte, ye may wel understonde'; only the greatest creators can afford so to belittle themselves. But the most curious turn that De Morgan gives to the narrator is that he generally speaks not as 'I' or 'we', but by personifying 'the story'; often with almost impudent effect, as when in telling us that his heroine 'adored Paris' he adds in parenthesis 'small blame to her, the story does so too'. And 'the story' is not omniscient:

How far was she aware of her handiwork? The story hesitates to say . . . However, the story hopes . . . Perhaps Lucy Snaith was innocence itself.

Or perhaps not.

Does this throw a new light on the 'second self'? Is it the author as storyteller, with the story as something given, with rights of its own, and himself as its servant? At times 'the story' seems almost to be his Muse—the nameless muse of Narrative. But this is too big a question to raise at the end of a lecture.

What I have tried to do here is to suggest some of the complexities of the relation between tale and teller, of which modern criticism of the novel seems to take too little account; for no one has examined the modes of narrative fiction with the perception brought to the dramatic mode by Professor Ellis-Fermor, or with so keen an understanding of the differences between them. Of the two, the novel is the freer form—'independent, elastic, prodigious' as Henry James had once called it—and it should not be denied its freedom to include the teller in the tale.

II

NOVELISTS AND NEAR-NOVELISTS

NOT WHOLLY by accident most of the recent books on nineteenth-century English literature remind us that, a hundred years ago, the dominant form, among the more purely literary forms, was that of the novel. Mr Ford's book on Dickens,[1] the first half of Mr Ray's big life of Thackeray,[2] and his collection of Thackeray's anonymous contributions to the *Morning Chronicle*,[3] the second half of Mr Haight's edition of *The George Eliot Letters*,[4] Mr Cockshut's critical book on Trollope[5]—all these books remind us of this directly.

The old dream that the epic was still a possible form, and the highest possible, was coming true less mechanically than in *Tom Jones*, and by a process something like that enunciated by William Morris in *The Dream of John Ball*: 'the thing they fought for comes about . . . and when it comes, turns out not to be what they meant.' Tennyson saw that 'the form of prose fiction' is 'all-comprehensive': it was seen to be inclusive as the epic had been: Milton obtruded passages of straight autobiography into *Paradise Lost*, and Dr Johnson saw no reason to wish them away—indeed he wished that Homer had done likewise. Henry James saw the novel as 'the most magnificent form of art', which was what the epic had been or had been held to be, up to the eighteenth century. Not that this standard was always reached. As in the eighteenth century and again in the twentieth there were novels and novels. 'It is not like a novel', said the publisher of *Felix Holt.* And in his chapter 'Popularities and Conventions' Mr Ford remarks that: 'When Allen Tate writes . . . that "the novel has at last caught up with poetry" we can safely assume that the word *novel* in this context connotes such

[1] George H. Ford, *Dickens and his Readers. Aspects of Novel Criticism since 1836*, 1955.

[2] Gordon N. Ray, *Thackeray. The Uses of Adversity* (1811–46), 1955.

[3] *William Makepeace Thackeray. Contributions to the Morning Chronicle. Now first reprinted*, ed. Gordon N. Ray, 1955.

[4] *The George Eliot Letters*, ed. Gordon S. Haight, vols. iv-vii, 1955.

[5] A. O. J. Cockshut, *Anthony Trollope. A Critical Study*, 1955.

works as *Emma*, *The Scarlet Letter*, or *Madame Bovary*, but that it does not connote the daily productions of contemporary fiction with their full-bosomed females leaning out from the dust-jackets.' We apply exacting criteria to *Paradise Lost*, and we must apply exacting criteria also to *David Copperfield* and *Middlemarch*. It is clear, moreover, that some of the critical principles evoked will be the same. And if we evoke more of these same critical principles for *David Copperfield* and *Middlemarch* than for *Emma*, that is because those two later novels are more fully like epic than Jane Austen's is. In one of Frederic Harrison's contributions to *The George Eliot Letters*, he speaks of reading in *Felix Holt* as he reads in Tennyson or Shelley or Browning, and of her 'put[ting] the subtle finish of a poem into the language of prose narrative'. And when the London manager of Blackwood's notes that George Eliot has the trick of standing away from her personages and seeing them as if from a distance, he is noting something like the trick of the epic poet. Browning thought *Romola* 'the noblest and most heroic prose-poem that I have ever read'.

The novel is also thought of as taking over some of the characteristics of drama. The debt to the drama is obvious in the novels of the theatre-loving Dickens, and we hear of the 'acts' and 'scenes' of *Felix Holt*.

2

The five books I began by naming concern the novel directly: others deal with it indirectly—Mr Duffin's vigorous and testimoniary *Reconsideration of Browning*[1] and the new letters of Mrs Browning.[2]

The author of *Aurora Leigh*, a poem as wildly popular as a novel throughout the latter half of the nineteenth century, is not wholly outside the category of novelist. At her best Mrs Browning is a minor George Eliot, though seldom wholly free from the erratic, the affected and what may be called the facetiousness of the intellect—but with a knack of writing

[1] Henry Charles Duffin, *Amphibian: A Reconsideration of Browning*, 1956.

[2] *Elizabeth Barrett to Mr. Boyd. The Unpublished Letters of Elizabeth Barrett Browning to Hugh Stuart Boyd.* Introduced and ed. Barbara P. McCarthy, 1955.

readable blank verse (a knack George Eliot did not have). As a novelist her novels might not have been good all through because she was too airy to get a lasting grip on her fictional people, but she could have managed episodes very well—witness certain memorable scenes in *Aurora Leigh*, especially those between Aurora and her aunt. And if we cannot wish to see Robert Browning as a novelist, that is because he is enough—just enough?—of a poet to have found in verse the proper medium for material which in less metrical hands would have gone into novels and stories. We recall that Henry James enjoyed himself showing how a novelist might have dealt with the material of *The Ring and the Book*, a poem the structure of which has suggested to twentieth-century writers ways of constructing a novel so that it makes its criticism of life mainly by the angles at which its bones lie. Structure of this status would have pleased Aristotle, who thought that the best plot was that in which the few main facts to be told were impressive merely by existing just like that. The great triumph of Browning, however, is not *The Ring and the Book* but those dozen supreme dramatic monologues such as 'The Bishop Orders his Tomb at St Praxed's', 'My Last Duchess', and a few poems like 'Youth and Art'. Though each of these is a fragment, it suggests a whole drama, not an episode of one. Every detail in them is what George Eliot and Henry James might have called a 'germ', a speck of mustard-seed potentialities. Ruskin said of the St Praxed's poem that he knew 'no other piece of modern English . . . in which there is so much told . . . of the Renaissance spirit'. He might also have said that he knew no small piece in which there was so much personal history and character. Mr Duffin notes that 'it tells no tale but gives a lightning impression [a series of lightning impressions?] of a personality, a situation and a civilization'. When you read 'My Last Duchess', you do not feel that it is a short poem stretching towards a play, so much as a play shrunk into a poem: it would seem that its details were selected from a fully worked-out bigger thing. It is customary to think of Browning's 'dramatic monologues' as offshoots of drama, but it would be truer to say that the form we see lying behind them is the novel form. Look, for instance, at 'Youth and Art'. The woman in that poem, thinking of the sculptor's failure, years ago, to propose marriage to her, asks:

> Why did not you pinch a flower
> In a pellet of clay and fling it?

—fling it in at her window from his window across the street. That is a detail presupposing a large functional setting that suggests a novel rather than a play. In *Madame Bovary* one piece of the action exists only as it is seen from a window across the way, and though this action in two places was realizable on the Elizabethan stage, it is not so on the modern. In a novel, however, Browning's detail could be enacted without contrivance, and would make the sort of action that is proper to the form. As it happens, a similar action (with, as it happens, similar psychological implications) occurs in *Jude the Obscure*—the country girls' flinging of 'the characteristic part of a barrow-pig' at Jude. If some of Browning's details—for instance, 'but don't jog the ice'—could go as comfortably into a modern play as into a novel, that is because since his day plays have learnt from novels. They cannot learn beyond a certain point. The dramatic form is suitable to a certain amount of material and to certain kinds or rather qualities of it. The amount should not be very large, and the kinds or qualities should be such as do not require the process of much development. In Elizabethan and Jacobean plays, for instance, passions blow up, or blow out, too quickly: there is a bolt from the blue instead of a cloud that starts no bigger than a man's hand, or there is a sudden flop instead of a leak. Many plays are unsatisfactory mainly because they are not novels. The novel can show development and show us it taking place in a setting that has 'solidity of specification'. The dramatist who came nearest to providing both these things was Ibsen. He was able to put development into his plays because he began them near the end of the action, revealing the past as people talked. He made the form of drama give him something as dense as a novel, but his method precluded his showing the full process of development. His plays are like novels that the author starts reading to us at a point in the last chapters, explaining as he proceeds by reference to things in the part unread. Nevertheless largely because of the way he constructed them, his plays are more nearly novels on the stage than the plays of other dramatists: for the Greeks, who like him began their action late, were not interested in 'solidity of specification'—a thing the novel cannot well do without, unless it makes up for it by unflagging and prolonged solidity of talk, as in Miss Compton-Burnett's novels. Ibsen's plays are Browning's dramatic monologues writ large. In both of them is much that belongs in the first place to the novel, however perfectly they have made it suit their own dramatic ends. When Mr Duffin asks if there is no art in Browning, the core of his answer is that Browning's art is that of the novelist: 'What of the brilliant art of presentation of figures and situations? . . . Instances could be multiplied to prove the possession of an art nowhere excelled—but equalled by Jane Austen and the great novelists generally. . . .'

3

Like their predecessors, the last four volumes of *The George Eliot Letters* have obvious importance for the critic of nineteenth-century novels both as things of art and things for the market. Literary importance, if not always commercial, attaches to a collection of any writer's letters. George Eliot's are unusual in that they themselves resemble a novel—the effect of Mr Haight's expert labours, in collecting them and making them as fully intelligible as possible, is that of adding a seventh to the long novels of George Eliot. Like fiction, the letters give us a strong feeling of progression. As we should expect from the evidence of her novels, George Eliot is much aware of the shape of life, of the shape it is taking and likely to take. And also of its surprises—as when the accumulating years bring her not only aches and pains but more cheerfulness than when she was younger. This progression, being recorded as it was lived through, does not lack that 'solidity of specification' which I refer to in Henry James's phrase but which George Eliot also had desiderated of a novel; that chorus of fearless, weighty, subtle commentary that sounds like the music of Brahms at some point in every page she wrote—he also on occasions can be clogged as well as weighty. It was said of the commentary in Thackeray's novels that even the most humdrum of them contained some touch of fine quality. It was said more than once of George Eliot's novels that the fine things came on every page: John Blackwood says it here of *Felix Holt.* And he says the same thing of the letters themselves—one of the delights of this edition is the literary criticism we get from those concerned with the publishing of her books.

This progression is not enough of itself to suggest the interest of a novel. To progression, however, is added suspense. George Eliot, as little confident of her powers as any great author has ever been, undertook when engaged on her two biggest novels to increase the pains of writing by a hazardous method of publication. And now that we have the letters complete, she makes us, as she made her willing and much involved associates, live through the long wearing excitements with her.[1] Her anxiety and self-distrust are chronic and severe: 'I have a great talent for anxiety'; 'the habitual tone of her mind', says Lewes, 'is distrust of herself'. Her physical health is always precarious—and in her letters, by the way, the principle of solidity of specification extends to the account of her ailments and diseases. With all this threateningly against her, she elects to publish *Middlemarch*, and *Daniel Deronda* later, in parts, and to begin publication before she has got far into the writing—so that, as she says on one occasion, 'there remains the terror of the *un*written', and, on a later, 'I dare not count much on fulfilling any project, my life for the last year having been a sort of nightmare in which I have been scrambling on the slippery banks of a pool, just keeping my head above water'. Meanwhile there had been the reaching of printing-house decisions, always in close consultation between the two groups—the Blackwoods and George Eliot-and-Lewes. The excitement and suspense is well conveyed by two sentences—Lewes's 'Ponder this; or suggest a better plan!' and Blackwood's 'I am most curious as to the result of the *Middlemarch* experiment'. How many parts in all and how big? At what price? At what intervals of publication?—'It will be a good plan, I think', says George Eliot, 'to quicken the publication towards the end'. What should they look like? In jackets of roman-lettered mauve,

[1] The correspondence from which the following quotations are taken is to be found in the fifth volume of Mr Haight's edition.

green, or grey?—'green is more effective (and less clerical) than the mauve'. What shall the 'lordship' be—i.e. the royalty? 'By the way', says Lewes, 'a thought strikes me. Would it not be well to have an advertisement sheet bound up with each part—as Dickens and Thackeray have had with their parts? (though not of course on the *covers*).' All these considerations are thoroughly aired in the hope of a thundering success, financial as well as everything else. Mainly the scheme of publication is aimed at 'inventing some mode of circumventing the Libraries and making the public *buy* instead of borrowing'. Nor is this all. How about publishing abroad? A member of the firm is so masterly as to get an Australian firm to pay for serial rights, and to pay as much as £200. And in Europe a good stroke is brought off and with satisfactory repercussions—'I fancy', smiles George Eliot, 'we have done a good turn to English authors generally by setting off Asher's Series, for we have heard that Tauchnitz has raised his offers'. And at home finally there is the excitement of the scheme in action—the watching of the sales of each part, both on its appearance and, in course of time, as a back number, and the consequent tending of the printing so as to keep up with the uncertain demand for these single parts. After all which come questions of complete editions in book form. Just when shall they be launched? And when shall the four bound volumes at two guineas be joined by the less handsome edition in two bound volumes at one guinea? And so to cheaper editions, down, or rather along, to the point where stereotyping and Collected Works begins. Suspense is strong as we follow all this hazardous mixture of mercantile campaign and psychological idiosyncracy. The play is for high stakes, and the cards are, as it were, the pages of some of the world's greatest fiction.

Then after *Theophrastus Such* (that little masterpiece of thoughtfulness and invention, that epitome of so much in the nineteenth century), when it looks as if there will be no more such swelling themes, when our interest seems as if it will confine itself to watching how, when Lewes is dead, George Eliot prepares her well-inured mind finally for death, we get a burst of novel-interest at its most explosive. Mr Haight prints—for the first time—a letter to John Walter Cross.[1]

[1] *George Eliot Letters*, vii, 211 f.

Thursday.

Best loved and loving one—the sun it shines so cold, so cold [she quotes 'The Idiot Boy', surely, because it is a poem about another Johnnie], when there are no eyes to look love on me. I cannot bear to sadden one moment when we are together, but wenn Du bist nicht da I have often a bad time. It *is* a solemn time, dearest. And why should I complain if it is a painful time? What I call my pain is almost a joy seen in the wide array of the world's cruel suffering. Thou seest I am grumbling today—got a chill yesterday and have a headache. All which, as a wise doctor would say, is not of the least consequence, my dear Madam.

Through everything else, dear tender one, there is the blessing of trusting in thy goodness. Thou dost not know anything of verbs in Hiphil and Hophal or the history of metaphysics or the position of Kepler in science, but thou knowest best things of another sort, such as belong to the manly heart—secrets of lovingness and rectitude. O I am flattering. Consider what thou wast a little time ago in pantaloons and back hair.

Triumph over me. After all, I have *not* the second copy of the deed. What I took for it was only Foster's original draft and my copy of it. The article by Sully in the New Quarterly is very well done.

I shall think of thee this afternoon getting health at Lawn Tennis and I shall reckon on having a letter by tomorrow's post.

Why should I compliment myself at the end of my letter and say that I am faithful, loving, more anxious for thy life than mine? I will run no risks of being 'inexact'—so I will only say 'varium et mutabile semper' but at this particular moment thy tender

Beatrice [They had been reading Dante together.]

That is one of the most richly doting love letters ever printed! The letters of the remaining fourteen months of her life are read in its lurid yet tender light. Eight months later we come to May 1880 when, after writing to her closest friends,[1] she marries Cross, twenty years her junior, the long-standing friend of Lewes and herself. I have referred to the structure of *The Ring and the Book*—here, at the point of highest intensity, it is repeated in some sort, or perhaps rather the structure of *Pippa Passes*: virtually the same letter sent on the eve of the wedding to five friends—like an undreamed-of summons requiring their soul of them—and their different replies. After this we expect

[1] The letters were not posted however until after the marriage had taken place.

silence. Instead, we get a reflorescence of gayest letterwriting; the old brilliant self of the days when she wrote for the *Westminster Review* and her first years with Lewes brightens in the Indian summer till the end, eight months later, told here with a proper completeness in letters by Cross, which Mr Haight prints for the first time. This is what we get, and it is enough for a novel-reader. What we should also have liked would have been a day-by-day account of what led up to the first love-letter and what was experienced between that and the wedding, and after. Samuel Richardson could have been entrusted to imagine it all, and George Eliot also. But the opportunity was not taken by George Eliot to be a reporter. We cannot help repining at the loss at the same time as we honour, in her case, as in everybody else's, the general law which she enunciates in one of her earlier letters—that some things are not copy for the pen. It is novels, after all, not letters, that tell us about those things we experience but do not write down. Some points of the intense process did get written down in a diary: Mr Haight is well aware of their weight, but they consist merely of a word or two.

It is possible that Mr Haight, who had Cross's letter-strewn Life as a starting point, foresaw something of the narrative interest of *The George Eliot Letters*. But the final result as it grew more clearly discernible must have surprised even him. I record my testimony, for what it is worth—which, into the bargain, is the testimony of a slow reader—that I have read every word of the seven volumes (barring the 150 pages of the index!), and could no more have laid down the story incomplete than I could have turned aside from *Daniel Deronda*. The novel that exists proverbially in all our lives is realized in these letters: in most collected letters what survives is that less tight and less enthralling thing, a biography.

4

Mr Ford's book deals with the fortunes of Dickens's novels at the hands of readers from the time of Boz to ourselves, and over 'the habitable world'. It is a theme of extraordinary richness, and its implications for the theory and practice of the novel are innumerable. Dickens may well be the most obvious genius who has used this form. Thackeray, even when he was speaking a little grudgingly, described him as having 'quite a divine genius so to speak'. To judge by the world-wide soundness of his continued fame, it is now time that his name should be added to that brief roll which received Shakespeare's 250 years earlier. Mr Ford has shown that to write of Dickens is to write about the novel form and about all novels written since. One mark of Dickens's greatness is that Mr Ford has had to spend as much space on the years when his reputation was, comparatively speaking, in the eclipse as on the years of its rise and long ascendency.

To look at what Mr Ford assembles from Victorian critics—with whom I am mainly concerned—is to see a great deal. This part of his book is largely a marshalling and alert discussion of remarks and passages drawn mainly from reviews of Dickens's novels and articles about them in periodicals, books of criticism and biographies. What a brilliant series they make!—so brilliant that when Mr Ford quotes a writer from the *Prospective Review* of 1851, whose 'appreciation of the handling of point of view in *Copperfield* . . . reads like a paragraph from Lubbock's *Craft of Fiction*', we are pulled up sharp by the coolheadedness of his comment: 'Such a passage is worth bearing in mind when one encounters the usual generalizations of literary historians concerning the total inadequacy of novel-criticism in mid-Victorian England.' Amidst all the brilliance of the Victorians here amply exhibited, we had forgotten that 'the usual generalizations of literary historians' exist. It is one of the great virtues of the work now being done on the nineteenth century that the generalizations are being forgotten. May new ones wait as long as possible! The more we read in nineteenth-century literature, the less we wish to sink its bright particulars. The same result follows a close reading in the literature of any century—it is always a process of testing generalities and finding them wanting. New generalizations come, and must come. But, if after making them, we go on reading primary documents, we see that the drive to make them is rather for the temporary comfort of our psyche than the continued repose of our intellect.

When reading nineteenth-century literature we have a

further dissuasion from making generalizations too early in that most of the great writers display multitudinousness rather than design. When we think of the stability of Dr Johnson—even of Swift and Pope—and then of the instability of Carlyle and Ruskin and Dickens (in so far as Dickens had views as moralist and critic of society), we see how far 'things have changed'—to leave the matter at its vaguest. Even Newman's point of view shows a 'development', though that is mainly on the surface—or rather in one department. These are difficult considerations, however, and here is no place to try to grapple with them. In so far as Mr Ford meets multitudinousness—a multitudinousness like that of a treasure house of gems in the *Arabian Nights*—he does what he can with it. He arranges it as neatly as he can, and he can himself think clearly—there is, for instance, a clear drawing out in Chapter 4 of what he means by 'explanatory criticism'; and in such a chapter as that on the changing views of readers about Little Nell, he gives us a taste of orderliness.

He would agree, however, that to turn away even from hard-won generalizations and to add to the reading that prompted them is to be aware once more of exciting problems. There can be few critics who can improve on Mr Ford's hard-won generalizations, but we are entitled, I think, to wonder how long they would stand a more thorough search for material. For instance, he starts at the year 1836, the date of *Sketches by Boz*, and notes that the work received 'fourteen notices and reviews (usually of a favourable sort)'. But another researcher, as I happen to know, found some twenty-five, and has a hunch that there are others undiscovered. And if so many for the *Sketches*, how very many for *Pickwick*, and so for all the rest? Mr Ford cannot but be 'sketchy' himself when he has taken more than a hundred years of Dickens criticism—to have taken twenty would surely have been enough. Moreover, taking so wide a field of time and so scattered a crowd of critics cannot but lead to a confounding of dates and of status. For instance, on page 41, where we are dealing with *Oliver Twist* (1839), we are given a quotation from a periodical of 1862; then a contemporary comment from Crabb Robinson's diary: over the page there is a comment from a review (1839) in the *Quarterly* by 'Richard Ford'. What is the precise worth of a remark made in 1862 about the readers of

1839? Who was Richard Ford? Was he *the* Richard Ford, the author of the *Handbook for Travellers in Spain*? Had the *Quarterly* a particular line, a particular axe to grind—see, for instance, Mr Ray's biography of Thackeray, page 222? Answers to questions like these may be difficult to find out: Mr Ford may know them, but till they are known, the material cannot really be weighed.

May I suggest another weakness? In Mr Ford's earlier book on Keats we were told about people's views on Keats. Here we are told about people's views on Dickens. Mr Ford asks us to assume that he holds views himself. We do assume it, and could perhaps infer them. But if so, that means that they are merely anybody's views. It is a question as to how best to spend one's time. It is a good way to spend it in reading and thinking about a thousand brilliant comments on x, but a better surely to try to discern the nature of x for oneself. Sometimes, as in the chapter 'The Poet and the Critics of Probability' we are given promising glimpses of what Mr Ford could himself do in the way of naked wrestle with literature—'Lear without his fool is not Lear', 'Dickens' method is to make [his] "strongly-marked" black characters probable by [giving] them not . . . virtues but . . . humour'.

5

Appropriately the first half of Mr Ray's life of Thackeray is written so as to be readable, and the prospective reader can be promised that he will neither halt nor skip. One merit is that the telling adheres intelligibly to chronology—a merit not always found in biographers, whose 'Meanwhile' and 'About this time' are often found undatable. The clear course of the story is not achieved at the expense of breadth. Mr Ray's distinction is that he is fully aware of the large context, particularly the social and the literary, in which his subject existed. An almost infinite amount exists to be learnt about both these, and, as we should expect of the editor of Thackeray's letters, Mr Ray has learned much. He is particularly instructive about the literary context in which jostle immortal literature and ephemeral, works like Scott's novels and *Eothen* and works contributed by third-rate writers to magazines and newspapers. No one knows more than Mr Ray about the contents of nineteenth-century periodicals, and it is knowledge indispensable to a good biographer of Thackeray. For therein lies the main interest of the first thirty-five years of his life. Thackeray's history as a man is not more interesting than many—the wealthy start (India, Charterhouse, Cambridge), the loss of the family fortune, Bohemianism abroad, his marriage and settling down to making money with his pen, the birth of his children, the insanity of his wife, the success of his journalism, the writing of great literature in essay, story, and novel form, ending (as far as this volume takes us) with *Vanity Fair*. But we read Mr Ray's account with avidity because it is about a journeyman of genius—genius most elegant and lively—of a writer flaunting uncomfortably under pseudonyms, and publishing in many places on many subjects (crying, after trying, 'I can't write the politics'), doing 'odious magazine-work which would kill any writer in six years', making friends and enemies, brushing against Bulwer Lytton, going through the long and even now not fully examined course of his ticklish relation with Dickens. The great interest of this part of the biography is that it is the biography of a delectable contributor to *Fraser's*, the *Foreign Quarterly Review*, *The Times*, the *Morning Chronicle*, and *Punch*. Mr Ray has been able to supplement the canon of Thackeray's journalism, notably as to his contributions to the *Morning Chronicle*, the most certainly attributable of which he has collected into a nicely produced volume. He knows the true value of these particular finds of his. They are of great charm; and of great interest—he notes that 'nowhere else does [Thackeray] speak so explicitly and at such length [on] what fiction ought to be'. But so is almost everything Thackeray wrote. My own point of divergence from Mr Ray the critic is that as a whole I should place as major much that he sees as minor. Of course *Vanity Fair*, with which the volume ends, is a St Paul's, but that does not prevent the smaller things from being as perfect as Wren's city churches. The tone in which to write of Thackeray's *opuscula* seems to me to be that of John Sterling when he asks of one of them: 'What is there better in Fielding or Goldsmith?'

6

Mr Cockshut is to be congratulated on an admirable first book. For a first book it is unusual. Trollope, in comparison with x or y, is a humdrum author whose appeal, one would have thought, is to older persons. If the young read him, one would not expect them to write on him—indeed writing on him offers any critic the difficulty Augustus John faced in the shapeless fatness of the master brewer—'I shouldn't know where to begin'. Of all great novelists—I know one reputable scholar-critic who goes so far as to rate Trollope as the best of the Victorian novelists, and his valuation cannot be dismissed at sight—he is the least seizable by the critic. Mr Cockshut attempts criticism, and is to be congratulated on doing so, especially since the result is put so lucidly. But though he has a chapter on technique, he is always slipping—slipping away into speaking of the matter Trollope's narrative is concerned in. He is at his best where he shows how that matter is made the propulsive force of the narrative. He writes well of Trollope's sense of society, his conception of the gentleman, of money, of property, of entail and primogeniture, and in the late novels of shady big finance of the international kind, and he well shows the role these matters play in the stories. But it is his over-mastering interest in these things that causes him to make a mistake of critical judgment. Because the matter of such a late novel as *The Way We Live Now*, with its international finance, is more strikingly interesting than the personal relations that adorn the earlier novels, Mr Cockshut thinks the later novels superior to those in the Barsetshire series and of the Barsetshire kind. He is also drawn to this view by his thesis that Trollope became savagely unhappy, and so more strikingly interesting, as the years rolled on. It is true that some of the later novels are exciting things, but surely, where they are more exciting, they have crudeness and a sort of mightless violence in place of the secure pastoralities of the Barsetshire novels. Those quieter writings are as genuine as Izaak Walton's. They possess—to revert to Mr Haight's volumes—what George Eliot saw in *Rachel Ray*, which she thought as 'natty and complete as a nut on its stem'.

III

HARRIETT MOZLEY

[I read Harriett Mozley's books in the 1940's, having been first led to them through some study of the literature of the Oxford movement and of the work of Charlotte Yonge; then, reading the periodicals of the 1840's, I noticed many references to them. Mr J. H. Mozley, then a colleague in the University, heard of my interest in his great-aunt's books and generously lent me her surviving letters; and the centenary of her death provided an opportunity to speak of Harriett and her work, more fully than was possible in my *Novels of the Eighteen-Forties*, in a talk in the B.B.C. Third Programme on 17 July 1952, entitled 'Newman's Sister Harriett and *The Fairy Bower*'. I cannot claim as a result that the interest of these works is more widely recognized, though I have now met several readers who 'have always known them'. And at least, a number of extracts from Harriett's vivacious letters have now been printed, in *Newman Family Letters*, edited and introduced by my friend Dorothea Mozley, and published in 1962.]

It is unsafe to affirm that any books of the past are forgotten. If I say it of Harriett Mozley's four books, *The Fairy Bower*, *The Lost Brooch*, *Louisa*, and *Family Adventures*, I do so with every expectation of stirring up a hidden ant-hill of readers who have always known them. I believe there are such readers, although I have not met them. By 'forgotten', then, I mean neglected by almost all the official sources of knowledge: escaping, for instance, those two great drag-nets in the *Cambridge Bibliography*, 'Minor Fiction' and 'Children's Books'; unmentioned in histories of nineteenth-century literature; never reprinted; not in the London Library; appearing very rarely on the second-hand book market. There are two exceptions: the books are rather secretively listed under the Dictionary of National Biography's article on the writer's husband, and they are referred to, not very favourably, by a recent biographer of the writer's brother. But she was a person, and an author, in her own right—not just Tom Mozley's wife and John Henry Newman's sister.

Newman said 'the only fault' of *The Fairy Bower* was that it was 'too brilliant'. One need not discount this as brotherly kindness; he was not, at least after 1833, noticeably biased in his family's favour. Several reviewers saluted the author as a second Jane Austen; all agreed that her book was quite different from any other 'tales for the young'. In the years of its fame it was read, as we say, 'everywhere'. In London, in Oxford—both 'by the party of hot-headed folks' and others, such as Frederick Temple, then an undergraduate; in Low Church circles too, and even beyond (the author heard of a Unitarian 'enraged beyond expression' with it.) Everyone, in 1841, seemed to the astonished author to be buying or borrowing *The Fairy Bower*. 'I wonder how it is', she wrote shortly after publication, 'that only 1,000 copies can have spread so universally'. Two more editions were soon called for. Where, I wonder, are those 3,000 or 4,000 copies now? I can account for only half a dozen. They cannot all have been read to pieces. Do they linger on private bookshelves, in libraries inherited from grandparents, known and loved by quiet people who perhaps have been reading literature all their lives without knowing it? For it is one of those books kept and re-read not only for sentiment but because it grows with the reader; one of that long-lived class once defined by Henry James as books which grown women can read to children without either's being bored. But literature it is; its place is as secure as its descendant's *The Heir of Redclyffe*, of which James was then speaking. As it is now 100 years this month since Harriett Mozley died, at the age of forty-eight, the occasion seems appropriate for attempting to reinsert her work into its niche in the temple of fame.

She wrote much more than the books I have named. But the complete evaluation of her work in some ten years of writing must await the recovery of all her anonymous tales, verses, and tracts. There is much flotsam which never reached even the harbour of the great national libraries. She and her work deserve a full-scale study; there is ample material in the surviving family letters, which the present owner has generously allowed me to read and quote. But short of such a study there are several possible angles of approach. Her books might be explored for the sake of Newman himself—for what they may reveal of the early influences of a shared domestic life (they decisively dispose, for example, of that persistent legend of an Evangelical family background), and for what they may imply of the clash of these two strong characters—who were never, after 1843, to meet again. 'There is that in Harriett', Newman is reported as saying, 'which I will *not* permit'; and she wrote, in 1845: 'J. H. N. is like a man who has made a disgraceful match.' This biographical approach has been suggested by Miss Maisie Ward, and she is sure to have successors. But the use of Harriett's stories as *romans à clef*, besides being a doubtful compliment, requires caution. *Family Adventures* was, indeed, founded on actual incidents and seems almost to proclaim reminiscence by its use, for five of its six child characters, of the Newmans' middle names; but the author begged her sister not to 'fix the characters on any individuals . . . they are not meant so'. Then, the first two tales might be considered as documents in the history of the Tractarian Movement: *The Lost Brooch* was once intended to be called *The Young Theologians*. Both books do indirectly convey certain of those doctrines, still more what the slang of their circle called the *ethos* of the 'party'. They were published by Mr Burns; their most favourable notices were in periodicals associated with the movement. But there are complications. Harriett was at no time at one with the movement; not only did each Romeward step drive her further back, but she had detached herself at a very early stage. She criticized some of the tracts severely, even to their writers, and in 1838, when proposing to dedicate a volume of verse to Queen Adelaide, she summed up her position: 'The Queen Dowager and myself are now the two most independent persons in Her Majesty's dominions bound by no parties or politics so we may both do anything we please'.

Moreover, she expressed a dislike of 'party' tales and novels, a dislike founded equally on disagreement with some of their principles and a shrinking from the overtly didactic method. There was 'a want of flexibility'; she desired 'books on sound principles, but *not dull*'. She quoted in mockery the High Church novelist Mr Gresley, who said he would give up writing if his books were found amusing; and it was the artist who mocked. But neither did she care for the praise of those who found *The Fairy Bower* 'a very pretty inter-*est*-ing book'; she preferred those who wrote to ask her, 'What does it *teach*?'—though she could not easily answer them. And, again, this is the artist's preference. She might make use of party sympathies; but she was not primarily, even in initial impulse, a party writer. Her own principles, and her delicate method of imparting them in fiction, she never positively defined, other than by saying, 'I am pretty sure no principles can be illustrated without definite individual characters'.

'What does it teach?' The 'problem novel' or 'discussion novel', soon almost to dominate contemporary fiction, had hardly yet appeared. But one problem is at least posed in *The Fairy Bower*—that of child nurture and education in the wealthier classes. Home or school, governess or parents, liberty or prohibitions? The story incidentally illustrated many different methods, even occasionally canvassed them in grown-up discussion; but there are no easy answers. About a dozen children appear, aged from ten to sixteen and disposed between several families. There are five mothers and one governess (fathers are at a discount, so far are we from *The Fairchild Family*). But none seemed intended simply as a model or a warning. The relation of cause and effect is blurred, even as in life. The worldly mother who delegates her duties to grandmother, boarding schools, and nursemaids, and in holiday time lets the children rip, as long as they do not discredit her socially, has not (so far) obviously better or worse children than the strict mother who employs a governess, forbidding dancing, cards and dice, encouraging Bible puzzles and capping of texts. The governess is in some respects an amusingly modern 'model'; she supervises introspective journal-keeping, rewards sin with kindness and gifts.

But 'what does it teach?' If instructors are known by their fruits, hers are a very mixed crop; Mary Anne is vain and deceitful, Constance upright and intolerant, and Fanny a romantic goose. From the upshot of the story we are meant to conclude, I think, simply that there are limits to what education can do, and that it is better to attempt too little than too much; that reverence is due to the young, but no fuss. The most sympathetically drawn mother is the least anxious; but even she makes mistakes. The positive values suggested are, perhaps, 'reserve' in religious discussion, very early training in obedience to a very few rules, and a trust in the unseen world. The most obvious conclusion, because asserted on the level of plot, is the fact that hardly one of the elders understands the children, and not one is aware of what is going on. For the grown-ups here are not guides through the museum of experience, like the Edgeworth and Sherwood parents; they are seen by the author with a more detached, even satirical eye. The shades of Mr and Mrs Bennet intrude upon the mother of Rosamund-with-the-purple-jar.

And here is a third possible approach to the book. It is a turning-point in the history of juvenile fiction, as was recognized not only at the time but a generation later:

They created the class of literature now termed 'books for the young', standing between the child's story and the full-grown novel. We do not mean that there were no such books before, but as a school they seemed to rise up in imitation of... *The Fairy Bower* and *The Lost Brooch*... Anything so curiously clever and covertly satirical was impossible, yet something more distinctly improving could be produced upon that same field.[1]

It is an expert in that field who speaks: Charlotte Yonge, who in her Preface to the 1886 edition of *Scenes and Characters* avowed her personal debt to the example of that 'memorable book', *The Fairy Bower*, which set up a 'wave of opinion' on which her own 'little craft' floated out. (Strange that the experts on Charlotte Yonge should overlook such acknowledgements.)

What was the novelty of *The Fairy Bower*? It is hinted in the preface:

an attempt rather to exhibit characters as they really are, than to exhibit moral portraitures for unreserved imitation or avoidance.... It introduces young persons to those scenes and situations of life which are their actual sphere and trial.

Recurrently, in tales for the young as in poetry, there must be a 'return to nature'. After the romances, Miss Edgeworth; after Mrs Sherwood, Harriett Mozley and, on a distant but parallel path, Harriet Martineau; after Charlotte Yonge, E. Nesbit. Perhaps the next revolution is about due.

[1] *Macmillan's Magazine*, September, 1869, p. 449.

Not even here, however, lies *The Fairy Bower*'s strongest claim to mature attention. Rather I would raise it above the smoke and stir of religious controversy, child-psychology, and literary history into the region of art. The critics who perceived 'another Jane Austen' were exaggerating, but not speaking at random. Nor was Tom Mozley, when he told his wife that her work was 'very good—*but it is a novel*'. She was put out; she did not really mean to be a novelist. 'Too deep for children, too shallow for grown-ups—just the unhappy medium', was what she feared she was tending towards. Her reviewers half agreed: 'her books are about, but not for, children'. But this fitted no category; hardly anyone in 1841 was writing 'about, but not for, children'. Her books, we now see, lie somewhere on that unmapped frontier that divides tales for the young from novels; only *Louisa* definitely crosses it, and earns the right to its title-page motto from *Sense and Sensibility*.

Jane Austen was admired by the author, indeed all but personally known to her.[1] The overlapping of their social circles reflects a real, if limited, relation. Both affirm the moral value of a sense of the absurd. And Harriett has caught a certain economy in ridicule. Young Fanny is writing a poem:

> 'What were you going to say, my dear?'
> Fanny said, some more verses, but she did not know what.

This Fanny, a minor but not unimportant character in *The Fairy Bower*, is a younger version of Catherine Morland, always relating her surroundings to the literary romance her head is stuffed with. When she protests that 'there can be no poetry or romance, if people always do exactly right. . . . All the interesting stories one hears in real life which approach to novels owe their very existence to someone or other doing what is wrong', she needs a Henry Tilney; she gets something not too remote: 'Supposing this is so, Fanny', returned Grace, 'it is no excuse for you and me doing wrong; we are not sent into the world for the purpose of making interesting stories'.

In the discussion raised by another of Fanny's vagrant

[1] In the *Times Literary Supplement*, 17 September 1954, I quoted a letter in which Harriett describes a visit to the Fowle family in 1838, and F. W. Fowle's recollections of Jane Austen.

impulses, the different world of the later and lesser writer is defined; her special position as critical observer of contemporary religious issues now underlies the comedy:

> 'Oh, I had rather be a nun than anything else in the whole world.'
>
> 'Really, Fanny, I am quite ashamed of you. . . . Don't you know that a nun is a Roman Catholic?'
>
> 'Oh, but a nun is the most unfortunate and interesting creature in the whole world!' cried Fanny, 'and they all look so miserable, and wander about and sing all night, and they wear long black garments, with a streaming white veil, and an immense long string of beads, with a cross at the end of it; and they go about curing all sick people, and binding up their wounds'.
>
> 'Fanny', cried Emily. 'What a medley you are making; I know what it is all from; I told you of a nun in one of Mrs Radcliffe's novels'.
>
> 'They would cut off all your hair', said Ellen, 'and then bury you, and shut you up in a convent, with bars, and you could never get out again. . . .'
>
> Fanny still persisted in her wish, if Isabella would be a nun too, and she said she would ask her.

There is a good deal of such interplay, but much more that simply establishes the diverse company of young people as lively, keen-witted, and boisterous. Mainly preoccupied with holiday fun, they 'think by fits and starts'.

The character through whose eyes much of the action and the finer moral distinctions are seen is the youngest and apparently most insignificant of them, Grace Leslie. Her situation is on one level simple enough to be 'for children': the first long visit to another family is a landmark in any small life. Grace spends a month of the Christmas holidays with the Wards, who have many other young visitors; her mother accompanies her, but deliberately stands aloof. For a mere child's tale, this has obvious possibilities; but the outward 'history of a month' (that is the sub-title) is but the gaily rippled surface of deep waters. For in that month Grace (like Miss Bowen's Portia) discovers and partly recognizes the world, the flesh, and the devil. In place, time, age of heroine (Grace is only ten) this world is miniature; but large dilemmas have to be faced, and heroic virtue attempted. *The Fairy Bower* is in fact, on a small scale, that story that never goes out of fashion and can hardly be written too often: the story of the girl lost in a dark wood—the story of the Lady in *Comus*, of Fanny Price, Dorothea Brooke, and Isabel Archer. On whatever scale, with whatever ending, sad, happy, or undefined, its truth and pathos always tell.

The title misleads, by hinting at fantasy; yet it is the right title, for what is called the 'fairy bower' is not only central to the plot, it is the 'golden bowl': a trifle in itself, but a climax, a hinge, and a symbol. In plain terms, it is a drawing-room alcove artfully decorated for the festive evening that is the high spot of the month's diversions. But the scheme for its decoration arose from a sudden vision of Grace's, impulsively and unfortunately communicated to an older girl, Mary Anne Duff, who 'wished very much to appear good and clever, and was always trying short cuts to both'. Here is a short cut: she announces the scheme and takes the credit. Grace misses the first step of the deception; then sees no moment to speak, and so becomes a party to the fraud, protecting Mary Anne, and tangling herself in a web of well-meant social and sentimental motives, her sensitive scruples making her feel responsible for the sin. The deception spreads into the baffling grown-up world; Mary Anne's new prestige contributes to the social elevation of her whole family. To speak now would be to bring crashing down an immense edifice. But the truth is suspected, notably by Grace's godfather (at times this story brushes against allegory). He first insinuates his suspicion, to the further confusion of the situation; calumny spreads (and a Harriett Newman would know what calumny can do) and then he makes the dramatic exposure. A lesser writer would have left Grace heroic and happy; but her tender conscience is dryly put in its place:

> Grace was of a susceptible turn, and if her mind was not duly strengthened, she might grow into a meek, sentimental character; always ready to blame herself, and take other people's faults upon herself; falling at length into a state of mind most painful to herself, and useless or tiresome to everybody about her.

Everyone wanted to hear more of Grace and her friends. So the author wrote *The Lost Brooch*, with the same young people six years older. It cost her far more pains than *The Fairy Bower*, which was 'dashed off on my first impulse'. It has more social comedy, more intricate moral interest than her first story, but is less poetically suggestive; and, being a continuation of the same characters, it resembles most sequels, in satisfying more than it surprises. To succeed it she planned and partly wrote a much more controversial and harder-hitting tale; developing, one may guess, the satire on suburban Evangelicals; but this seems never to have been completed.

'I long to be writing again, yet I feel pretty sure I have lost the power. I believe the Oxford folks have helped to put me in this state, for I feel as if every thing were about to be pulled to pieces.' That was late in 1841; the year of Tract 90; the year in which Harriett first foresaw Newman's future. In 1842 she did write again, but with a threefold change of direction. With *Louisa* she turned towards the novel, vividly displaying the social errors of an impulsive young bride, a slave to unconventionality, who deliberately visits the 'wrong' families in the belief that vulgarity implies goodness of heart. There is here no problem and no controversy: social comedy has won. But this story, which confirms her place in the Austen tradition, had no successor. She also wrote *Family Adventures*, intended for young children; but it lay unpublished for ten years, perhaps because its personal reminiscences seemed inopportune. But most of her literary energies went into juvenile journalism, so carefully anonymous that it is still largely untraced. These three 'different lines' were, she said, to be 'kept distinct'. This last line alone continued for a few years more.

That the progress of the novelist should cease is disappointing but not, I think, evidence against the genuineness of her gift. It is evidence rather of the difficulties of the divided life; and of certain difficulties peculiar to her and her time. The very success of her books disturbed her, as a threat to her domestic privacy, making her feel self-conscious in society; for a lady to be known to write was not yet a matter of course. The three memorable books were a brand from the burning. They took a toll of her always delicate health; months of feeling 'hunted' by proofs and reviews left her chronically sleepless, and there were her other anxieties. As sister, wife, and mother she could still write little tales and tracts, and contribute to the Mozleys' twopenny magazine (edited first by Anne Mozley, then by Charlotte Yonge), but after 1842 serious writing proved no longer possible. She was the sister of three incompatible and difficult brothers—John Henry, Frank, and 'poor Charles'; the first alone could have been a full-time occupation for the thoughts in 1843–5. She was the wife of the brilliant, impetuous Tom Mozley, always in and out of hot water, a hard-up clergyman in Oriel's worst living at Cholderton in Wiltshire, building a great new church against the wishes of his squire, alarming all shades of opinion with the *British Critic*, which he edited from the parsonage; and, in 1843, to Harriett's agony, threatening to 'Romanize'. Newman advised him to think it over for two years; but, as Tom said long after, he never could concentrate on one thing for ten minutes. So Harriett was saved; and Tom embraced his true destiny, in the top flight of journalism. He left the Tractarians and gradually migrated to *The Times*, after some years unsuitably divided between his parish and Printing House Square. When he became a chief leader writer in 1847 there was at least prosperity, but still less leisure; domestic and social life in Guilford Street proved even more exacting than on Salisbury Plain.

Harriett was not unhappy, did not protest. She had her own Grace—'my *live* daughter Grace', born in 1839—to guide through the labyrinth of growing up. The novelist survived only where many more mute inglorious Jane Austens survive—in letter writing. She seldom referred to any other writing. 'I must have more sympathy before I could write again.' She saw the influence of her books at work, but as she thought, often distorted; 'the Guy Fawkes of Grace Leslie in these books is inexpressibly unpleasant'. Both her beliefs and her art seemed for the time lost causes in the world. By 1847 her publisher Burns had 'Romanized' too; he could publish her brother's *Loss and Gain* but no more manuscripts of hers. She was, besides, changing her mind about the Evangelicals. They seemed no longer the Duffs, right-thinking but limited people in whom she would try to inculcate a salutary sense of the absurd; they now seemed the only upholders of true Church principles. 'The Oxford movement, or rather its movers, have weighty things to answer for', she wrote in 1846. Not of herself; she was a detached enough spectator of the Oxford movement by then. She might have come to think that gain out-balanced loss, had she lived. But at times I wonder if one of the 'weighty things' the Oxford movement had to 'answer for' was the loss of a distinguished novelist.

IV

THE HEIR OF REDCLYFFE[1]

AN ITALIAN newspaper of 1882 carried the mistaken report of the death of a celebrated English authoress, the Heir of Ratcliffe. She was, it was said, originally called Jong, but was made a Viscountess by Queen Victoria in recognition of her talent. This item of news was copied out by the daughter of the Dean of St Paul's and sent down to Otterbourne for Miss Yonge's amusement. In its complication of error lurks a truth: the truth of Charlotte Yonge's widespread contemporary fame and its origin in *The Heir of Redclyffe*, first published in January 1853. And although *she* never went to Italy—indeed very rarely left her corner of southwest England—she chose it as a suitable place for her hero, Guy Morville, to go to for his honeymoon, there to meet by chance the man who had wronged and misjudged him and whom he had finally forgiven, to nurse him through a fever, and die. Of the many long-drawn deaths in early Victorian fiction this was one of the most famous and least gratuitous. It is the high point, though not the conclusion, of a book remarkable alike for its fame, its representativeness, and some of its intrinsic qualities.

The author was twenty-nine when it was published. It was at least her twelfth book, out of a total which at her death in 1901 approached 200; and that although for many years she never wrote novels in Lent. But it was a new departure for her, both in kind and in popular response. With it, she stepped beyond her little public of Sunday-school teachers, to Mr Mudie's subscribers—to share the season's success with *Villette* and *Ruth*; with it she penetrated to what Saintsbury calls 'those undergraduate shelves which mean so much', the shelves of Morris and Burne-Jones and Birkbeck Hill at Oxford, of Hort and Henry Bradshaw and Henry Sidgwick at Cambridge. Birkbeck Hill, the future editor of Johnson, wrote to his

[1] This is the text of a talk in the B.B.C. Third Programme on 1 January 1953, the hundredth anniversary of the publication of Charlotte Yonge's novel.

betrothed in a melancholy mood: 'How glorious would be such a deathbed as Guy's, and how glorious for the survivor to be such as Amy!' That is typical of the way her hero and heroine magnetized youthful aspirations in the 1850's; and at a wide range of brow-levels. There was the curate who said there were but two books in the world for him: *The Heir of Redclyffe* was the other. Such excess, and the inevitable references in the orations of statesmen, aroused one late and loud dissentient voice, in Dickens's *Household Words*: 'Pusey-stricken fancies . . . romantic young ladies whose ideal man, name and all, is represented in Sir Guy Morville—the masculine, surely of Mrs Kenwigs's daughter Morleena, and invented in a kindred spirit of gentility.'

It is true that the book bears some of the superficial tokens of the mere best-seller. Yet it held its own for fifty years, reaching a twenty-second edition in 1876; and soon after being included in a collected edition with illustrations by Kate Greenaway—so 'modern', and so out of keeping. Old admirers observed with regret how the new generation thought their idol sentimental and priggish; as one critic said 'they cannot *see themselves* in Miss Yonge, and that is their chief demand from literature; for young people are not imaginative'. Another, in 1904, humbly consulted 'a young Sibyl of 19'; 'the oracle pronounced' that 'Eleven-year and twelve-year-old girls adore *The Heir of Redclyffe*. After twelve they don't care about Miss Yonge nowadays'. But novels read at eleven or twelve have a way of returning to mind; and I believe it is chiefly the survivors of that group who read her now. At this centenary of its publication *The Heir of Redclyffe* is out of print, even in two popular series of the classics.[1] The little rose-coloured volumes of 1853 are collectors' treasures; only later editions seep into the second-hand shelves as Victorian libraries are broken up. And literary criticism is silent now. Miss Yonge's own death occasioned several valuable studies; but histories of literature are perfunctory and often inaccurate in their treatment of her, and I think only two twentieth-century writers—Alice Meynell and Oliver Elton—touch the nerve of her work. Certain recent books contain

[1] In 1965 it was republished by Duckworth, with an introduction by Charlotte Haldane.

much useful material, but these survey her life and the social world of her novels rather than her art. Even in 1896, it was said that one-time 'blind affection' for her work was meeting its consequence in the 'faint praise of patronising remembrance'; and this has also proved prophetic. The book's status as a classic is accredited by its being read by characters in other classics; how many, I wonder, first met it in the third chapter of *Little Women*, where Jo is discovered eating apples in the garret and crying over *The Heir of Redclyffe*?[1] By the way, didn't we lose something when characters in children's books gave up reading? Sailing, pony-riding, and spy-catching, wholesome as such activities are, are somehow less convenient for emulation. *Little Women* reminds me of another possible intermediary: an early novel of Henry James. Almost simultaneously with Jo March, another New England girl 'sat down to a twentieth perusal of the classic tale of *The Heir of Redclyffe*'. Admitted, her male guardian (this is in *Watch and Ward*) dozed off when she read it aloud; but Henry James was not mocking her taste. Earlier, writing as a critic, he had coupled with the novel such phrases as 'first rate mind . . . a mind which is the master and not the slave of its material', even, though with a deprecatory 'almost', the word 'genius'. He was engaged in making a distinction interesting to students of Victorian novels: between those 'semi-developed novels' whose lesson is 'narrowed down to a special precept', and the genuine novels 'of which the meaning and the lesson are infinite'.

Now, the meaning and lesson of *The Heir of Redclyffe* could perhaps be reduced to 'a special precept': the forgiveness of injuries. But Charlotte Yonge did not begin with a precept as she had deliberately done in her earlier stories. She began with the idea of 'the penitence of a truly good man' and of two contrasted characters—'the self-satisfied, and the essentially contrite'. It was not her own conception, but suggested to her by a friend, Marianne Dyson, much older but less practised as a writer; of her Charlotte Yonge said, long after, 'Next to my father and Mr Keble, she turned the course of my mind'. Her imagination took fire; she built up the relation of the two main

[1] Miss Marghanita Laski tells me that in the American edition the book was *The Wide, Wide World*.

characters, Philip and Guy, partly in letters to Miss Dyson, with a growing excitement. Unusually, she spent a long time over the book—more than two years: all alongside such other activities as village school teaching, writing tales and tracts, and editing a new magazine. She shared it with family and friends; she was delighted when her mother said that Guy sounded like Mr Hurrell Froude—'I hope it is a sign that I have got the right sow by the ear'.

Family life was the scene of her story. The settled pattern of the Edmonstone household—parents, daughters, invalid son, and favourite nephew—is shaken up by the coming of the unknown cousin, Guy. The contrast of Philip and Guy is supported by others—between the sisters, Laura and Amy (kept in lower relief, as befitted girls), and later, between their respective engagements. The main contrast is subtly designed; it braces the whole book without ever becoming diagrammatic or didactic. Wealth and prospects belong to Guy, the heir; status in the Edmonstone family and superiority in intellect and self-control, to Philip. Both are young, handsome, and indeed honourable; but Philip is living on past virtue—he can never afford to be wrong, or to examine his own motives for being right. Serenely scoring off Guy in conversation, he shows himself an expert in what it is now the fashion to call 'lifemanship'. Especially skilful is the way Charlotte Yonge brings out contrasts of character by means of arguments about books; Byron's verse-tales and *I Promessi Sposi* are used as touchstones of moral taste, and so is Malory's *Morte d'Arthur*. The last is an unusual choice at that date (Guy shared it with Tennyson and Morris), and is treated by the sophisticated Philip with contempt—'very curious, in classical English; but it is a book no one could read through . . . a strange mixture of religion and romance'.

The choice of examples is not casual. The 'mixture of religion and romance' in *Morte d'Arthur*, still more in the tales of De la Motte Fouqué—*Sintram* and *Undine*—held a fascination for Charlotte Yonge. Writing *The Heir of Redclyffe* set free her own latent romanticism; attaching itself to Christian chivalry, it irradiated what might otherwise have seemed the narrow provincialism of the society she chose to reflect.

The 'meaning and the lesson' of *The Heir of Redclyffe*, though certainly not 'infinite', are considerably larger than those of her earlier stories. There, the reader sometimes feels imprisoned in the ethical assumptions peculiar to her time and class. Often a willing prisoner, thanks to her persuasive presentation; but only the very unspeculative could entirely accept, say, the awfulness of letting a farm to a Dissenter, or visiting a Mechanics' Institute ('Do you not know, Lizzie, that Socialists often hold forth there?'). There is no such limiting specification in *The Heir of Redclyffe*: sin is illustrated simply by Guy's bursts of fiery temper and fatalistic despair, by Philip's imperturbable self-righteousness, masking jealousy and spite. It is true that the guilt of Philip and Laura in concealing their engagement from her parents has been thought excessive (the first such criticism I have found is in 1861). But what is emphasized there is the self-seeking, the treachery to family affection; which is still translatable into modern terms. In short, I would claim that the moral content of *The Heir of Redclyffe* is easily disengaged from the social content, and is not seriously out of date.

On the point of 'gentility', mentioned in that adverse review which I have quoted, the novel perhaps is vulnerable. Its social world is small, almost feudal: Philip quotes *Locksley Hall*, but there is no awareness of a 'hungry people as a lion creeping nigher'. And though no one is more severe on worldliness than Charlotte Yonge, her own assumptions were perhaps a little more worldly than she knew. A streak of false romance occasionally interrupts the true. But authentic romance is there. Her achievement in making goodness romantic and attractive was not a slight one. The extraordinary thing is that part of Guy Morville's magnetism has a positive Byronic glamour, and not only in appearance: he is gay and melancholy by turns, misunderstood, outlawed, seemingly driven by fate. By fate: the potentially sensational elements in the plot are cunningly used. The evil strains in the Morville ancestry, the supposed curse, the predestined rivalry of Guy and Philip become tea-table talk; but they also form the other-worldly medium in which the characters are exposed and inter-related. All the characters *grow*, both through the 'trivial round' of family life and through their response to this dynamic situation. Take

Charles, the crippled Edmonstone brother, an especially perceptive character-study. He is not the stereotyped invalid of fiction, neither sweet influence nor savage misanthrope, but a little of both, and more the restless, irresponsible intriguer.

For his own entertainment, he thinks to provoke the rival cousins to display themselves; he receives less entertainment than enlightenment, is the first to realize their true natures, and by becoming Guy's partisan discovers himself. But the doom of the Morvilles is also transformed in another way—summed up in Laura's reminder to Guy: 'If you are a Morville, you are also a Christian!' (Is it only by coincidence that this remark recalls a remark of Newman's to one of his sisters?) Laura's words are in response to Guy's comparison of himself to Sintram, the knight of the German romance under 'a curse of sin and death'. The analogue of *Sintram* pervades the whole tale, recurring like a poetic image; it affects even the scene, the rocky coast of Redclyffe, in Guy's exile, representing the moon-rocks of the romance. It seems to carry the assurance of a happy ending; as Amy said, 'Sintram conquered his doom'. But Charlotte Yonge chose to go no further than the knight's ride with death.

Guy calls Amy 'My Verena': she becomes his bride, after long adversity, and his early widow; no matter to Charlotte Yonge that in the romance Verena was Sintram's mother, and had retired to a convent after his birth. The romantic parallel answers to the unsuspected firmness, even fanaticism, in Amy's character; thought by Philip to 'want bones and sinews', she is, superficially, just a charming, very charming, variant on the submissive young girl dear to Victorian novelists. But Amy, an Amelia Sedley who by-passes Vanity Fair, and is drawn by her author without ambiguities, has always the power of surprising the reader, as she does her relatives. 'It was as if a dove had flown in his face' was Philip's thought on one significant occasion. In her, too, Charlotte Yonge has made goodness attractive; if also, in the early phases of her widowhood, strange and other-worldly like Undine.

A commonplace novelist might have ended, as one reviewer saw, with Guy's death. Charlotte Yonge's mastery over her material is shown in the following nine chapters, with their continued narrative suspense—who is the heir? A question not fully resolved until the birth of the daughter, Mary Verena Morville—and their continued moral suspense, in Philip's slow self-discovery. The structural contrast is, of course, ironically completed with Philip's now reluctant inheritance of Redclyffe. (Charlotte Yonge generally punishes her worldly and self-sufficient characters by giving them what they once wanted.) And also, through these final chapters, we see the family pattern re-forming, and Amy's further progress traced through the dense material content of domestic life. It was, I think, Charlotte Yonge's keen sense of that life that kept her from vapid sentimentality: she once devised a scene in which a heroine in an emotional crisis sought her own room—only to find the maid was turning it out.

She resisted the pressure to write a sequel to *The Heir of Redclyffe*: I think she knew it was complete and, perhaps, for she was very humble, that she might not reach its level again. Keble warned her that a successful book might be the trial of one's life: but except that she was painfully shy of lion-hunters, it was no trial to her. The vast profits of the book fitted out a missionary ship; she soon set about a new serial, *The Daisy Chain*, which proved an even bigger success, and is the best of her many family chronicles. *The Heir of Redclyffe* belonged, as she saw, to a particular period: even from her narrow corner of observation, she could recognize changes in the time-spirit. In a novel of 1860, she made her rebellious young heroine say 'The last generation was that of mediaevalism, ecclesiology, chivalry, symbolism, whatever you may call it . . . ours is that of common sense'. It is to the Victorian 'age of chivalry' that *The Heir of Redclyffe* belongs. Reading it now, one can understand why it inspired the enthusiasm of William Morris; whose chivalry extended to wider horizons.

V

TROLLOPE'S STYLE

NOW THAT I have read almost everything that Anthony Trollope wrote—he wrote some forty novels, most of them long—I see with increased clearness that he is a giant among novelists, that he is big not merely in girth but in height. He stands firmly among the dozen or so giants of English fiction. Fortunately the Oxford University Press have made most of his books available in cheap reprints.

There is not a great deal of criticism of Trollope, but there will be much in the years to come. The following is offered as a contribution to the criticism of the style in which the novels are written.

Their style has no pretensions. It reveals its honesty in its preference for monosyllables. It likes plain words. It abhors the high-sounding. It creeps, and with the practised neatness of the centipede. But it is not the style of a man who abhors grace. Rather it is the style of one who knows how best to sustain grace without its seeming too much a thing of art. It has the beauty associated with the grey and white dress of Quaker women—we know, if only from pictures and photographs, how the severe and unadorned simplicity of Quaker clothes was not without its almost artful beauty—it could even transform a plain face into elegance. Trollope is so well satisfied with his one style that he scarcely used anything else. The upshot is that where his personages speak among themselves, or write letters to each other—and they do these things as often as possible—they speak and write, by and large, with his voice. I make the qualification 'by and large' because he does break up their spoken sentences a little, and leave some of them incomplete, when emotion or cunning and the like call for minor stoppages. But when there is nothing to arrest or complicate the spoken or written sentences of his personages, they flow on like Trollope's own. As a result his novels lie nearer to narrative poems than to the sort of novel that Dickens wrote. Speeches in the *Aeneid* and *Paradise Lost* are edited, as it were, by Virgil and Milton, and transmitted in their own style. There is no attempt on their part to endow their personages, who are individuals, with an individual style. The fallen angels have different characters, but they all use the same style in formulating their contrasted ideas. It is the same in Trollope. Pope said that if all the names of Shakespeare's personages were lost to us, we could supply them by reference to their style: it is one of those wonderful remarks about Shakespeare—Gray's 'Every word in him is a picture' is another—which the eighteenth century needs to be credited with. But if the names of Trollope's speakers were lost, the supplying of them would be quite impossible, unless there were some accidental and tell-tale peculiarity in the matter of the speech.

This is the first paragraph of a letter from Mrs Finn to the Duke of Omnium in *The Duke's Children*. Mrs Finn is a clever woman, and it is a formal letter, over which she took great pains. All that may be granted, and yet its consummate perfection is that of Trollope rather than Mrs Finn:

> As you will not come to me, I must trouble your Grace to read what I fear will be a long letter. For it is absolutely necessary that I should explain my conduct to you. That you have condemned me I am sure you will not deny;—nor that you have punished me as far as the power of punishment was in your hands. If I can succeed in making you see that you have judged me wrongly, I think you will admit your error and beg my pardon. You are not one who from your nature can be brought easily to do this; but you are one who will certainly do it if you can be made to feel that by not doing so you would be unjust. I am myself so clear as to my own rectitude of purpose and conduct, and am so well aware of your perspicuity, that I venture to believe that if you will read this letter I shall convince you. . . . (ch. xv)

Again, here are two parts of two letters in that late masterpiece, *Mr Scarborough's Family*. The first from Harry Annesley to his lover:

> Dear Florence,
>
> I wonder whether you ever think of me, or ever remember that I exist. I know you do. I cannot have been forgotten like that. And you yourself are the truest girl that ever owned to loving a man.

But there comes a chill across my heart when I think how long it is since I wrote to you, and that I have not had a line even to acknowledge my letter. You bade me not to write, and you have not even forgiven me for disobeying your order. I cannot but get stupid ideas into my mind, which one word from you would dissipate.

Now, however, I must write again, order or no order [they had been forbidden to correspond]. Between a man and a woman, circumstanced as you and I, things will arise which make it incumbent on one or the other to write. It is absolutely necessary that you should now know what are my intentions, and understand the reasons which have actuated me. I have found myself left in a most unfortunate condition by my uncle's folly. He is going on with a stupid marriage for the purpose of disinheriting me, and has in the meantime stopped the allowance which he had made me since I left college. . . .

But so it is, and I am driven to look about for myself. It is very hard at my time of life to find an opening in any profession. I think I told you before that I had ideas of going to Cambridge and endeavouring to get pupils, trusting to my fellowship rather than to my acquirements. But this I have always looked upon with great dislike, and would only have taken to it if nothing else was to be had. Now there has come forward an old college acquaintance, a man who is three or four years my senior, who has offered to take me to America as his private secretary. He proposes to remain there for three years. I of course shall not bind myself to stay as long; but I may not improbably do so. . . . I am to start in just a month from the present time. (ch. xlv).

And here is Florence in return:

Dear Harry,

Of course you were entitled to write when there was something to be said which it was necessary that I should know. When you have simply to say that you love me, I know that well enough, without any further telling.

Go to America for three years! It is very very serious. But of course you must know best, and I shall not attempt to interfere. What are three years to you and me? If we were rich people, of course we should not wait; but as we are poor, of course we must act as do other people who are poor. I have about four hundred a year; and it is for you to say how far that may be sufficient. If you think so, you will not find that I shall want more.

But there is one thing necessary before you start. I must see you.

There is no reason on earth for our remaining here;—except that mamma has not made up her mind. If she will consent to go back before you start, it will be best so. Otherwise you must take the trouble to come here,—where I am afraid you will not be received as a welcome guest. I have told mamma that if I cannot see you here in a manner that is becoming, I shall go out, and meet you in the streets, in a manner that is unbecoming.

Your affectionate—wife that is to be,

Florence Mountjoy.

Perhaps letters, being written things, are not the best test. The reproduction of conversation gives more scope for the representing of expression that is spontaneous. Even so, most of the speeches are beautifully shaped. Open the novels where you like and see if this is not so. The speeches are of the sort we should all like to be able to count on making—speeches that do not waste a word, which know exactly where they are going, and stride ahead with the utmost confidence. They are speeches like those of the Balliol men of the nineteenth century, who were said to be always exhibiting an effortless superiority—the superiority of perfect mastery. Coleridge spoke of the prospective power that an educated man is supposed to have over his expression—he foresees the end of a sentence the moment of embarking upon it. Few educated men have his power, as a matter of fact. But we feel that everybody in the novels of Trollope has it even though few of his personages are more than ordinarily educated or clever. The matter of everyday speeches—and Trollope's novels mainly afford opportunity for this sort of matter—is not difficult to master, but, even so, very few of us manage to do more than sketch our meaning, relying on other means (tone of voice, facial expression, movement of the hands, and so on) to complete it, and give it the proper shading.

But if Trollope's personages are usually Trollope himself when it comes to expressing their individual ideas, we can accept their unrealistic perfection of speech just because of the characteristics of Trollope's own style as described in my opening paragraph. That style is so pure and plain that it is indeed the style we should all prefer to speak and write if we had his sort of genius—Newman spoke of the simplicity that is an attribute of genius in general, and it certainly is an attribute of Trollope's in particular. It is a style for all purposes, being capable of handling the trivial and commonplace, and also the noble and splendid—it can indeed also handle the complicated when used by one who, like Trollope, always masters complexity so that it is reduced to its elements.

Those who are conversant with Dr Johnson's style in his letters and in much of the prose writing that he designed for publication will agree that Trollope's style is, to all intents and purposes, the style of Dr Johnson. Indeed, if we can stretch our imagination and think of the author of *Rasselas* as living a century later and as writing novels, he would have written novels very like Trollope's—perhaps in their matter, certainly in their manner. Here as a witness is a letter of Johnson, written like Harry Annesley's to a woman:

Dear Madam [Lucy Porter]

I suppose you are all frighted at Lichfield and indeed the terrour has been very general, but I am still of opinion that there is not yet any danger of invasion. The French fleet were within sight of Plymouth, but no gun was, I believe fired on either side. I had a note from Mr Chamier (the under Secretary of State) yesterday, that tells me. *The combined fleets* (of French and Spaniards) *are not in sight of land. They are supposed to be driven out of the channel by the Easterly wind. . . .*

Do not pay any regard to the newspapers; you will only disturb yourself. When there is any thing worth telling you, I design to let you know it. At present, it is the general opinion that the first action of consequence will be a great naval battle, and till that is over, all other designs, whatever they are, will be suspended.

I am, Dear Madam, your humble Servant
London. Aug. 24. 1777 [error for 1779]

Sam: Johnson.

The degree to which Trollope's general style is Johnsonian may be gathered from such a passage as that giving us the conversation of the Duke of Omnium and his son, Lord Silverbridge, in *The Duke's Children*:

'A club', said the Duke, as he sipped his coffee, 'is a comfortable and economical residence. A man gets what he wants well-served, and gets it cheap. But it has its drawbacks.'

'You always see the same fellows', said Silverbridge.

'A man who lives much at a club is apt to fall into a selfish mode of life. He is taught to think that his own comfort should always be the first object. A man can never be happy unless his first objects are outside himself. Personal self-indulgence begets a sense of meanness which sticks to a man even when he has got beyond all hope of rescue. It is for that reason—among others—that marriage is so desirable.'

'A man should marry, I suppose.'

'Unless a man has on his shoulders the burden of a wife and children he should, I think, feel that he has shirked out of school. He is not doing his share of the work of the Commonwealth.'

'I suppose I shall marry some day.'

'I should be glad to see you marry early', said the Duke, speaking in a low voice, almost solemnly, but in his quietest, sweetest tone of voice. 'You are peculiarly situated. Though as yet you are only the heir to the property and honours of our family, still, were you married, almost everything would be at your disposal. There is so much which I should only be too ready to give up to you!'

'I can't bear to hear you talking of giving up anything', said Silverbridge energetically. (ch. xxvi)

We might almost be reading a conversation in Boswell's *Life of Johnson*. Perhaps the only difference worth mentioning is that the Duke on one occasion inserts the tentative parenthesis 'I think.' Dr Johnson spoke as if the goddess of Truth herself were making him her mouthpiece.

One of the disadvantages of being born in the eighteenth century was that there had not yet occurred any of the literature of the nineteenth century. Dr Johnson had no great love for the novel form but he would, I think, have approved Trollope's contribution to it. In all honesty he could scarcely not have done so when the writer was so thoroughly Johnsonian.

VI

THE GEORGE ELIOT LETTERS I[1]

'It is the habit of my imagination', wrote George Eliot, 'to strive after as full a vision of the medium in which a character moves as of the character itself.' Such a vision of George Eliot is now more fully vouchsafed to her readers than ever before. The 'medium in which a character moves' is the more necessary for the understanding of a great writer who is also a woman. The bleak observation of Mr Wakem that 'We don't ask what a woman does, we ask whom she belongs to' was (mainly) out of date even when she wrote; but it remains true that we do ask 'whom she belongs to', wanting to know more than Cross could or would tell us about the daughter of Robert Evans, the sister of Isaac and Chrissey, Miss Evans of the *Westminster Review*, and 'Marian Evans Lewes', as well as 'George Eliot' and Mrs Cross. The magnificent Yale edition of the *Letters* gives us all we are ever likely to get, and it is a great deal. Most of the numerous passages 'pruned' from the letters by Cross (from motives understandable enough in 1885, so soon after the furore over Froude's *Carlyle*) are restored, and when this edition is complete, we shall have about 1,500 entirely new letters, collected by the present editor during the course of his twenty years' work. About a third are from other correspondents, and their inclusion is amply justified: for example, in the revelation of the anxieties and uncertainties—personal, artistic, and practical—which beset the writing and marketing of the first four novels, from 1856 to 1861.

This, so far, is the most fascinating part of the story. George Eliot's position in 1857 was delicate; she was doubly 'anonymous', with her friends unaware that Marian was 'George Eliot' and her publishers, perhaps fortunately, unaware that George Eliot was 'Mrs Lewes'. We are now enabled to see clearly the part played as critic and friend by that generous and canny Scot, John Blackwood, and by Lewes—stimulating, unselfish,

[1] *The George Eliot Letters*, vols. i-iii (1836–61), ed. Gordon S. Haight.

gay and sanguine, and manifestly enjoying the mystification ('Eliot' is 'that sensitive doubting fellow . . . you cannot think how shy and diffident') which is all part of the medium in which the awakening novelist moves. The letters are thick with new detail about the novels themselves, including George Eliot's specific justification of her material and methods against her publisher's occasional doubts; they will be an invaluable quarry for future criticism, as well as for the yet unwritten story of writer-publisher-reader relations in the mid-century, with all their social and literary ramifications. Does 'the Leviathan Mudie' deserve his discount if he takes only 500 copies of *Adam Bede?* Who should write to *The Times* about Liggins, that low-comedy character for whom the authorship was claimed? Is it right for George Eliot to answer 'No' to a direct question about her authorship? Should *The Mill on the Floss* be published in shilling numbers? How will the 'dropping of the incognito' affect 'the circulation in families'?

And through it all, from a mass of unspectacular but convincing detail, runs the evidence of the firm and intricately built personal relation of Lewes and Marian, independent of the sanctions of society, but never unmindful of them.

By the end of 1857, George Eliot knew that 'the long sad years of youth were worth living for the sake of middle age'. Cross's selection made those years seem too short. In this edition they fill the first volume, with many new letters, including one of vital importance to her father in 1842, in which she defined her changed religious position. But in the still earlier 'evangelical' letters, there is admittedly much that would not appeal to the Mrs Linnet of *Janet's Repentance*, who when reading the lives of preachers used to turn over the page 'whenever there was a predominance of Zion and the River of Life', looking for 'such promising nouns as "small-pox", "pony", or "boots and shoes" '. They contribute nevertheless something essential to the whole picture, giving us not only the 'medium' recalled in *Scenes of Clerical Life*, but the ranging intellectual interests of a provincial girlhood, and the first gauche movements of the style of one who at twenty already loved words, as 'the quoits, the bows, the staves that furnish the gymnasium of the mind'. At no period are her letters really intimate or easy in manner; they are more like William Wordsworth's than Dorothy's. But she is much more racy with Cross's prunings restored; from the earlier text we should not see how often George Eliot, like Mrs Transome, 'gave her thoughts a very sharp outline'.

The editing of letters is an especially searching test of scholarship; yet it receives few bouquets, since what the reader demands is simply the unobtrusive removal of all obstacles to understanding. In Professor Gordon Haight (already known from his *George Eliot and John Chapman*) these letters have their ideal editor, sensitive, tireless, and blessedly concise in conveying his abundant knowledge. The story he has to tell ends, for the present, with the writing of *Romola* in progress; with twenty more years of George Eliot's life to come, including *Middlemarch*, the remaining volumes will be eagerly awaited by many kinds of readers.[1]

[1] For reviews of the completion of the edition see above, pp. 28ff., and below, pp. 72ff.

VII

THE GEORGE ELIOT LETTERS II[1]

IT NEEDED courage for Mr Haight to start off his inquiries about George Eliot in the twenties. If he had been an Englishman it would have needed much courage. At that date no self-respecting young critic or researcher would have been seen dead with *Adam Bede* or *Daniel Deronda* within his rigid grasp. In those days we in England were all for the Elizabethan and seventeenth-century writers. In America no doubt there was more encouragement, but not enough surely to suggest that when the edition of the letters came to be published it would find so warm an enthusiasm for George Eliot as now exists on both sides of the Atlantic. Of course, where a novelist is concerned, there are likely to be two climates of opinion existing simultaneously: the opinion of literary critics and academics, and the opinion of common readers. These systems sometimes overlap. But they did not overlap in the twenties, when, to balance the critic's neglect, the common reader was assiduously borrowing the novels from public libraries or reading them in private inherited copies. The great Victorians have never ceased to be read except by those who write about their reading. From the start Mr Haight must have felt that he had behind him the silent approval of a host of common readers. It is interesting to find these common readers becoming more vocal now that they are being given the lead. They are now expressing their surprise retrospectively that the Victorian classics they have long remained faithful to have been forgotten by the critics who are vocal. They are *not* surprised that fashionable critics are now finding them great. They knew their greatness all along. George Eliot has always retained her interest universally as a social phenomenon. People who never opened any of her books acknowledged the historical interest of her marriage-less union with George Henry Lewes. Even in the twenties a prospective editor of her letters would at least know that there

[1] *George Eliot Letters*, vols. i-iii.

would be some welcome for any documents bearing on that. These two counts exhaust the encouragement that Mr Haight can have derived from outside. To them he added his own passion for the whole George Eliot matter.

We who have never edited any correspondence have enough imagination to see something of what the work involves. Broadly speaking, it is a business of collecting and explaining. Mr Haight has collected in the way that any real scholar undertaking to edit correspondence does collect—widely, resourcefully, with unbelievable luck. And with persuasiveness—only one of the batches of letters he tracked down has been denied publication by their present owner. The result is a huge number of letters which have never been printed before, or which have been printed in a garbled style, or not printed wholly. Notably, the numerous hitherto unpublished letters of George Henry Lewes to John Blackwood and John Blackwood's letters to George Eliot and Lewes—for Mr Haight prints letters to as well as from, when they have any importance. Of the importance of John Blackwood's, and of the much smaller number of letters by his brother and partner in the publishing business, William, I will remark two points of interest. They serve as indispensable annotations to the letters to which they are answers or which they call forth. And they contribute to the main narrative interest of these letters, which is not that of the 'marriage'—we are given few new details about that—but the remarkable interest of the history of the writing and publishing of *Scenes of Clerical Life*, *Adam Bede*, *The Mill on the Floss*, and *Silas Marner*. It is a fascinating story, replete with human interest—as also with bibliographical particulars, which have precision where the account by Cross, her husband-biographer, has vagueness. As a flame needs oxygen, George Eliot needed continuous encouragement both during the writing and after the publication of her work, and the main extra-domestic source and channel of this encouragement before the identity of George Eliot became common property was John Blackwood, who wrote with a blunt vigour and warmth beside which the letters he received from Lewes read awkwardly with would-be pleasant condescension. In the third volume the pleasantness of the correspondence between novelist and publisher is poisoned by sudden mistrust. For a time the letters to and from make painful reading. Hitherto George Eliot and Blackwood's had got on swimmingly. Or rather, had seemed to. For from the start there were latent difficulties over and above those that exist inevitably between publisher and successful author, however much below the surface. Until 1858 Blackwood's were corresponding with a shadow. At what point they guessed the identity of George Eliot we do not precisely know, but they were not assured of the correctness of their guess until February 1858 when *Adam Bede* was well under weigh. Hiding her identity, George Eliot felt from the start a sense of guilt. But what could she do? She was already at the top of the tree as literary journalist when she went to live with Lewes, whose marriage with Agnes Jervis had already broken up. When she came to write novels—that is, literature with the widest appeal—it was obvious that they would be denied the chance to prove their worth if they were known to be the work of a socially ostracized female. Deception was necessary for the sake of fairness to literature, and even for the sake of the public, who, as George Eliot well knew, would be the better for attending to the sort of works she meant to write, without being distracted by irrelevant gossip. A pseudonym was necessary. Its adoption, not unfair towards the public, was not wholly fair to her publisher, who was led to publish works issuing from a quarter that might damage him if and when it became known. This sense of guilt must have grown upon her when Blackwood's turned out to be so open, manly and generous. To the guilt on this score was added, when the writings sprang to fame, another more ordinary complication. Her letters express frankly her anxiety—it may be considered her practical need—to secure as much financial return as possible. Any successful author is tempted at moments to see his publisher as a mere merchant fattening himself on the precious life-blood of a master spirit. After much hesitation over who should publish *The Mill on the Floss* and how it should be published, she proposed terms to Blackwood's which were too clearly calculated to bind them hand and foot to what George Eliot thought right and proper—to a point indeed that made the Blackwood brothers unwillingly admit to each other that she was greedy. It may have been mainly because of Lewes that she succumbed to that unworthiness, or at best, unhappy necessity: when the matter was cleared up and Blackwood's cancelled their painful disappointments felt in private over a person who had struck them both by letter and in person as of sterling character, they absolved her as having acted under the influence of Lewes, whom they described in private as 'very keen'. The honourableness of Blackwood's is manifest. What their net profits out of George Eliot amounted to, up to this date and after, we do not know, but not every publisher would have disregarded the letter of the contract made for *Adam Bede*, and rewarded the author *pari passu* with their own rewards. The air finally brightens when they assure her that they felt no annoyance at having been, as it were, 'tricked' by a socially outcast genius, when for mercantile and other rarer reasons they prove to her that they are proud to publish her work, and wish to treat her in future, as they have in the past, with manly generosity. The last word comes in a letter of 1861 to a third party where George Eliot congratulates herself in having for publisher 'a man of such high character'. The only cause for regret is an aesthetic one—that John Blackwood persuaded George Eliot to review her description of Mrs Moss in *The Mill on the Floss*, and change 'a patient, loosely-hung, child-producing woman' to 'a patient, prolific, loving-hearted woman' —he praised the first reading as 'excessively good', but feared, at that date wisely, that 'some might take exception to it.'

This merest sketch of their relations at their most interesting point will show the reader that for all the uses to which George Eliot put the experience of Mary Ann Evans, she did not use the material that was most obviously rich—one can imagine the pleasure Trollope or Henry James would have found in using it for her. In the letters as they are arranged here we get the unfictionalized body of the material.

It is complicated in ways that one would like to go into—with blandishments and financial temptations coming from Dickens (that 'fallen angel', as one of Blackwood's assistants called him, but who had divined from the start that George Eliot was a woman) and others. One letter, hitherto unpublished, must be mentioned—a letter from Mrs Gaskell which begins with brilliant and devoted praise for the writings, but which, so as to 'be quite true in my ending', adds 'I wish you *were Mrs* Lewes. However, that can't be helped, as far as I can see, and one must not judge others'.

The reader of George Eliot's novels and Cross's *Life* must feel that he has now the amplest available materials for the study of the personality and character of Mary Ann Evans. Her character is thoroughly enough exposed to be found puzzling at times. There is some of the simplicity of nobility about it, and yet there is some pained elaboration. The sort of thing I mean is exemplified where she is writing to Mme D'Albert, the hostess who treated her kindly when she was abroad by herself after her father's death in 1849: 'You would not be very sorry, I hope, to receive a note from our hotel, telling you that we were there.' Perhaps some of it is more a matter of awkward expression than awkward sense: she is not always one of the masters of English prose. Never destitute of a fulness of meaning, she sometimes seems to have embarked on a sentence without due prospectiveness, the sentence as it proceeds being sometimes embarrassed by the remainder of the meaning.

The early letters, which almost fill the first volume, will greatly interest anyone seeking to learn more about the bearings of Evangelicalism on everyday life. Her religion prevents Mary Ann Evans from feeling at ease among worldlings, or among ordinary people when they take a slightly worldly fling. A list of disagreeable things includes 'the din of [man's] revelry'. She objects at having to make what seem too elaborate preparations for her brother's birthday party—though she may have objected because writing to Maria Lewis, her old teacher. But those same letters to Miss Lewis show her living a quite free intellectual life. She knows Young's *Night Thoughts* and Cowper's works through and through, and in the *Night Thoughts* at least there is, for all the stern tone, an almost heady intellectual gaiety: that poem, on which she was later to write her brilliant essay, adds to its solemn asseverations all the charms of the theatrical. And wonderful things are allowed in as light reading—Spenser's *Faerie Queene*, *Don Quixote*, and Southey's *Doctor*. She hears sacred music which, being Handel's, is of the theatrical sort. She responds constantly to 'all the sweet, peace-breathing sights and sounds of this lovely Earth'. Altogether we do not feel that her mind is any more starved than was that of young Milton. Indeed these letters are bursting with vernal ebullition. The young Evangelical must be seen in the light of the brilliant letter sent to Martha Jackson (Mr Haight thinks her the addressee) probably in March 1841, when she was twenty-one, and which is among the best of the letters hitherto unpublished:

Letters from a Town Mouse to a Country Mouse.

Dearest Rusticus,

. . . . In gloomy weather I shall fancy you with your feet on your fender, your double eye-glass over your nose, looking at me with friendly scrutiny as I tell you of my little affairs, or recall the impressions of my day's thought and reading. In fair weather, I shall fancy that we are strolling together round your five acres, which you contrive to expand into a large farm by elaboration of thought and handiwork, throwing as much soul into your indignant spudding of a single thistle as any ordinary Ofellus would spend over a crop large enough to seed the worlds in the Milky Way. I, your companion, pause mechanically where you pause—look at a cow when you look at her—watch the flight of a straw which you toss aside with your leisurely spud, and all the while chatter egoistically about my own thoughts and doings, complacently reflecting now and then, how very useful I am to you by keeping up your sympathy with a world where language is at a more sophisticated stage than Ba-a!

Towzer's nose pushes itself against my fingers, and then my fingers wander about his rough coat as I write. I am in the country, without the trouble of packing up: I see the autumn berries, I snuff the peculiar freshness of the autumn air between the hedge rows in the green lane, and the new soil the plough is turning over in the next field; or I wrap my cloak round me and enjoy the December hoar frost that defines every lingering brown leaf on the brambles or the young oaks; or I please myself in detecting the very earliest spring buds, and the delicate hints of colour on the bough tips; or I hear the swirl of the scythe as I watch the delicate grasses trembling under the eager flight and restless alighting of the humming insects; or I stand entranced before the glory of form and colour in the ripe full-eared corn field.

You will almost accuse me of valuing you as I do some painters' figures—for the sake of the landscape in which you are placed. Well! I suppose we are all loved (or despised) a little for the sake of our circumstances as well as for our qualities. The most heroic grocer would be under some disadvantage from the fact that you imagine him in company with pyramidal parcels of sugar, bladders of lard, and a general odour of tallow and the coating of cheese. And the most impudent thieving gipsy has the charm of the furzy common about her. What extrinsic charm have *I*, to make people care for me a little more than my qualities might deserve? Certainly none from the landscape about me, and as little from the carpets and curtains and other recommendations of an elegant interior which have often helped to fix a man's choice of his partner for life—(for who will pretend that a woman who is reached through a spacious entrance hall with Indian matting can appear as utterly commonplace as Miss Jackson seen through the open parlour-door as you enter the passage?). A little obloquy and a little celebrity are the two points of attraction in me beyond my personal qualities: apart from these I should be thrown back for the impression I make, on the sense or humour there might be in my conversation, or on the moral dispositions that might manifest themselves in my looks, voice, and actions. . . .[1]

Her mind—the mind we know so well from the novels, and admire so much—is already stretching itself in happy exercise, and already dealing with characteristic materials.

So much, brief as it is, in praise of the editor's collecting and what it tells us. As for his explaining, it is beyond praise. His annotations are as nicely worded as they are felicitously to the point. The twenty years he has spent on the collecting and editing have clearly been busily spent, and the moral triumph of the work is that its results are presented with the utmost economy. Of course Mr Haight is the last person to suggest that he understands every precise reference, that he has traced the source of every phrase enclosed in inverted commas. But when anything calling for annotation has not received it, the number of the calls that have been answered attests the pains of the frustrated search.

[1] *George Eliot Letters*, i, 85 ff.

VIII

THE GEORGE ELIOT LETTERS III[1]

NOTHING DIVIDES critical opinion so much as the letters of authors; no criteria are more elusive than those we apply to them. The letters of women writers would seem to be particularly vulnerable; no doubt the standard of charm set for them is higher. We remember that one critic called Jane Austen's letters 'trivial and dull . . . a desert of family gossip'; another heard in her sisterly jokes 'the whinnying of harpies'. One senses the irrational disappointment, even resentment, that in writing what she knew would please Cassandra, Jane Austen was not also concerned to please us: the expectation that the letters will give us something like the novels. Certainly readers seem to be more readily delighted by letter writers who have raised no expectations by published writings—forgetting that in the letters, say, of a Dorothy Wordsworth or a Jane Carlyle there is more *room* for complete self-expression, this medium being virtually their only one, their substitute for novels and poems. We seldom get it both ways.

The charm of spontaneous self-expression is not to be sought in George Eliot's letters, though now and then events shake it out of her; her letters belong to the tradition of Dr Johnson's, rather than Charles Lamb's. These are the letters of one who said 'I dislike letter-writing' and 'I do not willingly write or speak about my books'; Henry James wrote of her: 'her rich and complicated mind did not overflow in idle confidences . . . it was deeply reserved, and very far from egotistical'. Knowing her, he knew what *not* to expect from her letters when they were first published in 1885; he did not agree with the critics who found them disappointing. For opinion was divided then, as now. One reviewer, evidently expecting the letters to be more like the novels, said they seemed 'to conceal, as under a mask or domino, the vivacity and fertility which one naturally ascribes to the great author who understood labourers and

[1] *George Eliot Letters*, vols. iv–vii (1862–80).

butchers and farriers and sporting clergymen and auctioneers perhaps better even than she understood scholars and poets and metaphysicians'. To him her life seemed to supply 'a dusky background' to the novels, rather than to enhance the pleasure they give.

In the seven volumes of Mr Haight's edition of the *Letters*, with most of the letters from which Cross gave extracts now given complete, and twice as many more added, there is a much richer humanity, even if not quite the 'vivacity' of her humorous creations. We are given much more evidence of the width and liveliness of her sympathies, her concern with her correspondents' problems, domestic and intellectual; so that we understand why so many people turned to her in trouble. And the background of the life is by no means 'dusky'. She is, and on principle, reticent about her greatest source of happiness, her life with George Henry Lewes: but less reticent than Cross was on her behalf. The added letters contain such phrases as 'we are unspeakably happy' (though with an apology for giving such 'private news'); and much later, she looked back on 'twenty-four years of constantly growing love'. Sometimes there is a single qualification: 'as for us, we are alarmingly happy, and should have nothing to ensure us against the envy of the gods were it not for a few infirmities of advancing age'. The letters give so many details of these 'infirmities' as almost to supply a text book of psychosomatic illness (especially migraine and nervous indigestion); such detail runs counter to modern taste, but is typical of the Victorians' lack of reticence about ill-health (including death); and it is lightened by George Eliot's admission of exaggeration, and her enjoyment in finding picturesque comparisons for her haggard appearance—'I look like a persecuted witch', or 'I am as thin as a mediaeval Christ'. Again, there is the recurrent shadow of despondency about her work; for although in these last four volumes we meet her in mid-career, past successes gave her no confidence, only an added terror to the possibility of future failure. 'The habitual tone of her mind is distrust of herself', Lewes wrote, but his brighter influence turns even this depression into a family joke; and the reader learns to look forward to the recurrent, blissfully secluded holidays which signalize the end of each piece of writing, and in which the double happiness of achievement and affection unite. The 'duet of solitude', as she likes to call it, is much more in evidence in the letters than the famous Sunday afternoon receptions.

But these stand for something—for a status in society, achieved against odds by sheer intellectual eminence. These last four volumes of the *Letters* belong to the 'years of fame', and show us something of what fame meant to a Victorian novelist. Thanks to Lewes, she knew few of its troubles, little of the glare of publicity that shocked her in Dickens's later life with its 'feverish pursuit of loud effects and money'. For Lewes was, in Henry James's words, 'the most devoted of caretakers . . . a companion through whom all business was transacted . . . accident made rare, and exposure mitigated . . . he filtered the stream, and gave her only the clear water'. Some of the 'accidents' of fame are engaging in their fatuity, in that age when writers still had the glamour now reserved for film stars; we read of ladies pressing forward in the crowd to touch George Eliot's cloak, and of an authoress from New Jersey who submitted a novel called *Papa's Own Girl* for George Eliot's opinion; she may find crudities, but 'the work is certainly a significant one'. For once, George Eliot's dry comment to a friend has the vivacity of the novels: 'her letter seems to indicate a self-estimate in no need of consolation'. But, as the editor quietly remarks, 'not all the letters were transatlantic'. And not all feminine, either. One of her fans, an Englishman, was haunted by a dream that Mrs Lewes was desperately ill; if it was not so, would Lewes merely write 'Dream wrong' on the enclosed card and post it to him?

But George Eliot did value the more serious evidence of her growing influence and the new friendships it brought her, especially among younger men and women. Here, for instance, is a revealing remark: 'in proportion as I profoundly rejoice that I never brought a child into the world' [by the way, the editor has indexed this under 'Birth Control'] 'I am conscious of having an unused stock of motherly tenderness, which sometimes overflows. . . .' It 'overflowed', for instance, to Mrs Mark Pattison, Mrs Burne-Jones, and Elma Stuart. All these are her 'dearest daughters'; while, with a nice and perhaps prescient distinction, John Cross is 'dearest nephew'. The correspondence with these young friends makes a lighter supplement to the longer sequences to old friends, where the bond was a shared past: for instance, to Sara Hennell of Coventry, who had opened so many intellectual doors for her in youth, but herself remained essentially provincial, and had now grown rather peculiar and involved in her dim metaphysical speculations. But, as George Eliot wrote to Sara's sister, 'the old regard is much deeper than any new or transient irritations'. Her strong sense of the claims of 'old regard' makes one regret the more the disappearance of her letters to Herbert Spencer; whose later relation to her she defines in this precise and charitable comment:

> His mind rejects everything that cannot be wrought into the web of his own production. . . . We have long given up vain expectations from him and can therefore enjoy our regard for him without disturbance by his negations. He comes and consults us about his own affairs, and that is his way of showing friendship. We never dream of telling him *our* affairs, which would certainly not interest him.

Such incisive definition is also applied to contemporary public events, to all the most important intellectual movements, and occasionally, to contemporary literature. When George Eliot turned to novel writing in early middle-age, she was already a distinguished literary critic—a fact not generally realized, for her articles and reviews are still mostly uncollected and unknown.[1] But some of this loss is compensated by the new letters, which contain her views on most of the major works of the sixties and seventies. Some must have been suppressed by Cross because of their sharpness—for example, she is severe on Forster's *Life of Dickens*, on *The Ring and the Book* ('the subject seems to me unworthy of him'), on Pater's *Renaissance* (which she thought 'poisonous') and Mallock's *New Republic* ('a hateful book'). On the other side, there is her fervent tribute to Newman's *Apologia*, with the rare self-betrayal: 'a life how different in form from one's own, yet with how close a fellowship in its . . . spiritual needs and burthens'. Of contemporary

[1] This is less true since the appearance in 1963 of *Essays and Reviews of George Eliot*, ed. T. C. Pinney.

novels, she read at this date only what she expected to enjoy—which meant chiefly Trollope's. She found his books 'filled with belief in goodness, without the slightest tinge of the maudlin'; and she was also, unusually, aware of his art. Of his novel *Rachel Ray* she writes to him:

> I am much struck with the skill with which you have organized thoroughly natural and everyday incidents into a strictly related, well-proportioned whole—natty and complete as a nut on its stem.

And among minor and now forgotten novels, there is one which made an interesting appeal to her—*La Beata*, by Anthony Trollope's brother Thomas, which contains the germ of *Romola*.

That is only one of many details in the letters which are worth knowing and may affect future criticism of her own novels. It is also important to know of the slow and gradual growth of *Middlemarch*—'the various elements of the story have been soliciting my mind for years' she wrote; and to have Lewes's testimony that of all her characters, Dorothea was the most like her; and to have her own admission that Romola is 'ideal'—'I feel it acutely in the reproof my own soul is constantly getting from the image it has made. My own books scourge me'. That, I find the most haunting of her comments on her own work; but here is another one which may surprise some readers:

> I have always exercised a severe watch against anything that could be called preaching and if I have ever allowed myself in dissertation or in dialogue anything which is not part of the structure of my books, I have there sinned against my own laws.

But as regards the novels, what these letters give us above all, in incomparable fullness, is their publishing history: the strategy, the finance, the personal problems attending their various modes of publication. Most of the correspondence with John Blackwood is new, and makes it clear how large a part he played in her success—by his genial and particularized appreciation of her chapters as she wrote them, his skill in marketing, his readiness to experiment with a new format—notably the five-shilling parts of *Middlemarch*. Blackwood comes well out of the *Romola* affair, George Eliot's single defection—when she accepted £7,000 from Smith and Elder for serializing it in the *Cornhill*, and announced the fact to Blackwood in one of her very few ungracious letters. The London manager of the firm called it a 'disgusting transaction', but received the dignified reply from Blackwood: 'this going over to the enemy without giving me any warning . . . sticks in my throat but I shall not quarrel—quarrels especially literary ones are vulgar'.

The whole relation between George Eliot and her publisher deserves a detailed study in itself, and is also a major contribution to the unwritten history of the Victorian book trade. Anyone interested in the relative sales of cheap and expensive editions; or in the effect of the big circulating libraries; or the rates paid for articles by different periodicals, will find ample material, both in the letters and the appendices. There are even details about type and styles of binding; the *George Eliot Birthday Book*, admittedly very ornate, is apologized for—'we had to consider a colonial class rather as likely to be its largest buyers'.

I must be content with one more point, where the difference between publishing now and a century ago strikes me most forcibly—the speed of printing. She finished writing *Felix Holt* on 31 May; the printers had been on her heels, and the complete work, in three volumes, was on sale by 15 June. One trouble at least she was spared, the long suspense of modern authorship.

With the death of Lewes, the tale of her writings ends. The shock was great; for months it was as if she had died too. But then comes the final, unexpected chapter in her life—her marriage to John Cross, twenty years her junior. 'The one "change" I was unprepared for' said one friend; and she felt it herself; 'I am going to do what not very long ago I should myself have pronounced impossible for me'. She kept the secret from all her friends until after the wedding. The reader of the letters gets the surprise earlier, but it is equally dramatic. We have known only that Cross, who was a banker, and a family friend of some ten years' standing, had been visiting her to help with her financial affairs (though one note, 'I am in dreadful need of your counsel', suggests something more personal); then we learn that they had been reading Dante together; then, without warning, we have a letter to him beginning 'Best loved and loving one', and signed 'Beatrice'.[1]

As usual when she was going to surprise everyone, she went abroad, immediately on her marriage, leaving her stunned friends to recover as they could. On the whole they come out of it well—for one has to allow not only for the natural disappointment of old friends at not being confided in, but for the rigidity of the 'emancipated', to whom George Eliot's union with Lewes had become a symbol; and also for the particular doctrines of the Positivists, which forbade second marriages. But, as Frederic Harrison wrote to Cross: 'Every marrige is . . . a special and peculiar relation with its own conditions apart from any other marriage that ever was or will be'. Barbara Bodichon's response was the most spontaneous; and we may welcome the Victorian lack of inhibition that allowed her to write as she did: 'Tell Johnny Cross I should have done exactly what he has done if you would have let me and I had been a man'. Her brother, Isaac Evans, ended a silence of twenty-three years with his formal congratulations; a silence which, she said, 'has never broken the affection for you which began when we were little ones'—thus fulfilling in life the story of Maggie Tulliver and Tom. And indeed it is this seventh volume of the letters, least directly concerned with the novels, which is most nearly a novel in itself, rounding her life to its close, and restoring to our view the impulsive, even headstrong girl. The Indian summer of her life with Cross lasted less than a year; she died after a brief illness in the following December. With delicate timing, the editor ends with Cross's poignant letters to her friends—'And I am left alone in this new house we meant to be so happy in'.

Left alone, he dedicated himself to the task of biography; and on a singularly self-effacing plan, for the text of his *Life* largely consists of extracts from her letters and journals. This was the *Life* that Henry James read and reviewed, and from which he drew the impression of 'one of the noblest and most beautiful minds of our time'. That impression can only be deepened by the immensely fuller record that Mr Haight has assembled for us, and which I have tried to indicate by quoting almost exclusively from the *new* material. And the editor's

[1] See above, p. 31, where the letter is quoted in full.

expansion of the record, by including so many letters to and about her, is particularly felicitous, both for the variety it contributes, and the sense of saturation in the life of a period. But above all the living interest of the letters of George Eliot is that of the story they tell, the story of a life—and once more, in conclusion, I quote a contemporary opinion—a life 'serenely heretical, constantly aspiring, deliberately emotional'.

IX

TENNYSON'S SERIAL POEM[1]

THE *Idylls of the King*, like *Paradise Lost*, *The Prelude*, and *The Dynasts*, was a life-work, long prepared for by study and meditation and slowly perfected. But Tennyson's large design is unusual in that it grew and took shape partly in sight of his readers. The process may fairly be called serial publication, though of an uncommon kind; extending over forty-three years, with the intervals between instalments varying from seventeen years to one; the order apparently random; and the writer's reserve as to his intentions supplying a further element of suspense. The poem shares certain important characteristics with other Victorian serials, including the foresight and design which alone make possible the process of successful writing in instalments—as Dickens puts it, 'the whole pattern . . . is always before the eyes of the story-weaver at his loom'.[2] Another 'note' of serial publication is the peculiar closeness of contact between writer and readers and their sense of participa-

[1] 'Tennyson's Serial Poem' was given as the James Bryce Memorial Lecture at Somerville College, Oxford, on 28 May 1963. The references and some of the material in the notes have been added, but it has not otherwise been revised, and remains a lecture rather than an essay. Nor have I added references to an important study in a related field published in the following year, Dr Arthur Johnston's *Enchanted Ground: the Study of Medieval Romance in the Eighteenth Century* (1964), in which chapters vi–viii and the excellent bibliography are of obvious relevance to what I have said of the background of Tennyson's early reading and the rise of Arthurian scholarship.

Materials for the Life of Alfred Tennyson (4 vols., privately printed, 1895) is referred to as *Materials*, and *Alfred Lord Tennyson, a Memoir, by his son* (2 vols., 1897) as *Memoir*. I have also made use of Sir Charles Tennyson, *Alfred Tennyson* (1949) and *Six Tennyson Essays* (1954). The plan of this lecture has precluded discussion of Tennyson's handling of his sources in the *Idylls*, a subject on which much remains to be done; the most thorough treatment so far is in the editions of separate idylls by F. J. Rowe and G. C. Macaulay, and Herbert G. Wright, 'Tennyson in Wales', in *Essays and Studies*, xiv (1929) p. 71. See also A. Hamann, *An Essay on Tennyson's Idylls of the King* (1887), H. Littledale, *Essays on Tennyson's Idylls of the King* (1893) Richard Jones, *The Growth of the Idylls of the King* (1895). The only modern studies that seem to me of any value are F. E .L. Priestley's (see below, p. 82, n. 2) and Jerome Buckley's in *Tennyson, the Growth of a Poet* (1960).

[2] Postscript to *Our Mutual Friend* (1865).

tion, seen in their belief, warranted or not, that their advice and criticism might affect future instalments. And above all, there is the slow 'deepening [of] the impression'[1]—in George Eliot's phrase—because the publication is extended over a long period of time. The separate parts of Tennyson's poem were landmarks in many lives; one reader called it 'a strange memento of the passage of time'.[2] A man of fifty reading the accumulated series of ten in 1873 would recall reading the *Morte d'Arthur* as an undergraduate; but he would be over sixty before he saw the last instalment and nearly seventy before he read the last additional line. The enthusiastic James Knowles spoke of seeing the poem grow like Canterbury Cathedral—'far more poetical than St Paul's'—as 'round some early shrine, too precious to be moved, were gathered . . . a nave and arches, then rich side-chapels . . . then a more noble chancel. . . .'[3] Another recalled how 'gradually the astonished reader saw with delight the great plan of the work develop itself as idyll after idyll appeared in slow but steady succession'.[4] Others saw it not with delight but with satiety or even revulsion. For the 'deepening of the impression' worked both ways; if to one eminent Victorian who reviewed the poem 'it raises the character and the hopes of the age and the country which produced it', to another it was 'the ethics of the rectory parlour set to sweet music . . . making valetudinarians of us all'.[5] Some determined their views of the design before the poem was complete, and clung to them, resenting further additions 'with that reluctance which literary prepossessions always bring to an enlarging conception'; some, rereading the old parts in the light of the new, came to discern 'the absolute unity of the imaginative centre from the first piece to the last'; while others again, with curious logic, denied the possibility of any design in a work whose parts were written and published at

[1] Letter of 4 August 1872, on *Middlemarch* (*George Eliot Letters*, v, 297).

[2] *Blackwood's*, December 1872 (review of *Gareth and Lynette*).

[3] Letter in *Spectator*, 1 January 1870, signed 'J.T.K.'. Tennyson told Knowles 'your letter . . . is the best, and indeed might be called the only true, criticism of the Idylls' (*Nineteenth Century*, January 1893).

[4] A. Hamann, *An Essay on Tennyson's Idylls*, pp. 7–8.

[5] W. E. Gladstone, *Quarterly Review*, October 1859; John Morley, 'On *The Ring and the Book*', *Fortnightly Review*, March 1869, collected in *Studies in Literature* (1891), pp. 746–7.

wide intervals.[1] This was Buxton Forman's view, and it still persists in some quarters; and even Mr F. E. L. Priestley, in his valuable essay in 1949, while emphasizing the design, thinks that 'the real deficiency of the *Idylls* grows out of their piecemeal composition'.[2] Also persistent is the notion of Tennyson as a poet with no understanding of the needs of a large design, but an essentially lyric poet. But the poet who said, and showed, that 'every short poem must have a *shape*' would hardly suppose a long poem exempt; indeed Tennyson's critical standards for a long poem were exacting. 'Organizable lymph', such as he found in *Aurora Leigh*, was not enough; he demanded a 'compacted and vertebrate poem'.[3]

That was what he set out to make in the *Idylls of the King*; but from parts that would be seen gradually cohering into a whole. Form and procedure were interdependent. The form was new, and made new demands of its readers. One part of my theme is the growing shape of the poem, and the relation of certain idylls to the whole design; the other part is the course of the poem's reception, and this, if I may mention something so old-fashioned, bears on the literary history of fifty years and more.

For one of Tennyson's difficulties, as modern readers are not always aware, was that his matter was new. In 1842, Arthurian story was still strange to the ordinary reader, and even felt to be unacceptable as a subject for poetry; and this was undoubtedly one reason for the first long interval of seventeen years between the serial appearances. Here the spread of time and the slow deepening of the impression are particularly important. For by 1873, Arthurian story had become a household word; and part of the responsibility was Tennyson's, from the delayed effects of his own earlier work. There is no clearer instance of a poet creating the taste by which he was enjoyed; though that taste also eventually recoiled upon him, through his imitators, his rivals, and his sources themselves.

When he began his long poem in 1833, Tennyson was a

[1] [R. H. Hutton] *Spectator,* 8 February 1873, which includes comments on current criticism. The reviewers in *Blackwood's,* May 1870, and the obituarist in the *Quarterly,* January 1893, were among the objectors to piecemeal publication.

[2] *University of Toronto Quarterly,* xix (1949), p. 35.

[3] 'Personal Recollections by F. T. Palgrave', *Memoir,* ii, 506.

pioneer. He may have taken as a challenge the remark of Sharon Turner, in whose *History of the Anglo Saxons* in 1799 many of the Arthurian materials were relegated to a twenty-five-page appendix: 'If they should be found beneath the notice of the literati, they may be serviceable to some British Virgil.' No British Virgil had yet emerged; Arthurian matter was found more serviceable by the antiquarians—though they or their associates did produce two epics—Richard Hole's and Milman's; an unfinished Spenserian *Morte d'Arthur* by Reginald Heber, brother of the great collector; and the travesties by Hookham Frere and John Moultrie.[1] Scott was the only great Romantic with knowledge of this territory of romance, and in *The Bridal of Triermain* he chose to carry his knowledge very lightly. Tennyson owed more to *Marmion*; reading it as a child (as we know he did) he would find in the notes long quotations on the Chapel Perilous, Lancelot and the Sangraal—perhaps his first meeting with Malory. And in these very notes, in 1808, Scott announced that 'this curious work' was 'about to be republished'—for the first time since 1634. He had been preparing an edition himself (Scott's Malory is one of the great might-have-beens of literary history) but had just withdrawn in favour of Southey; Southey twice gave it up—it cannot have seemed a remunerative proposition—but in the end supplied an introduction to the reprint of Caxton in two handsome quartos published in 1817. But this 'bookseller's speculation' had been forestalled in the previous year by two cheap reprints of the

[1] Richard Hole, *Prince Arthur: or, the Northern Enchantment. A Poetical Romance in Seven Books* (1789); Henry Hart Milman, *Samor, Lord of the Bright City* (1818, revised 1839); Reginald Heber's *Morte d'Arthur* (written in 1812, first published in his *Life*, 2 vols., 1830); John Hookham Frere, *Specimen of a National Poem on King Arthur*, (1817–18). See also the verse adaptations in Gregory Lewis Way's *Fabliaux or Tales* with a preface by George Ellis (2 vols., 1800; 3 vols., 1815); the poems, and annotations, in John Leyden, *Scenes of Infancy* (1803) and *Scottish Descriptive Poems* (1803); John Moultrie's 'Sir Launfal' (written 1824, in *Poems*, 1837); Wordsworth's 'Egyptian Maid' (written 1828, published 1835). Only Leyden, Heber and Wordsworth are mentioned in M. W. MacCallum, *Tennyson's Idylls and Arthurian Story* (1894) and G. H. Maynadier, *The Arthur of the English Poets* (1907). The poems of Frere and Moultrie belong to the travesty tradition, represented also by Fielding's *History of Tom Thumb*, which continued popular in Kane O'Hara's version. There were two dramatic versions of Scott's *Bridal of Triermain*, an operetta by Ellerton in 1831, and Isaac Pocock's *King Arthur and the Knights of the Round Table: a new grand Chivalric Entertainment* (described in the *Morning Chronicle* as 'a horse-spectacle') in 1834, revived by Macready in 1842.

seventeenth-century text;[1] and it is these that should be treasured for their association with Tennyson, and with others. One of them, the Walker edition, was owned by another ardent Arthurian, Charlotte Yonge—in *The Heir of Redclyffe* she makes her hero, Guy Morville, defend it. I propose to quote the passage, as it serves to distinguish different points of view in the late 1840's which affected the reception of Tennyson's poem.

In the course of a game requiring the players to record their 'favourite character in history or fiction and time at which to have lived', Guy's choices are 'King Charles—Sir Galahad—the present time':

'Sir how much?' exclaimed Charles.

'Don't you know him?' said Guy. 'Sir Galahad—the Knight of the Siege Perilous—who won the Saint Greal.'

'What language is that?' said Charles.

'What! Don't you know the Morte d'Arthur? I thought everyone did! Don't you, Philip?'

'I once looked into it. It is very curious, in classical English; but it is a book no one could read through.'

'Oh!' cried Guy, indignantly; then, 'but you only looked into it. If you had lived with its two fat volumes, you could not help delighting in it. It was my boating-book for at least three summers'.

'That accounts for it', said Philip; 'a book so studied in boy-hood acquires a charm apart from its actual merits'.

'But it has actual merits. The depth, the mystery, the allegory—the beautiful characters of some of the knights'.

'You look through the medium of your imagination', said Philip; 'but you must pardon others for seeing a great sameness of character

[1] One in two 24mo volumes, published by Walker and Edwards, and one in three 24mo volumes, published by Wilks; both reproduce, inaccurately, the text of 1634, which itself was 'modernized', and printed from an imperfect copy of 1585. (The Wilks edition supplied the omitted matter.) It is certain that Tennyson used one of these editions; for example, he speaks of 'Brandagoras of Latangor' in *The Coming of Arthur*, where Caxton has 'Stranggore'. Hallam Tennyson in *Memoir*, i, 156, asserts that it was the Walker and Edwards edition, then in his possession, and 'much used by my father'. But in the Usher collection at Lincoln (catalogue, 268) is a copy of the Wilks edition, inscribed 'A. Tennyson' in Hallam Tennyson's hand. Perhaps he possessed one in boyhood and the other in the 1830's.

Tennyson must also have read Geoffrey of Monmouth, George Ellis's *Specimens of Early English Metrical Romances*, Scott's *Sir Tristram*, and Sharon Turner's *History*; the last-named is his source for the story of Nesting in *The Last Tournament*, related by Turner as a legend of King Alfred.

and adventure, and for disapproving of the strange mixture of religion and romance'.[1]

For many years we continue to catch echoes of these voices; the ignorant but curious—'Sir how much?'—the conventional and supercilious, and the devotee. Philip's is the voice of the *Quarterly Review*, the Establishment voice; Guy's is the poet's, the voice, let us say, of the young William Morris. By 1870, Charles has disappeared; there can have been no one left to say 'Sir how much?' at a time when, we are told, 'gentlemen of the turf were naming their racehorses after Arthur's knights'.[2] (It was rather later that children began to be named after them; 'Arthur' of course had been a favourite name throughout the century, but that was because of the Duke of Wellington.)[3]

But to return to the early 1830's, the period of Tennyson's earliest Arthurian poems; evidence of relative date is unclear, but it seems likely that his three lyrics *Sir Galahad*, *Sir Launcelot and Queen Guinevere*, and *The Lady of Shalott* preceded both the *Morte d'Arthur* and the draft schemes for long poem and play.[4] (*The Lady of Shalott* was published in 1832—to be received with discouraging sarcasm in the most influential reviews.) All three lyrics touch on characters that were to be used in the *Idylls*, but have no other connection with them, not even a common source; more suggestive is a single verse in the *Palace of Art*, also in 1832:

[1] *The Heir of Redclyffe* (1853), ch. x. For Sir Galahad, see also p. 97, n. 1 below.

[2] *Dublin Review*, April 1870. By 1878 undergraduates were calling themselves after Arthur's Knights; see *Ye Rounde Table* (1878), a periodical to which A. E. Housman contributed as 'Tristram'. In that year Stubbs, lecturing at Oxford, observed that 'in poetry it can scarcely be denied that Arthurian legend has begun somewhat to pall upon most ears'. Compton Mackenzie has recalled from his early childhood the tiles 'on either side of the asbestos gas-fire representing scenes from the *Idylls*' (*Octave One*, 1963, p. 233). The use of Arthurian names for locomotive engines dates from 1925; a 'Maid of Astolat' is still in service (see *The Times*, 24 October 1963).

[3] Charlotte Yonge, *History of Christian Names* (2 vols., 1863), ii, 128. Arthur is also a favourite name with novelists: Arthur Pendennis, Arthur Huntingdon, Arthur Clennam and Arthur Donnithorne.

[4] *Memoir*, ii, 122–5; the date suggested for the draft schemes is 1833, but they are evidently earlier than the *Morte d'Arthur*. At least part of *Sir Launcelot and Queen Guinevere* was written in 1830, and there is some evidence that all three are Cambridge poems.

Or that deep wounded child of Pendragon
Mid misty woods on sloping greens
Dozed in a valley of Avilion,
Tended by crownèd queens.

(Tennyson had hesitated about including these lines, and Hallam's bracing reassurance implies that the reason lay in their obscurity—'Don't be humbugged, they are very good; you may put a note if you will; yet Milton did not in *Paradise Lost*'.[1] Tennyson did not either, and in the contemporary context there is a certain defiance in the lack of notes to any of his Arthurian poems.) Thus early, Tennyson's imagination was caught by the closing scene of the king's life; this was the nucleus round which the rest formed, and no reader even of the pre-Vinaver Malory will be surprised.

Tennyson began his long poem at or near the end, and began it very early: the *Morte d'Arthur* was written by November 1833. It was worked on again in 1835, and FitzGerald long remembered Tennyson in that year reading from the manuscript in a boat on Windermere:

Nine years she wrought it sitting in the deeps
Upon the hidden bases of the hills.
Not bad that, Fitz, is it?

Published in 1842, the poem also was 'wrought' for 'nine years';[2] and one of the late additions, the prologue called *The Epic*, framed it in a modern setting,

At Francis Allen's on the Christmas Eve.

In apparently casual conversation it is recalled that one guest, Everard Hall, had had at college a gift for verse as well as for deep drinking—'What came of that?' (The question comes

[1] Letter of 10 October 1832, *Materials*, i, 111 (in *Memoir*, i, 90, the Pendragon reference is omitted).

[2] J. M. Kemble had seen a copy of the poem by November 1833 (*Memoir*, i, 130–1). For FitzGerald's note, see *Memoir*, i, 152–3. A copy of the poem in another hand is among the Houghton MSS at Harvard; the date is 1836 or later. It opens more explicitly:

After that battle where King Arthur lost
The flower of all the earth his Knights that made
THE TABLE ROUND. . . .

This copy lacks ll. 22–4 and 223–4, and reads 'waters wapping on the crag', (following Malory's 'I heard the waters wap') later revised to 'lapping'.

from the narrator, who is not the poet.) Frank, the host, interposes:

> he flung
> His epic of King Arthur on the fire!
> . . . these twelve books . . .
> . . . But I
> . . . pick'd the eleventh from this hearth.

And this 'eleventh book', the *Morte d'Arthur*, begins with a conjunction, 'So all day long the noise of battle roll'd', as if the preceding book had described the Battle of Camlan; and ends 'And on the mere the wailing died away'; all that could be left for the supposed twelfth book is a vision of the future and the return of the king. The return is glanced at in the epilogue, where the narrator dreams of 'Arthur like a modern gentleman'. In the final poem there is nothing of this, but rather the timelessness of a 'city building still And therefore built for ever'.

FitzGerald said the prologue was added 'to give a reason for telling an old-world tale'; a reason was felt to be necessary, as in Tennyson's *Godiva* and *The Day-dream*: a bridge for the reader from the everyday middle-class present to the romantic and legendary past—bringing it nearer, by admitting its distance. (If a precedent was needed there was Scott, with his artful recessions in *The Bridal of Triermain* from the nineteenth century to the eleventh and so to the sixth—linked stories within stories). But Tennyson's particular purpose here was also to dramatize certain doubts—and defiances—at one point almost trailing his coat: for the opening dialogue glances at that current and protracted critical insistence, which had been brought to bear on his own earlier poems, about the duty of the poet to deal with the present and not the 'exhausted past'. In the prologue Frank imputes to the incendiary poet the opinions of Tennyson's reviewers:

> He thought that nothing new was said, or else
> Something so said 'twas nothing—that a truth
> Looks freshest in the fashion of the day,

and Everard adds:

> 'Why take the style of those heroic times?

For nature brings not back the Mastodon,
Nor we those times . . .'

His epic, with its 'faint Homeric echoes, nothing-worth', was 'much better burnt'.

The 'burning' of the epic stands, I believe, for Tennyson's private decision against epic as the form for his long poem; but the reference to the other eleven books—not burnt, not written, but already in his mind, and two of them partly planned or even composed—makes the prologue also a disguised prospectus. When the *Morte d'Arthur* took its place as the *Passing of Arthur* in 1870, Tennyson's advertisement noted that it was 'connected with the others in accordance with an early project of the author's'. Meanwhile, the closing scene of the story could stand as self-contained even for readers unfamiliar with its earlier stages. Indeed, it is so self-contained, and seems to commit the poet to so little in what should precede it, that some have interpreted it as evidence that the whole was not yet foreseen even in outline. It might lead us to expect that the preceding narrative would include no more than Merlin's prophecies, the receiving of Excalibur, the deeds of the Round Table and the final battle; there is no reference to Lancelot or Guinevere nor any of the dead knights. It is the story of glory departed, of a great king defeated and dying; a Christian king, in 'a broken chancel with a broken cross', with supernatural aid and prospect of healing; the Round Table is an image of the mighty world, but there is no allegorical conflict, nothing that could be interpreted as 'sense at war with soul'. In spite of 'I perish by this people which I made', the tragic emphasis is not on betrayal, but rather on the inherent condition of man in time, loss, change, death. But these may prove the deepest levels of the poem. And the winter landscape—the icy caves, the tingling stars, the long glories of the winter moon, Sir Bedivere 'clothed with his breath and looking as he walk'd Larger than human on the frozen hills'—where Malory specifies no season—suggests that Tennyson had already foreseen the 'symbolic year'.

But on the case he had put in the Prologue the verdict of 1842 was clear, or he chose to think so. Twenty-five years later, thinking perhaps that all that was then still unwritten might have been behind him, he said, 'I had it all in my mind, could have done it without any trouble. The reviews stopped me'. Their general tenor was encouraging to the writing of a long poem, but insistent that it ought to be on a contemporary theme; John Sterling in the *Quarterly*, sympathetic to the volumes as a whole and therefore the more impressive where disapproving, classed the *Morte d'Arthur* among 'fancy pieces', 'borrowed from those conceptions of past ages that have now become extremely strange or quite incredible to us'. The poet who 'rushes away with us into the ruins and sepulchres of old supernatural beliefs . . . can make no direct impression on our feelings . . . The miraculous legend of "Excalibar" [*sic*] does not come very near to us . . . a mere ingenious exercise'.[1]

It was evident that in such a climate a long poem on King Arthur would risk neglect and misunderstanding; Tennyson was not 'stopped', but the order of his writing and publication was altered, and he cherished his design more secretly, saturating himself in the subject, and missing none of the new texts that were being edited—such as the *Thornton Romances* in 1844, the *Brut* and the alliterative *Morte Arthure* in 1847, and the *Mabinogion* in Lady Charlotte Guest's translation in 1838–48. Also in 1848, Tennyson's enemy Bulwer Lytton began to publish his *King Arthur* in twelve books; the notes and a motto from the *Brut* on the title page gave it a factitious air of mediaevalism, but as Lytton said, he had 'borrowed but the names', 'preferring to invent for myself an entirely original story'. (Tennyson's opinion is not recorded.) In the summer of 1848 Tennyson spent two months exploring Cornwall, and met a genuine fellow enthusiast, near where

> . . . the long wave broke
> All down the thundering shores of Bude and Boss.

Hawker of Morwenstow recorded 'much converse on Arthur and his Queen', and 'lent him books and manuscripts about King Arthur which he carried off, and which, perhaps, I shall never see again'.[2]

[1] *Quarterly Review*, September 1842.

[2] From Hawker's MS account of the visit, given in C. E. Byles, *The Life and Letters of R. S. Hawker* (1905), pp. 190–4. Tennyson sent him a copy of the *Idylls* in 1859, and of the *Holy Grail* in 1869.

By now the seed of Tennyson's Arthurian poems was flowering in many minds, especially young minds. Both Morris and Burne-Jones had read them in boyhood; when they met as undergraduates in 1853 (in an Oxford where 'all reading men were Tennysonians') this was an immediate bond. In his first term Jones wrote to a school friend:

Learn Sir Galahad by heart; he is to be the patron of our order. I have enlisted one in the project up here, heart and soul. [It was of course Morris.] Signed General of the Order of Sir Galahad.

Neither had yet read Malory; it was two years before Jones found a bookshop with a copy of Southey's edition, and he could not afford it; but Morris could, and it became their bible. And so to the *Oxford and Cambridge Magazine*; Rossetti's illustrations; the ten frescoes in the Oxford Union; and Morris's *Defence of Guinevere*. At Cambridge, the collection called *Cambridge Essays* in 1855 contained George Brimley's long article on Tennyson, twenty-five pages of it devoted to the *Morte d'Arthur*. One other example: Frederick Furnivall's reading of Tennyson's *Morte d'Arthur* as a youth of seventeen was, he said, 'the beginning of his enthusiasm for mediaeval literature'; which led (the link is explicitly made by Furnivall himself) to his Roxburghe Club editions of Arthurian romances and the founding of the Early English Text Society; among the first seventy-five subscribers was 'Alfred Tennyson, Farringford'.[1]

By 1855 Tennyson had planned the final shape of his long poem; but the two items that he chose to write first were as distant as possible from the *Morte d'Arthur*: in order of writing they were *Nimue* (afterwards *Vivien*), and *Enid*, from the *Mabinogion*, partly written during two months in Wales, exploring Welsh manuscripts and studying the language.[2] These two were evidently chosen because they were self-contained stories which could stand together as a contrasting pair; and

[1] J. W. Mackail, *Life of William Morris* (1899), ch. 2–4; *Memorials of Edward Burne-Jones* (2 vols. 1904), i, 77, 104, 116–17; *Frederick James Furnivall, a Record* (1911), p. xlvi, p. 11. Tennyson's name as a subscriber is in E.E.T.S., *Arthur ... from the Marquis of Bath's MS*, ed. Furnivall (1864).

[2] Coventry Patmore and his wife helped him by copying Welsh ballads and elegies from manuscripts in the British Museum (Sir Charles Tennyson, *Alfred Tennyson*, p. 302; and see the letter from Emily Tennyson quoted in Joanna Richardson, *The Pre-eminent Victorian*, 1963, p. 101.)

that was how he meant to publish them, under the title *Enid and Nimue: the True and the False*[1]—in itself a small temporary unity, but ready to take its place in the larger design. When he decided to write and add two more, *The True and the False* was still to be the main title; its rejection has been taken to imply a change of purpose, but I think wrongly. For the 'true and the false' remains as one of the large, simple antitheses that are among the 'vertebrae' of the whole poem. It is not a crude contrast, for it is crossed by the doubtful question of what is true and what is false: Leodogran's doubts of Arthur's claim to be King; Merlin's 'truth is this to me and that to thee'; and the confusion that falls on Arthur's heart before the final battle,

> I know not what I am,
> Nor whence I am, nor whether I be King.

Midway in *Enid* stands the narrator's comment, which so far appears to be simply evoked by the immediate situation—Geraint's doubts of Enid's truth:

> How many among us at this very hour
> Do forge a life-long trouble for ourselves,
> By taking true for false, or false for true
> Here, thro' the feeble twilight of this world
> Groping. . . .

But this surely announces one of the great uniting themes of the poem. Tennyson is also laying foundations for his main narrative: the ground of Geraint's mistrust and Nimue's malice is the same—'the rumour [that] rose about the Queen'—and, as a motive, it is his invention.

Enid has nevertheless been felt to be too self-contained, too long and leisurely a narrative to be consistent with the final proportions of the completed whole. It is self-contained by its happy ending; faith is restored, the tyrant Edyrn is 'nobly changed'. And the amplitude of description can be justified, in a story designed to fall early in the sequence—standing first in 1859, second and third in the final arrangement—as part of the unfolding of a world seen by a traveller moving through it:

[1] Title of the trial issue, printed in May 1857 (*Materials*, ii, 180).

> [The] little town with towers, upon a rock,
> And close beneath, a meadow gemlike chased
> In the brown wild, and mowers mowing in it;

the fortress 'white from the mason's hand', Yniol's castle in decay; and especially of the wild world of 'lawless turbulence' outside Camelot, the 'naked hall' of Doorm, the forest where

> . . . Many passed but none regarded her . . .
> A woman weeping for her murdered mate
> Was cared as much for as a summer shower;

and 'the common sewer of the realm', which the king will cleanse, 'clear the dark places and let in the law'. Another of the poem's large antitheses, Order and Disorder, is already established.

The reception of Tennyson's poems generally began before publication through the submitting of manuscript or trial printing to friends. And his immediate reason for not publishing these two idylls alone was, according to Palgrave's MS note[1], 'a remark upon Nimue which reached him'. I believe we can identify that remark and its source. Burne-Jones, now, as will be recalled, a devotee of Malory as well as of Tennyson, protested with 'pained face and eager expostulation' against the use of the beautiful name Nimue, the Lady of the Lake, for his wily enchantress; so Tennyson 'good-naturedly changed it to Vivien'.[2] In any case it was only the name that he had taken from Malory; his source was the story in the 'Continuation of Merlin'.[3] He not only revised, but held back both poems until he had written *Elaine* and *Guinevere* as a second balancing pair. As a general title *The True and the False* was equally appropriate, and it was used for the next trial-printing, but along with a sub-title *Four Idylls of the King*. Out of this came the final title *Idylls of the King*; the word 'Idylls', modest and precautionary, limited his claims and commitment (*Idylls* I think is more limiting than *Four Idylls*); but the presence of the word 'King', underlined by the motto from Joseph of Exeter, 'Flos regum

[1] In his copy of the trial issue, given to him by the poet 27 December 1857, and now in the British Museum (C.59.a.25).

[2] *Memorials of Edward Burne-Jones*, i, 182.

[3] It was easily accessible, being included in Southey's edition of 1817 and in the notes to the *Mabinogion*.

Arthurus', hinted at the poet's larger intentions. At the same time there was nothing that openly suggested, as the *Morte d'Arthur* prologue had done, that these four were part of a prospective whole. Readers were left to take them either way.

The group of four is also calculated to form a temporary unity, formally balanced and with the main lines of the narrative now exposed and, in *Guinevere*, gathered to a climax that could be a conclusion. *Elaine* is the largest in reference, emotionally and pictorially, yet the most compact; at once the complete story of Elaine, and a centre casting rays into the past and future of Lancelot, Guinevere, Arthur, and the Round Table—a true 'idyll of the King'. Sir Charles Tennyson chose it as an example of Tennyson's narrative power, in rebutting Mr T. S. Eliot's strange statement that Tennyson 'could not tell a story at all'. There is here a particularly beautiful use of that narrative device common to nearly all the idylls: beginning in the middle of a situation with a new character, and then winding back to account for it:

> Elaine the fair, Elaine the loveable,
> Elaine, the lily maid of Astolat,
> High in her chamber up a tower to the east
> Guarded the sacred shield of Lancelot. . . .
> How came the lily maid by that good shield
> Of Lancelot, she that knew not ev'n his name?

So each idyll seemed a fresh start, and it was possible for readers of the four to take each as a single unit; 'four poems of unequal length, each of which bears a lady's name' was the cautious approach of one reviewer, and several, guided by the separate titles, treated them as contrasted studies in feminine character; one saw the common theme as 'love—its diseases and counterfeits'.[1] But their interconnection was also discerned at a deeper level—'a set of stories with continued allusion to a latent thread'—with 'a moral unity and a living relationship'; the connection with the 1842 *Morte d'Arthur* was generally seen and aroused considerable speculation as to what the form portended, along with some advice. Sometimes the compactness of treatment was welcomed: the reviewer who said 'length—interminable length—is the bugbear inseparable from the name of

[1] *Blackwood's*, November 1859; *Macmillan's*, November 1859.

Arthur', but 'we need not fear from Tennyson another twelve cantos of fable, mythology, and antiquarian learning' was surely thinking of Bulwer Lytton's misconceived experiment. The word 'Idylls' was often objected to as misleading—these poems were not pastoral, not pictures of common life; they should have been called Books, and could be regarded as 'long episodes for a grand epic Arthur'. 'We do not despair of seeing Mr Tennyson achieve . . . the structure of a full-formed epic.' In this writer's view, the subject was suitable—'it is national; it is Christian'; in another's, 'the disproportion and incoherence of the materials [was] fatal' to epic, and Tennyson's choice of form showed a true instinct.[1] But whatever name was given to the series, the consensus of opinion was that the poet would and should continue it. His choice of a subject from the past was no longer seen as a radical objection, for he had shown his power of bringing the past into the present; this is generally applauded, though with a note of surprise if not of warning: Tennyson had 'given new life' to 'exquisitely beautiful fossils'; 'Say what people like, the world in general cares uncommonly little about King Arthur'; 'the subject seems most remote'; 'we have no belief in Arthur', the legends 'belong to fairyland', are 'a forgotten cycle of fables', 'the rugged creation of crusade romance'; though it was also conceded that there might be advantages in 'a world-famous hero of whom nothing whatever is known'. These representative quotations (from six different reviews)[2] suggest that some ignorance as well as distaste for Arthurian story still prevailed, outside the circle of scholars and of Pre-Raphaelite poets and painters; only a few reviewers at this date comment in any detail on Tennyson's treatment of his sources; he is not yet charged with misrepresenting Malory. And the idylls are still treated as if they were alone in the

[1] *National Review*, October 1859; *Bentley's Quarterly Review*, October 1859; *Blackwood's*, November 1859; *Edinburgh Review*, July 1859; *Quarterly Review*, October 1859; id., April 1869. Bagehot was the reviewer in the *National Review*, Anne Mozley in *Bentley's Quarterly*, J. M. Ludlow in *Macmillan's*.

[2] *Westminster Review*, September 1859; *Bentley's Quarterly Review*, October 1859; *Contemporary Review*, April 1868; *Edinburgh Review*, July 1859; *Saturday Review*, 16 July 1859; *Dublin University Magazine*, April 1860. The only reviewers to show any first-hand knowledge of the sources are Ludlow, Anne Mozley, and Patmore; Patmore's knowledge is evident much earlier, in his articles in *Lowe's Edinburgh Magazine* in 1846, which may have been known to Tennyson.

field—without reference to Arnold, Owen Meredith, or Morris,[1] and naturally no one noticed the anonymous *Queen Iseult* in *Undergraduate Papers* in 1857, written in fact by Swinburne of Balliol.

The great majority of the reviewers were enthusiastic; and though in my quotations I have left them anonymous, we can in fact identify several distinguished names—J. M. Ludlow, Anne Mozley, Bagehot, and Coventry Patmore (author of *two* long anonymous reviews, in the *Edinburgh* and the *North British*—he had read the *Idylls* before publication, and betrays the fact by quoting the unrevised text). Gladstone also had seen them and he persuaded the *Quarterly*'s editor, Whitwell Elwin, to allow him a free hand in reviewing them, in a particularly high-minded and eloquent piece of criticism, urging the poet to make the *Idylls* the basis of an epic and emphasizing the noble morality of the King in *Guinevere*; the review carried great weight at the time, but was the kind that might eventually, in Tennyson's phrase, 'set his foes blessing'. There were as yet few foes, but several who voiced their doubts more privately. Ruskin, as a devotee of *Maud*, showed some disappointment with 'the increased quietness of style', and said 'so great power ought not to be spent on visions of things past but on the living present'; to Elizabeth Browning in Italy, the *Idylls* seemed 'far-off, flat, and cold'; Carlyle thought Tennyson was treating his readers like infants or old ladies, though 'the lollipops were superlative'; Bulwer Lytton thought Tennyson 'a poet adapted to a mixed audience of school girls and Oxford dons', though he knew very little about either. The diversity is summed up in the picture of the aged Crabb Robinson, at a eulogistic lecture on the *Idylls* by George Macdonald, 'for ever whispering "*May* be so—may be *not*".'[2]

[1] Arnold's 'Tristram and Iseult' in *Empedocles on Etna* (1852); Owen Meredith's 'Elayne le Blanc', 'Queen Guenevere', and 'The Parting of Lancelot and Guinevere' in *Clytemnestra* (1855); Morris's *Defence of Guenevere* (1858). The *Constitutional Review*, September 1859, alone makes passing reference to Arnold and Owen Meredith. Other Arthurian poems published since 1842 are F. W. Faber's *Sir Launcelot* (1844, revised for 2nd edn. 1857) and Lowell's *Vision of Sir Launfal* (1848), both largely imaginary. See also p. 98, n. 2 below.

[2] Ruskin to Tennyson, September 1859 (*Memoir*, i, 452–3; E. T. Cook, *Life of John Ruskin* (2 vols., 1911), i, 465). Elizabeth Barrett Browning to William Allingham, 9 October 1859, *Letters to William Allingham*, 1911, p. 104; *Correspondence of*

But Tennyson received every encouragement, private and public, to continue his serial, and further instalments within a few years were generally expected. He was now, however, much more impervious to praise or blame: 'He reads the reviews and is amused to find how often he is misunderstood' was noted by Caroline Fox in 1860. Tennyson was again visiting Cornwall: 'The Welsh claim King Arthur', she says, 'but the poet gives all his votes to us'.[1] It is in Lyonnesse that the story begins and ends, and at this time Tennyson evidently had the *Coming of Arthur* particularly in mind. By 1862 he had 'arranged all the intervening Idylls', and records of his reading and travels show that his thoughts were often on them;[2] but he postponed the writing of the long-pondered *Holy Grail*, because, as he said in response to urgent entreaties from friends, he was 'not in the mood'; with the result that at least five long poems on the Grail were published before his.[3] They did not influence him, unless negatively; but their existence is one cause of the completely different climate of opinion when his long-expected next instalments appeared at the end of 1869. By 1860 the rush of popular interest, obviously accelerated by his own volume, is already evident. We read in one magazine that 'a familiarity with the *Morte d'Arthur* has lately become almost indispensable' for novel-readers; in another, that 'Arthur is come again!'; the knights 'crowd upon us everywhere in prose and poetry';[4] a little anonymous volume of verses, called *Arthur's Knights*,

Carlyle and Emerson (2 vols., 1883), ii, 339–40; *Henry Crabb Robinson on Books and their Writers* (3 vols., 1938), ii, 798 (8 June 1860); *The Life of Edward Bulwer, first Lord Lytton* (2 vols., 1913), ii, 431, 471. Another early dissentient was Matthew Arnold, who failed to find in the *Idylls* 'the peculiar charm and aroma of the Middle Ages' (letter of 17 December 1860; *Letters*, i, 127; and see p. 101, n. 1 below).

[1] Caroline Fox, *Memoirs of Old Friends* (1882), p. 324.

[2] Besides visiting Cornwall, he went to 'Camelot' (Winchester), and in 1859–61 was reading the stories of Gareth, Pelleas, and Tristram in the *Morte d'Arthur*; he also talked of writing on the Quest of the Sangraal.

[3] James Russell Lowell, *The Vision of Sir Launfal* (1848); [Anon], *Arthur's Knights, an adventure from the Legend of the Sangrale* (1858); George Macdonald, 'The Sangreal', in *Good Words* (1863); R. S. Hawker, *The Quest of the Sangraal, Chant the First* (1864); Thomas Westwood, *The Quest of the Sancgreall, The Sword of Kingship, and other poems* (1868). Westwood's letters in *A Literary Friendship* (1914), contain interesting comments on Tennyson's *Holy Grail*. J. S. Stuart Glennie, *King Arthur: or the Drama of the Revolution* (2 vols., 1867, 1870) also touches on the Quest.

[4] *Fraser's*, August 1860; *Blackwood's*, September 1860.

first privately printed in 1858, 'for the amusement of those young people who have some curiosity about the Early English romances and few means of gratifying it', was twice reprinted, and Thomas Wright's preface to his 1858 edition of Caxton's Malory said that some knowledge of these stories was 'absolutely necessary for those who would understand those Middle Ages which have of late years been so much talked of'. But the need was still felt for a popular modernized abridgment for those deterred by the 'antiquated spelling and quaint style'; it was met by a Christmas gift book of 1861, 'particularly designed for boys', and dedicated by permission to Tennyson by J.T.K. (This is Knowles, and it was the means of his introduction to the poet.) Meanwhile a very well-informed account of Arthur's Knights, with long quotations in Middle English and Old French, was running in the magazine edited by Charlotte Yonge;[1] and finally in 1868 came the popular and long-loved Globe edition, Caxton's text modernized and expurgated.[2] In the higher reaches of scholarship, the early 1860's saw Furnivall's Roxburghe Club editions of Lovelich ('our great Victorian poet has glanced over these pages') and of the French *Queste*. This has one of Furnivall's vast sprawling introductions—odds and ends of scholarship, muscular Christianity, romantic feminism, and references to social evils; it also includes the first extended objection to Tennyson's representation of the King in the *Guinevere* idyll, on the grounds that a king who had committed incest had no right to condemn. I abridge drastically his torrential and discursive pages:

To any one knowing his Malleore . . . to come on Arthur rehearsing to his prostrate queen his own nobleness and her disgrace, the revulsion of feeling was too great, one could only say to the 'Flower of Kings', 'If you really did this, you were the Pecksniff of the

[1] Ellen L. Millington, *King Arthur and his Knights*, in the *Monthly Packet* (edited by Charlotte Yonge), 1859 to 1864. Miss Yonge's own *History of Tom Thumb* (1855) is a storehouse of Arthurian lore for the general reader; and an anonymous version of 'The Legend of Sir Galahad' had appeared in the *Monthly Packet* in 1852–3.

[2] 'What is wanted, therefore, is an edition for ordinary readers, and especially for boys, from whom the chief demand for this book will always come; and such an edition the present professes to be . . . Such phrases or passages as are not in accordance with modern manners have been . . . omitted or replaced' (Introduction by Sir Edward Strachey).

period' . . . I quite admit that Mr Tennyson . . . has a right to combine the legends as he will (and whatever he has done or may do with them the English world will be grateful) but I desire to point out that . . . [and so to an account of Arthur's own sin, concluding] If any one is to be blamed for men's lusts, let it be *men*.[1]

I have paused over Furnivall because he represents a new type of reader, who knows some of Tennyson's sources and turns them against him.

The result of all this editing was that there was more and more material for the several minor Arthurian poets of the sixties to draw on; most however drew chiefly on Tennyson, successfully copying only the inessentials.[2] The exception was Hawker, poet of the unfinished *Quest of the Sangraal*, who said truly, 'I know I am dogmatic, proud, and mysterious. But I am not a plagiarist'.[3]

Tennyson wrote his *Holy Grail* idyll in 1868; he had 'seen the subject clearly for some time', and the whole poem was completed in a fortnight and hardly afterwards revised. The manuscript shows no hesitation over the radical decision of *how* to tell the story—narrated at a distance by Percival in the monastery.[4] A year later it was published with *The Coming*

[1] *La Queste del Saint Graal* (Roxburghe Club, 1864), pp. vi–vii. It was perhaps because of such reference to the incest episode that Tennyson made the disclaimer in 'To the Queen', 1872:

> him of Malleor's, one
> Touch'd by the adulterous finger of a time
> That hover'd between war and wantonness.

[2] For example, W. J. Linton's 'The Old Legend of King Arthur' in *Claribel and other Poems* (1865), transparently imitative of Tenyson's *Morte d'Arthur*, and Sebastian Evans's 'Arthur's Knighting' in *Macmillan's Magazine*, August 1869.

[3] C. S. Byles, *Life of R. S. Hawker* (1905), pp. 456–7; Hawker was complaining of a notice in the *Church Review*. He republished his poem in *Cornish Ballads* (1869), but never completed it.

[4] 'I feared for years to touch the subject of the "Holy Grail" and when I began, finished it in a fortnight'. The poem was written in September 1868, and the complete manuscript survives, in MS Eng. 952, notebook 38, in the Houghton Library. This consists of 52 pages, beginning with a prose draft of about 18 pages, interspersed with passages of verse. This carries the narrative to the close, but does not include Percival's meeting with Bors and his account of his meeting with Lancelot; and Percival's confession is evidently a later addition. The verse draft follows, and is substantially that of the published idyll, though in slightly different order and with many minor stylistic differences. Further changes

of Arthur, *Pelleas and Ettarre*, and *The Passing of Arthur*—the old *Morte d'Arthur* enclosed in a new beginning and end.[1] At the same time the old idylls were republished, some with new titles, '*Merlin* and Vivien', '*Lancelot* and Elaine'—which emphasized their relation to the whole. Tennyson gave much thought to his titles; the *Coming* and the *Passing* were substituted at a late stage for *The Birth of Arthur* and *The Death of Arthur*,[2] and are titles appropriately more mysterious, suggesting process rather than event. But the whole volume, as if to allay suspense, was called *The Holy Grail and other poems*; a note directed the reader how to order them in the series, and gave a collective title, *The Round Table*, to the six now framed by the *Coming* and *Passing*. When the accumulated eight are seen together, the narrative unity is at once plain; this is the story of Arthur as King, in victory and defeat; the founding and breaking of his 'goodly fellowship'; the original emphasis of the *Morte d'Arthur* is restored and the Round Table idylls fall into place as illustrative, marking the stages of decline.

Many reviewers, eager to grasp and assess what they supposed to be the completed poem, had studied the new and old poems in sequence, and dealt at elaborate length with the 'noble design' and its 'essential unity'.[3] Some hastened to label it 'a great epic', and discovered a continuous allegory with Arthur as the conscience, the soul, or even 'the Crowned Soul'. To the term 'epic' Tennyson strongly objected as a 'misnomer',[4]

were no doubt made when the poem was copied for the press the following month, and in the trial-printing of November 1868, of which no copy survives.

The first five pages of the prose draft were printed in *Materials*, iii, 141–5.

[1] The opening makes it 'That story which the bold Sir Bedivere . . . told . . . in the white winter of his age'. The additions amount to 144 lines before the *Morte d'Arthur* begins, and 30 lines at the end. Further additions were made in 1873, and also to the *Coming of Arthur* and *Pelleas and Ettarre*.

[2] The British Museum has a copy of the trial-printing of the four new idylls (Ashley 2104) and some manuscript drafts (Ashley 4521). The titles are 'The Birth of Arthur', 'The Holy Grail', 'Sir Pelleas' and 'The Death of Arthur'. This appears to be the sole surviving copy, given by Tennyson to Locker-Lampson. Wise dates it 1868; but the composition of these idylls was not completed until May 1869.

[3] The fullest reviews are those of Hutton (*Spectator*, 25 December 1869), Alford (*Contemporary Review*, January 1870) and the *Edinburgh Review*, April 1870.

[4] Letter to Sir George Grove, 2 December 1872; Grove had sent him a copy of Hutton's article in the current *Macmillan's* (C. L. Graves, *Life and Letters of Sir George Grove*, 1903, pp. 197–8.).

and of course rightly; though he had borrowed occasional devices from epic, the narrative was not continuous, heroic action was not central, and he did not speak as an epic poet, but more humbly, as 'he that tells the tale'. But the allegorical interpretation he not only welcomed, but encouraged in advance; Knowles was preparing the ground for it a year before the publication of the new volume.[1] This endorsement we can understand; the discrepancy between the critics' view of allegory and his was not yet obvious, the emphasis was where Tennyson wished it to be, on the King, and he was seen to be more or other than 'that grey King, whose name a ghost . . .' or 'him of Malleor's'. Later, when the substitution of abstractions for characters became a kind of ingenious parlour-game, Tennyson resisted—'I hate to be tied down to say *this* means *that*, when the thought in the image is so much more than any specific interpretation'.[2] The 'thought in the image', the poetic word 'shadowing', and even the line he added twenty years later as a corrective, 'ideal manhood closed in real man',[3] indicate his intention better than 'any specific interpretation'. The worst are those that apply the substitution to a whole situation; as when Arthur's didactic tone in *Guinevere* is defended on the grounds that the soul rebuking sense is bound to sound didactic.

[1] Knowles had met Tennyson in 1866 and had become a close friend. He added the following passage to the Preface of the revised third edition of his *Legends of King Arthur* (1868):

> Arthur . . . stands evidently for the Soul, the moral conscience, as the Round Table does for the passions; and everywhere the struggle of the Spirit with the Flesh is painted. The very title 'Idylls of the King' implies something more and other than mere legends of Arthur, and contains an allusion to the King within us; else why was not the book named 'Idylls of King Arthur'?

Compare his letter in the *Spectator*, 1 January 1870, and Eversley edition, v, 488–90. One or two other reviews may also have been officially inspired. Alford's claim that his exposition in the *Contemporary Review*, January, 1870, 'is not . . . a mere invention of our own' suggests that he had discussed the question with Knowles; he did not renew his early acquaintance with Tennyson until the following March. Lytton showed some resentment of this priming of reviewers in the Preface to his *King Arthur*, published in a revised edition in the autumn of 1870: 'it is the wise fashion of authors now-a-days to delegate such tasks to friendly reviewers, instructed and secured beforehand.'

[2] *Tennyson and his Friends* (1911), p. 302, reported by the Bishop of Ripon; cf. Eversley edition, v, 490: 'he often said that an allegory should never be pressed too far.' The extreme of ingenious allegorizing may be found in MacCallum's book.

[3] In 'To the Queen' in the edition of 1891, immediately after 'shadowing sense at war with Soul'.

Many of Tennyson's admirers took up the Gladstonian line and saw the controlling design in the high moral purpose of the poem; they were anxious to counter the growing criticism of the Idylls as ornate, over-elaborated, sentimental, 'exquisite insulated pictures',[1] a line of attack in which Arnold was among the 'audacious light troops'. But the defenders overplayed their hand and provoked much further controversy. There is in this body of reviews a tone of polemic and exhortation which often obscures their real perceptiveness, and only Richard Holt Hutton seems to me to see the poem in itself as it really is—insisting on an 'imaginative centre', not allegory but in George Eliot's phrase 'an unfolding of far-resonant action', which 'paints the waste places of the heart and the strength of the naked soul'.[2] The *Holy Grail* fulfilled all expectations, but its interpretation was almost a touchstone of each critic's private bias—'truth is this to me and that to thee'. Percival shows 'the hardening effects of fanaticism'; 'religion [is] blown into mere fantastic shapes of superstition'; the King 'lacks the guiding star of specifically Christian faith'; the *Dublin Review*, which a few years earlier had held it a theme which only a Catholic could treat as it should be treated, was satisfied, and detected only one heresy; the *Tablet* found 'much gold and little alloy', although guessing that the author's theology might differ from theirs, whereas the *Inquirer* saw the influence of 'modern free-thought'; the Dean of Canterbury welcomed it as a useful lesson for that party in the church which was more concerned with 'millineries' than evangelism—(1870 was the year when the Ritual Commission reported). All this illustrates the lack of the free play of mind of which Arnold had recently com-

[1] The defensive attitude is particularly clear in Alford's article, which counters specific criticisms in the article in *Temple Bar*, May 1869, where the phrase 'exquisite insulated pictures' occurs. This article (by Alfred Austin) was widely read, and was approved by Arnold (*Letters*, ii, 9; and Austin, *Autobiography*, 2 vols., 1911, ii, 1–2); compare Arnold's criticisms in his final Homer lecture (*Last Words*, 1862) and his later comment in an unpublished letter to Gosse in 1882 (quoted by R. H. Super, *Times Literary Supplement*, 28 October 1960); and also Bagehot's article in the *National Review*, November 1864. Hutton (*Spectator*, 25 December 1869) admits to having regarded the 1859 *Idylls* as 'an exquisite series of cabinet pictures', but now sees the whole as 'a great tragic epic'.

[2] R. H. Hutton, *Spectator*, 2 December 1871, reprinted in *Brief Literary Criticisms* (1906); and *Macmillan's*, December 1872, reprinted in *Literary Essays* (1876).

plained; but at least hardly anyone now thought the stories remote from contemporary interests.[1]

The 1870 reviewers, even those who claimed Tennyson's confidence, were unanimous in one assumption; they believed the poem complete. Why not? It had a beginning and an end and quite a lot of middle. But Tennyson himself was never in doubt. The poem was still growing; the imputed 'allegory' might be complete, but the balanced shape of the poem was not. He had in mind a more comprehensive picture of the Round Table, a more nearly continuous narrative, and a more symmetrical pattern. The *Last Tournament* and *Gareth and Lynette* (begun ten years earlier) were worked on together through the next two years,[2] though published successively; the *Last Tournament* appeared in the Christmas number of the *Contemporary Review*, now edited by Knowles, (the same day as the first part of another serial, *Middlemarch*, and Hutton wrote a leader in the *Spectator* comparing them), and again in a volume with *Gareth* nearly a year later, in 1872. The reader was directed where to place them and told that 'the whole series would shortly be published in their proper shape and order', and some months later the series appeared, in the final volumes of a collected edition then in progress. (It should have appeared before, but Tennyson held it up by further revision.) The earlier reference to the 'whole series', and the number ten, suggested that they really were complete this time, and Hutton, reviewing this edition, spoke for many when he said 'let him be Anathema Maranatha if he ever adds to or alters

[1] J. T. K., letter in *Spectator*, 1 January 1870, and *Contemporary Review*, May 1873; *Literary Churchman*, 5 February 1870; *Dublin Review*, April 1864 and April 1870; *Tablet*, 25 December 1869; *Inquirer*, 18 December 1869; Henry Alford, *Contemporary Review*, January 1870. The *Wesleyan Methodist Magazine*, April 1870, was the only one to complain of the 'rubbish of mediaeval superstition'.

[2] *Gareth*, first thought of in about 1861, was being worked on in the autumn of 1869. In MS Eng. 952, notebook 40, a prose sketch of the opening of *The Last Tournament* is interpolated in the Gareth story, linked to it by a reference to the guilty love of Queen Bellicent for Sir Lamorack, afterwards discarded. *The Last Tournament*, first thought of as 'a poem on Tristram and Isolt' in 1859 (*Materials*, ii, 218) was finished by May 1871 (*Memoir*, ii, 104), and was set up as if for volume publication (Ashley 2101 consists of the proofs, rather than a trial edition) before appearing in the *Contemporary*. *Gareth* was not finished until July 1872, and was further revised before publication with *The Last Tournament* in October, and again for the edition of 1873.

it again, to the distraction and confusion of all who possess this edition'. A few weeks later Tennyson, meeting him, informed him 'with a grim smile', 'I must have two more idylls at the least'.[1] This was the one afterthought to his design, and by chance we can date his change of mind; the American edition of *Gareth and Lynette* and the *Last Tournament* was printed from advance sheets and contains a note saying that, with them, the series was concluded—but Tennyson deleted that note before the English edition appeared.[2] He wrote his final idyll, *Balin and Balan*,[3] in 1873, but did not publish it for twelve years, whether for the sake of purchasers or because he had not decided whether to make it into one or two. But before turning to the purpose and effect of these last additions on 'the proper shape and order', I want to mention one curious aspect of the reception of the series in 1873. By then the *Idylls* had been entangled in a controversy partly irrelevant to them, and to read the reviews is almost to participate in a nineteenth-century battle in the mist. Critics of the *Idylls* are now using terms like 'reprisals' and Tennyson's 'bodyguard'.[4] They group themselves around Buchanan's attack on the 'Fleshly School of Poetry', especially Rossetti, first published in Knowles's *Contemporary Review* (October 1871), and Swinburne's counter-attack in his pamphlet *Under the Microscope* (July 1872); in their reviews of the completed *Idylls* Buchanan, Knowles, and others carried on the campaign, introducing, for example, abuse of 'certain . . . dyspeptic or nervously deranged gentlemen who think poetry ought to be a sort of galvanic battery' and find Tennyson 'not half wicked enough' and 'abominably slow', who object to Poetry's teaching virtue, but don't mind if it

[1] The ten idylls first appeared together in the Library edition, vols. v and vi, in January 1873; Hutton reviewed them in the *Spectator*, 8 February 1873. Tennyson's remark to Hutton is given in *The Diary of Alfred Domett*, ed. E. A. Horsman, 1953, p. 79.

[2] See Edgar Shannon, 'The Proofs of *Gareth and Lynette*', *Papers of the Bibliographical Society of America*, xli, 1947, p. 321.

[3] The three manuscript notebooks containing drafts of this idyll are described by Sir Charles Tennyson in *Six Tennyson Essays*, pp. 169–77; the long addition to *Merlin and Vivien*, which first appeared in 1874, was originally part of it. *Balin and Balan*, was published in 1885, and described as 'an introduction to *Merlin and Vivien*'.

[4] *Blackwood's*, December 1872.

teaches vice, or who find the Christian ideal in the *Idylls* effeminate, when it is they who are effeminate, 'bleating after passion'.[1] All this was not only provocative, but did harm to their cause and cannot have been welcomed by Tennyson. For Swinburne had been implicated not only as pamphleteer but as poet. Soon after the *Grail* volume came out he wrote to William Rossetti that like Gabriel he had been 'stimulated to fresh Arthurian exertion by the *Morte d'Albert*' (a joke he often repeats); and in December 1871, the same month as the *Last Tournament* appeared, the result was seen in the Prelude to *Tristram and Iseult*.[2] That great rhapsody on love is his implicit and permanent comment; but he was stimulated to a different form of exertion by the irritant of the reviewers' emphasis on Tennyson's 'profound and exalted morality'. In what is really a parenthesis in his argument in *Under the Microscope*, he mischievously turned the tables by accusing Tennyson of lowering and degrading the moral tone of Arthurian story, making 'Arthur a wittol, Guinevere a woman of intrigue, Lancelot a co-respondent', and Vivien, about whom he takes a very high moral tone, 'a prostitute'; more particularly, he attacks Tennyson for missing the 'Hellenic dignity' of Malory's story as the tragedy of a doomed king under the shadow of his own sin. Once again, we see a younger writer turning Malory against Tennyson. The fullest reply to Swinburne was made by Hutton six months later (Swinburne thought it very unsatisfactory because it said nothing about co-respondents or prostitutes); but on the main point, Hutton says, very reasonably, that 'Tennyson, as every true poet—Mr Swinburne himself for example—had to choose between the various inconsistent elements in the Arthurian legends'.[3] Tennyson never replied,

[1] Robert Buchanan, in *St. Paul's*, March 1872; [J. T. Knowles], 'The Meaning of Tennyson's King Arthur', *Contemporary Review*, May 1873. The recent 'effort . . . to depreciate Tennyson' is also referred to in the *Catholic World*, May 1872; and Swinburne's views are approved in *Athenaeum*, 26 October 1872.

[2] *The Swinburne Letters*, ed. Cecil Y. Lang, 6 vols., 1959–62, ii, 78 (letter of 28 December 1869); see also ii, 212–13 (on Hutton's comments on *Under the Microscope*) and iv, 260 (on *The Last Tournament*). Swinburne attacked the Idylls again in 'Tennyson and Musset', *Fortnightly*, February 1881. The 'Prelude' first appeared in *Pleasure: a Holiday Book*, published in 1871; the completed *Tristram of Lyonesse* in 1882.

[3] *Macmillan's*, December 1872; see *Literary Essays*, p. 402.

though he did include in his Epilogue the line 'Art with poisonous honey stol'n from France'; he rated the controversy at its true worth, and in 1891 he wrote to Swinburne thanking him for an ode on his eighty-second birthday, saying 'I am and always have been your admirer'.[1] And on Tennyson's death Swinburne wrote those wonderful lines:

Far above us and all our love, beyond all reach of its voiceless praise,
Shines forever the name that never shall feel the shade of the changeful days . . .

The last additions to the idylls, *The Last Tournament*, *Gareth and Lynette*, *Balin and Balan*, and some substantial passages elsewhere,[2] tell us much about Tennyson's matured intentions; and here we have an advantage over his contemporaries; as one wrote regretfully: 'If we could put all the old arrangements out of our mind, and fancy ourselves reading the Idylls [in their right order] for the first time, which with all deference to Mr Tennyson is impossible. . . .'[3] For the poet there were related problems: late additions had to be shaped to fit into an existing and already complex pattern and to look as if they had always been there. He did this with great skill. For example, up to 1870 the reader had heard nothing of King Mark; in the serial order, he met him in the *Last Tournament* in 1871, in *Gareth* in 1872, in *Merlin and Vivien* in 1874, and finally in *Balin and Balan*. So in the completed series Mark appears to be an integral part of the narrative, appearing in the second, fifth, sixth and tenth Idylls.

Tennyson also used the opportunity of his additions to make the pattern clearer still by catching up some old threads and stitching them into the new. *The Last Tournament* is our final view of the whole Round Table in decline, complementary to *Pelleas and Ettarre*—this is underlined by Pelleas's reappearance as the Red Knight—as a picture of collective as distinct from

[1] *The Swinburne Letters*, vi, 21.

[2] These include the description of the battle against the heathen, and the song 'Blow, trumpet' in the *Coming of Arthur*, the long passage connecting Vivien with King Mark in *Merlin and Vivien*, the song in *Pelleas and Ettarre*, and the King's speech in his tent in *The Passing of Arthur*.

[3] *Blackwood's*, December 1872.

individual disillusion and corruption. 'The glory of the Round Table is no more', and Lancelot 'saw the laws that ruled the tournament Broken, but spake not'. Recurrent words are 'broken'—'broken music', broken vows—and 'red', to be drawn together (with another backward reference) in the most terrible of the King's accusing words to Guinevere:

> The children born of thee are sword and fire,
> Red ruin and the breaking up of laws.

The very narrative method of *The Last Tournament* reflects disruption: the action begins and ends in Camelot in two days of autumn gloom, but its movement ranges outwards in space to the eastern marsh, westwards to the castle of King Mark, and backwards in time through Tristram's dream and memories, forward through Arthur's first premonition:

> . . . whence the fear lest this my realm
> Reel back into the beast, and be no more,

words which haunt Lancelot 'like birds of prey' (which is also an image now seen recurring in three consecutive Idylls). Other fine threads carry us farther back, especially to Elaine, that other 'dead innocence' and those other jewels. *The Last Tournament* is the most 'compacted and vertebrate' of all the idylls, and complaints about the compression and subordination of Tristram's story are wide of the mark; Tennyson has not, as Swinburne thought, 'degraded and debased' it; he 'had to choose' and has chosen wisely, and for a story which is there to *be* subordinate, to enforce the sense of broken vows, ruin and calamity, and the slow attrition of time.

This idyll lengthened the falling curve of the poem; *Gareth and Lynette* restores the balance and is there to show us *what* has been lost, the *glory* of the Round Table, the spring of the year and the music that is unbroken, 'melody on branch and melody in mid-air'. (I speak of it in its final form; the manuscripts show several layers of writing, and it was at one time designed to be more heavily shadowed and therefore to fall later in the sequence.)[1] With its happy ending it is necessarily, like *Geraint and Enid*, a self-contained narrative, but the subsidiary narrative links are clearer—with the *Coming* through

[1] See p. 102, n. 2 above.

Bellicent, with the catastrophe through Modred and King Mark, with the whole series through Lancelot. Like *Enid*, too, it is leisurely in exposition, setting the scene, but by a different method; alone of the idylls, its narrative begins at the beginning, for Camelot is to dawn upon us from a distance, through hearsay and daydream; with Gareth we approach it slowly, and see through his eyes the sculptured detail of the symbolic gates, enter the city and the court and learn the meaning of the vows by seeing them kept. As a trial and triumph of faith the story is parallel in substance to *Enid*, but also with likenesses and unlikenesses at a distance to *Pelleas and Ettarre*—Pelleas, that other boy-knight, who also gazes up at Camelot:

> Blackening against the dead-green stripes of even,
> 'Black nest of rats'.

Throughout *Gareth* there are covert anticipations of the future—in Lynette's cry

> O King, for thou hast driven the foe without,
> See to the foe within!

and in the invented names of the Knights guarding the loops of river round Castle Perilous—the Morning Star, Noonday Sun, Evening Star, and Night who is also Death, but being slain is a child 'fresh as a flower new-born'; the whole emblematic of the individual life, and summed up in the line describing the rock-carvings—'The war of Time against the soul of man', text for so much in the poem.

By his latest additions Tennyson heightened the contrasts between the beginning and end of the poem, and many of his shorter additions in 1873 served the same purpose; for example, in contrast to the battle in the mist there is Arthur's first battle against the heathen, when

> . . . the world
> Was all so clear about him that he saw
> The smallest rock far on the faintest hill,
> And even in high day the morning star.

This is the battlefield where Lancelot and the King 'sware on the field of death a deathless love', and Arthur said 'Man's word is God in man'; the lines have their echoes—Arthur and

Guinevere 'sware on the shrine of Christ a deathless love', the emphasis of the enlarged *Coming of Arthur* is more than ever on unity and mutual trust: 'Arthur and his Knights for a space Were all one will. . . .' His latest additions make it clear how closely related in his mind were the formal, the narrative, and the moral shape of his poem. When he told Hutton with a grim smile in 1873 'I must have at least two more', he added the reason, 'to make *Vivien* come later into the Poem, as it comes in far too soon as it stands'. In the end, when the old implied promise of twelve books was fulfilled by the addition of *Balin and Balan*, and the division of *Geraint and Enid* into two,[1] *Merlin and Vivien* falls centrally, the sixth of twelve instead of the third of ten; and the combined effect of *Balin and Balan* and the long addition to *Merlin and Vivien*[2] is to draw Vivien into the main story as an emissary of King Mark. Much more emphasis thus falls upon 'the foe without', the 'little rat that borest in the dyke', and this extends the moral meaning; as the voice in the *Vision of Sin* says, 'the crime of sense became The crime of malice, and is equal blame'; Balin curses 'the tale, the told of, and the teller'. And the death of the two loving brothers Balin and Balan at each other's hands forecasts the final battle:

> When friend and foe were shadows in the mist,
> And friend slew friend not knowing whom he slew.

By one other late addition to *Merlin and Vivien* Tennyson drew together the themes of his poem and some of its leading images. Merlin

> Walk'd with dreams and darkness, and he found
> A doom that ever pois'd itself to fall,
> An ever-moaning battle in the mist,
> World-war of dying flesh against the life,
> Death in all life and lying in all love,
> The meanest having power upon the highest,
> And the high purpose broken by the worm.[3]

The passage is dramatically relevant, but these premonitions

[1] The two titles first appeared in 1886, but the idyll was divided into 'I' and 'II' in 1873.

[2] See p. 105, n. 2 above.

[3] First published 1873; there is a manuscript draft in notebook 39, which looks, from its position, as if it might be intended for *The Passing of Arthur*.

are not there simply to define his state of mind. At about the same date Tennyson added the King's despairing words before the final battle:

> I found Him in the shining of the stars,
> I mark'd Him in the flowering of His fields,
> But in His ways with men I find Him not . . .
> For I, being simple, thought to work His will
> And have but stricken with the sword in vain.

In the course of its uniquely long serial progress the pessimism in the poem had been deepened, with Tennyson's own advancing years and his maturer vision of the possibility that realms and civilizations might indeed reel back into the beast and be no more. The pressure of time and change affected the poem, which is itself concerned with time and change. In the *Morte d'Arthur* of forty years before Bedivere said:

> And I, the last, go forth companionless,
> And the days darken round me, and the years,
> Among new men, strange faces, other minds.

Tennyson added no twelfth book, no vision of the Return of the King, no reference to a far-off divine event. But the thirty lines added at the end of the *Morte d'Arthur* in 1869 relieved the darkness of the conclusion by continuing the narrative a little further, with a simple statement of what is seen in the world of space and time. And when, after some hesitation,[1] he decided on his last line, he chose to suggest a beginning rather than an end. Bedivere saw:

> Straining his eyes beneath an arch of hand,
> Or thought he saw, the speck that bare the King,
> Down that long water opening on the deep
> Somewhere far off, pass on and on, and go
> From less to less, and vanish into light.
> And the new sun rose bringing the new year.

[1] In the trial-printing, the poem ends with 'From the great deep to the great deep he goes', and the line 'Then rose the new sun bringing the new year' occurs earlier.

X

A WORD FOR BROWNING

AN EXPERIENCE that recently befell me as a teacher may have interest for others, at least for people who wish well to Browning.

Speaking for myself, I have always wished him well because I am constantly being drawn back to him. I have always had an undeniable love for those hundreds of bits and pieces of him which could not be bettered for energy (and sometimes farouche vigour), for clarity, easy brilliance, individuality (they are quite unlike anything by any other poet), for a sort of democratic lack of airs and graces, for their nearness to good prose or good exclamatory speech without leaving off being good metre. Here are a few of the passages that haunt me: I take them all from a single source, the *Men and Women* of 1855:

> Beautiful Evelyn Hope is dead!

(in which the leaden blankness of 'dead!' is a shock supervening on the dactylic euphony);

> What did I say?—that a small bird sings
> All day long, save when a brown pair
> Of hawks from the wood float with wide wings
> Strained to a bell: 'gainst the noon-day glare
> You count the streaks and rings.[1]

> ... the great opaque
> Blue breadth of sea without a break.

> I seem to see! we meet and part: 'tis brief;
> The book I opened keeps a folded leaf,
> The very chair I sat on, breaks the rank;
> That is a portrait of me on the wall—
> Three lines, my face comes at so slight a call:
> And for all this, one little hour's to thank.

> ... A simile!
> We mortals cross the ocean of this world

[1] Browning comes near being Hopkins at times. In other words Hopkins received vital help from Browning.

Each in his average cabin of a life—
The best's not big, the worst yields elbow-room.
Now for our six months' voyage—how prepare?
You come on shipboard with a landsman's list
Of things he calls convenient—so they are!
An India screen is pretty furniture,
A piano-forte is a fine resource,
All Balzac's novels occupy one shelf,
The new edition fifty volumes long;
And little Greek books, with the funny type
They get up well at Leipsic, fill the next—
Go on! slabbed marble, what a bath it makes!

And so on to the rest of the long paragraph. But there is something humourless in stringing out things so excellent and so plentiful. How can any critic of poetry not take things like this to his bosom—provided he has a bosom to take them to?

And there is so much more than this to praise in Browning. Of all our poets he is the most fertile in originality of design—of design in the widest sense, design of thinking and design of form. He has more good ideas for poems than anybody else. We have only to read Mrs Sutherland Orr's classic *Handbook* to see him as a poet utterly original when it comes to what we call 'inspirations' and 'bright ideas'. No poem is like another, either in form or substance. They are each as distinct as short stories by different authors, and they often share the substance of short stories. A hundred instances spring to mind, but I limit myself to one as showing how dazzling is his choice of matter. Mrs Orr's account of 'Adam, Lilith, and Eve' is as follows:

'ADAM, LILITH, AND EVE' illustrates the manner in which the typical man and woman will proceed towards each other: the latter committing herself by imprudent disclosures when under the influence of fear, and turning them into a joke as soon as the fear is past; the former pretending that he never regarded them as serious.

Here is the poem itself:

One day it thundered and lightened.
Two women, fairly frightened,
Sank to their knees, transformed, transfixed,
At the feet of the man who sat betwixt;
And 'Mercy!' cried each—'if I tell the truth
Of a passage in my youth!'

Said This: 'Do you mind the morning
I met your love with scorning?
As the worst of the venom left my lips,
I thought "If, despite this lie, he strips
The mask from my soul with a kiss—I crawl
His slave,—soul, body and all!" '

Said That: 'We stood to be married;
The priest, or someone, tarried;
"If Paradise-door prove locked?" smiled you.
I thought, as I nodded, smiling too,
"Did one, that's away, arrive—nor late
Nor soon should unlock Hell's gate!" '

It ceased to lighten and thunder.
Up started both in wonder,
Looked round and saw that the sky was clear,
Then laughed 'Confess you believed us, Dear!'
'I saw through the joke!' the man replied
They re-seated themselves beside.

And yet Browning is often a poet it is more exciting to talk about and remember than to read. He is so careless, or rather (because he did care) so imperfect an executant! We start to read him with enthusiasm, and are encouraged by his gift for beginning a poem as splendidly as Donne could. As we proceed we find perfection flawed. We find obscurity of the worst kind—the obscurity that comes of expressing badly an idea that could so easily have been expressed well. Or rather could so easily have been expressed well in prose, or in a metre that did not call for rime. Browning (whose rimes can be as brilliant as anybody's) will often take for his rime a word not required by his sense, or a *mot* the reverse of *juste*. The marvellous first two lines of 'The Lost Leader' are ruined because they are followed by two which for rimes use words that ideally they do not want, words that cry aloud to be released from their discomfort:

Just for a handful of silver he left us,
  Just for a riband to stick in his coat—
Found the one gift of which fortune bereft us,
  Lost all the others she lets us devote . . . !

For 'of which fortune bereft us' read, in easy prose, 'which we did not possess,' or 'which we could not give him', or 'which it was not in our power to supply', or something like that. For 'she lets us devote' read 'which it *was* in our power to give,' etc. The idea is clear and simple, but because of the exigencies of metre and rime Browning can only provide it with clumsy English. Wherever we turn in Browning we are likely to come up against these elementary clumsinesses and *bêtises*.

There is the danger, however, that we see as such what is not so. An instance of insensitive reading on my part was shown up by a student of mine when we were studying that remarkable poem 'Women and Roses'. I quote enough of it to make my point:

> I dream of a red-rose tree.
> And which of its roses three
> Is the dearest rose to me?
>
> Round and round, like a dance of snow
> In a dazzling drift, as its guardians, go
> Floating the women faded for ages,
> Sculptured in stone, on the poet's pages.
> Then follow women fresh and gay,
> Living and loving and loved to-day.
> Last, in the rear, flee the multitude of maidens,
> They circle their rose on my rose tree.
>
> Dear rose, thy term is reached,
> Thy leaf hangs loose and bleached:
> Bees pass it unimpeached.

When I got to 'unimpeached', I groaned aloud. But one of my students had the inspiration—showed the Good-Samaritan kindness towards Browning—to look up *impeach* in the *O.E.D.*, whereupon he found it to have had a meaning, now obsolete, that served Browning's purpose well. *Impeach* used to mean *hinder*, *impede* (cf. Fr. *empêcher*). In Holinshed's *Scottish Chronicle*, for example, comes the sentence: '. . . to impeach the Englishmen from setting on land any vittles there'. A poet like Browning, who sets out to be 'free of [language's] four corners', has every right to use a word in an obsolete sense. This he was doing, quite legitimately, and I had 'impeached' him for using a word in a wrong sense, merely because I thought he was capitulating to the cruel need for a rime. The moral is clear. Because Browning is sometimes defeated by the English language we must not think he is defeated as often as we ignorantly suppose.

And so to my second point. Browning sometimes uses words more precisely, with more exactitude of sense, than I for one had given him credit for. Here is that brilliant little poem 'My Star':

> All that I know
> Of a certain star,
> Is, it can throw
> (Like the angled spar)
> Now a dart of red,
> Now a dart of blue,
> Till my friends have said
> They would fain see, too,
> My star that dartles the red and the blue!
> Then it stops like a bird;—like a flower, hangs furled:
> They must solace themselves with the Saturn above it.
> What matter to me if their star is a world?
> Mine has opened its soul to me; therefore I love it.

In the tenth line Browning is using exactly pointed imagery. By 'stops like a bird' he means 'stops throwing out twinkles' as a bird stops working its wings.

My third and last point shows me to be a reader who, when he re-reads a difficult passage, discovers the same sense in it as before—a sense which, if it is the wrong sense or an unsatisfactory, muddled sense, will lead him to pronouce the passage obscure when in fact it may be capable of a demonstrable plainness. One of the great poems of the nineteenth century, a poem as great as a great poem of Donne's or Wordsworth's—a poem to make the hair of the mind, as it were, to stand on end—is 'By the Fireside'. Until recently I always thought the expression of the fourth and fifth stanzas disgraceful. Whenever I read them I was irritated by a sense of identical obscurity. Let the reader try them for himself:

I

> How well I know what I mean to do
> When the long dark Autumn evenings come,
> And where, my soul, is thy pleasant hue?
> With the music of all thy voices, dumb
> In life's November too!

2

I shall be found by the fire, suppose,
  O'er a great wise book as beseemeth age,
While the shutters flap as the cross-wind blows,
  And I turn the page, and I turn the page,
Not verse now, only prose!

3

Till the young ones whisper, finger on lip,
  'There he is at it, deep in Greek—
Now, then, or never, out we slip
  To cut from the hazels by the creek
A mainmast for our ship!'

4

I shall be at it indeed, my friends!
  Greek puts already on either side
Such a branch-work forth as soon extends
  To a vista opening far and wide,
  And I pass out where it ends.

5

The outside-frame, like your hazel-trees—
  But the inside-archway narrows[1] fast,
And a rarer sort succeeds to these,
  And we slope to Italy at last
And youth, by green degrees.

There is nothing difficult in 2 and 3, and nothing more than pleasantly and resolvably puzzling about 1. But my blindness to the course of the thinking in 4 and 5 has now been enlightened by the help of students. In the light of their findings I shall attempt a paraphrase:

You little know what he will be doing if you think he will be doing Greek ('I shall be at it indeed, my friends!' is an echo of what the children said, but it does not mean what it meant when they said it: whatever he is doing now it won't be Greek, for he is day-dreaming). His study of Greek will have already—even before the children have slipped off—given way to day-dreaming. This dreaming he compares to 'a branch-work', to the sprays of bushes, and they form a vista down which he roams to where they end, and he

[1] Browning later changed 'narrows' to 'widens,' deciding that it was better to suggest what the vista looked like to one walking down it.

finds himself in another sort of place (not yet named or precisely indicated). His day-dreaming begins as English day-dreaming—as day-dreaming about the things round and about him in that particular time and place, with the children at play. He compares it, therefore, to a vista that begins as an English thing with hazel-trees. The first part of the tunnel down which he wanders is made of English hazels (of home thoughts). But the tunnel soon becomes one made of other trees, trees of a kind rarer (to an Englishman) than hazels, foreign trees, presumably olives since

> . . . we slope to Italy at last
> And youth, by green degrees.

His day-dreaming is about the past, his youth, and about an incident in it (suggested by his children), his courtship, which took place in Italy. And so to the next stanza:

> 6
> I follow wherever I am led,
> Knowing so well the leader's hand . . . !

He follows day-dreaming, but his dreams are governed by his thought of his leader (the wife he is to apostrophize in stanza 21:

> My perfect wife, my Leonor,
> Oh, heart my own, oh, eyes, mine too,
> Whom else could I dare look backward for . . . ?)

The moral of all this is that I was not alert enough in my re-readings of the poem. I had never had the wit to see that 'I shall be at it indeed, my friends!' had changed its sense. Its tone had escaped me. Speaking coolly, I do not think I can be heavily blamed for missing the tone, because it is easy to suppose that if the branch-work is put forth by Greek it will be a development *of* Greek, problems raised by it. But I now see that I ought to have spotted the existence of a shift in the sense retrospectively, after seeing what is the upshot of the following lines. My difficulty here points to the root of the trouble with Browning as a user of language. His task of expressing is often occupied in conveying one meaning and only one (he is not often an 'ambiguous' poet), but he did not look on expression as a means of achieving the one meaning wanted while excluding all other meanings. The power to exclude the unwanted is surely the mark of a good writer (as of a good reader) when only one meaning is concerned.

Anyway it is plain that the ideal reading of Browning is that done in a company of readers. This was a truth discovered in his life-time, when the first little group of devotees put their heads together. No doubt it was a group of earnest Bostonians. How sensible they were! We have missed something by the dissolution of the Browning Society. But we can resuscitate it informally in our university seminars, and shall no doubt do so increasingly as our nineteenth-century literature comes to be studied as closely as we are now seeing it deserves to be.

XI

CLOUGH'S *BOTHIE*

ARTHUR HUGH CLOUGH was to publish few books in his life of some forty-two years. On the face of it this was a strange shortcoming—he was a powerful writer in an age when there was inevitably much rushing on from manuscript to print. A repugnance from obtruding, however, was stubbornly a part of him. When poems of his did attain to print, his deliberate unworldliness was evident in their very titles. That of his first—*The Bothie of Toper-na-fuosich*—could not well have been less ingratiating either then or, after the revision of the placename half of it, at any later time; and when William Thomas Stead enterprisingly chose to include the poem in his Penny Poets, he sensibly revised the title to read *The Love Story of a Young Man*, or *The Bothie of Tober-na-vuolich*, explaining himself in his preface:

> Great poets are often but poorly qualified for the position of a news editor. They are first-class as poets, but they sometimes break down when serving up their work to the public. They can produce the goods, they cannot dress their shop window.

Even the word 'bothie', which became fairly well-known later, was unfamiliar in 1848. Now, a century later, we may again need to be reminded that it means a keeper's hut. And, as a punishment for his sublime ignoring of the general reader, Clough had to face the charge that his title was indecent. *Blackwood's Magazine* was to suggest in error that it had been foisted on him by 'some very unscrupulous Gaelic wit'! It seemed that his avoidance of the ingratiating had led him into pretentiousness, as unlikely a fault of his as a wish to be gratuitously indecent. The *Dipsychus* MS shows that indecency—as it was measured at the time—was within his range when necessary, and even the text of *The Bothie* itself. Clough was not the kind of man some of his contemporaries chose to think: they complimented him on his 'purity', and thought it to his credit; it was an age that admired, or affected to admire, ignorance of seamy and especially sexual matters, but for Clough there was no virtue in ignorance of any sort, and he wished his knowledge to be as complete as that of anybody of his own or any other time. His most recent editors[1] cannot understand the charge of indecency: they find the placename, which Clough had picked up on a holiday in Scotland, to mean 'the well of the frightful [woman]', and conclude that it is difficult now to guess at the supposed impropriety—though surely it is plain enough, and especially after the publication of his letter of 15 February 1849 to Tom Arnold, who was in Australia:

You remember Toper na fuosich, in the map, on Loch Ericht—and how I made out afterwards that Dallungart was the present name. Good reason why! for now that I form tender recollections of you and Shairp under the blanket together and of that Madonna-like Mother and two children—now that I, I say, have published the name to all the drawing rooms and boudoirs (of course) of all the world—What think you?—It turns out, they tell me, to mean what Horace calls 'teterrima belli causa'—!—O mercy!—It is too ludicrous not to tell some one, but too appallingly awkward to tell anyone on this side the globe:—in the Gath and Ascalon of the Antipodes you may talk of it, and laugh at your pleasure. Do you know too that in the boat on Loch Ericht I asked the boatman 1st where it was, and 2nd what it meant. He replied, the bairds' well, which I could not understand. Did he mean the *bairns*' well? homunculorum fons et origo.[2]

Clough told Allingham, seven years after publication, that 'I was so disgusted with the mishap of the name, that I have never had pleasure in [the poem] since'.[3] Later he changed the title to *The Bothie of Tober-na-vuolich*, which he 'improvise[d] without enquiry'.[4] But whatever English readers can have made of the title in 1848 or later, they must have found it offensively grotesque. Nor did the title of his second volume strike them as any more attractive. Advertised as forthcoming in the first edition of *The Bothie*, it was made up of poems by himself and his friend Thomas Burbidge, and called *Ambarvalia*—the ignorant were

[1] *The Poems of Arthur Hugh Clough*, ed. H. F. Lowry, A. L. P. Norrington and F. L. Mulhauser, 1951.

[2] *The Correspondence of Arthur Hugh Clough*, ed. F. L. Mulhauser, 1957, i, 244.

[3] id., ii, 498.

[4] id., ii, 514.

expected to consult Lemprière's dictionary and find, to their surprise in view of the sobriety of the poems themselves, that it meant 'a joyful procession round the ploughed fields in honour of Ceres, the Goddess of Corn'.

Nor apparently were its first readers taken with the get-up of the book. Clough's friend, Professor W. Y. Sellar, in an anonymous review of the posthumous volume of mainly reprinted *Poems*, welcomed the new volume partly on material grounds—he found it a delightful book to handle. This indeed it is. It is one of those many publications of the mid-nineteenth century that we are now coming to prize for their appearance. Sellar's welcome, however, partly expressed relief—for him the new volume replaced an eyesore:

> The uncouth shape in which *The Bothie* was first sent into the world, was a real drawback to its success [he means its wide success—it was much read in Oxford], and to the pleasure of reading it. Mr Macmillan [the publisher of the new volume] has satisfactorily shown, that whatever may be the other objections to the admission of hexameters into English literature, the length of the lines is not incompatible with elegance and convenience in the volume which contains them.[1]

We ourselves do not find the 1848 book repellent. It is tall and thin, flexibly bound (in my copy at least) in that dark slaty-purple favoured at the time for books of sermons, its title-page spaciously set out in red and black, and its text pleasantly printed in the unassuming type that is used for most nineteenth-century books. The printer was Charles Whittingham the Second of the elegant Chiswick Press, but he or Clough or the publishers—Francis Macpherson of Oxford and Chapman and Hall of the Strand—were responsible for something that we can indeed agree to be uninviting. Being English hexameters, Clough's lines are long, and his paragraphs usually very long, so that the appearance of the page, designed to take them, resembles a high broad brick wall with one edge jagged. This effect was mitigated, as Sellar noted, when Macmillan's chose a shorter and narrower page, obliging the longest lines to spill over and so provide relieving patches of blank paper.

[1] *North British Review*, xxxvii, August to November 1862, p. 324.

2

Sellar mentioned the hexameter, and without enthusiasm. English versions of the ancient and foreign metre have never attracted readers very much, though they have often attracted poets. English hexameters had been written in the sixteenth century and again, following the German example, in the later eighteenth century. In 1821 Southey published his *Vision of Judgement* and discussed the previous use of the measure in his preface. In 1847 came Longfellow's *Evangeline,* the year before Clough's *Bothie.* After these experiments the metre aroused much discussion, 'occupy[ing] a most disproportionate amount of human intellect'.[1] Its use was canvassed especially for translations of Homer. Altogether it has always seemed on sufferance in English, if only because the poets who used it—Clough included—felt obliged to air their views on the relationship between the ancient system of quantity and the English system of stress, not seeing that when once adopted into English the line of six stresses set the classical metre that inspired it at defiance. Matters of quantity and stress are quite beyond the competence of all but phoneticians, and poets, though they have not always known it, are anything but that! As metrical theorists, they have failed to write sense because they have failed to see that where the hexameter is concerned, all that an English reader requires is (*a*) six stresses, the first of them falling on the first syllable of the line; (*b*) one or two syllables, not necessarily of the same degree of weakness, following each of the stressed ones, and (*c*) a closely similar final cadence, beginning with the fifth stress and running in one or other of these ways (to take instances from the opening lines of *The Bothie*):

> . . . thrown the hammer;
> . . . Hector so called it;
> . . . upraised elbows,

where '-raised' is a syllable bearing a stress intermediary between weak and strong.[2] As Southey and Longfellow had

[1] A. P. Stanley, anonymously reviewing *The Poems and Prose Remains,* 1869, in the *Westminster Review,* N.S. xxxvi, July 1869, p. 381.

[2] My quotations are all from the first edition. Clough revised it, but may not have completed the process—he did not live to see another edition through the

used the measure, the six stresses were very rarely in doubt: take for instance those lines from *Evangeline*, which as it happened Mrs Henry Wood was to prefix to *East Lynne*:

> Truly the heart is deceitful, and out of its depths of corruption
> Rise, like an exhalation, the misty phantoms of passion;
> Angels of light they seem, but are only delusions of Satan.
> This is the cross I must bear; the sin and the swift retribution.

But the trouble with the metre used in this way is that it reads monotonously—it becomes as tiresome as the metre of *Hiawatha*. Clough may have seen this defect. He avoided it, however, only at the cost of occasionally making his metre uncertain at a first reading, and sometimes persistently clumsy. I may say here and now that for several reasons *The Bothie* is a poem that requires to be read repeatedly. In his fine essay on Clough, John Addington Symonds testified to this, and to the rewards of close familiarity: 'He is a poet who will bear being frequently read; and who, each time we read him, astonishes us with some fresh beauty, or some new reach of thought.'[1] But to read *The Bothie* 'until it shines', as Pope would have said, is a lot to ask of readers, especially after the quickening of the pace of life in the nineteenth century and later.

As to Clough's metre, it pleads to be rehearsed. Many lines, if we forget classical metre, 'read themselves': for example:

> Skilful in Ethics and Logic, in Pindar and Poets unrivalled;
> *Shady* in Latin, said Lindsay, but *topping* in Plays and Aldrich;[2]

or:

> This was the letter of Philip, and this had brought the Tutor:
> This is, why tutor and pupil are walking with David and Elspie.[3]

But other lines require practice before all six stresses can be pegged out along the line: for instance:

> Do as I bid you, my child; do not go on calling me Mr;[4]

press. The texts printed after 1848 accordingly are all to some extent editors' texts. The text of 1848 is one for which Clough was fully responsible, and the reader who prefers later versions can readily find them. The Oxford edition lists all the variants.

[1] *Fortnightly Review*, N.S. iv, July to December 1868, p. 617.
[2] ch. I. [3] ch. VI. [4] ch. VII.

in which 'not' is stressed. The metrical variety that results from these subtleties is delightful, but it can only be discovered by application. One point of caution: the modern reader must allow for changes of accent since Clough's day: in the following lines I mark the obsolete accentuation, which must be observed if the metre is not to stumble:

Noble ladies their prizes adjudged for costúme that was perfect;[1]
Came and revealed the conténts of a missive that brought strange
tidings;[2]
When she thought of all these, and these contémplated daily.[3]

That the metre is to be a subtle one is advertised in the first syllables of its first line, which form the beautiful beginning:

It was the afternoon; . . .

Because of the rule about stressing the first syllable of the line, we are required to stress 'It'. To make the stress strong, however, would be absurd because that particle cannot bear such treatment—when wishing to stress the impersonal pronoun in speech we substitute a periphrasis such as 'that one'. 'It' must be stressed, therefore, with a lighter stress than we give to 'aft-' in 'afternoon', with the sort of stress that chiefly comes of lingering on a syllable. Because of this comparative weakness of stress, we give to 'was' a compensatory stress, but again not a strong one. And the two weak stresses give us a slow, sliding, quiet opening: 'It was the . . . '. The metre stood in the way of the original popularity of the poem, and still does. I shall show more fully later why this is a pity.

Several other things in the poem offered difficulty, and in airing the most salient of them I shall also be exhibiting some of the virtues of the poem, and introducing the reader who does not know *The Bothie* to the constituents of its story. The best service we can render Clough's re-emerging reputation is to prepare the not ill-disposed reader for the anfractuosities of the poetry, and merely by airing them make them less formidable.

3

It was as a vehicle for translating Homer that English hexa-

[1] ch. I. [2] ch. IV. [3] ch. VIII.

meters came to be much in evidence during the mid years of the nineteenth century, and this was partly owing to Clough. Though *The Bothie* was given out as a pastoral—it has 'A Long-Vacation Pastoral' as its subtitle—it was also a piece of mock-epic, of the complex kind in which the mockery is loving mockery, as in *The Rape of the Lock*. To quote again from Sellar's review:

Mr. Clough was well known at Oxford to be an excellent scholar; and it is to his careful revision that we owe our only trustworthy translation of Plutarch's Lives. [His] poems prove, further, that he had a very living sympathy with the great writers of antiquity—a gift which does not always accompany even an exclusive devotion to classical studies. Readers of the poems will often come upon modes of thought and expression, which recall old familiar tones in Homer and Plato, in Virgil, Horace, and Lucretius; and they will remark how, in the darkest time of his despondency, a new life and inspiration seem to come to him from the art and ruined grandeur of antiquity.[1]

Sellar sees that the object of the mockery ranges beyond Homer, but, as we should expect of a narrative poem, it is the epic that Clough imitates most abundantly. Epic imitations of this sort please frankly—they remind the reader, if he knows the right things, of an ancient method of narrative that is still venerated on grounds of antiquity, being honoured, especially at times when there is too little writing of pure narrative, for its straightforward serviceableness. But for the reader of mock-heroic there has always been a complication of pleasure. The poet often reproduces the ancient method not only in modern language but with modern matter expressed in it, indeed matter as modern as possible, his hope being to prompt a variety of feelings—of wonder (that the ancient world was as busy with practical things as is that of today), of amused contempt (for the lauded modern things have not yet attained the longevity that gives them dignity), of laughable surprise (to find ancient and modern set side by side), of pride (that we do have something new equivalent to the old). In taking some obvious instances of imitation or 'mocking' I shall be showing how brilliantly Clough adapts the ancient modes.

[1] op. cit., p. 328.

Epic poets make a point of marshalling a crowd of things by naming them in order of importance or of chronology. Accordingly Clough writes:

Be it recorded in song who was first, who last, in dressing

—in dressing for the dinner that concludes the Highland sports! And so we are introduced to the members of the reading-party as at various intervals they take their place in the four-wheeler waiting to convey them to the dinner, their characters being disclosed by means of the time of their appearance and by their dinner outfits (a sort of modern equivalent of armour):

Hope was first, his Honour, and next to his Honour the Tutor.
Still more plain the Tutor, the grave man, nicknamed Adam,
White-tied, clerical, silent, with antique square-cut waistcoat
Formal, unchanged, of black cloth, but with sense and feeling beneath it;
Skilful in Ethics and Logic, in Pindar and Poets unrivalled;
Shady in Latin, said Lindsay, but *topping* in Plays and Aldrich.
Somewhat more splendid in dress, in a waistcoat work of a lady,
Lindsay succeeded; the lively, the cheery, cigar-loving Lindsay,
Lindsay the ready of speech, the Piper, the Dialectician,
This was his title from Adam because of the words he invented,
Who in three weeks had created a dialect new for the party,
Master in all that was new, of whate'er was recherché and racy,
Master of newest inventions, and ready deviser of newer;
This was his title from Adam, but mostly they called him the Piper.
Lindsay succeeded, the lively, the cheery, cigar-loving Lindsay.
Hewson and Hobbes were down at the *matutine* bathing; of course too
Arthur Audley, the bather par excellence, glory of headers,
Arthur they called him for love and for euphony; so were they bathing,
There where in mornings was custom, where over a ledge of granite
Into a granite bason descended the amber torrent.
There were they bathing and dressing; it was but a step from the cottage,
Only the road and larches and ruinous millstead between.
Hewson and Hobbes followed quick upon Adam; on them followed Arthur.
Airlie descended the last, splendescent as god of Olympus;
Blue, half-doubtfully blue, was the coat that had white silk facings,

Waistcoat blue, coral-buttoned, the white-tie finely adjusted,
Coral moreover the studs on a shirt as of crochet of women:
When for ten minutes already the fourwheel had stood at the gate-way,
He, like a god, came leaving his ample Olympian chamber.[1]

This same passage illustrates other epic imitations. Lindsay is called 'cigar-loving', and the sort of epithet it is, is plain from its name: it is a Homeric epithet and a compound one. And his cigar allows a more brilliant imitation because Homer often calls Zeus 'cloud-compeller',[2] which epithet fits without change a person noted for his tobacco-smoking. 'The grave man, nicknamed Adam' is also Homeric, and the phrase recurs as it would have done in Homer—and was particularly amusing to friends who spotted the thirty-year-old Clough himself as very like the tutor. Again the one and a half lines describing the *matutine*—a slang phrase for morning bath—recur here and there when mention of the bathing pool recurs, and this is in the Homeric manner. They can bear the repetitions, and have the strange effect of deepening the melancholy of the gay and serious poem, a melancholy to which the falling rhythm of the hexameter contributes: the repetition of the little picture suggests that the hither-and-thithering of the human beings acts itself out in the midst of the eternal stability of rock and water.

Again there is straightforward imitation in the linking of the narrative items by simple conjunctions prominently placed, which mark as with chalk the footsteps of the story:

Then was the dinner served, and the Minister asked a blessing,
And to the viands before them with knife and with fork they beset them;
Venison, the red and the roe, with mutton; and grouse succeeding;
Such was the feast, with whiskey of course, and at top and bottom
Small decanters of Sherry, not overchoice, for the gentry.
So to the viands before them with laughter and chat they beset them.
And, when on flesh and on fowl had appetite duly been sated,
Up rose the Catholic Priest and returned God thanks for the dinner.
Then on all tables were set black bottles of well-mixed toddy,

[1] ch. I. Clough's italics.

[2] *OED* which has no reference to Clough, cites the use by *The Times* of 1865 of 'cloud-compeller' as a synonym for a smoker. Clough seems to have been consciously improving on Pope here who had described his foggy goddess of Dulness as 'cloud-compelling'.

And, with the bottles and glasses before them, they sat digesting,
Talking, enjoying, but chiefly awaiting the toasts and speeches.[1]

Epic poets frequently give us numerals—it is another indication of their love of important particulars. Clough clusters numerals as often and thickly as possible: the best instance comes at the beginning of III, which outdoes anything in the ancient epics, and so achieves a more pointed mockery:

So in the golden morning they parted and went to the westward.
And in the cottage with Airlie and Hobbes remained the Tutor;
Reading nine hours a day with the Tutor Hobbes and Airlie;
One between bathing and breakfast, and six before it was dinner,
(Breakfast at eight, at four, after bathing again, the dinner)
Finally two after walking and tea, from nine to eleven.

There are two passages in which Clough sets the epic complications working elaborately. The first is the account of the after-dinner speeches. At one point in the *Iliad* the poet begs the omniscient muses to let him know the names of the captains of the Greek army, adding 'But the common sort could I not number or name, nay, not if ten tongues were mine, and ten mouths'. What are men in Homer become words in Clough:

Spare me, O mighty Remembrance! for words to the task were unequal,
Spare me, O mistress of Song! nor bid me recount minutely
All that was said and done o'er the well-mixed tempting toddy,
Bid me not show in detail, grimace and gesture painting,
How were healths proposed and drunk with all the honours,
Glasses and bonnets waving, and three-times-three thrice over,
Queen, and Prince, and Army, and Landlords all, and Keepers;
Bid me not, grammar defying, repeat from grammar-defiers
Long constructions strange and plusquam-thucydidëan,
Tell, how as sudden torrent in time of speat[2] in the mountain
Hurries six ways at once, and takes at last to the roughest,
Or as the practised rider at Astley's or Franconi's
Skilfully, boldly bestrides many steeds at once in the gallop,
Crossing from this to that, with one leg here, one yonder,
So, less skilful, but equally bold, and wild as the torrent,
All through sentences six at a time, unsuspecting of syntax,
Hurried the lively good-will and garrulous tale of Sir Hector.

[1] ibid.

[2] 'Flood'—Clough's note.

Left to oblivion be it, the memory, faithful as ever,
How the noble Croupier would wind up his word with a whistle,
How the Marquis of Ayr, with quaint gesticulation,
Floundering on through game and mess-room recollections,
Gossip of neighbouring forest, praise of targeted gillies,
Anticipation of royal visit, skits at pedestrians,
Swore he would never abandon his country, nor give up deer-stalking;
How, too, more brief, and plainer in spite of Gaelic accent,
Highland peasants gave courteous answer to flattering nobles.
  Two orations alone the memorial song will render;
For at the banquet's close spake thus the lively Sir Hector,
Somewhat husky with praises exuberant, often repeated,
Pleasant to him and to them, of the gallant Highland soldiers,
Whom he erst led in the fight;—something-husky, but cheery, tho' weary,
Up to them rose and spoke the grey but gladsome chieftain:
  Fill up your glasses once more, my friends—with all the honours,
There was a toast which I forgot, which our gallant Highland homes have
Always welcomed the stranger, I may say, delighted to see
Fine young men at my table—My friends! are you ready? the Strangers.
Gentlemen, I drink your healths,—and I wish you—with all the honours![1]

Has any other writer, in prose or verse, ever displayed the good intentions of a-syntactical after-dinner speakers, let alone displayed them more delightfully? And delightfully all the more because of what he makes of his relationship to the resuscitated muse of ancient epic. On another occasion the muse is invoked to the detriment of all the newest means of information across a distance:

  So in the golden weather they waited. But Philip came not.
Sunday six days thence a letter arrived in his writing.
  But, O Muse, that encompassest Earth like the ambient ether,
Swifter than steamer or railway or magical missive electric
Belting like Ariel the sphere with the star-like trail of thy travel,
Thou with thy Poet, to mortals mere post-office second-hand knowledge
Leaving, wilt seek in the moorland of Rannoch the wandering hero;

[1] ch. I.

and so to a beating about the Highlands from a station up in the sky till the wandering Philip is located in 'mountain-top and moorland':

I see him,
Lo, and he sitteth alone, and these are his words in the mountain.[1]

Perhaps the outstanding characteristic of the ancient epic is its formal simile—there are 250 of them in the *Iliad* and *Odyssey*. Often the matter of these similes is zoological. Clough has one short imitation in a passage I shall quote later—that describing the 'belly-flop' of the corpulent Hobbes when diving. A longer, and so a more epical one, comes in the passage I have just quoted describing the after-dinner speeches. On another occasion the beast has a longer stay, but by virtue of the means of metaphor rather than simile; Philip Hewson, who is to emerge as the hero of the poem, embarks on one of his speeches to the assembled party of tutor and undergraduates as they idle in the cottage after returning from the dance that concluded the sports. When he warms to his work we get:

But he with the bit in his teeth,—scarce
Breathed a brief moment, and hurried exultingly on with his rider,
Far over hillock, and runnel, and bramble, away in the champaign,
Snorting defiance and force, the white foam flecking his quarters,
Rein hanging loose to his neck, and head projected before him.[2]

I have called the figure metaphor rather than simile, but it is half way between the two: Philip is not called a horse outright, as it would be the function of a metaphor to call him; he is called 'he' and the horse's nature rather joins his own than replaces it, which is more like the effect of a simile.

It is owing to the mockery of the epic simile that we get one of the most remarkable things in the poem, the dawn simile which has the love of Philip for Elspie as its long-deferred major term:

But as the light of day enters some populous city,
Shaming away, ere it come, by the chilly daystreak signal,
High and low, the misusers of night, shaming out the gas lamps,
All the great empty streets are flooded with broadening clearness,
Which, withal, by inscrutable simultaneous access

[1] ch. IV. [2] ch. II.

Permeates far and pierces, to very cellars lying in
Narrow high-back-lane, and court and alley of alleys:
He that goes forth to his walk, while speeding to the suburb,
Sees sights only peaceful and pure; as, labourers settling
Slowly to work, in their limbs the lingering sweetness of slumber;
Humble market-carts, coming-in, bringing-in not only
Flower, fruit, farm-store, but sounds and sights of the country
Dwelling yet on the sense of the dreamy drivers; soon after
Half-awake servant-maids unfastening drowsy shutters
Up at the windows, or down, letting-in the air by the doorway;
School-boys, school-girls soon, with slate, portfolio, satchel,
Hampered as they haste, those running, these others maidenly
 tripping;
Early clerk anon turning out to stroll, or it may be
Meet his sweetheart—waiting behind the garden gate there;
Merchant on his grass-plat haply, bare-headed; and now by this time
Little child bringing breakfast to 'father' that sits on the timber
There by the scaffolding; see, she waits for the can beside him;
Mean-time above purer air untarnished of new-lit fires:
So that the whole great wicked artificial civilized fabric,—
All its unfinished houses, lots for sale, and railway outworks,—
Seems reaccepted, resumed to Primal Nature and Beauty:—
—Such—in me, and to me, and on me the love of Elspie![1]

Here, by the way, surely is the most comprehensive description of the dawn in English. In 'A Description of the Morning' Swift had limited himself to recounting the humdrum or discreditable business of the urban human beings who are up and about: there is not a word about the light in the sky or on the earth. Wordsworth, also in the city, had noted only what is as glorious in the city as in the Lake District:

Never did sun more beautifully steep
In his first splendour, valley, rock or hill. . . .

In the magnificent account of the dawn in *The Prelude*, however, he stoops from the sublime to notice that near at hand

. . . in the meadows and the lower grounds
Was all the sweetness of a common dawn,
Dews, vapours, and the melody of birds
And labourers going forth to till the fields.[2]

[1] ch. IX.
[2] IV. 329 ff. Though written earlier, *The Prelude* was not published till 1850.

Clough stands midway between those who dwell only on the squalor and those who dwell only on the sublimities.

Because of the epic, it may be noted, Clough used some archaic English. We get 'Lo, and he sitteth . . . ' and 'erst' and 'anon'—to draw on the passages I have already quoted. He was not a poet given to using archaic diction, or, more generally, archaic language, when he could avoid it. In this he differed from Arnold, who assumed—perhaps because he was lazy or busy over other things—that poetry was sometimes the better, as in the eighteenth century, for using words and phrases on the score of their presence in earlier poetry. Sometimes Clough's use of English was startlingly modern in *The Bothie*, and later I shall indicate one particular way in which its diction was characteristically up-to-the-minute. But now and again he furnished it with old-fashioned English, and that, I think, because he found the metre otherwise too difficult. As it happened, however, he had the best of excuses, being engaged on writing mock-epic. But mainly it is a case of claiming indulgence—this is how I see it—because of the meritorious hard work being put in on other things. He was not a writer to use archaisms by choice. This is one of the several principles of his poetics that he shares with present-day poets.

A final word on the relation of his poem to the epic. How did it strike contemporary readers? There was no lack of knowledge of the ancient epics in Clough's day—all scholars then knew Greek, and most 'common readers' knew Pope's *Homer*, and perhaps also Dryden's *Virgil*. Nevertheless a poem imitating the narrative method of the epic as closely as Clough's did is by so much a learned poem, and for some readers must therefore have been a forbidding one. Over the last century other brilliant realistic narrative poems had made no such demands—Gray's 'Long Story', Cowper's 'John Gilpin', poems of Crabbe, Wordsworth's 'Idiot Boy', *Peter Bell*, and *The Waggoner*. These poems seemed, in comparison, unassuming additions to the ballads you could buy in the streets.

4

Another difficulty lay in the subject—in that part of it

concerning an undergraduate reading party. Clough is a realist —he writes of things as frankly in verse as if he was writing of them in prose. The things he writes of in *The Bothie* cannot but include 'shop'—'set books' and names of the latest clothes. And the comments on these and all other things cannot, since Clough is thoroughly competent, avoid being given in the Oxford slang of 1848. I have already quoted uses of 'shady' (i.e. unreliable) and 'topping'. We also hear that Philip is to 'go up at Easter'—i.e. be examined at that point in the academic year. Hope tells the tutor that

> . . . a Cambridge man I know, Smith, a senior wrangler,
> With a mathematical score hangs-out at Inveraray.[1]

Here 'man' is used of a member of a university, in this instance a graduate member, and 'hangs out' is a slang term first recorded in the nineteenth century ('score' is merely another numeral). The purport of most of the slang words would be plain to most readers, but there is one term which might have puzzled them or been understood in a wrong sense. The party usually bathe near the cottage, but after a time stumble on a bathing place even more delightful, and

> There they bathed, of course, and Arthur, the glory of headers,
> Leapt from the ledges with Hope, he twenty feet, he thirty;
> There, overbold, great Hobbes from a ten-foot height descended,
> Prone, as a quadruped, prone with hands and feet protending;
> There in the sparkling champagne, ecstatic, they shrieked and shouted.
> 'Hobbes's gutter' the Piper entitles the spot, profanely,
> Hope 'the Glory' would have, after Arthur, the glory of headers:
> But, for before they departed, in shy and fugitive reflex
> Here in the eddies and there did the splendour of Jupiter glimmer,
> Adam adjudged it the name of Hesperus, star of the evening.[2]

I shall revert to the second half of this passage. It is not easy to follow, especially if we do not know that 'headers', a nineteenth-century word for a dive headforemost, had also the Oxonian sense, for which Clough is our sole authority, of the practitioner of that kind of dive, and that 'gutter' was Oxford slang for the stomach-flat fall on to water which we now call a

[1] ch. II. [2] ch. III.

'belly-flop'. Eric Partridge's *Dictionary of Slang* has no earlier use of this latter word than one some dozen years later, when he finds it current at Winchester. Unless we know the sense of the word we miss seeing that Clough uses it to crown his vivid account of Hobbes's attempt at a dive, which is part of the character of that corpulent, brilliant, erratic, ridiculous, young man. When the poem was revised, one delightful touch of general slang was omitted, the current word for penny, for *copper*, which replaces it in the later version:

For it was told . . .
How they had walked, and eaten, and drunken, and slept in
kitchens,
Slept upon floors of kitchens, and tasted the real Glen-livat,
Walked up perpendicular hills, and also down them,
Hither and thither had been, and this and that had witnessed,
Left not a thing to be done, and had not a *brown* remaining.[1]

Another of these general slang words, not confined to Oxford, has established itself in the language: we hear that Elspie Mackaye is

stopping
Just above here with her uncle. . . .[2]

The most elusive slang word occurs in a passage that is studded with them:

And there was told moreover, he telling, the other correcting,
Often by word, more often by mute significant motion,
Much of the Cambridge coach and his pupils at Inveraray,
Huge barbarian pupils, expanded in infinite series,
Firing-off signal guns (great scandal), from window to window
(For they were lodging perforce in distant and numerous houses)
Signals, when, one retiring, another should go to the Tutor:—
Much too of Kitcat, of course, and the party at Drumnadrochet,
Mainwaring, Foley, and Fraser, their idleness horrid and dog-cart;
Drumnadrochet was *seedy*, Glenmorison *adequate*, but at
Castleton, high in Braemar, were the *clippingest* places for bathing,
One by the bridge in the village, indecent, *the Town-Hall* christened,
Where howbeit had Lauder been bathing, and Harrison also,
Harrison even, the Tutor, another like Hesperus here, and
Up the water of Eye, half-a-dozen at least, all *stunners*.[3]

[1] ch. III, Clough's italics. [2] ch. III. [3] ibid., Clough's italics.

The word 'adequate' is one beloved of the writers of logic, and this explains its adoption as undergraduate slang. Locke had called 'ideas' adequate when they 'perfectly represent those Archetypes which the mind supposes them taken from; which it intends them to stand for', and Mill's *Logic* two years before *The Bothie*, had stated that 'the only adequate definition of a name is . . . one which declares the facts'. The point of slang is that it is used as much as possible. It is the result of an attempt to cut out other diction for the sake of isolating and stabilizing the 'set' who use it ('set' in this sense was a term originating at Rugby in the nineteenth century), and making them self-sufficient—they flaunt their private understandings. In this sense 'adequate' was a slang word, as 'topping' and 'stunner' were, and it is amusing to note that a little later Arnold used it as one of his repeated critical terms. Having been a term for logicians, it was now also claimed by him for critics, and no doubt he smiled to himself that for him and his fellow Oxonians it had cheerful memories of youthful over-use.

Clough sees the use of slang as ridiculous. His mockery of it may be gathered from the way he crowds slang words together, as in the passage I have just quoted, and also from the following passage which is a *locus classicus* of the thing, like the account of the after-dinner syntax. Lindsay is mourning the shortness of his stay with Hope's people at the castle:

Only one day to have staid who might have been welcome for seven,
Seven whole days in castle and forest—gay in the mazy
Moving, imbibing the rosy, and pointing a gun at the horny![1]

We may note that Dick Swiveller in *The Old Curiosity Shop* had already used both 'mazy' (dance) and 'rosy' (wine), but I can find no authority for 'horny'. Clough is laughing at slang for the double reason that it is ridiculous when used over much, and that it expands infinitely unless we are careful. I have equated 'mazy' with *dance*, but it may already have indicated a particular dance, the waltz. In 1864 Mrs Henry Wood used it as an epithet so as to suggest this particular sense for the noun.[2] Part of the amusingness of the word, as used in slang, is that, like

[1] ch. III.

[2] *Lord Oakburn's Daughters*, ii, 326: 'Whirling round the room in the mazy waltz. . . .'

'rosy' it began as a word in the high poetry of Spenser, Milton, and Pope.

The Saturday Review, noticing the collected poems, did not find Clough's slang repellent or difficult: it described *The Bothie* indulgently as 'full of the harmless slang in vogue at Oxford';[1] in 1848 Kingsley, who was a 'Cambridge man', had seen all round the subject, making it the occasion for one of his sermons:

> The exclusively Oxonian allusions and phrases may be objected to, and certainly a glossary of a dozen words or so would have been a convenient appendage. But we think the author perfectly right in having introduced his Oxford slang. The thing existed—it was an integral part of his subject. Oxford men have peculiar phrases, peculiar modes of life and thought—he had no right to omit them. For ourselves, we cannot sympathise in the modern cosmopolitan spirit, which cries down all local customs, phrases, and costume; and wants to substitute a dead level uniformity for that true unity which is only to be found in variety; which prefers, as Archdeacon Hare well instances, the dead blank regularity of a modern street, to the rich and harmonious variety of a pile of old Gothic buildings; which would civilise Highlanders by making them abjure kilts and take to paletots, and is merciless to all peculiarities—except its own.[2]

5

The lines about Hobbes's gutter[3] illustrate another difficulty that crops up from time to time—that of following the sense. I find the lines quoted to mean that Lindsay profanely, but wittily, called the place 'Hobbes's gutter'; Hope wished to call it 'the glory' in compliment to Arthur Audley, the best diver among them, while the tutor was for asserting the claims of what was more exquisitely sensuous—before they had left the pool they had remarked the reflection on the waters of Jupiter, and accordingly the name he wished to call it by was that of the evening star, 'Hesperus'. Here is another passage to illustrate the difficulties of understanding the syntax. I am quoting, it will be remembered, from the first edition. Clough found the passage

[1] op. cit., XII, 1861, p. 564.
[2] *Fraser's Magazine*, January to June 1849, p. 109.
[3] See above, p. 132.

difficult to compose—not surprisingly when he was talking with complete frankness of the process of adolescence, mental and physical. The Oxford editors show us that some of the physical had been shed by the time the composing reached the 1848 text, and more was to be shed in later revision. The process of shedding no doubt kept pace with the growing taboos of the time, which had become strict by 1860. In 1848 Clough could still print a passage so outspoken as the following, though I quote the passage to call attention to the teasing (but solvable) syntax: Hobbes is speaking:

Never I properly felt the relation of man to woman,
Though to the dancing-master I went, perforce, for a quarter,
Where, in dismal quadrille, were good-looking girls in plenty,
Though, too, school-girl cousins were mine—a bevy of beauties,—
Never (of course you will laugh, but of course all the same I shall
 say it,)
Never, believe me, revealed itself to me the sexual glory,
Till in some village fields in holidays now getting stupid,
One day sauntering 'long and listless', as Tennyson has it,
Long and listless strolling, ungainly in hobbadiboyhood,
Chanced it my eye fell aside on a capless, bonnetless maiden,
Bending with three-pronged fork in a garden uprooting potatoes.
Was it the air? who can say? or herself, or the charm of the labour?
But a new thing was in me; and longing delicious possessed me,
Longing to take her and lift her, and put her away from her slaving:
Was it to clasp her in lifting, or was it to lift her by clasping,
Was it embracing or aiding was most in my mind; hard question!
But a new thing was in me, I too was a youth among maidens:
Was it the air, who can say? but in part 'twas the charm of the
 labour.
I was too awkward, too shy, a great deal, be assured, for advances,
Shyly I shambled away, stopping oft, but afraid of returning,
Shambled obliquely away, with furtive occasional sidelook,
Long, though listless no more, in my awkward hobbadiboyhood.
Still, though a new thing was in me, though vernal emotion, the
 secret
Yes, amid prurient talk, the unimparted mysterious secret
Long, the growing distress, and celled-up dishonour of boyhood,
Recognised now took its place, a relation, oh bliss! unto others;
Though now the poets, whom love is the key to, revealed themselves
 to me,

And in my dreams by Miranda, her Ferdinand, sat I unwearied,
Though all the fuss about girls, the giggling, and toying, and coying,
Were not so strange as they had been, so incomprehensible purely;
Still, as before, (and as now) balls, dances, and evening parties,
Shooting with bows, going shopping together, and hearing them
 singing,
Dangling beside them, and turning the leaves on the dreary piano,
Offering unneeded arms, performing dull farces of escort,
Seemed like a sort of unnatural up-in-the-air balloon-work,
(Or what to me is as hateful, a riding about in a carriage,)
Utter divorcement from work, mother earth, and objects of living,
As mere gratuitous trifling in presence of business and duty,
As does the turning aside of the tourist to look at a landscape
Seem in the steamer or coach to the merchant in haste for the city.[1]

The reader will see why I suggest that *The Bothie* needs to be read repeatedly, though this is an unusually teasing passage. He will also see that the poem is one well worth understanding.

6

To these difficulties of expression may be added one of structure. *The Bothie* deals with a party of people, and introduces them as a party. We all know how hard it is to find our whereabouts when the first scene of a story introduces all the characters at once. Such a story as Anthony Berkeley's *Jumping Jenny*—surely one of the most brilliant of detective novels—may have lost readers because its first crowded scene asks so much all at once. Clough has a clear idea of all the actors in his story—as we have seen he can even differentiate them according to their tastes in waistcoats—and this did not go unrecognized: Sellar noted that:

There is not one of the personages of the 'Bothie', or even of 'Amours de Voyage', where the sketching is much slighter, whose individuality is not as thoroughly impressed upon as as if they had been delineated in a three-volume novel by Mr. Trollope. We are made to understand by most happily selected touches, and delicately illustrative phrases, not only what they are in themselves, but precisely how they affect one another. It becomes as impossible for us to attribute a remembered remark to the wrong person as it would be in a play

[1] ch. II.

of Shakespeare. To say that Clough's dramatic faculty was strong might convey a wrong impression, as we imagine he was quite devoid of the power of representing a scene of vivid action; but the power of forming distinct conceptions of character, and expressing them with the few touches that poetry allows, is one of the gifts for displaying which we may regret that he had not ampler scope.[1]

(The regret, by the way, need not be too bitter: after all Clough wrote *Dipsychus* as well as the poems Sellar mentions.) It is necessary for the reader to keep the 'men' separate because of their contrasts and their inter-action, particularly by means of the remarks they throw in whenever any topic is being expressed at length—as when Philip is developing his idea that women are more sexually attractive when they are familiar with hard work (Chapter II), and when half the party report their adventures after splitting off for a while from the base at the cottage. Unless we keep the 'men' separate we miss all the inter-action of their intellect and personalities.

7

Let me revert to the metre, and for the purposes of praise. English hexameters are difficult to write because the first foot of the line begins with a syllable that is stressed. In most English metres, the basis being iambic, the line begins with a syllable that is unstressed:

> The child is father to the man;
>
> A linnet that had lost its way;
>
> To bottomless perdition there to dwell;
>
> And justify the ways of God to man.

The English hexametrist is denied an iambic opening to his line, and is therefore denied such 'natural' things as a noun with its article and runs of words like 'they mingled', 'the Piper', 'of architectural', 'and lo' and 'at Castleton'. When he cannot avoid such phrases, he had no option but to give the weak syllable to the close of the previous line:

So it was told. . . .

[1] op. cit., pp. 382 f.

How to the element offering their bodies, down-shooting the fall, they
Mingled themselves with the flood and the force of imperious water.
  And it was told too, Arthur narrating, the Piper correcting,
How, as one comes to the level, the weight of the downward impulse
Carries the head under water, delicious, ineffable; how the
Piper, here ducked and blinded, got stray, and borne-off by the current
Wounded his lily-white thighs, below, at the craggy corner;[1]

or

Philip shall write us a book, a Treatise upon *The Laws of Architectural Beauty in Application to Women*;[2]

or

Rounded the craggy point, and now at their ease looked up; and
Lo, on the rocky ledge. . . .[3]

or

Drumnadrochet was *seedy*, Glenmorison *adequate*, but at
Castleton. . .[4]

And accordingly Clough in an introductory note apologized for the way 'a word will often be required to be transposed by the voice from the end of one line to the beginning of the next'. He does not impose this requirement often, and in revision he removed some of the offending instances (he need not have done so, the reader finds them pleasant when infrequent). To be often denied, when he is beginning a line, the sort of phrases in question is a severe limitation. On the other hand the hexameter has a compensation in the rhythm that closes the line. Unique among English metres, except for some others imitated from ancient lyric metres, the hexameter offers a rhythm into which English phrasing glides effortlessly. Indeed the *tum*-te-te-*tum*-te of the line ending is a common rhythm in Old English metre, a rhythm so common that its loss in the metres favoured from Chaucer onwards is a major loss. It is also a common rhythm in speech, and so in written prose. Of the sentences of

[1] ch. III.
[2] ch. II.
[3] ch. III.
[4] ibid.

Stead I quoted at the outset[1] the last two ended with an instance of it: 'work to the public' and 'dress their shop window', and indeed the whole last sentence is a hexameter complete, or would be if it figured in a hexametric poem, for only then should we give an accent to 'They':

They can produce the goods, they cannot dress their shop window.

That the reader did not spot the accidental metre shows how native to our speech the rhythm of the hexameter is. But it is the run of its last two feet that is so English. Anybody can readily recall scores of phrases of the rhythm most characteristic of the ending of the hexameter—'gammon and spinach', 'Saturday morning', 'Waterloo Station', 'fabulous prices', 'All's well that ends well'. Clough took full advantage of the opportunities for making phrases coincide with this rhythm. Instances crowd in the passages I have already quoted. And the finest phrases of the poem coincide with the rhythm in question, especially when we extend it backward to include the fourth foot of the line:

> tender of game-law;[2]
>
> awkward hobbadiboyhood;[3]
>
> the celled-up dishonour of boyhood;[4]
>
> brief-kilted hero;[5]
>
> perfection of water;[6]
>
> consolement of waistcoats.[7]

The hexameter, when we forget its origins, invites the use of English at its most native. Altogether, so English is the rhythm that the use of slang may be said to have been attracted by it. If the metre is fed with words such as these:

> That's right,
> Take off your coat to it, Philip, cried Lindsay, outside in the garden,
> Lindsay, cigar-loving hero, the Piper, the Dialectician,

[1] See above, p. 118. [2] ch. III. [3] ch. II
[4] ibid. [5] ibid. [6] ch. III.
[7] ch. IV. When Arnold praised his dead friend at the close of the Homer lectures he commended two line-end phrases from *The Bothie*—'dangerous Corrievreckan' and 'where roads are unknown to Loch Nevish'—and Emerson lifted 'joy of eventful living' for the 'Power' chapter in his *Conduct of Life* (1860); two of these three phrases, however, have the *tum*-te-*tum*-te that is alternate to the *tum*-te-te-*tum*-te rhythm (see above, p. 121).

Take off your coat to it, Philip.
Well, well, said Hewson resuming;

Laugh if you please at my novel economy; listen to this, though;[1]

and this:

Ah, you have much to learn, we can't know all things at twenty;[2]

—if the metre accommodates such conversational rhythms as these, it encourages the writer to be more conversational still, and give us slang expressions.

In summary, then, we have in *The Bothie* a raciness of language that Dryden, Pope, and Byron would have appreciated, and which in their more exclusively iambic rhythm they strove, on occasions, to achieve.

The hexameter had other advantages in that it could beautifully accommodate certain sorts of matter. Clough showed it to be a good metre in which to reproduce discussion. And also to reproduce protracted stillness, or circling or gliding movement. When the engagement of Philip and Elspie is ripening we get this:

Ten more days did Adam with Philip abide at the changehouse,
Ten more nights they met, they walked with father and daughter.
Ten more nights, and night by night more distant away were
Philip and she; every night less heedful, by habit, the father.
Happy ten days, most happy; and, otherwise than thought of,
Fortunate visit of Adam, companion and friend to David.
Happy ten days, be ye fruitful of happiness! Pass o'er them slowly,
Slowly; like cruise of the prophet be multiplied, even to ages!
Pass slowly o'er them ye days of October; ye soft misty mornings,
Long dusky eves; pass slowly; and thou great Term-Time of Oxford,
Awful with lectures and books, and little-goes and great-goes,
Till but the sweet bud be perfect, recede and retire for the lovers,
Yea, for the sweet love of lovers, postpone thyself even to doomsday!
Pass o'er them slowly, ye hours; Be with them ye Loves and Graces![3]

And to illustrate the circling and gliding movement there is the expression of the water-imagery that is salient in the latter half of the poem; for instance:

But a revulsion wrought in the brain and bosom of Elspie;

[1] ch. II. [2] ibid. [3] ch. VI.

And the passion she just had compared to the vehement ocean,
Urging in high spring-tide its masterful way through the mountains,
Forcing and flooding the silvery stream, as it runs from the inland;
That great water withdrawn, receding here and passive,
Felt she in myriad springs, her sources, far in the mountains,
Stirring, collecting, rising, upheaving, forth-out-flowing,
Taking and joining, right welcome, that delicate rill in the valley,
Filling it, making it strong, and still descending, seeking,
With a blind forefeeling descending, evermore seeking,
With a delicious forefeeling, the great still sea before it;
There deep into it, far, to carry, and lose in its bosom,
Waters that still from their sources exhaustless are fain to be added.[1]

With such passages we may link that in which the light of dawn is described as it quietly pervades the town.[2] I can compare such passages only to passages in late Mozart or Beethoven where the music does not progress so much as hover—hover in bemused expectation that power will in time accumulate to enable it to bound forward: a good instance comes in the finale of Mozart's great C major piano concerto (K. 503), where for twenty-two bars the scurrying but tethered notes sway from side to side as if awaiting the opening of a great door that will allow them to burst through and onward.

Finally we may note the general advantage the hexameter has in being a sad metre—sadness is always worth having in poetry,[3] especially when, as here in *The Bothie*, its sadness can be mingled with high-spirits, and a sort of average struck. The announcement of a wedding is a happy announcement, but also a solemn one, and the hexameter can therefore express it perfectly:

There, when shearing had ended, and barley-stooks were garnered,
David gave Philip to wife his daughter, his darling Elspie;
Elspie the quiet, the brave was wedded to Philip the poet.[4]

8

I hope by now I have persuaded the reader new to Clough that *The Bothie* is a poem to read for its story, which I shall not

[1] ch. VII.
[2] See above, p. 129.
[3] See my *Pope and Human Nature*, 1958, pp. 58f.
[4] ch. IX.

spoil by recounting it. What lies in store I may indicate in general. The reader will not find himself in a poem like, say, Wordsworth's 'Vaudracour and Julia', where the love-making is 'poetical', that is, in which only the beautiful things about love are allowed a say. Instead he will find himself in a novel, or, since the work is as comparatively brief as some 2,000 lines, in a *nouvelle*. I say *nouvelle* rather than short story because the scale of the work allows the author all the elbow room he requires—there is room for long speeches in full and for scenes down to their particulars—when Elspie takes the initiative at a point where the lovers are drifting momentarily apart, we get this:

She stepped right to him, and boldly
Took up his hand, and placed it in hers; he daring no movement;
Took up the cold hanging hand, up-forcing the heavy elbow.[1]

There can be few love stories as complete as Clough's because he takes a complete man as his hero, a man complete with body, mind and soul. The item of mind is not frequently met with in fiction. Philip is an undergraduate in close touch with his tutor, and both of them are aware of the movement of thought in a time of upheaval—in a word of the writings of Carlyle. *The Bothie* shows the impact of love on a man with a strong intelligence—one who, for instance, sees the need for a finer social justice, or at least, since he comes round to allowing aristocrats their place, for a timely criticism of social values; on a man who sees that to work hard, whether with mind or body, is a fine thing, and worth being paid for doing, even when it is a woman who does it; who sees that high social rank can prove as thwarting as low social rank. Elspie responds to the emancipated intellect in Philip. At one point she makes him retract a first principle. If women are to be emancipated, what happens if they want to get the sort of education that men secure as a matter of course:

But I will read your books, though,
Said she, you'll leave me some, Philip.
Not I, replied he, a volume.
This is the way with you all, I perceive, high and low together.
Women must read,—as if they didn't know all beforehand:

[1] ch. VII.

Weary of plying the pump we turn to the running water,
And the running spring will needs have a pump built on it.
Weary and sick of our books we come to repose in your eye-sight,
As to the woodland and water, the freshness and beauty of Nature,
Lo, you will talk, forsooth, of the things we are sick to death of.
What, she said, and if I have let you become my sweetheart,
I am to read no books! but you may go your ways then,
And I will read, she said, with my father at home as I used to.
If you must have it, he said, I myself will read them to you.
Well, she said, but no, I will read to myself, when I choose it; . . .[1]

For Elspie had already asked the question:

> Should *he—he* have a wife beneath him? herself be
> An inferior there where only equality can be?[2]

One of the interests of *The Bothie* is that it gives us one half of the Oxford of its time, the other half being given by Newman's *Loss and Gain*, which followed it a year later. Clough's intellect can stand comparison with Newman's, and he had a harder task as a narrator because he had to show an intellect in love with a woman not with a mainly mental ideal—Newman's hero is in love with the Christianity of the Roman church. Newman's hero aspires to solitude, Clough's to society: 'a relation, oh bliss! unto others'.[3] And that relation is hard to master in words. Philip thinks at every turn of the story. His mind in love remains as hardworking as Donne's had been, and so provides a combination of passion and cerebration that is not commonly shown by story-tellers. Donne's thinking probes the private nature of love, while Philip sees love as part of the social order. Accordingly Donne's thinking is more fiery. But to make a comparison with Donne at all is to claim for Clough a degree of literary importance that has too long been denied him.

[1] ch. VIII.

[2] ch. VIII. Clough overlooked the metrical error: 'an' should have been placed at the end of the preceding line and an additional foot provided for the following line.

[3] ch. II.

XII

CLOUGH: THOUGHT AND ACTION

THE SURPRISING thing about the Clough letters[1] is that even though the present collection runs to 656 pages, we still have not been given more than a large fraction of the whole. 'Of the 1,311 letters available for publication, 279 have been printed complete, 292 have been partially printed, and 740 have been omitted.' In due course of time, let us hope, we shall be given the Clough letters complete. Even then we shall always lack, it seems, what must have been as good as anything known to be preserved. When Professor Lowry published the letters of Matthew Arnold to Clough in 1932, he noted Arnold's remark, nine years after Clough's death, that 'I am troubled at having absolutely nothing of Clough's except his name in one or two books.' One letter has survived from Clough to Arnold, and this Professor Lowry printed. Unfortunately it is just a letter from Rome about the siege, and we have got the same news and nearly the same comments in other letters. But we should like the complete series because they were the letters Clough sent to 'my most intimate friend'. So he describes Arnold when introducing his fiancée to his past life. He adds '(or has been)'—because in future she, Blanche Smith, was to have all that intimacy. Judge by the letters to Blanche, Clough's intimate letters are, for all their quietness, as wonderful as anything we get from English letter-writing: the note is struck unhesitatingly in the first two letters we are given:

. . . What was the true apple? do you know? I believe its true name was 'Love is everything.' Women will believe so, and try and make men act as if *they* believed so, and straightway, behold, the Fall, and Paradise at an end etc., etc.

Love is not everything, Blanche; don't believe it, nor try to make me pretend to believe it. '*Service*' is everything. Let us be fellow-servants. There is no joy nor happiness, nor way nor name by which men may be saved but this. . . .

[1] *The Correspondence of Arthur Hugh Clough*, ed. F. L. Mulhauser, 1957.

. . . Do you think that though you and all womankind together cast me off that Truth would not be true, earth beautiful, the sky bright, honour honour, and work work—only a little harder. I tell you, yes; take it as you will. I ask no girl to be my friend that we may be a fond foolish couple together all in all each to the other. If one that has dreamt of such unreality will open her eyes and look about her and consent to be what alone in plain fact she can be, a help-mate—that is a different thing. I will ask no one to put off her individuality for me; nor will I, weak and yielding as I am, if I can help it, put off mine for anyone.

We have not been given even the extant letters complete, but we cannot altogether complain since some of the space saved has been spent generously on letters *to* Clough. Every set of letters, we see, is a part of a vast correspondence, the correspondence of an age. The letters Clough wrote were in his day only one of innumerable centres. Even in his short life of forty-two years, he corresponded with, say, a hundred persons, many of whom were well known in their day and are well known still, and all of whom corresponded with their hundreds. Some of the vast context of letters—all of which no doubt will be printed sometime—is represented here by chosen letters from friends—for instance, from W. G. Ward (grieving that in a letter from Clough there was nothing 'which might not equally have done to be printed as an essay for the world at large'), from Emerson ('Four dollars a week in the country, and six in the city, will buy good private board—which includes furnished lodgings, but excludes washing'), from Tom Arnold ('Those are indeed happy who can still hope for England'), J. C. Shairp ('Therefore I wish . . . to read the Bible simply with the heart rather than head'), from Froude ('At any rate [when writing history] one has substantive stuff between one's fingers, to be moulding at, and not those shine and sea-sand ladders to the moon "*opinions*" '), from R. H. Hutton, ('Bagehot . . . thinks a College education is quite incompatible with business habits'), from Bagehot himself ('Do you expect to find America "instructive"? . . . I rather like that rough, active pecuniary life'), from Carlyle ('I say, *Be* it, then, as Demiurgus Russell, and the National Palaver, will!'), and so on. (There is no letter from Newman, but a telling remark in a letter of Clough's: 'Everybody liked [Emerson]. . . . Some people thought him very like Newman. But his manner is much simpler.') Here, then, are more than 600 pages of letters with a generous amount of print per page.

The stage is now set for a revival of Clough's reputation, for we are already indebted to the present editor, along with Professor Lowry and Mr Norrington, for a splendid edition of the poems. If the revival comes it will be indeed a revival, for Clough's poems were much reprinted in the 1870's and 1880's and were even included in Stead's Penny Poets. Clough has never lacked his devoted readers, and they have been very numerous in the aggregate. For a certain sort of revival it is perhaps, too late. A quarter of a century ago the complete, unbowdlerized edition of 1951 might have made a stir. Then we were all reading Mr Auden, who has many points of resemblance to Clough—lively general intelligence, interest in revolutionary Europe, skill to write, as it were, on the harpsichord, with something of the exciting toneless rattle of machinery. On the other hand, if the revival comes along today it will be a more knowledgeable one. In the 1930's we were too ignorant to appreciate in Clough anything more than such dateless things as 'The Latest Decalogue' and that 'number' in *Dipsychus* which has for refrain 'How pleasant it is to have money heigh-ho!' Now we are more competent in matters Victorian, and so more ready to understand his thought about, for instance, the several versions of Christianity current in England in the 1840's, the status of women, the principle of wages for work even when done by 'ladies', the state-planning of industry as an alternative to *laissez faire*.

For Clough is one of the most searching thinkers of his time. 'Do we not work best', he asks, 'by digging deepest?' And because of the very soundness of the ideas he discovers he is one of the concisest of writers. The first of his letters, written at the age of ten, partly consists of an account of a visit to the zoo, and the many animals mentioned are so firmly pinned down by their familiar or strange names that the letter has some historical interest as a catalogue. All through his life he tried to give things their right or, failing that, their apparently best, names. The words he used were either those that referred directly to concrete things, or those that he could define to his own satisfaction.

As a schoolboy we cannot but see that he was acting partly out of character. He took over without enough thinking the beliefs and methods of Dr Arnold, whom he had several reasons for reverencing—as adult mind, as headmaster, as priest, as father (his own being far away in America). The letters he wrote to his younger brother show him as an executive of Arnold's even outside the parish. But even in these letters there is a search for things that are as definite as animals in the zoo: 'You say you are tempted every hour. I do not know what to in particular'; or, to another young correspondent, 'I got hold of that moment just after I had read your letter to try to write what I really felt in really true words'. Later, when he reached Oxford and had outgrown the wish to tamper with the religious life of others, he wrote that little poem confessing his 'strange distorted youth', but, as a proof that it had not been altogether distorted, the poem makes a cross-reference, as it were, to the letter just quoted—in that letter he sought for the fact of feeling and its faithful expression in words, and here for a true ground of feeling, a ground that could be felt to be a real part of his being, secure, approved: he speaks of seeking 'one feeling based on truth'. At twenty-two we find him testing even the diction of his poems by the same one standard:

> I am afraid that there may be something of affectation in them or at any rate of calling things by wrong names and better names than they deserve, which I seem to detect in all the things I wrote in the [school] Magazine: but on the whole I venture to believe them fairly truthful. . . .

He looked to words, as it were, to guarantee the integrity of his ideas. When he is expressing an idea he is like someone who is whittling down a block of wood so as to be able to grasp it more firmly: he qualifies what he says from all the angles he is aware of. To demonstrate his grasp take a well-known statement:

> I think others are more right, who say boldly, We don't understand it, and therefore we *won't* fall down and worship it. Though there is no occasion for adding—'there *is* nothing in it—' I should say, Until I know, I will wait: and if I am not born with the power to

discover, I will do what I can, with what knowledge I have; trust to God's justice; and neither pretend to know, nor without knowing, pretend to embrace: nor yet oppose those who by whatever means are increasing or trying to increase knowledge.

These and the rest, surely, are words of a strong man. He called himself 'weak and yielding' in the love-letter quoted earlier, but it was in a context that towered with strength. It is only the unthinking who make the mistake of judging him merely on some of his acts. Professor Mulhauser thinks his 'weakness' was because of something psychological, his shyness, but it was rather because of the strength of his intellect. Goethe had remarked how easy it is to act, how hard to think. Clough's mind required to know as much as possible before it allowed the desires to form and the will to be put in motion.

When he was exploring the possible means of livelihood in New England, supposing Blanche came out and they were married, he explored them with endless scrupulousness almost as if no happiness hung on them. The will was only one element in a whole—of wishes, abilities bodily and mental, all the possible opportunities, the nature and worthwhileness of this sort of work and of that. He reduced the role of the will because he was aware of claims from so many quarters. For the Elizabethans 'will' sometimes meant 'lust', and for Clough the one seemed almost as detestable as the other. In *Amours de Voyage*, just as if he was speaking of lust, he speaks of 'the ruinous force of the will'. Ward wrote of his 'lack of asserting your own will'. He did not care for the act of asserting because his incomplete mind included an inevitable ignorance of the results. It was like sending off a boulder down hill. His 'philosophy' was something like Newman's, who believed that when an act is done 'the whole man moves' in doing it. For most of us, unlike Newman and Clough, in the moment of action the whole man has little of the intellect included in it. Clough's decision to resign from the Oriel Fellowship may not have taken quite so long to form as Newman's, but the process was essentially the same. Clough resigned when his act had, as it were, enough really firm ground to stand on—he did not give in his resignation in a trance or in excitement. He acted deliberately and therefore strongly, and there was more strength in the act than in those of many men who are called strong-minded but who are merely strong-willed.

The trouble about Clough was the trouble his integrity sometimes gave to others. In the world of practice action must often be on weak or incomplete grounds. If he had no overmastering desires on his own account, others had for him, and, being more ready to act wildly, they had no compunction in thrusting action upon their hesitant friend. The reason for his hurried departure from New England to a choice of jobs in London was a brisk letter from Frederick Temple, then headmaster of Rugby, who, though he could not undertake to choose for him, ordered him home so as to make him choose: 'Such a need for returning here to consult will not occur again. So at any rate I decidedly advise your coming here with all speed.' To which Clough replies by booking a ticket and writing to Blanche:

> I sail with this from New York—but this may reach you first—But my views are for America.—I hardly know why I should come, but Temple was imperative—

Looking back from his desk in H.M. Council Office, Downing Street, he described his 'precipitate' flight as 'half-voluntary': Temple had supplied the missing half. But it was half-voluntary because for eight months his open mind had been quietly receiving and tending the many kindly impressions so that the claims of New England had come to be as complex and engaging as any he could imagine in England. It was the very thoroughness of his knowledge that kept the will waiting. Such a degree of awareness is not usually an enviable gift in a crisis, but it gives an unusual interest to life during those long stretches when it does not matter whether choices are made or not.

Clough would have as little as possible to do with two practical principles much respected at the time—the Butlerian principle of accepting a strong probability as likely to be a certainty, and the principle of acting before thinking out, when 'the whole man' was straining at the leash to move. It was held, by Carlyle as well as Newman, that when your power of thinking gives out, an act of will precipitating you into the midst of what your problem rises out of will solve it for you: by worshipping, you find there is a God; by acting as if in support of a cause, you find that you believe in it. Clough's reply to this expedient argument was the pointed line in *Amours de Voyage*:

> *Action will furnish belief,*—but will that belief be the true one?

He honoured his power of thinking things out too much to accept such aids to practice, come what might. It was from the depth of himself that those six lines came:

> It fortifies my soul to know
> That, though I perish, Truth is so . . .

The letters of Clough are the letters of one who took that hard stand. Our only regret is that, unlike Newman, he did not write down the whole of his thinking. There are few letters from Oxford, and what exist are mainly news for friends abroad. He was a great purveyor of news because he could select what mattered: his letters from Rome during the siege of 1849 are first-rate reporting and first-rate commentary. He wrote little except under stimulus. Fortunately his being engaged during his eight months in America meant that he kept up a continuous commentary in letters to Blanche, both on the place and on this thoughts about it. These remarkable letters will be much read in New England. But all the letters together show us how difficult it is to live when we are endowed with a mind virile enough to think some way into the meaning of it all.

XIII

MATTHEW ARNOLD IN OUR TIME

EARLY THIS century when Quiller-Couch noted that the poet Arnold 'was not popular in his own time', he slammed down his hand on the future, adding 'and never will be'. If the standard of popularity is that set by Gray's 'Elegy', no doubt he was right. But by a lower standard not so surely. Look at the present state of Arnold's bibliography. During the last decade no other English poet of the nineteenth century, or earlier, can show so many reprintings—except the poet who died the year after Arnold, Gerard Manley Hopkins. These reprintings culminated in 1950 when the Oxford University Press reset the poems complete with textual apparatus, and so produced an edition, which, until the poems are fully annotated in the way so clearly pointed out by Lowry and Tinker's *Commentary*, must remain final. And now, as added testimony, comes this handsome addition to the Reynard Library.[1] On bibliographical evidence, then, Arnold is something of a popular poet. For those who agree that he is a great poet as Keats and Hopkins are great poets, for those who gaze in delighted awe at Mr Garrod's superlative—'the greatest of the Victorian poets'—this is a pleasant state of affairs, inviting the critics who speak mainly or only of his defects to look at him again.

The defects that have been much deplored are technical defects, which certainly exist, though not perhaps so numerously as some people believe. Quiller-Couch charged Arnold with his crop of 'Ah!'s; and 'far worse' with his crop of italics, 'a device almost unpardonable in poetry. . . . Nor had Arnold an impeccable ear for rhyme'. Then—at a bound to come nearer to our own day—there is Dr Leavis, who took a sonnet of Arnold's and rejected it as, among other things, showing throughout a 'dead conventionality of . . . phrase'. And finally Mr Bateson, who a year ago believed that Arnold's most famous poem, 'Isolation', was 'only saved from banality by its last line. . . .

[1] *Matthew Arnold: Poetry and Prose*, ed. John Bryson, 1954.

The clumsiness and conventionality of the writing [is] embarrassingly obvious'.

At the present moment, then, there is a collision between critics deploring defects and readers reading. Does this mean that Arnold's readers do not mind technical defects? Some readers no doubt do not spot them—technical defects do not exist as objects for which an alternative is seen to be desirable except for those who have made a close study of the art of expression. These exceptional readers do spot them, and are pained by them. But blind to these things or seeing them clearly, readers read and re-read the poems of Arnold. Mr Eliot, who in 1933 found little to interest him in Arnold's technique, also found him, even at that date, 'a poet to whom one readily returns'. Evidently in practice the defects do not prove fatal. That is what Quiller-Couch discovered over Arnold's rhythm: '. . . if we hesitate to follow the many who have doubted his ear for rhythm, it is not for lack of apparently good evidence, but because some of his rhythms which used to give us pause have come, upon longer acquaintance, to fascinate us.' Evidently what Arnold requires of his readers is an eye to see what is plain as a pikestaff, and a patience to appreciate virtues that do not show themselves so quickly.

The sonnet Dr Leavis took was that on Shakespeare, one of the sixteen poems of Arnold's selected for that interesting anthology, *Fifteen Poets*, which, published by the Clarendon Press in 1941, made so cheerful a contribution to the war effort. Do we not all remember the text of this sonnet vaguely—a poem so long as a sonnet cannot hope to have its text remembered better than vaguely? And does it not include at least one line and several phrases which we remember pointedly? (Mr Auden once said compendiously that poetry was memorable speech, and it is not a bad test of a rough and ready kind.)

'Others abide our question, thou art free.' What is wrong with this memorable line? It is neither banal nor dead nor conventional. I know nothing better as the opening of an address to Shakespeare. It is better even than Landor's:

> Shakespeare is not *our* poet, but the world's.

Faced with that sublime theme, we do not feel that Arnold lets us down. And to turn to the poem that Mr Bateson carps at—for carping it seems—that poem is great overwhelmingly! The word 'overwhelmingly' can stand a pointed application. The defects of the poem are flooded over not only by that last line—

The unplumb'd, salt, estranging sea

—but by

Oh then a longing like despair
Is to their farthest caverns sent,

and also by the general tone of the poem. Speaking of the separateness of individual souls, it speaks in tones that in the nineteenth century would have been called piercing. 'Piercing' indeed is too weak a word: its tones are trenchant. Arnold is one of the really powerful emotional forces that have found expression in our poetry. If you want to read of aching hearts, longing, frustration, the depths of blankness and isolation, you must go to him, to Tennyson, and to few others. Earlier in this century Arnold's poems were valued for their Keatsian landscape; there was a strong Oxford cult of 'The Scholar Gypsy' and 'Thyrsis'. I suggest that he is popular now because of his hundred short poems that show him as marvellously gifted in the expression of sorts and shades of emotion. And also as a psychologist: as for instance in this fragment:

Below the surface-stream, shallow and light,
Of what we *say* we feel—below the stream,
As light, of what we *think* we feel—there flows
With noiseless current strong, obscure and deep,
The central stream of what we feel indeed.

Or in this paragraph from 'The Buried Life':

Only—but this is rare—
When a belovèd hand is laid in ours,
When, jaded with the rush and glare
Of the interminable hours,
Our eyes can in another's eyes read clear,
When our world-deafen'd ear
Is by the tones of a lov'd voice caress'd,—
A bolt is shot back somewhere in our breast
And a lost pulse of feeling stirs again:

The eye sinks inward, and the heart lies plain,
And what we mean, we say, and what we would, we know.
A man becomes aware of his life's flow,
And hears its winding murmur, and he sees
The meadows where it glides, the sun, the breeze.

'A bolt is shot back somewhere in our breast': what other poet so well knows what it feels like to have feelings?

In theory, of course, we wish that Arnold had written with a Miltonic perfection of diction, or rather that he could have been counted on to write with it always. But in practice the wish is defeated. As we read him we see that to go on talking about defects is as if you objected to a scratch on a fist that was knocking you down. There is something wrong with literary principles that can allow defects like Arnold's to outweigh virtues like his.

When we leave Arnold's poetry for his prose, it is necessary to make a sharper division between his readers, the division marking off the scholar and the general reader. Nowadays scholars are delightedly busy reading Arnold's prose because they are seeking a better understanding of the nineteenth century than that current a few years ago. Arnold, who spoke so much about his own times, is for these scholars a figure of central and fascinating interest. But what of the general reader? Can we recommend Arnold's prose to him? Writing for the general reader of his own time on the themes he did, Arnold cannot hope to hold the general reader of our own time by his matter. The general reader of today must read the Matthew Arnolds of today. For instance, if he is interested in social philosophy, an outstanding interest of Arnold's, he goes to Arnold's descendants—Margaret Mead, say. So numerous are these descendants that there is little time for the general reader to explore their literary sources. Even so, he can go to Arnold's prose. And chiefly, as it happens, for a reason the reverse of that which has kept some critics away from his poems. He can go to it for its technical felicities. There are defects in Arnold's prose, and great ones, but they are scarcely defects of technique. What was wrong with his prose was owing to lack of knowledge and grasp—defects which were inevitable then, and which probably are still, the matter investigated being so immense, subtle and impalpable. Arnold takes races, civilizations and eras, and moves them about—so he assumes—as if they were vases on the mantelshelf; his airy manner of thinking is sometimes pretentious, as Buckle's sometimes was. Nor is his diction always firm and sure; as a literary critic, for instance, he uses abstract terms—beauty, truth, and so on—without acknowledging their hardly accessible content. But his general technical accomplishment is a delight. His tone, so riling at the time for its victims, is for us, who do not find his subject matter so pressing, great comedy. Mr Bryson goes so far as to speak of his 'adorable insolence of . . . manner'. Look, for example, at the Preface, especially in its earlier form, to the *Essays in Criticism*. Or, taking the first paragraph of his 'Literary Influence of Academies', note how readily one falls into the trap of the opening sentence, only to find oneself put in one's place among the thousand ready British voices cited in the second. Or, despite its German framework, the whole of *Friendship's Garland*. Or there is the buoyant evolution of his argument in the essays on Johnson, Wordsworth, and Byron. We can still read prose the matter of which is superficially out of date for the fun of seeing it expressed just so.

XIV

'YES: IN THE SEA OF LIFE'

THE POEM of which these are the opening words[1] has been more often singled out by critics for superlative praise than any other poem of Arnold's. Already in 1867 Swinburne could refer to it as 'the famous verses, cited and admired even by critics sparing of their priceless praise';[2] to Saintsbury in 1908 it is simply 'Mr Arnold's finest poem by far'.[3] In the belief that some part of the poem's power consists in its waking of echoes from our reading, and that these also lay within Arnold's reading, I have collected some of these and attempted to relate them to the poem. (Of some that have escaped notice in print I believe many readers, especially nineteenth-century readers, to have been at least half-aware.) These are presented not in any foolish confidence of completeness, or of a new illumination of the poem. I am moved partly by dissatisfaction with what has been previously written about the poem, not only with the vagueness of eulogy but often with the stated or suggested views of its themes, and with such comment as there has been on parallels and sources. The last two are found in interdependence. Sometimes a too simple view of its themes has provoked undue emphasis on a single parallel. When John Duke Coleridge in an early review[4] charged Arnold with imitation of a

[1] Published in *Empedocles on Etna, and other poems*, 1852; reprinted in 1853, 1854, 1857, 1869, in the *Selections* made by Arnold himself in 1878, and in all later editions of *Poems*. There is nothing to show in what year it was written. In 1849 Arnold was contemplating publishing another volume of short poems in 1850 (letter quoted by Mrs Humphry Ward, *A Writer's Recollections*, 1918, pp. 42–3). The courtship of Miss Wightman in 1850 need by no means preclude the writing of a Marguerite poem in that year or later. The poem was not revised except in punctuation and title. The 1852 text is given on p. 179 below; for the titles, see pp. 171 and 177 below.

[2] Review of *New Poems* in *Fortnightly Review*, October 1867; reprinted in *Essays and Studies*, 1875.

[3] Preface to *Pendennis* in Oxford edition, p. xxvi; cf. *Corrected Impressions*, 1895, p. 153, and *Matthew Arnold*, 1899, p. 30.

[4] Of the 1853 *Poems*, in the *Christian Remembrancer*, xxvii (3 April 1854). The religious complexion of the periodical has to be remembered, as well as J. D. C.'s sense of family property. But J. D. C. was Arnold's friend and Arnold took the review with

passage in *Christabel*, he was under-interpreting the poem as well as (not quite disinterestedly) imputing a wrong or over-conscious motive. When Saintsbury aligned the poem with 'the grim *Nequicquam!* of Lucretius' and with the later 'Strangers Yet',[1] he was either writing loosely or over-specializing the poem's emotional reference; when, in another place, he called it 'simply an extension of a phrase in *Pendennis*',[2] his tone has the overstatement of discovery. And (to come to recent authorities) when Tinker and Lowry in their valuable and much-used *Commentary*[3] disregard this last and mention only the echoes of Coleridge and of a single phrase of Horace, and when M. Louis Bonnerot rejects both these as origins of the image (which was never claimed) in favour of a letter of Arnold's to his sister,[4] there seems some lack of discrimination. All these 'parallels', and others, are of some but varying relevance to different levels of the poem's meaning and purpose. Looked at together they may appear more clearly, and perhaps also expose the poem more clearly. It will stand, and reward, some searching. Its single, branching image, sustained and growing from the first line to the last, the compactness and tension along with the deceptively plain statements, and the tremendous concentra-

some amusement: 'My love to J. D. C., and tell him that the limited circulation of the *Christian Remembrancer* makes the unquestionable viciousness of his article of little importance' (*Letters*, i, 35). Arthur Stanley took up the cudgels on Arnold's behalf, rather on grounds of ethics and etiquette than literary criticism (*Life and Correspondence of Lord Coleridge*, 1904, i, 211–12). He says: 'I think that the passage about "the rocks" [*sic*] has no lineal connection with *Christabel*.'

1 *Matthew Arnold*, 1899, p. 31. 'Strangers Yet' is by Richard Monckton Milnes, Lord Houghton; it appears in *Poetical Works*, 1876, ii, 85, with the date 1865 and a note that it has been set to music by Mrs Bernard. It expresses the commonplace sentiment that even those nearest in blood and affection are essentially strangers; the best lines, and the only ones at all near to Arnold, are:

> Oh! the bitter thought to scan
> All the loneliness of man:—
> Nature, by magnetic laws,
> Circle unto circle draws,
> But they only touch when met,
> Never mingle—strangers yet.

2 Preface to *Pendennis*, p. xxvi; reprinted in *A Consideration of Thackeray*, 1931, pp. 186–7.

3 C. B. Tinker and H. F. Lowry, *The Poetry of Matthew Arnold: a Commentary*, 1940, p. 156.

4 *Matthew Arnold, Poète*, p. 68 n.

tion of the climax make it the firmest and perhaps indeed the greatest of Arnold's lyrics.

2

Of all earlier poets, Horace has most to do both with the poem's inherent and its overt meaning, and has given most to its words. The echo from Horace[1] is the stronger for being climactic in Arnold's poem.

Who renders vain their deep desire?
  A God, a God their severance rul'd;
And bade betwixt their shores to be
The unplumb'd, salt, estranging sea.
(ll. 21–4)

nequiquam deus abscidit
  prudens Oceano dissociabili
terras, si tamen impiae
  non tangenda rates transiliunt vada.
(*Odes*, I. iii. 21–4)

Further, Arnold's repetition of 'A God' recalls Horace's 'deus, deus nam me vetat' (*Epodes*, xiv. 6)[2] associable with the lines from the Ode by the idea of prohibition, though here the context is comparatively trivial and formal.[3] But what is given and taken from the Ode is by no means confined to the lines quoted. In their context Horace's lines imply much more of Arnold's

[1] So far as I know, it is noted only in Tinker and Lowry, with acknowledgement to a remark of Professor Arnold Whitridge (Arnold's grandson); but most readers of both poets must have been aware of it, and aware that the likeness extended to *deus abscidit* as well as to *Oceano dissociabili*.

[2] Noted by Archibald Y. Campbell, *Horace*, 1924, p. 143 n. The Carlyle passage noted below (p. 165, n. 2) also contributes something to Arnold's emphasis.

[3] That Horace's *Oceanus circumvagus* (*Epodes*, xvi. 41), in conjunction with *beata petamus arva divites et insulas*, was the starting-point for Arnold's image in the first line, as recently suggested by Paul Turner ('*Dover Beach* and *The Bothie*', *English Studies*, xxviii (1947), p. 176), seems to me more dubious; I can believe that it was in Arnold's mind, and that at any time between 1848 and 1850 this Epode would have had many special meanings for himself and Clough (Mr Turner notes that the lines head the ninth section of *The Bothie*); but not that anything in the image or words of 'Yes: in the sea' is taken from them. Horace uses *circumvagus* for the encirclement of the whole earth by the sea. Mr Turner points especially to l. 5, but the intimate connection between the sea and the islands seems to me lacking for Horace; his word implies nothing of the close particular embrace of 'enclasping flow'. I should put this 'parallel' in the 'salmons-in-both' category.

thought. *Dissociabili* (already noticeable by its novelty) carries the more weight from its use in a poem on the parting of friends; Horace is addressing Virgil on his departure for Greece and begs the ship to carry him safely *et serves animae dimidium meae*.[1] Further, in reflecting on the daring of the sailor, he implicitly compares it with the proud rashness of Prometheus and Daedalus; the tone may be half-teasing and self-teasing in relation to the occasion (he is supposed to be wishing his friend a safe voyage) but he is reflecting seriously upon desperate endeavours, unconquerable human aspirations. Thus Horace touches each verse of Arnold's poem, including the lines which express most clearly the vain but deep desire of the isolated individual to communicate with others. Arnold says man's desire is vain, Horace that the divine ordinance is vain if man defies it; but Arnold has not really reversed Horace's emphasis on man's defiance, for Horace is partly ironic. The Ode as a whole leaves him looking at least with detachment at Jove's thunderbolts and man's impiety.

Nequiquam, hardly articulated, overhangs Arnold's whole poem. Is it also, as Saintsbury implied, the more deeply reverberating *nequiquam* of Lucretius—the futility of man's striving and protesting against things as they are, and the special futility of the lover's hope of happiness?

> nequiquam, quoniam medio de fonte leporum
> surgit amari aliquid quod in ipsis floribus angat.[2]

or, more specifically,

> nequiquam, . . .
> nec penetrare et abire in corpus corpore toto:
> nam facere interdum velle et certare videntur.[3]

For all his interest in Lucretius,[4] I do not believe that Arnold intended to express precisely what Saintsbury calls 'that function of the riddle of the painful earth', and Saintsbury's

[1] Line 8. Cf. Arnold's

> So far apart their lives are thrown
> From the twin soul that halves their own.
>
> ('Too Late', ll. 3–4, also in 1852 volume.)

[2] *De Rerum Natura*, iv. 1133–4.

[3] ibid., iv. 1110–12.

[4] See *Commentary*, pp. 292–7.

own previous comment, 'the poet's affection—it is scarcely passion—is there, but in transcendence; he meditates more than he feels', itself defines a difference. Arnold's meditation is on the common human lot, which not even lovers can escape. The *amari aliquid* adds only extra saltness to the sea. And the sea is at the same time the sea of life; it is not simply ironic to call its flow enclasping; what divides is itself consoling ('fold closely, O Nature, thine arms round thy child').[1] The 'vain . . . desire' *may* include, deep in the roots of the poem, the desire 'penetrare et abire corpus in corpore toto', but in the poem includes it only as the greater includes the less. To point the distinction by means of Sir Thomas Browne:

> United souls are not satisfied with imbraces, but desire to be truly each other; which being impossible, their desires are infinite, and must proceed without a possibility of satisfaction.

It is the soul which suffers, the desire to communicate that is frustrated. If the more specialized meaning is suggested, it is I think the reader's doing; to most readers it would probably not even occur. To say that Arnold is not writing particularly for or about lovers may be open to question; to say that he is not writing particularly about passion frustrated in the moment of fulfilment is put beyond question by the island-image itself.

If the poem as written bears any trace of Lucretius, it is in the word 'salt' in the last line (*amari aliquid*), and this is much fainter than the trace of Horace in 'estranging'. The line, and each word of it, is locked into Arnold's context; 'estranging' carries far more emotional weight here than does Horace's *dissociabili*. Both are thinking of the actual sea that parts friends as well as islands, but only to Arnold does the sea between islands *stand for* the separateness of all friends—all men—as distinct from those only geographically parted. What 'estranging' also owes to the equally weighty 'unplumb'd'[2] and 'salt' which adjoin it is beyond calculation. Richard Holt Hutton, a perceptive and neglected critic, and one of the few who has not merely called the line Arnold's greatest (in those or other words), has suggested something of it:

[1] 'Parting.'

[2] In Donne's *Sermons*, xxxvii, is 'a bottomless Sea which no plummet can sound'.

without any false emphasis or prolix dwelling on the matter, it shadows out to you the plunging deep-sea lead and the eerie cry of 'no soundings', it recalls that saltness of the sea which takes from water every refreshing association, every quality that helps to slake thirst or supply sap, and then it concentrates all these dividing attributes, which strike a sort of lonely terror into the soul, into the one word 'estranging'.[1]

Within this great achievement there is included the smaller but still rare one of felicitous and exact translation; and at first sight one might think that when John Conington used 'estranging main' in his verse translation of Horace's Odes in 1863 he was simply setting the seal of approval on Arnold's own choice of word.[2] But the currency of felicitous translation is partly, even largely, an oral one; and by chance the evidence survives that this choice of word was made by one who taught both Arnold and Conington.

There is one characteristic of [Tait's] teaching which must not be passed over, and that was his power of selecting more than usually spirited and appropriate English words as the equivalents of those employed by the Greek or Latin author who was the subject of the lesson. That well-known old pupil of his, Mr. E. A. Scott,[3] who was for thirty-six years a Rugby master . . . dilated more than once to his School House pupils in the early sixties on this power of his old master. After the lapse of forty-five years only one or two of those felicitous translations remain 'in the cobwebby corner of memory's bin'. . . . Another was the translation of 'dissociabili Oceano' . . . by 'with the estranging main', the very words which Conington, who was himself in the Sixth Form under Tait for at least a year,[4] subsequently employed in his translation of the Ode referred to.[5]

Arnold was not, of course, a sixth-former under Tait, having left school in 1841; but the years in which Tait was Tutor of Balliol (1835–42) included Arnold's first year as an under-

[1] *Literary Essays*, pp. 335–6 in 1900 edition; first appeared in *British Quarterly Review*, April 1872.

[2] The Loeb editor, C. E. Bennett, also adopts it.

[3] Edward Ashley Scott, master 1859–95, at school 1842–8. This is the Scott who, with J. C. Shairp, then a master, visited Clough's Highland reading-party in 1847 (W. Knight, *Principal Shairp and his Friends*, 1888, p. 106).

[4] He left Rugby for Oxford in 1843.

[5] S. Selfe, *Chapters from the History of Rugby School*, 1910, pp. 83–4.

graduate.[1] It is, of course, not entirely impossible that Arnold suggested to his tutor the word which Tait afterwards passed on to his Rugby sixth-formers; but the probabilities are in Tait's favour, and a minute fraction of the praise Arnold has received for this great line might be transferred to the credit of the most versatile of Victorian archbishops.

3

Arnold's first verse contains a general statement about the conditions of human existence—'we mortal millions live *alone*'. The first verse is not, then, about those who long to be together when apart, or who when not parted long to be more together; it is not even only about each individual's personal loneliness; it is about the isolation of 'mortal *millions*', the vast sum of isolations. The image is not of two islands (and I do not think it narrows itself into that even in later verses), or of a group of islands, but of all the islands in the sea, 'dotting the shoreless watery wild'. 'All men are isolated'; that sentiment is too 'natural', too little 'new', for its long history and countless variations to add to or reveal anything in the poem. The famous sentence in Donne's *Devotions* varies by explicit contradiction: 'No man is an *Iland*, entire of it selfe; every man is a peece of the *Continent*, a part of the *Maine*.'[2] I shall not venture into the question whether this variation is more typical of Donne's century and Arnold's of his, nor do I believe it would be rewarding; Arnold and his contemporaries, even more than Donne and his, though perhaps on a different level, showed that they felt themselves 'involved in mankind'; and affirmation, questioning, and contradiction of man's island nature are but different faces of the same thought. Still in a Christian context, that thought appears in a poem from that volume which all Victorians knew in childhood or youth, *The Christian Year* of John Keble, Arnold's godfather:

[1] Arnold (who had approved of his appointment to Rugby) also taught the lower fifth form under him for a few months from December 1844 to April 1845, in the interim between his examination and the award of the Oriel fellowship, and possibly again for a short period in 1850.

[2] *Devotions upon Emergent Occasions*, 1624, xvii.

Why should we faint and fear to live alone,
    Since all alone, so Heaven has will'd, we die,
Nor even the tenderest heart, and next our own,
    Knows half the reasons why we smile or sigh?
Each in his hidden sphere of joy or woe,
    Our hermit spirits dwell, and range apart. . . .[1]

To Keble this separateness is a necessary part of the imperfect human condition, not to be regretted since it makes man aspire to heaven. To others it was simply necessary and to be accepted:

When I spoke of myself as an island, I did not mean that I was so exceptionally. We are all islands—

Each in his hidden sphere of joy and woe,
Our hermit spirits dwell and roam apart

—and this seclusion is sometimes the most intensely felt at the very moment your friend is caressing or consoling you. But this gradually becomes a source of satisfaction instead of repining.[2]

These are not offered as parallels; though there is certainly a real affinity between Arnold and George Eliot, and it is not surprising to hear from Arnold himself in 1876 that she said 'that of all modern poetry mine is that which keeps constantly growing upon her.'[3]

But there are two nearly contemporary elaborations of the idea which were likely to have been half-consciously recalled by Arnold and by many of his early readers; indeed, they illustrate one current in that 'main movement of the mind of the last quarter of a century' which he said in 1869 he believed his poetry to represent.[4] Two of the many different directions in which the notion of general isolation could be slanted are represented in Carlyle's *Past and Present* (1843),[5] and Thacker-

[1] Twenty-fourth Sunday after Trinity.

[2] J. W. Cross, *George Eliot's Life*, 1884, p. 167 of 1892 ed.; letter of May 1854, written to Mrs Bray just before she left the country with Lewes.

[3] *Letters*, ii, 126.

[4] *Letters*, ii, 9; letter to his mother.

[5] The parallel with Carlyle has not been noted before. Arnold's Oxford generation (that of *Tom Brown at Oxford*) were particularly enthusiastic about Carlyle. The earliest letter we have from Arnold to Clough (1845; *Letters to Clough*, p. 55) is partly in Carlylese. Arnold and Clough visited Carlyle together in June 1848 (ibid., p. 16).

ay's *Pendennis* (1849);[1] the one resentful of the isolation of workers and masters in modern society; the other exposing with rather more bitterness than compassion the real isolation of the domestically intimate. Carlyle speaks of isolation and Thackeray also of islands; but in both passages it is the momentary poetic quality and the picturesque suggestions that bring them into contact with the poem. With Carlyle there is also his emphatic rejection of divine agency, which may help to account for Arnold's equally emphatic assertion of it.

In his final Book, the 'horoscope' of the future, Carlyle is appealing against industrial anarchy to the 'captains' who must arise; against the formal tie of cash payment to the closer bond of love and loyalty such as the feudal baron knew:

> It was beautiful; it was human! Man lives not otherwise, nor can live contented, anywhere or anywhen. Isolation is the sum-total of wretchedness to man. To be cut off, to be left solitary: to have a world alien, not your world; all a hostile camp for you; not a home at all, of hearts and faces who are yours, whose you are! It is the frightfulest enchantment; too truly a work of the Evil One. To have neither superior, nor inferior, nor equal, united manlike to you. Without father, without child, without brother. Man knows no sadder destiny. 'How is each of us', exclaims Jean Paul, 'so lonely, in the wide bosom of the All!' Encased each as in his transparent 'ice-palace'; our brother visible in his, making signals and gesticulation to us;—visible, but forever unattainable: on his bosom we shall never rest, nor he on ours. It was not a God that did this; no![2]

Carlyle's general argument has little connection with this poem, though much with Arnold's later development; but when he speaks of 'isolation' he passes beyond the socially unhealthy separateness of men in industrial England to imply a separateness still more terrible, because less curable. The quotation (a favourite with Carlyle)[3] from Richter, the change to the first person, extend his reference from the 'condition-of-England question' nearer to Arnold's 'mortal millions'; 'the wide bosom

[1] Published in numbers, 1848–50; chapter xvi appeared early in 1849. This likeness was noted by Saintsbury (loc. cit.), and independently by J. T. Hackett, *My Commonplace Book*, 1919, p. 266. Mrs Sells accepts it (from the latter source) in her article 'Marguerite', *MLR*, xxxviii (1943), p. 294, n. 1.

[2] Book IV, ch. iv; p. 367 in edition of 1843.

[3] See the essay 'Jean Paul Friedrich Richter again' (1830), in *Miscellanies* (1839), iii, 72 of 1869 edition.

of the All' touches the 'enclasping flow'; and Arnold counters, even in reiteration, Carlyle's 'It was not a God that did this; no!' (Not that 'a God' means the same to both writers.) But nearest of all to the poem is Carlyle's poignant and 'romantic' image for frustrated communication (an image set going by the word 'enchantment') of our brother man in his transparent ice-palace, making signals 'visible, but forever unattainable'; arousing, that is, a 'longing like despair'. Arnold (not necessarily in this verse, but in his half-conscious recollection of the whole passage) has responded, as he so often does,[1] to the poet in Carlyle. Often as he might contend, in the sphere of fact and policy, against the particular recommendations of this 'moral desperado',[2] he could have said at any time of his life what he writes to Clough in 1848, 'it is the style and feeling by which the beloved man appears'.[3]

And now Thackeray. The immediate excuse for his general statement of human isolation is trivial enough: it is Mr Smirke's disappointment at losing Pendennis as a pupil, and losing therefore his one outlet for his secret and absurd adoration for Helen Pendennis. The comic irony of the curate's preoccupation with his own feelings, in the midst of the larger disquiets of his superiors at the moment of Arthur's launching on the world, inspires Thackeray to remind the reader, with ample and disturbing satiric detail, how little the members of any household really know of each other's thoughts. After exposing in turn son, daughter, and grandmother, he concludes:

> And as for your wife—O philosophic reader, answer and say—Do you tell *her* all? Ah sir—a distinct universe walks about under your hat and mine. All things in Nature are different to each: the woman we look at has not the same features, the dish we eat from has not the same taste to the one and the other. You and I are but a pair of infinite isolations, with some fellow-islands a little more or less near to us. Let us return, however, to the solitary Smirke.

For a moment the button-holing address to the reader modulates into soliloquy. Upon the rather shabby area of family life

[1] And as he did to the sentence in the previous chapter (IV. iii), 'Much lies among us, convulsively, nigh desperately, *struggling to be born*', and to a great deal in *Sartor*.

[2] *Letters to Clough*, p. 111.

[3] ibid., p. 75. See below, p. 217, 'Matthew Arnold and Carlyle'.

in which Thackeray's investigations have previously been moving, uncovering secrets, raising suspicions ('settling like a meat-fly'), there breaks, in that one sentence, a sudden shaft of insight; its very unexpectedness and brevity take the eye and the memory. Unexpected, for it is not led up to; Thackeray's people are not trying to communicate, nor does he suggest that they should; they are each other's dupes, and until this point the fact has seemed mainly to amuse him. Still, into that one sentence so much suggestion is packed that we could well assume (with the closeness of date) that it was among the later, more immediate stimuli of Arnold's poem. This is still far from saying with Saintsbury that the poem is 'simply an extension' of Thackeray's sentence; for Arnold says much more.

4

Arnold's islands were not always islands. 'For surely once, they feel, we were Parts of a single continent.' Here what might appear a 'stock' development disguises complicated associations and echoes. When we read these lines (and the bleakly straightforward manner of the first claims a different kind of attention from the nightingale-moonlight lines and the 'longing like despair'), we may not be wholly satisfied with the 'balance or reconcilement . . . of the idea with the image'. This longing for unity may be something that 'we mortal millions' feel; is it important to the poem that they should feel it? First, what is that 'once' for which they desperately long? It would be too trivial (for the poem) if it were no more than a happier period in the individual's life or love; this is the longing of all islands, of mortal millions. I think we can exclude, too, the 'historic' past of Carlyle's social thinking, and also of Arnold's own later 'Dover Beach' and 'Obermann once more' ('the sea of faith Was once too at the full' . . . 'the past, its mask of union on'). In the Platonic 'Self-deception' Arnold wrote of a further, an absolute, past, out of time; men 'claim the glory Of possessing powers not our share' because 'before we woke on earth, we were', desiring the 'treasuries of God'; but a Power beyond our seeing 'staved us back, and gave our choice the law'; 'decided What the parts, and what the whole should be'. 'Before we woke on earth' is most likely to be the poem's 'once', and the natural association with other poetry is perhaps with Wordsworth's 'native continent' from which men's spirits cross by an isthmus to earth and human life.[1] Or more vaguely, with the poetically (and philosophically) commonplace equation of island = man's life (the part, the Many); continent = God, 'Nature' (the whole, the One).[2] That is, the separation hinted in 'parts of a single continent' is that of creature from creator. No particular passage need be even at the back of Arnold's mind; but some lines that may have fastened on his imagination occur in Browning's *Christmas Eve*.[3] Browning sees the creator as standing 'a hand-breadth off, to give Room for the newly-made to live'; man's separateness in receiving his gift of reason is his privilege and opportunity—

> Man, therefore, stands on his own stock
> Of love and power as a pin-point rock,
> And, looking to God who ordained divorce
> Of the rock from his boundless continent

—recognizes the kinship between his own love and power and this manifestation of God's love and power. Removed though Browning's whole intention is—his poem is a hammering out of his personal faith, Arnold's poem only faintly brushing against problems of belief in its passing—in their mode of expression the two poets seem here to touch. The common element of meaning is a divinely enforced separation imaged in the contrast between continent and tiny island ('dotting' the sea; 'pin-point rock'); and Browning's poem as a whole also emphasizes the individual's isolation from his fellows and his need to share and communicate ('For I, a man, with men am linked . . . no gain That I experience must remain Unshared'). This and the poem's other themes are a reminder that it was likely to interest Arnold in 1850, even had he not with Clough been an

[1] *Prelude*, v. 536–8.

[2] Wordsworth's image is of two continents, with the emphasis on separation by distance, difference, and time, not by severance; Young's in *Night Thoughts*, iv ('From Nature's *continent*, immensely wide, Immensely blest, this little *Isle of Life*, This dark, incarcerating Colony Divides us'), is obscure as an image, but presumably implies the same general notion.

[3] Published 1 April 1850.

interested (and critical) reader of Browning before that date.[1]

The relation of Arnold's lines to this area of meaning (whether he recalled Browning or not is a side-issue) leaves them, perhaps, still unsatisfying. The non-human forces in the poem raise almost too great a variety of suggestions. The sea of life with its 'enclasping flow' ('water as the Mediator between the inanimate and Man')[2] suggests the mysterious, infinite, impenetrable; 'a God, a God', in so far as he is more than Horace's *deus*, suggests the arbitrary and uncompassionate.[3] But these conceptions are poetically and triumphantly united in the central irony of the poem by the last line; the enclasping sea, the echoing straits are *also* unplumb'd, salt, and estranging. The idea of the 'single continent' is comparatively unintegrated. It demands more connection with the other 'unknown Powers' than it fulfils; its assertiveness seems to claim an intellectual assent to a continuous meaning on all levels which is not completely there.

5

As a mere statement about geographical islands, the lines are fully acceptable. Granted that islands could feel, they would be correct, even up to date, in feeling they were once part of a single continent; the reader of 1852 who had been brought up on Lyell could accept the statement as a scientific one. But this kind of association and appeal are not commonly Arnold's concern in the way they are Tennyson's. If he desired any association it was with the legendary, poetic tradition as formulated, for instance, in Collins's 'Ode to Liberty'. There is here no plainly verbal contact, but to my mind there is a vital connection with at least one of Arnold's underlying meanings.

> Beyond the measure vast of thought,
> The works the wizard Time has wrought!

[1] *Letters to Clough*, p. 97. The letter is undated, but probably not long after September 1848. Arnold's knowledge of *Christmas Eve* is suggested by a much later echo, in 'Obermann once more' (cf. part xi).

[2] ibid., p. 92 (letter from Switzerland, September 1848).

[3] As in 'I hear a God's tremendous voice, "Be counsell'd, and retire!" Ye guiding Powers, who join and part' ('The Lake'); cf. 'the Powers that sport with man' ('Destiny').

The Gaul, 'tis held of antique story,
Saw Britain link'd to his now adverse strand;
No sea between, nor cliff sublime and hoary,
He pass'd with unwet feet thro' all our land.
To the blown Baltic then, they say,
The wild waves found another way,
Where Orcas howls, his wolfish mountains rounding;
Till all the banded West at once 'gan rise,
A wide wild storm ev'n Nature's self confounding
With'ring her giant sons with strange uncouth surprise.
This pillar'd earth so firm and wide,
By winds and inward labours torn,
In thunders dread was push'd aside
And down the should'ring billows borne.
And see, like gems, her laughing train,
The little isles on ev'ry side!
Mona, once hid from those who search the main,
Where thousand elfin shapes abide,
And Wight, who checks the west'ring tide;
For thee consenting Heav'n has each bestowed,
A fair attendant on her sov'reign pride:
To thee this blest divorce she ow'd,
For thou hast made her vales thy lov'd, thy last abode![1]

Little more here in common, it would seem, than the tradition of two lands, once united, now separated, with the multitude of 'little isles' as a decorative adjunct. But the lands are Britain (with her 'attendant train') and the mainland of Europe; Collins's note[2] supports the tradition by arguments 'from the correspondent disposition of the two opposite coasts'. For Collins's purpose of saluting Liberty in a patriotic poem of 1747,

[1] 'Antistrophe', 64–88 (*The Poems of William Collins*, ed. Walter G. Bronson, 1898). Collins believed himself the first to make poetical use of this tradition. But cf. Drayton, *Poly-Olbion*, Song xviii, and Selden's note.

[2] On l. 67. His further note on l. 81 supplies an independent cobweb thread connecting the lines with Arnold; for it records the legend of a mermaid off the Isle of Man who fell in love with a beautiful young man who deserted her, whereupon she hid the island in enchanted mist as a revenge. This has not been previously noted in connection with 'The Forsaken Merman', though the latter poem has been related to the Arnolds' visit to the Isle of Man in the summer of 1845 (where he wrote 'The Gipsy Child') and some of the still current mermaid-legends cited, in Penelope Fitzgerald's 'Matthew Arnold's Summer Holiday', *English*, vi (1946), p. 77. This further link with the note may have tied the poem more firmly to Arnold's memory.

the separation is a 'blest divorce' (a sentiment which could have been thought timely in 1848–50);[1] to Arnold it was for his personal life a matter only for regret. For, of course, entwined with his sense of isolation of all islands and all mortal millions is his awareness of himself, on his own native island, and of the estranging sea between himself and France and Switzerland, both for all they symbolize to him, and for their connection with the poem's recipient. This is a 'Switzerland' poem.[2] It is headed 'To Marguerite' in the editions of 1853 and 1854, 'To Marguerite, continued' in 1869 and thereafter, and on its first appearance in 1852 had a title of Wordsworthian precision, not paralleled elsewhere in the volume—'To Marguerite, in returning a volume of the Letters of Ortis'. Particular hypotheses about when and where Arnold wrote the poem are here immaterial (what we know of his habits of composition does not warrant the tying up of any poem's writing to a single time or place); but wherever or whenever he returned that borrowed volume, the notion of an actually separating sea, past, present, or to come, must have been in his mind. He is thinking, as in other poems, of several modes of separation; but the geographical is at least among them.[3] The idea is deeply in the image; Arnold's poem, like Horace's ode, is in part about an actual sea separating himself and another. Such a sea can indeed hardly be looked at or thought of without suggesting something that is not sea; the particular sea of the Straits of Dover is not as definitely present in this poem as in 'Dover Beach'; but the titles, and especially the original title, make it a necessary part of what we receive. And lines 15–18 are the clearest reminder of it, whether or not the link with Collins's ode is a true one.

6

With personal separation (not of *all* mortal millions but of Arnold and another or others) in mind, consider again the

[1] As by 'the Tory member's eldest son' in *The Princess* (lines added in 1850 edition): 'God bless the narrow seas! I wish they were a whole Atlantic broad.' (The Atlantic was broader then.)

[2] It was included in the group so entitled as soon as the group was formed (in *Poems*, 1853) and never left it, though its number in the series and its title were several times altered.

[3] As in 'Parting' (1852).

associations of 'estranging'. The common colloquial sense of 'estrangement' is not to be overlooked. That other kind of separation or isolation underlies the poem, although no one line exposes it, and it is clearest when we think of the poem not alone but as part of the whole constellation of 'Switzerland' and allied poems. That is, the parting of friends that comes from 'growing apart'. The image of lands once united and now divided touches common speech here; we speak of a rift or a gulf. It is for this separation, or rather for its extreme cases (a quarrel, a misunderstanding, caused by slander), that Coleridge used a similar image:

> Alas! they had been friends in youth;
> But whispering tongues can poison truth;
> And constancy lives in realms above;
> And life is thorny; and youth is vain;
> And to be wroth with one we love
> Doth work like madness in the brain. . . .
> They parted—ne'er to meet again!
> But never either found another
> To free the hollow heart from paining;
> They stood aloof, the scars remaining,
> Like cliffs which had been rent asunder;
> A dreary sea now flows between;—
> But neither heat, nor frost, nor thunder,
> Shall wholly do away, I ween,
> The marks of that which once hath been.[1]

John Duke Coleridge[2] charged Arnold with imitating these lines, not in 'manner' but in 'thought'; 'would they [Arnold's lines] have been written but for the famous passage in *Christabel*?'[3] The question (even apart from the general issues it raises) could not be answered with the expected negative unless we thought that this kind of estrangement was the main theme of Arnold's poem, which is impossible. But there is a connection;

[1] *Christabel*, ll. 408–13, 418–26.

[2] See p. 157, n. 2 above.

[3] An indication of how famous it was is found in a letter from Jane Carlyle to William Allingham, in the early 'fifties: 'For years and years we [the Carlyles and Mill] have "stood apart like rocks, &c. &c. &c." (I forget the quotation in spite of reading it anew in every young lady's thrilling novel).' (*Letters to William Allingham*, ed. H. Allingham, 1911, p. 141.)

it may be partly dependent on the connection with Collins's ode (does Coleridge recall its 'no sea between, nor cliff', its wild storm, wrenching the lands apart?) but it lies more in the sense of hopelessness and tediousness in severance—

> A dreary sea now flows between
>
> The unplumb'd, salt, estranging sea.

Coleridge's objective statement of the old breach between Sir Leoline and Sir Roland de Vaux is here sharpened, troubled, elaborated by his own consciousness of misunderstandings with friends; his poem at this point is not simply narrative, any more than Arnold's is simply a general reflection. The ghost of 'I' and 'you' vexes the detached 'we' and 'they'.

The implied 'you' is not only Marguerite. Several passages in Arnold's letters in years around 1850 speak of, or suggest, a growing apart from those nearest to him. 'As I become *formed*', he writes to his sister Jane in January 1851, 'there seems to grow a gulf between us, which tends to widen till we can hardly hold any intercourse across it.'[1] Something of the same feeling affected his relation with Clough in the years between 1849 and 1853; the admissions in the letter of 1853 confirm part of what can be read between the lines in earlier letters, and partly explain the curious blank in the latter half of 1850.[2] Clough's phrasing in his letter of June 1849, 'Our orbits therefore early in August might perhaps cross and we two serene undeviating stars salute each other once again for a moment amid the

[1] *Letters*, i, 14. Jane Arnold had married W. E. Forster on 15 August 1850; Arnold was engaged, and married in June 1851. Bonnerot, p. 68 n., links the passage with the poem. But he does not (p. 69) distinguish sufficiently between this image and that of the separate course of ships. The latter image Arnold frequently used (e.g. in 'Human Life', 'The Future'), and used, for separation and perhaps estrangement, in two other 'Switzerland' poems ('A Farewell', 'The Terrace at Berne'; compare Clough's 'Qua cursum ventus', written with W. G. Ward in mind in 1845). The movement of ships and the sense of temporal change make this an essentially different image. Islands can never meet again and ships can.

[2] The one surviving letter (*Letters to Clough*, p. 116) suggests that they had not known of each other's doings for some months. Clough had been in Venice (and writing *Dipsychus*), Arnold abroad on a journey of which nothing is known except that he was 'not . . . at Geneva', as Clough had expected, and that he followed Miss Wightman to Calais ('Calais Sands' is dated in the MS 'August 1850') and went on to the Rhine (Tinker and Lowry, *Commentary*, pp. 116–72.) This is the biggest and most important gap in our knowledge of Arnold's life in his writing years.

infinite spaces',[1] half mocks their essential solitude and independence. The phrase anticipates Arnold's in 'A Farewell'; when, after this life, the 'true affinities of soul' appear, 'then we shall know our friends' and 'may to each other be brought near And greet across infinity'. There is estrangement in the same poem, as in 'We were apart', and in 'Parting',[2]

> a sea rolls between us
> Our different past . . .
> Far, far from each other
> Our spirits have grown;
> And what heart knows another?
> Ah! who knows his own?

But these others are more simply poems of the *heart*, striving to know itself and another; the special attraction and frustration they express affect 'Yes: in the sea' only in so far as it is one of a series of poems. The exclusion of 'I' and 'you' (as of the mountains and lakes of Switzerland) points its impersonality; in this it is unique in the series. 'The unplumb'd, salt, estranging sea' belongs nearly as much, and as little, to Arnold and Clough, Arnold and his sister, even possibly to Arnold and Fanny-Lucy, as to Arnold and Marguerite; quotations from the letters and other poems near in date show that the inevitability of estrangement was playing upon his mind from more than one direction.

7

One kind of isolation that the poem surely never suggests is that of the romantic outlaw, wanderer, exile from and enemy of society. Its meaning seems removed from the Werther-ish sphere represented by the Letters of Ortis named in the original title. (It is doubtful if any reader would relate Foscolo's work to the poem[3] at all but for that title. Arnold never elsewhere

[1] *Letters to Clough*, p. 108. The orbits did not cross that year because Arnold chose to remain at Thun.

[2] 1852, but at least partly written by September 1849.

[3] In fact no one to my knowledge has even referred to it, apart from Mrs Iris E. Sells (*Matthew Arnold and France*, 1935, pp. 101–2) and a passing reference by Saintsbury suggesting that 'Ortis' may have been a common source for Thackeray and Arnold. See also Isabel Macdonald's 'novel' about Arnold, *The Buried Self*, 1949.

mentions author or work, nor have they ever been accounted an influence on his thought). It has its own limited relation to the poem, simply as being the story (told mainly in letters) of a man peculiarly isolated, by political circumstances and by temperament. The few reflections Ortis makes upon his isolation, however, are not and could never be Arnold's:

l'homme, ouvertement ou en secret, est toujours l'implacable ennemi de l'humanité.[1]

chaque homme naît ennemi de la société, parce que la société est ennemi de chaque individu.[2]

Je suis donc obligé de revenir à cette affreuse vérité, dont l'idée seule me faisait frissonner autrefois, et que depuis je me suis habitué à méditer et à entendre avec tranquillité, 'Tous les hommes sont ennemis'.[3]

No farther than this does Ortis generalize his own unhappy fortunes; and this is not Arnold's direction, either in this poem or elsewhere.[4] Nor could the attraction of Foscolo for Arnold be inferred from that of Sénancour, which some have found surprising; Foscolo has not, I think, the 'gravity and severity which distinguish [Sénancour] from all the other writers of the sentimental school.'[5] Arnold probably saw him as one of those 'fathers' who 'water'd with their tears This sea of time': at one with the Byrons and Shelleys whose 'groans' and 'lovely wails' availed nothing to the later generation.[6]

But a book that is not important or influential may none the less, read at a certain time and place, be an immediate stimulus, the spark to fire a long train of feeling and reflection. This the Letters of Ortis, even if mere chance had brought them in

[1] *Jacques Ortis*, 1881, p. 99. My quotation is from the translation by Alexandre Dumas, since this, first published in 1839 and again in 1847, seems likely to be the version that Arnold and Marguerite read. (Cf. Sells, *Matthew Arnold and France*, p. 101.) The original Italian work was first published in 1798, but much altered by the author in later editions. He died in 1827.

[2] ibid., p. 201.

[3] ibid., p. 230.

[4] The poem which does sometimes recall Ortis is *Empedocles*; it is the 'finger of reason' which points Ortis 'to the tomb'. The connection might be worth exploring.

[5] Arnold's note to 'Obermann once more' in *New Poems*, second edition, 1868.

[6] 'Stanzas from the Grande Chartreuse', 1855; perhaps written 1851, and the verse about Shelley probably as early as 1849.

Arnold's way, could have been; at a stage when all forms of literary introspectiveness interested him (and that is an interest very personal to the reader and often difficult in a given case to justify critically). Ortis's exile from Italy, his frustrated hope of happiness in love, his progress towards the final act of disowning the world in suicide, had many claims on Arnold's response. Perhaps enough to justify the affirmative which opens the poem ('Yes, Ortis was isolated—and we all are'). The mountains and woodland scenes, the passages of love might carry a peculiar significance; the more since it was not by mere chance that Arnold read Ortis. The title names the human agent. He would inevitably relate the volume's content to its owner, perhaps to his own action in returning it—across an estranging sea. That 'together they perused' the book in candlelit evenings in the Hôtel Bellevue at Thun is Mrs Sells's fancy picture; but one must still admit it very likely that she did really lend him the book (the detail would be a very odd one to invent) and that it meant something to one or both of them. Suppose she, as is common with lenders, thought more highly of it than he, this very realization would add to the poetic stimulus, to the relevance of the volume to the poem.[1]

8

But the sea between criticism and biography is uncomfortable sailing. The important thing now about Marguerite is not who or what she was, but that Arnold put her into his poems. Not only into those which name her in text or title, or are linked by the formal grouping or by common details of person and setting with those which name her; or even only into the whole of the 1852 volume.[2] She is, has been poetically made, a part of the experience which was among the material of *all* his poems: a part, and not a separable part. Switzerland, Obermann, the poet's conflicting desires for 'solitude' and 'the world without', the felt contrast between cities and mountains,

[1] This is perhaps to indulge fancy as much as Mrs Sells in another way. But at least one need not, in reaction against the Kingsmill–Trilling view of the relation, assume that because Marguerite read Ortis the two were necessarily in intellectual sympathy.

[2] H. W. Garrod, *Poetry and the Criticism of Life*, 1931, p. 39, was the first to emphasize its remarkable unity.

between the hot glare of the day and the coolness of snow and moonlight and clear water, are equally inseparable parts. It is artificial (even for those engaged in biographical detective-work) to argue about which are 'Marguerite' poems. This particular poem, if met only under its 1857 title of 'Isolation', might have been tacitly accepted as 'not a Marguerite poem', and at most would have aroused speculation and debate.

Even with all its titles, it is farther removed from its Marguerite source than its predecessor[1] in the series. 'We were apart; and day by day'. The relation between these two poems is puzzling, the more so since it was not made apparent from the beginning. In 1869 Arnold finally tied the poems together by entitling the second one 'To Marguerite, continued' and shifting the title of 'Isolation' to 'We were apart'. There is no parallel to this in Arnold's successive reshufflings of his shorter poems; some poems are split into two, but no other poem first appears alone and then in such close contact with another. Was 'Yes: in the sea' originally written as (or always felt to be) a continuation of 'We were apart'? (The stanza is the same, and is one rarely used by Arnold.) If so, its 'Yes' then comes to affirm a subsidiary statement in the last verse of the preceding poem; 'happier' men are so because they do not know their loneliness; they only 'dream'd two human hearts might blend', their faith releasing them from 'isolation without end Prolong'd'. But it is just as likely that that last over-packed verse was deliberately written to make a hinge between the two poems, so that the second might counteract the slightly embittered and arrogant personalities of the first.

If 'Yes: in the sea' is the second part of a two-part poem, it is 'continued' in a different direction. The first poem states an experience of separation, the inconstancy of one heart, and the proud withdrawal of the other in realization of its essential moonlike loneliness, and in remorse for ever having stooped to vain mortal love. The second moves beyond the lovers' case, seeing it only as an extreme and particular instance of the universal human situation. The link is, 'If even lovers cannot really communicate, then men are isolated indeed'. This Arnold has said elsewhere:

[1] In editions from 1857 on.

Alas, is even Love too weak
To unlock the heart and let it speak?
Are even lovers powerless to reveal
To one another what indeed they feel?
. . . I knew they [the mass of men] liv'd and mov'd
Trick'd in disguises, alien to the rest
Of men, and alien to themselves—and yet
The same heart beats in every human breast.

('That we have all of us one human heart'; 'parts of a single continent'),

Ah, well for us, if even we,
Even for a moment, can get free
Our heart, and have our lips unchain'd:
For that which seals them hath been deep ordain'd.

('A God, a God their severance rul'd').

The lines are part of 'The Buried Life',[1] where Arnold's theme is primarily man's isolation from his own deeply concealed true self (what he elsewhere calls the 'unlit gulf'[2]—the 'central stream of what we feel indeed');[3] from its 'subterranean depth' come 'airs, and floating echoes' bringing 'a melancholy into all our day'—like the music from the moonlit hollows across the straits, the longing in the island caverns. That poem has of all Arnold's the nearest affinity to 'Yes: in the sea'.[4] It is also a further reminder that for Arnold, as has been well said, 'l'amour fut une fenêtre ouverte sur le mystère de la vie humaine'.[5]

The subject of 'Yes: in the sea' is human life; and 'the same heart beats in every human breast'. The poem draws part of its strength from the common stock of experience; it represents Arnold's own multifold experience of what was read and thought as well as what was proved upon the pulses. What Arnold affirms in his opening 'Yes' is, finally, something like 'I know

[1] 1852; ll. 12–23, 26–9.
[2] 'The Youth of Nature', in *Poems,* 1852.
[3] Verse in *St. Paul and Protestantism.*
[4] On the difficulty of communication see also 'Poor Matthias' (1882), ll. 157–72, especially l. 169, 'Brother man's despairing sign', and ll. 171–2, on the 'Sundering powers'.
[5] Bonnerot, p. 78.

now the truth of what so many have written'. Into the poem drift 'airs and floating echoes': 'Isolation is the sum-total of wretchedness to man' . . . 'You and I are but a pair of infinite isolations' . . . 'Each in his hidden sphere of joy or woe' . . . 'A dreary sea now flows between' . . '*dissociabili*—translate as "estranging" '.

Text of 1852

TO MARGUERITE,

IN RETURNING A VOLUME OF THE LETTERS OF ORTIS.

Yes: in the sea of life enisl'd,
With echoing straits between us thrown,
Dotting the shoreless watery wild,
We mortal millions live *alone*.
  The islands feel the enclasping flow,
And then their endless bounds they know.

But when the moon their hollows lights
And they are swept by balms of spring,
And in their glens, on starry nights,
The nightingales divinely sing,
And lovely notes, from shore to shore,
Across the sounds and channels pour;

Oh then a longing like despair
Is to their farthest caverns sent;
—For surely once, they feel, we were
Parts of a single continent.
Now round us spreads the watery plain—
Oh might our marges meet again!

Who order'd, that their longing's fire
Should be, as soon as kindled, cool'd?
Who renders vain their deep desire?
  A God, a God their severance rul'd;
And bade betwixt their shores to be
The unplumb'd, salt, estranging sea.

XV

RUGBY 1850: ARNOLD, CLOUGH, WALROND, AND *IN MEMORIAM*

An eyewitness account of Matthew Arnold as a young master at Rugby from the recollections of one who was then a schoolboy; a visit from Clough with the newly published *In Memoriam* under his arm, and Arnold's comments thereon: this might be expected to figure in bibliographical and critical studies of one or more of the three poets. That it does not[1] may argue that it has been overlooked or forgotten; or possibly that it has been considered and discarded as manifestly fictitious. In either case it is worth while to look at the context and the inherent probability of the account, its corroboration from other sources and the qualifications of the witness.

Arnold and Clough appear, under their own names, in *The Three Friends: A Story of Rugby in the Forties* (Oxford University Press, 1900). The author was the Rev. Arthur Gray Butler, then almost seventy years old. He had been a boy at Rugby from 1844 to 1850, under A. C. Tait, who succeeded Dr Arnold; half a century after, when he was a Fellow and Tutor at Oriel, he published his one prose work,[2] this unpretentious and charming school-story. 'Hovering between fact and fiction', he says in the Preface, it is designed 'to give a picture of the Rugby I knew and loved, at a time subsequent to that described so inimitably in *Tom Brown*'. It is a pleasant if desultory tale, a prose idyll rather than a novel; its substance is the events of three school-

[1] There is an incidental reference, with a brief quotation, in Alan Harris, 'Matthew Arnold: the unknown years', *Nineteenth Century*, cxiii (April 1933), 502. Sydney Selfe, *Chapters in the History of Rugby School*, 1910, pp. 78–9, also quotes one sentence and identifies 'Fulton'. W. F. Connell (*The Educational Thought and Influence of Matthew Arnold*, 1950, p. 15, n. 1) is aware of Butler's book but considers it 'sadly astray' in details.

[2] His other publications are two historical dramas (*Charles I*, 1874, revised 1907, and *Harold*, 1892, revised 1906), a volume of poems, *The Choice of Achilles*, 1900, and reminiscences contributed to various biographies (see below, p. 193 n. 4).

years, especially as affecting two friends, Gordon and Fleming.[1] Clearest among the background figures of the staff are the headmaster, Tait, and a young tutor called Fulton. There is no reference to Arnold until the ninth chapter, 'By-play', last but one in the book. (Gordon and Fleming are now in their third and last year in the sixth form and discussing their futures.)

'How would you like to be a Master here?' Gordon asked.

'Not clever enough!' said Fleming. 'I could never do that First Class work at Oxford.'

'Oh, couldn't you? You could do anything if you tried; and you'd be up to all the fellows' tricks; and they'd do twice as much for you as for some of the men here.'

'Did you hear of Mat Arnold the other day,' asked Fleming, 'when they brought in news that it was a half-holiday? "Thank Heaven!" he said aloud, and the Form cheered him.'

'He's not the stuff to make a Master of,' said Gordon, grimly. 'Fancy him teaching little chaps τύπτω and the verbs in μι! How could he? There's not a bit of the Dominie about him. He's much too great a swell.'

'Oh, he'd do it fast enough if he had to do it,' said Fleming... Gordon shook his head.

'He'd never be a Fulton,' he said....

'No,' said Fleming, 'of course there's no one like Fulton as a Master. But Arnold, if he got something he liked, might make you feel—well, something that Fulton couldn't. And he's A1 at Fives.'[2]

The boys go to visit Fulton, 'to eat strawberries', and find him and Arnold talking on the lawn. Arnold is 'lolling back in an easy chair', watching the clouds, 'as he indolently stroked the head of a great stag-hound'; the two are engaged in a discussion on the subject of marks, which Fulton supports as a necessary incentive in the Lower School.

'Ah, my friend Fleming,' said Arnold, turning to the new arrivals,

[1] The third friend appears to be 'Twining', but he is more shadowy, and has left by ch. viii; the wild 'O'Brien' is perhaps a better candidate. I have not attempted to identify the boys; some of Butler's own experiences, and probably his characteristics, are represented in both Gordon and Fleming, but neither can be a self-portrait. The dedication 'to George Joachim Goschen, our leader at school' (he was head boy in 1850) may suggest another possible model. There are half a dozen references to Butler in A. D. Elliot's *Life of Lord Goschen*, 2 vols., 1911, but no reference to the book.

[2] This and the following passages quoted are from ch. ix, pp. 100–5.

'you are just in time to mediate between me and Mr Fulton' (the Mister was uttered somewhat unwillingly); 'he says that these little creatures, whom I have the honour of teaching, by a whim of our good Tait, must be treated like young pigs, poked at and prodded everlastingly, till they are taught to squeak intelligibly. What do you say? As one who knows something of these barbarians' (this was said playfully), 'do you believe in the prodding system?'

The debate is clearly intended to have a wider application: Arnold believes that 'to teach the world one should give wings to the few', Fulton that 'it is the many we have to do most for'. But Arnold mockingly turns the question aside:

'They gather round me after lesson to know what marks I give them—it's the only thing they care for—with an eagerness, a ferocity, which is quite appalling. . . . These strawberries are delicious. I observe, by the by, you take the smallest ones. I understand. Quite professional! Are they the sweetest?'

'No! But someone—was it you, Arnold?—had already taken the biggest. Pray don't say anything. I understand. Quite instinctive! You always loved distinction.'

Arnold picks out one strawberry for admiration—

'an imperial one, quite the grand style. Ripe too all over! I wonder how much of me would ever come to ripeness if I was a School-Master?'

But this mild fooling, slightly reminiscent of a well-known scene in *The Importance of Being Earnest*, is dissipated by the unexpected appearance of a visitor,

strongly-built, with a grave, thoughtful look, and expressive eyes that lighted up a somewhat sombre countenance.

'Clough!' shouted the Tutor.

The ensuing passage deserves quoting in its entirety; and with it and its context before us it may be possible to see what proportion of truth of fact or of impression it can contain.

'In the name of the Prophet, Clough!' said Arnold, 'fresh from Oxford damps and metaphysics to breathe real youth and freshness at Rugby! Well! They have not killed me yet, dear, as you said they would: not even their whole schooldays and First lessons! Dear creatures! They are very kind to me, on the whole, though they made me an April fool one day. But a plague on pedagogy, when you are here! What is that under your arm?'

'A new book of poems, Mat,' said Clough, simply, 'just out. It marks an era.'

'Yours,' said Arnold inquiringly, 'yours, beloved?'

'No! something far higher! Something for the highest heaven! It is one of the Immortals.' And he handed him, as he sat down, a little brown volume, from which Arnold read eagerly, '*In Memoriam, A.H.H.* No author! Who is A.H.H.?'

'They say it is Arthur Hallam,' replied the other, 'and the author shines out in every line. It must be Tennyson. Read No. 56!'

And then turning to the Tutor and the two boys, after a few words about Oxford, he fell easily into Rugby talk. He was not a great talker himself, but he loved to hear others talk, and was a sympathetic listener. The boys, especially, interested him; and, as their awe of the great man faded, they chattered away freely, delighted to find that he knew the country even better than themselves. . . .

Meanwhile Arnold was heard murmuring to himself, 'Beautiful! Luminous! A new metre! A masterpiece! It must be Alfred.' Then at last turning to Clough, and handing him the book, he said, with faltering voice, all the light playfulness, with which he cloaked real earnestness, departed, 'Read! My voice is wasted in much teaching.' And pointing with his finger, 'There!' And Clough read, in a soft low voice, like far-off music:

[The first and last two verses of No. lvi, 'Peace, come away', are then quoted.]

'Another,' said Arnold, lying back, and playing with the great staghound's ears, 'another!' And again Clough read, not as picking out favourites, but letting eyes and fingers choose for him, one after another of those immortal poems, which took the heart of England by storm, and have been the delight and strength of the English-speaking race ever since.

And as often as he stopped, Arnold would say, almost in a whisper, 'Another!' till at last, closing the book, Clough said, 'It must be Tennyson. Who else could it be? And his greatest work!—Did you know Hallam, Mat?'

Then Arnold murmured something about 'Immortal!' and recovering himself with a sigh, replied, 'Hallam? Oh, yes, I saw him once. He was unlike other men. But it needed friendship to understand it. Ah, Clough, when we have that villa in the Caucasus we used to talk of—'

'The Caucasus,' said the young Tutor, starting up. 'Bless me! Why, here we are forgetting Third lesson. Come along!' Arnold groaned, and they all laughed.

The question of marks is revived by the entrance of Fulton's sister bringing him his mark-list. Arnold teases her; he would have guessed who would be top and who would be bottom ('about a dozen of them'); so why not have saved the 'bother' of adding up marks? And with a final flourish, he is gone:

'Amid the general decay of virtue at the present moment, let us not forget punctuality, and Third lesson! Good afternoon!' The boys went off, avowing Clough and Arnold were both splendid fellows and *In Memoriam* was the finest poem in the world . . . and the School bookseller had much to do to supply the demand for it.

The only further reference to Arnold is in the final chapter:

Fulton . . . wrote to Arnold, who had left Rugby suddenly, vowing that his villa in the Caucasus was not to be purchased there.

2

The scene quoted purports to have taken place at Rugby in June 1850; the month is specified, strawberries are being eaten, the Rugby term ended in the second half of June, and *In Memoriam* was published on June 1. Can the actors—Arnold, Clough, 'Fulton', and (presumably) A. G. Butler himself—have been together at that time and place? I shall show that they can, if not in those precise roles. 'Fulton' is identified by Selfe (on the high authority of 'the Dean of Wells'[1]) with Theodore Walrond; he was a master at Rugby from 1848 to 1851,[2] and had a boarding-house at 12 and 14 Hillmorton Road.[3] He and Arnold were old friends, but, so far as we know, never actually fellow masters; Arnold's Rugby teaching was probably confined to a few months between December 1844 and March 1845, and by 1850 he was in the third and last year

[1] T. W. Jex-Blake, 1832–1915; Butler's contemporary at Rugby (1844–51), at University College, Oxford, and again as master at Rugby (1858–68). He was headmaster (1874–85). He wrote Butler's obituary notice in the school magazine, *The Meteor*, 3 February 1909.

[2] The *Rugby School Register* gives the date as 1853, but other evidence makes it clear that Walrond was tutor at Balliol (1851–6). The *Register's* date might be accounted for by a temporary return for a brief period in 1853.

[3] *Rugby School Register*, 1902, ii, p. xv; cf. *Three Friends*, p. 56.

of his employment as Lord Lansdowne's secretary.[1] That he had often visited Rugby since his father's death we know from his letters to Clough and from other sources;[2] he was on excellent terms with Tait, his old Balliol tutor, and wrote to him in 1842 heartily approving his appointment.[3] He was certainly at Rugby in November 1849, concerned in the election of Tait's successor, Goulburn, and discussing it with the masters. Most of them were old friends, and some were his own Rugby and Oxford contemporaries, recently appointed; besides Theodore Walrond there were 'Plug' Arnold, G. G. Bradley, and J. C. Shairp. The letters of both Clough and Arnold show that Rugby under Tait was not only their old school but a sort of colony of Oxford (and especially Balliol) where contemporaries would meet freely and frequently to discuss the affairs of school, university, and world. When a master was ill, some old Rugbeian who was a recent graduate would be called in to take over the absentee's teaching for a week or two, and it is even possible that Arnold was doing this in June 1850. There is certainly nothing either in Arnold's known habits or in the few records of his movements for the summer of 1850 to prevent us from assuming that he was at Rugby for a short visit in June.[4]

Clough, too, was a frequent visitor to Rugby, and was cer-

[1] The obituary notice in *The Times* (17 April 1888) refers only to a period of teaching after leaving Lord Lansdowne and before the Inspectorship, but this notice contains other demonstrable inaccuracies.

[2] The records of the Debating Society from 1845 show him as 'a frequent visitor' (W. H. D. Rouse, *A History of Rugby School*, 1898, pp. 289–90. It is possible that these records survive, but I have not been able to consult them). It was not until about 1848 that Arnold's last brother left the school.

[3] W. Benham and R. Davidson, *Life of Archbishop Tait*, 1891, p. 115. Clough had written to the trustees in support of Tait's candidature (Selfe, pp. 68–9).

[4] The demands of his secretaryship would probably not allow a long one. Parliament was in session from 9 April to 16 August, save for the Whitsun recess, which fell in May. There is evidence (in *The Times* reports) of Lord Lansdowne's presence in London on 7, 22, 26, and 28 June, and his absence at Bowood is not noted until 6–8 July. Of direct evidence of Arnold's doings this summer there is very little, with a gap in the published correspondence from May to October. In May his mother and sister Jane were visiting him in London, and on 15 August he was at Rydal, for Jane's (postponed) marriage with W. E. Forster (Mrs Humphry Ward, *A Writer's Recollections*, 1918, pp. 35, 46; *The Times*, 19 August 1850) and left almost at once. The manuscript of 'Calais Sands' is dated 'August 1850,' and Arnold's preoccupations in the late summer may be inferred from this poem and the related 'Faded Leaves'. See also Clough's letter to Tom Arnold, quoted in *Commentary*, p. 170.

tainly there in October 1850,[1] on his return from Venice (when Arnold just missed him), and perhaps also in June; the tone of a letter to Shairp from London on 19 June[2] conceivably suggests a recent meeting. (He did not leave England until after 23 July, when the session at University Hall was over.) We are therefore free to suppose Arnold and Clough at Rugby in mid-June, even if it is untrue that Arnold was teaching and that Clough was 'fresh from Oxford damps and metaphysics'. And the natural objective for them both would be the house of their old friend Theodore Walrond in Hillmorton Road.[3]

That Walrond was an intimate friend of both poets at this time, there is plenty of scattered evidence in the letters and elsewhere.[4] The friendship evidently dated from schooldays. Theodore Walrond entered the School House at Rugby in 1834, three years before Clough left for Balliol; he and Arnold were sixth-formers together, and he was captain of the school at the time of Dr Arnold's death. He was tutored by Clough for the Balliol scholarship in the long vacation of 1841, and went to Balliol as a scholar in 1842, taking a first class in 1846.[5] He was thus an exact contemporary at school and university of Matthew's next brother, Thomas, who recalled their friendship half a century later in these words:[6]

[1] *Letters to Clough*, p. 116.

[2] *Poems and Prose Remains*, 1869, i, 168. The letter of January 1850 (p. 113) also shows his close contact with Rugby masters.

[3] Probably the house where Arnold lodged when teaching at Rugby in 1844–5. It was then the Rev. Algernon Grenfell's 'house', and Arnold took Grenfell's place during his last illness. Grenfell died on 6 March 1845; Richard Congreve was appointed in April and succeeded to the same house. (*Rugby School Register*, 1901, i, x, xix, xxii; and cf. *Letters to Clough*, p. 56.)

[4] See below. No biographical notice of Walrond existed, apart from a brief obituary in *The Times* of 20 June 1887 and a longer one in the *Annual Register*, until John Curgenven's article appeared: 'Theodore Walrond: friend of Arnold and Clough', *Durham University Journal*, xliv (1952). This was not available to me when the present essay went to press; the valuable new information contained in it includes the interesting fact that when Walrond stood, unsuccessfully, for the headmastership of Rugby in 1869, A. G. Butler was one of his supporters. (The later-published *Correspondence of Arthur Hugh Clough*, ed. F. Mulhauser, 1957, contains many new references to Walrond, and I have added a few of them, 1964).

[5] *Rugby School Register*, 1901, i. 274, and *The Times*, 20 June 1887.

[6] 'Arthur Hugh Clough: a Sketch', *Nineteenth Century*, xlii (1898), 106–7. Cf. W. Y. Sellar's letter to W. Knight, in *Some Nineteenth Century Scotsmen*, 1903, p. 264: 'When I was an undergraduate, A. H. Clough, the two Arnolds, Walrond, and Shairp, formed a kind of quinque-lateral'.

After I came up to the University in October [1842], Clough, Theodore Walrond, my brother and I formed a little interior company, and saw a great deal of one another. We used often to go skiffing up the Cherwell, or else in the network of river channels that meander through the broad meadows facing Iffley and Sandford. After a time it was arranged that we four should always breakfast in Clough's rooms on Sunday morning. These were times of great enjoyment.

At a much briefer distance of time, Matthew Arnold, writing to his brother in Tasmania in 1857, also recalled it:

You alone of my brothers are associated with that life at Oxford, the *freest* and most delightful part, perhaps, of my life, when with you and Clough and Walrond I shook off all the bonds and formalities of the place, and enjoyed the spring of life, and that unforgotten Oxfordshire and Berkshire country. . . . 'The Scholar Gipsy' . . . was meant to fix the remembrance of those delightful wanderings of ours in the Cumner hills before they are quite effaced—and as such, Clough and Walrond accepted it.[1]

In 1843 Walrond and Clough were on holiday abroad together, and in 1844 all three were together in Patterdale, on a reading-party (Walrond reading, and Arnold fishing).[3] At this point the Butler family enters the picture: George Butler, an elder brother, had a reading-party at Grasmere,[4] and joined Walrond's party on Helvellyn:

when we got into a mist, and through the mist, near the top, loomed out Walrond and Clough and Matthew Arnold. . . .[5]

In March 1845 Arnold at Rugby wrote to Clough at Oxford, with 'my love to Walrond';[6] in the late summer Clough visited

[1] Ward, p. 54. Others recalled the 'Decade', the select debating society of which the three were members, e.g. Lord Coleridge, in W. Knight, *Principal Shairp and his Friends*, 1888, pp. 411–12.

[2] *Poems and Prose Remains*, i, 90; *Correspondence*, p. 125.

[3] ibid., i, 93; *Correspondence*, pp. 129–34.

[4] This is described by Josephine E. Butler, *Recollections of George Butler* (n.d.), p. 37, and (much more fully) in an article by George Butler in *Longman's Magazine* (October 1888, xii, 621–35).

[5] J. E. Butler, p. 48; recollections of Spencer Perceval Butler, a younger brother who was a member of the reading-party, and at Rugby 1841–7. George Butler was at Harrow, and at Exeter College; he would know Arnold and Clough as fellow members of the 'Decade'.

[6] *Letters to Clough*, p. 55.

Walrond at his home at Calder Park near Glasgow, after a Highland expedition, in which Thomas and Edward Arnold had also shared;[1] and in 1847 Walrond and Thomas Arnold visited Clough on that famous reading-party at Drumnadrochet[2] on which some incidents in *The Bothie* were founded, Walrond perhaps figuring in the poem as 'Arthur, the glory of headers'.[3] In November 1847 Walrond, Clough, and Matthew Arnold dined at Balliol and attended a meeting of the 'Decade'.[4] In July 1848 Arnold (without permission) confided to Walrond Clough's intention 'to resign his fellowship';[5] in August Walrond became a master at Rugby,[6] and Clough visited him there in November, when Arnold wrote to Clough crowing over them both for their misjudgment of Edward Arnold's prospects in the Schools.[7] Clough's letters of 1849 imply a continued correspondence with Walrond, and Walrond and Shairp were the only two besides Arnold to whom he showed the manuscript of *Amours de Voyage*.[8]

In November 1849 Arnold was at Rugby, walking to Thurleston and Kenilworth with Walrond ('don't you envy me', he writes to Clough),[9] and again in October 1850, just missing Clough on the latter's visit after his return from Venice, about which Clough had evidently been uncommunicative ('Walrond seems to have learnt nothing of your late goings on').[10] The 'little interior company' of undergraduate days, already reduced by Thomas Arnold's emigration in 1847, was by now beginning to disperse. But Walrond, like Clough, was at Arnold's wedding in June 1851;[11] he stood godfather to his second

[1] Knight, op. cit., pp. 87–8; and cf. *Poems and Prose Remains*, i, 97 ff., and Thomas Arnold's article cited above; also *Correspondence*, pp. 150–3.

[2] Knight, pp. 103 ff., with reminiscences written by Thomas Arnold, and Edward and George Scott, as well as Shairp's (previously printed in *Poems and Prose Remains*, i, 28–30).

[3] Knight, p. 110 (letter from Edward Scott).

[4] ibid., p. 115.

[5] *Letters to Clough*, p. 87.

[6] *Rugby School Register*, i, xvi; *Correspondence*, p. 199 shows that he had also taught there temporarily in February.

[7] *Letters to Clough*, pp. 94–5; the editor misinterprets this letter.

[8] *Poems and Prose Remains*, i, 116, 165.

[9] *Letters to Clough*, p. 113; and cf. *Letters*, i, 11.

[10] *Letters to Clough*, p. 116.

[11] Harris, p. 509.

son in 1853;[1] and when Arnold wrote to Clough in New England about his 1852 poems, he still implied the three-fold cord.[2]

> I doubt whether I shall ever have heat and radiance enough to pierce the clouds that are massed around me. Not in my little social sphere, indeed, with you and Walrond; there I could crackle to my grave—but vis à vis of the world.

(That 'crackling' in a 'little social sphere', with both 'heat and radiance', is just what Arthur Butler shows in *The Three Friends.*) In the autumn of 1854 Arnold and Walrond once more explored the Cumnor country together.[3] The 'great town's harsh heart-wearying roar' asserted its claims; but the friendship ended only with their lives. When Walrond died in 1887, Arnold 'felt as if part of his life had been taken from him'.[4]

> Sellar was once saying to Matthew Arnold how *good* Theodore Walrond was, and Arnold replied, 'Ah, we were all good at Rugby!' 'Yes,' said [Sellar], 'but he has remained good!'[5]

The 'goodness' of Walrond was valued by all who knew him. Max Müller used to call him his 'English conscience', and Lord Bowen acclaimed him as 'the modern Hercules, whose choice was always the choice of virtue'.[6] It is a virtue that shines through the portrait of 'Fulton'; and the intimacy pictured in Butler's story, with its quick modulation from banter to earnestness, corresponds with, even if it does not literally exemplify, an amply attested reality. Butler has written of 'three friends' in more than his ostensible sense.

That Butler himself had come to know Walrond well when at Rugby is suggested by the chance records[7] of a boating-party

[1] *Letters*, i, 48.

[2] *Letters to Clough*, p. 126; and cf. p. 129.

[3] *Letters*, i, 38; by this time Walrond was back at Oxford, where he held a Balliol Fellowship (1850–7), acting as tutor (1851–6), when he was appointed Civil Service Examiner. Later letters show that he telegraphed to Arnold reports of the progress of the election to the Professorship of Poetry in 1857 (Ward, p. 55), and spent a long holiday abroad with him in 1858. Walrond married Charlotte Grenfell in 1859 and became Secretary to the Civil Service Commissioners in 1863. He wrote Dr Arnold's life for the *DNB* in 1885 and began to prepare a full biography of Arthur Stanley.

[4] *Recollections of G. D. Boyle*, 1895, p. 182.

[5] E. M. Sellar, *Recollections and Impressions*, 1907, pp. 327–8.

[6] H. S. Cunningham, *Lord Bowen*, 1893, p. 140 (at a speech at Balliol in 1877).

[7] E. Graham, *The Harrow Life of Henry Montagu Butler*, 1920, p. 60; Josephine E. Butler, *Recollections of George Butler* (n.d.), p. 87.

at Oxford in 1851, with his younger brother, Goschen, and Walrond, and a picnic party to 'Witchwood' with his older brother, Goschen, and again Walrond. Butler's own history was repeating the pattern laid down by his young elders: scholarship, first class, Oriel fellowship, return to Rugby as assistant master.[1] There was even a reading-party at Grasmere in 1853[2] to echo that of 1844; while Butler and Goschen founded an 'Essay Society'[3] to take the place of the expiring 'Decade', to which his elder brother had been proud to be elected in 1841.[4] Arthur Butler's brothers indeed complete the chain. By 1844 he would know their contemporaries by repute. When he himself entered the School House at Rugby in August at the age of twelve, he would join the 'huge form'[5] to which Matthew Arnold, waiting for something to turn up after his inglorious second class, came to 'teach small boys τύπτω' at £100 a term. There, perhaps, he heard him 'thank heaven' when a half-holiday was announced: and may have guessed, as boys will, how Arnold was likely to spend it.[6]

But the ninth chapter of *The Three Friends* claims to be the fruit of maturer observation. In June 1850 Arthur Butler was a sixth-form boy, in his last term, perhaps his last week, at school; and what he then saw would be the more clearly photographed on his always retentive mind[7] by the sentiment of valediction. He was going up to University College, Oxford;[8]

[1] Butler taught at Rugby (1858–62), along with his old schoolfellows T. W. Jex-Blake, Edward Scott, and Philip Bowden-Smith.

[2] *Recollections of John Henry Bridges*, 1908, p. 62 (from Butler's contributions), and G. C. Brodrick, *Memories and Impressions*, 1900, p. 88.

[3] Brodrick, p. 100; *Charles Henry Pearson*, 1900, p. 72; *Life of Lord Goschen*, i, 24.

[4] *Recollections of George Butler*, p. 31.

[5] *Letters to Clough*, p. 56, letter of March 1845. If Butler had three years in the Sixth, like 'Gordon' and 'Fleming', this seems very likely. C. H. Pearson, at Rugby (1843–6), started in the Lower Fifth at the age of twelve, 'a class of more than sixty', and recalls the masters as being 'over-taxed by the great size of their divisions, numbering from 40 to 70' (*Memorials*, 1900, p. 13).

[6] In sending a message by Clough to Richard Congreve, the Rugby-Oxonian who was to succeed him, Arnold commends the 'stabling' as well as the apricot marmalade.

[7] See below, p. 194, n. 5.

[8] He had matriculated in March, but the *Life of Tait* shows that he was still at school when the headmaster departed in May. He was obviously mistaken when he said in his contribution to the *Life of Stanley* (i, 358) that he entered University College in 1849.

Clough, Arnold, and Walrond represented his own future.

The hypothesis that Butler himself knew Arnold and perhaps Clough (and the former not merely as one of a 'huge form' of over sixty) has some independent evidence; in 1909 those who recollected Arthur Butler were able to say that at Rugby he 'laid the foundations of lifelong friendship with members of the Rugby circle, including, of older men, Dean Stanley and Matthew Arnold',[1] and that 'it was a revelation to have a tutor who had known in the flesh our literary heroes, Clough and Matthew Arnold, and loved to talk of them'.[2] It is true that the evidence for any 'life-long friendship' with Arnold is wanting,[3] as not with Stanley.[4] But my conviction that the ninth chapter is fact rather than fiction has other sources.

3

It proclaims its essential authenticity as a portrait of Arnold in the very turn of his speech; there is a *panache* at once recognizable to those familiar with the letters to Clough and personal anecdotes of the young Arnold. This is something that could not be faked, could not be concocted out of remote childish memories and a maturer knowledge of Arnold's published writings or even a maturer acquaintance with the man. The Arnold of the 'unknown years' is now partly known to us, but was hardly known to mere readers of Arnold in 1900. (About that time the recently published letters were criticized by their nominal editor for their 'obscuration' of Arnold's 'over-flowing gaiety'.)[5] But the Arnold his Oxford friends knew, with affectation and banter masking earnestness and melancholy ('I

[1] *The Times*, 18 January 1909, p. 13; and *The Haileyburian*, 19 February 1909, p. 169.

[2] *The Haileyburian*, p. 178 (letter from an Oriel pupil).

[3] Henry Montagu Butler knew Arnold well in the sixties, when he was living at Harrow and had two boys in the school, and the note of a visit to 'old Mrs. Butler' (the mother) in 1871 (*Letters*, ii, 58) suggests a family friendship.

[4] See below, p. 194, n. 5.

[5] G. W. E. Russell, *Matthew Arnold*, 1904, p. viii; the letters had been 'severely edited' before they came into his hands, and were further censored in proof. And see Saintsbury's complaint of the complete obscurity of Arnold's early years (*Matthew Arnold*, 1909).

laugh too much and they make one's laughter mean too much');[1] the exuberance and nonchalance, the gay speculative intellect, the 'Olympian manners', the flourishes of affection,[2] are all caught in Arthur Butler's picture of that June afternoon in Hillmorton Road. Suspended between the claims of a villa in the Caucasus and of Third Lesson, eating strawberries in 'the grand style',[3] and discoursing semi-allegorically on end-of-term marks ('the best . . . is what we want'), 'much too great a swell to be a Dominie'—this is recognizably the Matthew Arnold of the early poems, the few 1845 letters ('For me, I am a reed, a very whoreson Bullrush; yet such as I am, I give satisfaction'),[4] the Arnold observed in 1850 by Charlotte Brontë ('seeming foppery', but with a 'real modesty' and 'intellectual aspirations' under 'assumed conceit' and 'superficial affectation'),[5] and by Crabb Robinson:

> a very gentlemanly young man with a light tinge of the fop which does no harm when blended with talents, good nature, and high spirits;[6]

even the Arnold who defeated George Bradley's attempt to impress visiting parents by refusing food in these startling terms:

> 'No thank you, my darling, I've just bitten off the tails of those three bull-pups of yours.'[7]

Butler's presentation of Clough is comparatively the merest outline, and would not by itself carry any evidence of authenticity; it is true to what is well known of Clough's appearance

[1] *Life and Correspondence of Lord Coleridge*, i, 145 (letter of 1844); and cf. Thomas Arnold—'His keen bantering talk made him something of a social lion among Oxford men' (*Passages in a Wandering Life*, 1900, p. 56), and Max Müller, *Auld Lang Syne*, 1898, pp. 111–12, and *My Autobiography*, 1901, pp. 272–3.

[2] The 'dear' and 'beloved' reported here match the frequent address of 'my love' to Clough, which the American editor imperceptively called a 'somewhat curious expression' (*Letters to Clough*, p. 59). But Margaret Woods, George Bradley's daughter, had already testified that 'it was thus he used to address his friends' (*Essays and Studies*, xv (1929), 8).

[3] Arnold was already using the phrase privately in 1850; *Letters to Clough*, p. 115.

[4] *Letters to Clough*, p. 56.

[5] Letter to James Taylor, 15 January 1851 (*The Brontës*, 1932, iii, 199).

[6] *Correspondence with the Wordsworth Circle*, ed. Edith Morley, 1927, ii, 743.

[7] Margaret Woods; cf. n. 2 above. From her reference to G. G. Bradley's age, the date was probably 1848, and the incident is further evidence of the frequency of Arnold's casual visits to the school.

and quiet manner, but could easily have been gathered from hearsay or a reading of the memoir of 1869. But there is one minor figure in the scene who is worth pausing over for a moment: the 'great staghound' whose head Arnold is 'indolently' stroking. This is surely Gruim, the 'Scotch staghound of great power and beauty',[1] the constant companion of another master and Balliol friend of Arnold, Clough, and Walrond—J. C. Shairp. The picturesqueness of the school scene and its scope for harmless flamboyance is again suggested by what we read of Shairp in his friends' and pupils' reminiscences:

All old Rugbians of the time will remember the impression he at once created, as he stalked about, sometimes with a plaid around him, and a long crook in his hand, and a noble deerhound at his side. . . .[2]

The particular old Rugbeian who wrote those words was Arthur Butler. And one of Bradley's reminiscences adds another important link, for it shows Shairp walking right through a cricket game absorbed in a newly published book—*In Memoriam.*[3] Another biography containing reminiscences by Arthur Butler shows how firmly other parts of *The Three Friends* are compounded out of fact. The recollections of Tait as headmaster and incidents of his reign, in his first volume of *The Life of Archbishop Tait*, to which Butler contributed, nowhere contradict and in many respects tally closely with the material of *The Three Friends.*[4] A detailed comparison confirms the impression that a large part of the novel is intended as history, though individual characteristics may be blended and periods telescoped.[5] Something of Shairp's well-known friendliness

[1] Knight, p. 131; contributed by Archbishop Tait.

[2] Knight, p. 134; Gruim's name is on p. 136, and his existence is mentioned also by Hodgson (Knight, p. 154).

[3] Knight, pp. 139–40; contributed by Bradley.

[4] ch. vi, and cf. Butler, Bradley, and others in *Life of Tait*. The trouble with the Sixth, Tait's illness, the scenes at his departure, and minute details of the 'mutiny' of 1848 appear in both biography and story.

[5] 'The story . . . opens with an incident of the game for which we can vouch, though the date, we think, is an anachronism. . . . He certainly leaves an impression of more intimacy between masters and boys than we ever remember as existing' (Review in *Athenaeum*, 12 January 1901, p. 50). 'Fulton' was 'fresh from Oxford' in 1847 (ch. iv), a year before Walrond's appointment.

with the boys[1] may be glanced at, along with the deerhound, in 'Fulton'; he was at the time almost equally intimate with Arnold and Clough. Something also, perhaps, of Butler himself when he returned as a master in 1858,[2] for example, in Fulton's balancing of the claims of athletic and academic distinction:

> And then the Tutor smiled, and thought of his own achievements in old days, in both fields of prowess; and as a cup won at Henley met his eye, he said to himself, 'After all, which did give me the greatest pleasure, that or the Balliol? It was a near thing between them.'[3]

For Butler himself was remembered at Rugby for athletic prowess in cricket, fives, and football,[4] and for giving his name to 'Butler's Leap', as well as for his scholarship at University College, his Ireland and double First.

Arthur Butler's credit as a witness is high. He knew Rugby well, as boy and later as master; as undergraduate at University College (for one year under Arthur Stanley, who became a lifelong friend), as Headmaster of Haileybury and as Fellow and Tutor of Oriel, he had the ideal atmosphere for preserving and rehearsing his recollections; the reminiscences contributed to the biographies of Tait, Shairp, and others[5] show the piety and felicity, and the picturesque choice of detail, with which he could present them; and where they can be checked, the excellence of his memory. Both at Haileybury and Oxford he was remembered as one who had known great men in their early days, and delighted to talk of them. A Rugbeian reviewer of *The Three Friends* approved the portraits of Arnold and Clough as

[1] Knight, ch. viii; see especially reminiscences contributed by Davey and Hodgson. Shairp was (in 1846) another of Tait's Balliol appointments, and one applauded by Arnold (Knight, p. 137).

[2] *The Meteor*, 3 February, pp. 6–7; obituary notice by T. W. Jex-Blake, and letter from 'A.S.'

[3] *The Three Friends*, p. 51.

[4] *The Meteor*, 3 February, pp. 6–7.

[5] R. E. Prothero and G. G. Bradley, *Life and Correspondence of Arthur Penrhyn Stanley*, 2 vols., 1893, i, 358–9, 428, ii, 12; *Charles Henry Pearson, Memorials*, ed. W. Stebbing, 1900, pp. 144–50; *Recollections of J. H. Bridges*, 1908, pp. 60–7; *Frederick Temple: a Memoir*, ed. E. G. Sandford, 2 vols., 1906, pp. 172–5, 214–19. The liveliest records of Stanley as an Oxford tutor in 1850–1 came from Butler; and the words 'Even after more than fifty years many recollections come back to me with force and vividness' (*J. H. Bridges*, p. 60) typify the impression made by all his contributions.

drawn from the life. Much of the tale, including all that concerns Tait as headmaster and the 'mutiny' of 1848, can easily be shown to be authentic. It would, on the face of it, be unnatural that he should invent a scene for Arnold and Clough to enact under their own names. The main substance of that scene conflicts with no other biographical records (the only possibly fictitious element is Arnold's role as a master in 1850, and even that cannot be proved so) and is confirmed by what is known of Arnold's frequent visits to Rugby and his intimacy with its masters. Moreover, the detail of that intimacy, the imponderables of tone and turns of phrase, is that of contemporary letters and recorded conversations, mostly still unpublished in 1900. It is not then rash to plead for the acceptance of the ninth chapter as a contribution to the biography of Arnold.

But that may not be its only value.

4

Whereas the value of the personal portraits in Butler's story is corroborative and picturesque, making defined and dramatic a general impression of the young Arnold and his friends which we can draw from other sources, his delighted recognition of *In Memoriam*, if accepted, contributes something new to our view of Arnold as poet and critic. From what has preceded it in the chapter it derives a persuasiveness which might be lacking if it stood alone. Lacking, not so much because no other evidence exists that Arnold and Clough liked *In Memoriam*; but because some details may at first sight seem to some readers unconvincing. There is at least one factual inaccuracy; Arnold was a boy of ten when Hallam died, so that even if he had met him, he would not speak of him like this: 'Hallam? Oh, yes, I saw him once. He was unlike other men. But it needed friendship to understand it.' (The personal acquaintance of Tennyson and Arnold at this date—which is, I think, implied in the 'Alfred'—is, though not well attested, not impossible;[1] and the

[1] Hallam Tennyson says that his father 'had known [Arnold] at Coniston, as a young man just entering on life' (*Memoir*, ii, 225). Tennyson was at Tent Lodge, Coniston, in the late summer of 1850, but no meeting is recorded. They certainly met at Coniston in 1857, and were then already friends (Charles Tennyson, *Alfred Tennyson*, 1949, p. 306); in 1855 Tennyson writes 'I have already an affection

quick assurance of his authorship of the anonymous poem is a response shared by many early readers.)[1] It may be that Butler is 'hovering', to use his own word, nearer to 'fiction', eking out a memory with invented detail; the 'tone' of earnest conversation is generally less easy to recall than banter. And there is another possibility, a reason why Butler might 'hover' towards fiction just here. He is concerned to emphasize a pattern in recurrence. The friendships of Tennyson and Hallam, of Arnold and Clough, of Gordon and Fleming, are implicitly compared; *In Memoriam*, 'Thyrsis', and in its tiny way *The Three Friends*, dissolve into a single evocation of youthful friendship.[2] With this intention in mind he might wish to enlarge his memories. But that surely is all that can be said against the passage. Details may be invented; but to turn suddenly from reporting to invention in the main *fact* of the chapter—that Clough and Arnold read *In Memoriam* together at Rugby in the month of its publication, and were delighted—would seem strange.[3] It is best to accept it as true in essence if not in all details; and then to consider how it both modifies and accords with our present view of Arnold's response to Tennyson.[4]

for him' and speaks of 'The Merman' as 'an old favourite of mine' (*Memoir*, i, 410). It could be assumed that they met in London before 1850 (Arnold was 'a young man just entering on life' any time from 1844) and that Hallam Tennyson had confused this with the 1857 meeting.

[1] T. R. Lounsbury, *The Life and Times of Tennyson (from 1809 to 1850)*, 1915, pp. 617–19.

[2] 'Thyrsis' is referred to on p. 108 as 'another noble garland of friendship'. There is also a reference to the 'glorification of school friendships' in *Coningsby*, and a quotation.

[3] And, as it happens, contrary to a stated principle of Butler's in his historical plays: 'we may not construct scenes and characters out of our own imagination, and then, as has been said "do some historical events or personages the compliment of borrowing their names". Even where invention is permitted, it must be within narrow bounds, and jealously guarded from transgression.' *Charles I*, 1874, pp. xvii–xviii.

[4] In Clough's case there is less to discuss; what little is recorded of his views is already favourable to Tennyson, with the single exception of his 'Decade' speech, and that appears to have been pro-Wordsworth rather than anti-Tennyson. Arnold's letters to him clearly suggest that Clough thinks better of Tennyson than he does, and that at that date he stands nearer to him as a poet, at least in intention. Clough did not resist imitation (*Letters to Clough*, p. 61, and cf. 'Natura Naturans') and is in one important respect more Tennyson's kind of poet than Arnold's; the line through *The Princess*, *The Bothie*, and *Maud* as narratives of contemporary life is clear, and was recognized by some contemporary critics. Clough's friendship with

As I said, it contributes something new—it could not have been confidently guessed; yet it can be recognized as not merely possible, but even as helping to explain the remarks on Tennyson that Arnold made elsewhere. At least it is not a specific contradiction; for (unless it be obliquely referred to in 'The Scholar Gipsy', as many contemporaries believed but Arnold denied)[1] *In Memoriam*, Tennyson's greatest poem, appearing at the outset of Arnold's own career as a poet, receives no mention from him in letters or published work.[2] And the reader of Arnold's generally impatient remarks in the letters to Clough:

1847: 'dawdling with [the] painted shell [of the Universe]'
1855 (the *Maud* volume): 'a lamentable production . . . thoroughly and intensely provincial'
1861: 'I care for his productions less and less'[3]

and of the more reasoned censures in the last Homer lecture and the later letters, is left asking 'But what about *In Memoriam*?' There is no answer: the poem is never named, nor is Tennyson even referred to in letters between 1848 and 1853. At least then a space is left into which the first impressions recorded by Butler ('beautiful, luminous') may be slipped. And there are bits of the pattern which show some relation to them. Caring 'less' implies having cared 'more'; and there is a more revealing admission:

> One has him so in one's head, one cannot help imitating him sometimes; but except in the last lines I thought I had kept him out of 'Sohrab and Rustum'. Mark any other places you notice, for I should wish to alter such.[4]

Tennyson in the last ten years of his life was close; he visited Farringford, heard and admired the first three Idylls before publication (*Poems and Prose Remains*, pp. 232, 235; *Correspondence*, pp. 522, 539, 547, 557, 565) and in the last year of his life joined the Tennysons 'in the valley of Cauteretz'.

[1] Lines 182–90. Some of the evidence and arguments are set out by Tinker and Lowry (*Commentary*, pp. 209–11) but not the use of the stanza on the title-page of Joseph Jacobs's 1892 study of *In Memoriam*, nor the argument from the context, which suggests a living writer. But it is impossible to press the identification in face of Arnold's definite statement thirty years later that he intended Goethe, surprising though this may seem.

[2] William Knight in his *Retrospects* (1904), recalls: 'I remember and can now hear, his musical quotation of the lines "Leave thou thy sister when she prays [here follows the rest of the stanza, xxx. 6–8]" ' (p. 196). And see p. 199, n. 2 below.

[3] *Letters to Clough*, pp. 63, 147, 154.

[4] *Life and Correspondence of Lord Coleridge*, i, 210; letter of 1853.

These sentences in a letter to John Duke Coleridge perhaps best formulate Arnold's mixed response: a fascinated familiarity with Tennyson's poetry, and a self-protective resistance to it, especially in his own poetry, and especially in one poem. The familiarity is consistent with Butler's account, as also the recorded enthusiasm for Tennyson in Arnold's Oxford set after the appearance of the 1842 volumes, when his 'name' was 'on everyone's lips . . . portions of [the poems] repeatedly set for translation into Latin or Greek verse . . . read and re-read so habitually that there were many of us who could repeat page after page from memory'.[1] And though it may be assumed that Arnold, like Clough, would oppose the motion up for debate at the 'Decade' about 1844, 'That Tennyson is a greater poet than Wordsworth',[2] the compliment implied in such a motion should not be overlooked.

The resistance to Tennyson as a poetic influence is a reaction natural in a poet half a generation younger, as yet unestablished, and fighting, as a poet, for his independent life. Fighting, perhaps against the spell laid upon his own poetic sensibilities, certainly against the tendency of critics to 'place' his own early poems as Tennysonian. Reviewers and friends (J. D. Coleridge was both) had noted Tennysonian echoes, both in *The Strayed Reveller* and the *Poems* of 1853, *Blackwood's* actually rebuking the unknown author for being too imitative in 'Mycerinus', and being 'directly reminded of one of Alfred's early extravaganzas' by 'The Forsaken Merman'.[3] In November 1853 Arnold had Clough as well as Coleridge to contend with, and wrote to him twice in five days defending himself against the charge of being Tennysonian in 'Sohrab'. He concedes one or two lines—'rather Tennysonian—at any rate it is not good'.[4] In the same letter the belittling of 'The Scholar Gipsy', Clough's favourite in the volume,[5] as having only a 'pleasing melancholy' may

[1] This is recalled by Bradley from October 1842; he had been away from Oxford for a year and had then met Tennyson at the Lushingtons' (*Memoir*, i, 205–6). Cf. Knight, p. 57.

[2] *Poems and Prose Remains*, i, 25; Shairp's recollections. Bradley reports that Shairp also spoke for Wordsworth (Knight, p. 139).

[3] September 1849, pp. 340–6; and cf. *Fraser's*, May 1849, pp. 570–86.

[4] *Letters to Clough*, pp. 145–6.

[5] *Poems and Prose Remains*, ii, 214; letter to C. E. Norton, 1853.

be one more move against the Tennysonian, and perhaps particularly against *In Memoriam*, parts of which 'The Scholar Gipsy' approaches in '*couleur locale*'[1] as well as in mood. Arnold had his own view of it; it was a poem for the 'interior company' who shared the same reminiscences, not for the 'complaining millions of men' who needed something to 'animate and ennoble'.[2]

The 1853 Preface also shows Arnold trying to uproot and reject a kind of poetry which is congenial to one part of his nature, and which is of the same kind as *In Memoriam*. The Preface never mentions Tennyson; but it implies him, in more than one passage, and if *Empedocles* is to be rejected, so too is *In Memoriam*, as the 'dialogue of the mind with itself' (there could not be a more apt description),[3] as the 'allegory of the state of one's own mind', and as representing a 'situation . . . in which the suffering finds no vent in action . . . something morbid . . . something monotonous . . . painful, not tragic'. Again, Tennyson's manner is glanced at when Arnold pleads for 'the subordinate character of expression'; clearly, the 'hand' which he offers to guide the 'young writer' bewildered by the 'number of existing works capable of attracting [his] attention' will lead him firmly away from Tennyson, as from Keats and Alexander Smith ('Keats, Tennyson, et id genus omne', who must cause 'perplexity' to 'young writers');[4] away from 'exquisite bits and images', from poetry that adds 'zest to our melancholy and grace to our dreams'.[5] Away from all this; towards what, the Preface is there to define, and 'Sohrab and Rustum' to exemplify. 'In its poor way Sohrab and Rustum animates';[6] it pleased him better than anything else he had done, the material

[1] Letter to Tom Arnold, 1857 (Ward, p. 54).

[2] *Letters to Clough*, p. 146.

[3] I think this is confirmed by a passage in an unpublished letter cited, as a footnote to this article, by R. H. Super in *TLS*, 28 October 1960: When asked his opinion of a manuscript poem by William Alexander, he replied (21 July 1860): 'Though no one without real poetical feeling could have written it, I confess it does not quite please me. It seems to me to belong to the "In Memoriam" type of poems; poems which have no beginning, middle or end, but are holdings forth in verse, which, for anything in the nature of the composition itself, may perfectly well go on for ever.'

[4] *Letters to Clough*, p. 97; letter of (?) late 1848.

[5] ibid., p. 146.

[6] ibid., p. 147.

was good, and that was everything; it was galling to be told on all sides that even this poem was Tennysonian, and to have 'The Scholar Gipsy' preferred.[1] 'But this is not what we want.'

In Arnold's later judgments on Tennyson he makes his grounds for complaint more specific. That he should become harsher in the early eighteen-sixties is explicable. While he increasingly demanded that literature should be 'adequate', should powerfully apply 'ideas' to life; while he advanced, not merely with the times but ahead of them, as one of the 'sharp-shooters, the quick-witted audacious light troops',[2] Tennyson receded further from him. But as Tennyson became less 'adequate', he became more popular. Arnold was alive to the danger of 'culture' here. Allowing Tennyson 'temperament and artistic skill'[3] and 'poetic sentiment',[4] he saw him as 'deficient in intellectual power'[5]—his 'reach of mind is petty'.[6] In short, he is 'not . . . a great and powerful spirit in any line'.[7] Again the context shows that Arnold is fighting, this time for the superiority of Wordsworth and Goethe, the priests and sages of poetry. He had been fighting especially for Wordsworth in the last Homer lectures, on which he commented:

> Tennyson's devoted adherents will be very angry with me, but their ridiculous elevation of him above Wordsworth made me determined to say what I did.[8]

It is in this that we come nearest to the centre of his objection; and the reaffirming of one of the positions taken up in the 1853 Preface is clear.

In his final lectures Arnold, with his critics in mind, is concerned to draw distinctions important to him. He brings out the 'true Homeric plainness' and the 'natural simplicity' of Wordsworth, partly through a contrast, by description and example, with Tennyson's 'subtle sophistica-

[1] The preference persists, but especially perhaps among Oxford men, for whom Arnold admitted that he primarily wrote it.

[2] 'Joubert', lecture of 1863; *Essays in Criticism* (1865).

[3] *Letters*, i, 127 (1860).

[4] ibid., ii, 9 (1869).

[5] ibid., i, 127 (1860).

[6] *From a Victorian Post-bag*, 1926, p. 75 (letter to Llewelyn Davies, 1863).

[7] *Letters*, i, 239 (1864).

[8] ibid., i, 165 (1862).

tion', 'distilled thoughts in distilled words'.[1] To this he devotes some four pages,[2] of which one sentence sufficiently indicates his position. Spedding, he has said, is wrong in finding Homeric plainness of thought and speech in Tennyson:

> I answer that these I do not find there at all. Mr Tennyson is a most distinguished and charming poet; but the very essential characteristic of his poetry is, it seems to me, an extreme subtlety and curious elaborateness of thought, an extreme subtlety and curious elaborateness of style. In the best and most characteristic productions of his genius, these characteristics are most prominent.

He gives half a dozen examples, mainly from heroic poems, of a 'way of speaking . . . the least *plain*, the most *unHomeric*, which can possibly be conceived'. Then, to show that, when Tennyson tries to be simple, he 'can only attain a semblance of simplicity', 'artificial simplicity', or '*simplesse*', he puts two passages from 'Dora' beside two from 'Michael'. No examples are drawn from *In Memoriam*, and it may be by inference excluded from condemnation in this footnote:

> In lyrical poetry, in the direct expression of personal feeling, the most subtle genius may, under the momentary pressure of passion, express itself simply. Even here, however, the native tendency will generally be discernible.

Lyric poetry, when Tennyson is being thought of, is a very large exclusion; but Arnold is, here as in the 1853 Preface, pre-occupied with the Great Poem and the Grand Style. This admitted, it would still be open to Arnold to allow natural simplicity to

> He put our lives so far apart
> We cannot hear each other speak.

Apart from this passage, there is no overt reference to Tennyson in Arnold's published work. But, perhaps because

[1] In a letter to Palgrave discussing his own poems in 1869 (G. W. E. Russell, *Matthew Arnold*, pp. 41–3), Arnold incidentally draws a further distinction, and a severe one, between Virgil's 'natural *propriety* of diction and rhythm' and the style of the *Idylls*, 'something dainty and *tourmenté*'. He here admits that 'Sohrab' has 'something, not dainty, but *tourmenté*'.

[2] pp. 54–8 in the first edition of *Last Words*, 1862; pp. 413–16 in the Oxford edition (1914).

of what he had said in his lecture, he was asked two years later to review the *Enoch Arden* volume for the *Spectator*—and was much tempted. The poem itself he thought 'very good indeed—perhaps the best thing Tennyson has done';[1] but he could not write about Tennyson without saying all he thought, and that might be attributed to 'odious motives'. (One recalls his wish to keep free of 'the ignoble saturnalia of personal passions'.) Here is already shaping itself his principle of not writing about contemporary literature:

> In general I do not write about the literary performances of living contemporaries or contemporaries only recently dead.[2]

—a self-denying ordinance which explains many omissions in his criticism. He wished that Stopford Brooke had ended his survey of English literature at 1832:

> No man can trust himself to speak of his own time and his own contemporaries with the same sureness of judgment and the same proportion as of times past.[3]

In other words, 'disinterestedness' on contemporary literature was impossible. What Arnold did publish, still more what he wrote privately of Tennyson, confirms this; the murmur of impersonal (not 'odious') axe-grinding is always there—Tennyson is not Homer, or not Goethe, or not Wordsworth, not a 'complete magister vitae'; and so 'not what we want'.

But the strength of Tennyson's influence, on poetry, on standards of criticism, and up to a point on Arnold himself, is measurable by Arnold's resistance. It suggests some degree of captivation. There are besides many indications that Arnold's view of poetry was not uniformly austere, not solely controlled by 'what we want', what is 'important for us'. Inconsistent, out-of-date personal tastes break through; and one poet, first damned for the 'harm he has done to English poetry', wins upon Arnold by his 'natural magic'. (It is too often forgotten that Arnold gives this equal weight with 'moral profundity'.) There is a breach in the wall. And Arnold's own instinctive

[1] *Letters*, i, 239 (1864). Cf. letter to J. D. Coleridge, op. cit., ii, 125–6—'one of the two or three very best things Tennyson has done'.

[2] *Letters*, ii, 376 (1888).

[3] Review of 1877, collected in *Mixed Essays*, 1879.

pleased response is half betrayed even in the moment of resistance: the 'exquisite bits and images' of 'modern poetry' were after all 'exquisite'; 'the most subtle genius' is not a phrase of condemnation, and it is admitted that even this, in lyric, may 'under the momentary pressure of passion, express itself simply'. When brought together and related to his own work in criticism and poetry, Arnold's strictures on Tennyson make sense, and are not merely severe; they are certainly not discordant with delight in *In Memoriam.* No admirer of both poets, least of all one who thinks *In Memoriam* Tennyson's greatest poem and 'Thyrsis' Arnold's, could be content to suspect Arnold's silence on that poem to be that of insensitiveness. I hope my resuscitation of Arthur Butler's story may be seen as bringing an authentic voice into that silence: perhaps even a 'floating echo' from Arnold's deep-buried 'central stream of what we feel indeed'.

XVI

ARNOLD: THE LECTURER AND JOURNALIST

MATTHEW ARNOLD'S audience was delighted with his lecture on translating Homer in the autumn of 1860, and more delighted still when it swelled from one to three. It was a triumph for the Professor of Poetry. His earlier lectures had not gone so well because he had chosen subjects that were too grandiose. But it was different with the Homer lectures where he was 'very sure of [his] ground'. Altogether he was emboldened to cancel the arrangement he had made with *Fraser's Magazine*: 'I should get at least £30', he told his mother, 'so it is a temptation, but I think as they are my first published Oxford lectures it is more decorous to publish them as a book than as magazine articles.' Decorousness did not depend for Arnold on conditions of publication. His prose writings began and ended with that adornment over the thirty years during which he appeared frequently. But though decorous he was always something of a journalist.

We can see why these lectures were a temptation also to *Fraser's*. In the mid-nineteenth century and earlier the question of how best to translate and trans-metre Homer was a warm subject of debate in the journals, including *Fraser's* itself, and here sparkled the last and truest word on the subject. In addition the editor knew that the pleasure of being decorous did not for Arnold exclude the pleasure of being personal. At any moment he might break out into personalities—amusingly, and even sometimes with a gay offensiveness.

There is a tell-tale remark that startles us in Professor Neiman's volume:[1] Arnold is discussing certain theological writings, and suddenly interposes: 'I wish to lay aside all ridicule, into which literary criticism too readily falls.' It

[1] *Essays, Letters, and Reviews by Matthew Arnold*, ed. Fraser Neiman, 1960.

startles us because we do not now think of ridicule as a *modus operandi* of criticism. But it had been that for many critics from the Restoration days onwards, and in Arnold's lifetime there had been the outrageous use of it by Macaulay. Arnold himself makes outrageous use of it sometimes. But few people would deny a place for the outrageous in journalism. And Arnold's gifts were as near to those of the journalist as to those of the poet and sober critic. Paper warfare—for Professor Newman, whom Arnold attacked, retaliated, as any spirited person would, and Arnold returned with his *Last Words*—is one of the cheering characteristics of journalism as much as are its reports of cricket or boxing.

In that century lecturing, journalism and literature intermingled. There was less standing on dignity than there had been for Addison or Johnson, for Gray and Wordsworth. Many masterpieces were read to audiences before they became books—and Dickens reversed the process. 'Magazine day', the first of the month, saw parts of novels by Dickens and Thackeray stacked up beside copies of *Blackwood's* or *Fraser's*. Great novels appeared bit by bit among magazine articles about horse-breaking or cholera. Newman's *Apologia* was a series of pamphlets supervening on a pamphlet duel. The mid-nineteenth-century authors seem to hold off from books for as long as possible, trusting their splendid utterance to air or ephemeral print. Journalism got into the bones of literature. The four volumes of *The Ring and the Book* appeared one at a time, and a reviewer dubbed them 'a newspaper in blank verse'.

Journalism is certainly in the bones of all the prose literature of Arnold, which was both decorous and mercantile, both a thing to remember and a tract for the times. The preface to the *Poems* of 1853 had been that, and *Fraser's* wanted the Homer lectures because they were drawn from the same tap. Trying to weight the Homer lectures towards decorousness, Arnold elected to publish them in book form. But never again—unless we count *England and the Italian Question*, which, designed either 'for a pamphlet, or for *Fraser*', did in fact appear as a pamphlet—never again did he prefer a book to articles. Instead he made the best of the two worlds, writing articles which later he brought together into a book.

But not all his articles achieved the more decorous permanence of book-form, and on his death it was plain to everybody that enough pieces remained scattered to make a second series of *Essays in Criticism.* A third series followed in 1910, and even as late as 1914 the Oxford University Press generously added to their two-shilling volume of *Essays* five other essays 'now for the first time collected'.

That marked the end of what we might call the posthumous phase of collecting. In the 1950's set in the researcher's phase. For Arnold has now reached that high point of greatness at which publication *in toto* is both inevitable and desirable. Already much that remained obscure has been garnered in, and more is promised. In 1952 came the edition of the *Notebooks*, and in 1953 Mr Allott's five *Uncollected Essays*, and we are led to expect the near publication of the 'diary-notebooks' by Mr W. B. Guthrie, of the University of Virginia, and indeed the publication in time of all the letters under the editorship of Professor A. K. Davis, Jr., of the same university—all the letters and all of them in full shape, for Arnold's family twice subjected to censorship the text of the Russell collection of 1895. Certain other of Arnold's contemporaries have reached this peak of greatness, and when all the collecting is complete we shall have been persuaded—if we still need to be—to a truer sense of the liveliness of the literature of the mid-nineteenth century.

Certainly in the volume under review (which reminds us that all the great writers of the age were rebels against what was really illiberal in it) there is no trace of the heavy and the dull. As an instance take one of the longer pieces, rescued by the Oxford *Essays*, and now again by Professor Neiman. The title threatens the heaviest dullness—'Dr Stanley's Lectures on the Jewish Church'. Its purpose is to draw edification from the different ways Holy Writ was being treated by two up-to-date scholars—the Regius Professor of Ecclesiastical History at Oxford, soon to be Dean of Westminster, and the Rt. Rev. John William Colenso, Bishop of Natal, who had shown up the technical impossibilities in the early part of the Old Testament record. Professor Neiman rightly claims that the article is important for the understanding of Arnold's intellectual development. But it could have this importance and still be heavily dull. Duteously turning to read it, we soon meet a passage that only Arnold could have written:

I cannot tell what may, in the end, be the effect of the Bishop of Natal's book upon the religious life of this country. Its natural immediate effect may be seen by any one who will take the trouble of looking at a newspaper called Public Opinion, in which the Bishop's book is the theme of a great continuous correspondence. There, week after week, the critical genius of our nation discovers itself in captivating nudity; and there, in the letters of a terrible athlete of Reason, who signs himself 'Eagle-Eye', the natural immediate effect of the Bishop's book may be observed. Its natural ultimate effect would be, I think, to continue, in another form, the excessive care of the English religious world for that which is not of the real essence of the Bible: as this world has for years been prone to say, 'We are the salt of the earth, because we believe that every syllable and letter of the Bible is the direct utterance of the Most High', so it would naturally, after imbibing the Bishop of Natal's influence, be inclined to say, 'We are the salt of the earth, because we believe that the Pentateuch is unhistorical'. Whether they believe the one or the other, what they should learn to say is: 'We are unprofitable servants; the religious life is beyond'.

And so to the peroration, at once modest and proud:

And you are masters in Israel, and know not these things; and you require a voice from the world of literature to tell them to you! Those who ask nothing better than to remain silent on such topics, who have to quit their own sphere to speak of them, who cannot touch them without being reminded that they survive those who touched them with far different power, you compel, in the mere interest of letters, of intelligence, of general culture, to proclaim truths which it was your function to have made familiar. And, when you have thus forced the very stones to cry out, and the dumb to speak, you call them singular because they know these truths, and arrogant because they declare them!

The liveliness and general interest of these sample pieces are typical of what we find in the rest of the *Essays, Letters and Reviews*, which range in subject from an address to the Wordsworth Society to an article on university reform, and from a preface to the literary exhibits in *The Hundred Best Men* to an article on ordnance maps (a little masterpiece closely woven as a rug, and written to expose the inferiority of British maps to Swiss and German).

The notes in Professor Neiman's volume call in the main for research in ill-mapped fields. Reading in them we are haunted by Mark Pattison's remark about Milton—that the full understanding of the poetry is the reward of consummated scholarship. One needs a great deal of scholarship to follow the sense in Arnold's prose works, and some of it must lie in the rough and tumble of his time. To learn a few bleak biographical particulars about, say, 'the Rev. W. Cattle' is only the beginning of wisdom. Arnold's gibbeting of him and the rest cannot be appreciated till we have met them in the life of the times, in the newspapers so as to get them 'twopence coloured'. When Arnold writes 'Our days go by, and the hour with Mr. Yates in the *World* is followed by the hour with Mr. Labouchere in *Truth*, and this fascinating course of reading leaves us with little leisure or taste for anything else . . .', or 'it was Professor Fawcett, and not the Bishop of Bordeaux, who took the bit in his teeth', we need a great deal of knowledge for full understanding.

The notes we are given must be something of a disappointment unless the note-maker has virtually become a mid-nineteenth-century person himself. And that is asking what can very rarely be forthcoming. Professor Neiman has given us texts, and some useful guidance towards understanding all they contain of solid and airy matter, and it is for each of us to acquire the stranger parts of erudition for ourselves. We need to work as hard in the interest of understanding Arnold as of understanding Pope, and must do it partly in the same sort of field, for the preface to the *Essays in Criticism* in its first form (reprinted here by Mr Neiman) is to the nineteenth century what *An Epistle to Dr Arbuthnot* is to the eighteenth. And it is significant of change that Pope's apologia is in verse, and Arnold's, without loss of brilliance, in prose.

XVII

SWINBURNE

THAT SWINBURNE'S letters are being published, and published with all possible completeness and editorial competence, comes as a shock. Here are the first two handsome volumes, and four more are to follow.[1] Joining the letters of Thackeray, Trollope, George Eliot, and Clough, all of which have appeared since the war, an edition of Swinburne's letters would seem to lack the ample justification of its predecessors—those four of his contemporaries are now being read, or, if not, are receiving the respect of those who mean to read them. But Swinburne? Few older people have returned to his poetry, perhaps not even to his critical writings; few younger people seem to have read either the poetry or the prose. *Lesbia Brandon* was first published in 1952, but copies soon reached the remainder counter. Though copyrights have expired, there is no indication that any publisher is following up with a great new complete edition the few slim volumes of selected poems that appeared in the 1950's. What, then, is the justification for a new edition of the letters, five times larger than its predecessor, an edition which, as Mr Lang fatalistically notes, is costing a 'staggering' amount in printers' bills?

There is, to begin with, the justification obvious to scholars: that, being the letters of an author universally ranked as important in his day, they contribute facts and opinions about contemporary literature. To read them is to learn more about the Pre-Raphaelites—Rossetti, Morris, Simeon Solomon in particular—about the emergence of Blake's fame, and the further emergence of Keats's; about the impact on Englishmen of Victor Hugo, Baudelaire, and Whitman; to gather from statements, hints, and tones how the great writers senior to Swinburne were continuing to strike their juniors. It is also to learn much about contemporary publishers. And to some extent

[1] *The Swinburne Letters,* ed. Cecil Y. Lang, vols. i–ii, 1959. Vols. iii–vi were published 1960–2.

the general reader can join the scholar because Swinburne's commentary itself is literature, especially now that we have the text of his letters complete.

The pleasure of getting a letter from him must always have been vivid, and sometimes overwhelming. It might contain, for instance, one of those vituperative phrases that only he could make so magniloquent. In one letter Kingsley, the great muscular Christian, is referred to. He had, it seemed, rashly written a piece of art-criticism. Swinburne had come across the advertisement, and, announcing it to his correspondent, rose to what he felt to be an occasion: Mr Lang at last makes the words public: '[an] incredible announcement of a malodorous emanation from the kennel of Kingsley'. Being glorious, such things are not mere vituperation. They are fragments of literary criticism, lively enough to count as literature, and so are for the general reader as well as the student of the history of literature.

There is more for the general reader, also. Mr Lang does not claim that Swinburne's letters are 'great' letters, but there are gains as well as losses in not belonging to the grander order. 'Great' letter-writers can be bores unless we admit their assumption that the letter may slide into the essay (an assumption we might have expected Swinburne to adopt). But how delightful is the letter-form that is used as it should be used, to convey to an absent person what, if he were present, would be conveyed by word of mouth. It is even delightful when the sender is not more than a fairly ordinary person. From time to time most of us receive letters about nothing very much which a third person would enjoy reading if the scrawl were made print and any practical urgency removed by the passage of time. Swinburne's letters are those of an extraordinary person, but they have their moments when the stuff of ordinary letters attains memorability: 'two violent snowstorms on the Derby day! . . . I think we shall all have to emigrate'; 'the damnable unventilated air of the [British] Museum'; 'stopped (as usual, being in a special hurry) at a bookstall'; 'On n'a pas trop d'amis dans ce f— monde, and we can't *afford* to misunderstand each other; I can't at least'; 'I want tin'; or, to take a youthful example, 'In beginning my letter to you, I hear a voice that says "Make lime of his bones": but I resist the gentle intimation and merely ask what the and cetera you mean by never answering me all this time? If the priceless freight has miscarried, I shall do something spasmodic'.

Some of these letters, however, are great letters in the sense of the word that owes nothing to the essay. There is the glowing one, for instance, in which Swinburne describes his meeting with the worshipped Mazzini so as to win the sympathy of his mother: 'They say a man's highest hopes are usually disappointed: mine were not . . .'. And there is the quite early letter about de Sade, remarkable for the completeness of its account of the psychology of flagellation—it contains this passage, for instance:

> Seriously is [de Sade] not exactly a typical monk? not voluptuous, not sensual, hardly cruel in the proper sense of the word, but alternately bestial and spiritual, and often both at once? the aspiration, and laborious service of his 'ideal', being as great and deep as the appetite it works through.

Or there is the letter about Carlyle, or the long letter about Landor's works, or the early letters to Watts (-Dunton), when that efficient person was helping to set Swinburne's tangled professional finances in order, letters in which Swinburne voluminously states his haughty, bitter views about Buchanan, the author of *The Fleshly School of Poetry*. These private letters rank with the many he sent to the press—most of them standing up for important principles besides being elaborately and superbly vituperative—and which we must thank Mr Lang for reprinting here for the first time.

These pleasant and substantial things for the general reader and the scholar may lead all of us to read the poetry itself, to read it or to reread it; for letters are the easiest way into the work of an author due for re-examination. Forty years ago Mr Eliot said some damaging things about that poetry, and he spoke for most people then and since that date. No adverse judgment, however, can stand permanently against an important writer. We ourselves change, given time; and the spirit of the age, to which we subtly conform, also undergoes changes. And so we return to things that had once to be discarded in order that we might give our undivided attention to different things.

Up to a point Mr Eliot's verdict still stands firm. It still seems true that Swinburne was often carried away by his own pulsating rhythm, only to be deposited in the shadows and windy places of verbiage, or even nonsense. A poem ends only when the poet, like the dancing dervish, is at long last exhausted. The dance of words proved too dazzling for many of his contemporaries. They raved over *Atalanta in Calydon* in the way they had raved over *Festus* and the poems of Alexander Smith. Every age has poets it raves about. We have them ourselves, and the surprising thing is that they are not unlike Swinburne, or at least more like than we have seen. The *Poems and Ballads* of 1866 has its twentieth-century modernity. It contains, for instance, such a line as this:

> Their blood runs round the roots of time like rain.

Is not this a line that could be written nowadays, a line from which strangeness, not to say obscurity, rises like a mist from the unwonted juxtaposition of the commonest words, words that are the names of the oldest things? He speaks of 'the deep sharp sea' and 'the hot hard night'. We like such things in the moderns, and there they are to be liked in the despised Swinburne.

But if we are not drawn to his poetry because he is sometimes one of ourselves, we shall be drawn to it, as time goes on, because we are reading the other writers of the mid-nineteenth century. Rereading his better contemporaries will make us more willing to read him. They are indeed his betters, because they have so many more things to say, and so many new things, because so much of their meaning is of the sort that comes home to the business and bosoms of mankind, because they could write so much more weightily, incisively, variously, memorably—indeed for all the reasons that led Swinburne himself at some time or other to praise many of them finely and pungently.

We shall read Swinburne if only because we shall see him as complementary to the rest. Like them he was a rebel. All poets to some extent must be. But being younger than the great mid-nineteenth-century writers, his rebellion was partly against them. The great Tennyson was too 'narrow-toned' at times—over politics, for instance—and sometimes seemed to be fumbling what he dared not bite. Browning and Clough were too unmusical and ratiocinative. Arnold was not a sure technician—not even in that Swinburnian poem 'The New Sirens' which Swinburne persuaded him to reinstate in the canon. But Swinburne was never narrow-toned, never unmusical, never unsure of his technique, and only faintly ratiocinative. He supplied as many colours as he saw to be lacking, and supplied them lavishly because the gap seemed wide. He was aware of a gap in the life that was being represented in the literature: human life included more of the highflying, and of mindless abandon. There is a significant remark when he is engaged on writing 'A Song of Italy': 'If I finish this poem at all to my satisfaction, there will be a bit of enthusiasm in verse for once—rather'.

To take one instance: in mid-nineteenth-century literature there was much said about the sea, much that was sublime or beautiful, but there was not enough said to match what Swinburne saw in a sea that was doing its worst—or best, as he would have said. His letters show how strongly he felt about stormy sea. He exulted in rough sea bathing. Few have felt more painfully the longing to fling out arms and legs in turbulent water: 'I am dying for it—there is no lust or appetite comparable!'; 'my craving (ultra Sapphic and plusquàm-Sadic) lust after the sea'; a sea-picture by Hook 'made me thirsty to be in between the waves'; his daring is near to devilry—he prefers to bathe on dangerous coasts, and is once swept two miles out, and only rescued by the merest luck. When he was eighteen he crossed the Channel in appalling conditions, and at the age of seventy recalled the glorious experience in metre. The result is not only a stupendous poem about sea, air and sky, but also about the poet. No other poet would have felt himself so much a part of it all, and the proof of it lies in one phrase especially:

> Filled full with delight that revives in remembrance a sea-bird's heart
> in a boy.

Among the other gaps that Swinburne filled, two are striking. First, that of passionate political poetry. 'The Eve of Revolution', written in 1870, is a miracle of sustained flight and din as of trumpets. *Flight* is the word—its feet scarcely touch the ground —but then that is in order for a poem at a political crisis when feeling and not intellect is what runs high. Then there is his contribution to the mid-nineteenth-century account of love—to use the general word to begin with. Swinburne's letters show him as 'abnormally' sexed, glorying in the thoughts and pictures of flagellation and perversities, and they hint at participation in the actualities of them. (For the first time we have these letters complete.) Plainly this particular glorying could not be transferred bodily into the public poetry, though some of it is less abnormal than was believed at the time. But what of it—feelings and their objects—could indeed be transferred was transferred without loss of reality. The account of passion, even if of abnormal passion, is an account of a reality. It does not insult the power of the passion, as the speaker of 'Locksley Hall' insulted it when in a famous line he made the fancies of a young man turn to thoughts of love lightly. The epithet that Swinburne awards to 'kisses' is 'heavy'.

The only solid ground for disapproval was, and is, that these feelings and their objects occupy too much space, and that they fail in variety. Swinburne misjudged the size of the gap. There was room for an exhibition of love or lust of the sort particularly interesting to himself, but a greater writer would have covered more of the total subject, and covered it with less display. The letters show him eager to shock the Philistines. He was too eager—it was part of his general failure to outgrow the feelings of an undergraduate. There is an amusing moment in a letter addressed from Oxford:

> One evening—when the [painting of the] Union was just finished—Jones and I had a great talk. Stanhope and Swan attacked, and we defended our idea of Heaven, viz., a rose-garden full of stunners [Rossetti's slang for beautiful women]. Atrocities of an appalling nature were uttered on the other side. We became so fierce that two respectable members of the University—entering to see the pictures—stood mute and looked at us. We spoke just then of kisses in Paradise, and expounded our ideas on the celestial development of that necessity of life; and after listening five minutes to our language, they literally fled from the room! Conceive our mutual ecstasy of delight.

Such things are delightful in an undergraduate. Swinburne, however, did not outgrow them. But that his shocking poems were published at all—and published by the respectable Moxon, until he dropped them—was a proof that there was more to them than unusual sexual feeling. They were the work of a poet who wished to say as much about the usual matter of poetry as about Dolores and the rest. Swinburne was not chalking on public walls.

His poetry appealed to the young and will do so again. It is poetry that cries out to be read aloud. Swinburne himself took every opportunity to present it to friends in this vocal way, and there are descriptions of his rapt performances. That his poetry requires the music of the exalted speaking voice is both its strength and weakness. It can stand that test, and it cannot so well stand the other test; that of a *lumen siccum*. Swinburne is usually a lyric poet, and we do not ask of a song what we ask of poetry in which music is not preponderant. But if Swinburne is not a great poet, he is a great minor poet as Collins, say, and Christopher Smart are, and as we still think that Dylan Thomas is. Unlike these poets he is also a writer of first-rate criticism, and perhaps the best of it comes in the letters, expressed without airs and graces because to an audience that was unprovocative, consisting only of a like-minded friend.

XVIII

MATTHEW ARNOLD AND CARLYLE[1]

THE CONJUNCTION of these two names may seem surprising; and, indeed, the very name of Carlyle in a lecture on English poetry. Carlyle's obvious place is among the Master-minds; and as such he was the subject of a noble discourse delivered here in 1940 by Sir Herbert Grierson. Speaking of Carlyle as a 'prophet', Sir Herbert illuminated his argument by Spinoza's distinction between the prophets of the Old Testament and the New—a distinction which, as it happens, points to one of the radical differences between Carlyle and Arnold, between Hebraism and that 'sweet reasonableness' which Arnold admired and attempted to pursue. Carlyle was felt as a Master-mind by most Victorian writers, and particularly by those who, like Arnold, were young in the 1840's. The complexity of Arnold's response to this mastery, his acceptance and his rebellion, I have thought worth examining,[2] for the sake especially of the light thrown on some of his poems.

Arnold's statements about Carlyle themselves offer something of a challenge. The extreme points are represented by two remarks, one made in youth, the other in late middle-age; the

[1] This lecture was reviewed by Kenneth Allott in *MLR*, liii (1958), p. 302 and by J. P. Curgenven in *RES*, NS, x(1959), p. 108. It received some comment, and a valuable expansion of its argument, with, I think, confirmation of its main conclusions, in a long article by David J. DeLaura, 'Arnold and Carlyle', *PMLA*, lxxix (1964), p. 104. While necessarily covering some of the same ground, Mr DeLaura concentrates mainly on Arnold's critical and social writings of the 1860's, which could not be thoroughly explored in a Warton lecture on English poetry. See also Fraser Neiman, 'The Zeitgeist of Matthew Arnold', *PMLA*, lxxii (1957), p. 977. But I believe that as far as Arnold's poetry is concerned, my reference, in the following footnote of 1956, to the neglect of Arnold's response to Carlyle is still true in 1964.

[2] It has been neglected by all critics except Professors Tinker and Lowry, who refer to Carlyle several times in passing (*The Poetry of Matthew Arnold: a Commentary*), Professor Louis Bonnerot, who considers his influence on several poems (*Matthew Arnold, Poète*, 1947), and Mr Frederick Page, in 'Balder Dead' (*Essays and Studies*, xxviii (1942), p. 60) a modest but stimulating essay in which that poem is related both to Carlyle and to Arnold's religious thinking. My instances, except as noted under *Empedocles on Etna* and 'Stanzas from the Grande Chartreuse', are new.

first calls Carlyle 'the beloved man', the second is 'I never much liked Carlyle'. The difference is less than it appears, for the second statement refers to Carlyle's 'preaching', the first to the 'style and feeling' of his work; and I believe that Arnold responded especially to the poet in Carlyle, to what he called his 'surpassingly powerful qualities of expression'. This is the Carlyle who haunts Arnold's poems—sometimes almost independently of their subjects. I shall give one instance, before proceeding to my main argument. The Scholar Gipsy has little in common with the Carlylean hero, yet a leading image of the poem and one of its most familiar phrases come from *Heroes and Hero-Worship*:

> But I liken common languid Times, with their unbelief, distress, perplexity, with their *languid doubting* characters . . . impotently crumbling-down into ever worse distress . . .—all this I liken to *dry dead fuel*, waiting for the *lightning out of Heaven* that shall kindle it.

You will recognize this in the lines:

> Rapt, twirling in thy hand a *wither'd spray*
> And waiting for the *spark from heaven to fall*. . . .
>
> Free from the sick fatigue, the *languid doubt*. . . .
>
> Thou waitest for the spark from Heav'n! and we,
> Light half-believers of our casual creeds. . . .

If this parallel is meant to operate as meaning, that is, to be recognized and allowed for by the ordinary reader, it would affect the interpretation of a poem that has attracted much attention from recent critics.[1] But Arnold can hardly mean by the 'spark' simply what Carlyle means:

> . . . I said, the Great Man was always as lightning out of Heaven; the rest of men waited for him like fuel, and then they too would flame;

and all that is certain is that, even when he had diverged from the doctrine of *Heroes*, he remembered one of its symbols. And

[1] It was not observed in two recent and valuable critical studies: G. Wilson Knight, '*The Scholar Gipsy*: an Interpretation' (*RES*, N.S., vi (1955), p. 53), and J. P. Curgenven, '*The Scholar Gipsy*: a study of the growth, meaning, and integration of a poem', *Litera*, vols. ii–iii, 1955–6.

that I believe to be characteristic both of him, and of a whole way of looking at Carlyle.

For much of the fascination exerted by Carlyle in the nineteenth century was that of a poet, and therefore long outlasted the acceptance of his teaching. It was John Henry Newman, of all people, who called Carlyle 'quite fascinating as a writer'.[1] The extreme statement of the paradox comes from an equally unexpected source, Gerard Manley Hopkins:

> I do not like his pampered and affected style, I hate his principles, I burn most that he worships and worship most that he burns, I cannot respect (no one now can) his character, but the force of his genius seems to me gigantic.[2]

If we accept this, it cuts away at a blow all the twentieth-century reasons for neglecting Carlyle. It was the *Reminiscences*, posthumously published by Froude, that Hopkins had in mind in saying that no one could now respect Carlyle's character; a hasty judgment, but one that persisted until recently. Arnold himself foresaw some distaste as a result of Froude's biographical 'revelations'; but he thought it an *unfortunate* effect. 'Unluckily, he has begotten a distaste for Carlyle', 'One of the bad effects has been to tire people of Carlyle'.[3] No one foresaw the main cause of the recession. Leslie Stephen wrote at about the same time that Carlyle's opinions were now a matter of history, and might be judged as calmly as Burke's or Milton's. The next two generations did not judge them calmly, as we know.

Of his own generation, Arnold himself is the best witness to the strength of Carlyle's influence, in a lecture delivered to an American audience in 1883. Its opening is well known:

> Forty years ago, when I was an undergraduate at Oxford, voices were in the air there, which haunt my memory still. Happy the man who in that susceptible season of youth hears such voices! they are a possession to him for ever.

Whose were these voices? One was Newman's, and the passage that follows is always quoted in books on Newman or the Oxford Movement: 'that spiritual apparition, gliding' into St Mary's,

[1] *Letters*, ii, 300.

[2] *Letters of Gerard Manley Hopkins*, ed. C. C. Abbott, 1938, p. 59.

[3] *Letters*, ii, 358, 369 (letters of 1887).

whose words were 'a religious music—subtle, sweet, mournful'. Much less often quoted are the words in the next paragraph, on 'the puissant voice of Carlyle . . . reaching our hearts with true, pathetic eloquence. Who can forget the emotion of receiving in its first freshness such a sentence as . . .' and there follows a quotation from Carlyle on Edward Irving. And it is only the first of nine quotations from Carlyle distributed through the lecture; the persistence of his 'fascination' for Arnold is emphasized by their tenuous connection with the subject, which is Emerson.

The first words of that lecture, 'Forty years ago, when I was an undergraduate at Oxford' define our starting-point. Arnold went up to Balliol in 1841, just at a time when the growth and spread of Carlyle's fame was at last manifest. Its force was the greater because belated; Carlyle had been writing for twenty years (and lecturing in London for four successive seasons); so that a beginner in 1841 would receive the full impact of *Sartor Resartus*, *The French Revolution*, the five volumes of *Miscellaneous Essays* (including the collected criticism of German and English literature, and those great fountains of nineteenth-century thinking, 'Signs of the Times' and 'Characteristics'); then, in 1840, came *Chartism* and *Heroes and Hero-Worship*, and in 1843, *Past and Present*. According to one reader, it seemed that suddenly Carlyle's 'phrases were in all young men's mouths'.[1] Many readers recorded or recalled the astonishing effect he had upon them; and in these tributes, a certain kind of metaphor recurs: 'Running like wildfire'; 'his daring theories moved me like electric shocks'; 'he carries one off one's legs like a hurricane'; 'a sort of spiritual volcano . . . his language had the electric effect of a moral discharge'; 'a beacon . . . a voice [like] ten thousand trumpets';—mere samples of testimony, from different and independent witnesses,[2] all about Arnold's age and undergraduates in the 1840's. They include representatives of four universities; but in Oxford the impact of Carlyle

[1] David Masson, *Carlyle Personally and in his Writings*, 1885, p. 67; compare Mark Rutherford, *Pages from a Journal*, 1900, p. 12.

[2] Masson (loc. cit.), Charles Gavan Duffy, *My Life in Two Hemispheres*, 1898, i, 52, J. C. Shairp (W. Knight, *Principal Shairp and his Friends*, 1888, p. 156), R. H. Hutton (obituary article in *The Spectator*, 1881, collected in *Brief Literary Criticisms*, 1906), Froude, *Carlyle's Life in London*, 1884, vol. ii, ch. xi.

was especially strong. Not only 'intellectuals' were affected; Thomas Hughes's Tom Brown, 'the commonest type of English boy of the middle class', had 'scarcely ever in his life been so moved by a book' as by *Past and Present*[1] (and this was autobiographical; to the end of his life Hughes kept Carlyle's works in a 'small prophetic bookcase'). Of Arnold's immediate circle of friends, J. C. Shairp is typical. He recalled the very moment of his discovery of Carlyle in 1840.[2] He had just come to Balliol as a Snell Exhibitioner, and was in low spirits:

> He had been tired by his morning's reading, depressed by the weather, which was too bad even for an Oxford 'constitutional,' and had gone, in a state of intellectual depression, into a bookseller's shop, had seen and immediately bought the four or five volumes of *Miscellanies*, which had just appeared, and carried them back to his rooms. The first essay on which he came was that on Edward Irving, which he read and re-read, walking about his room, feeling himself, as he said, possessed and carried away by a new passion.

This was also the essay that Arnold chose to quote as an instance of the 'voices heard in youth'. Shairp's history is in another way a diagram of Arnold's own; for after twelve years of reading Carlyle he came to feel that he had read him 'perhaps too eagerly', so that his influence became too overmastering. A more complex case is Arthur Hugh Clough, who became particularly close to Carlyle both in his writings and in personal friendship; an eager reader, from about 1839, and probably a stimulant to Arnold's interest. Clough too became critical—as when, bidding farewell to Emerson in 1848, he said, 'Carlyle has led us all out into the wilderness and left us there.' But *The Bothie* was still to be written, and it has been aptly described as 'Teufelsdröckh in hexameters'.[3] Other admirers in Arnold's immediate Oxford circle were his brother Tom and Anthony Froude; and these, like Arnold, were for a time equally responsive to the voice of Newman. Froude called Carlyle and Newman the 'two writers' who 'have affected powerfully the present generation of Englishmen';[4] when it became painfully clear, after Newman's secession in 1845, that the two voices were calling from different

[1] *Tom Brown at Oxford*, 1861, ch. xxxv.
[2] Knight, p. 38; contributed by W. Y. Sellar.
[3] By Maurice Hewlett, in *Extemporary Essays*, 1922.
[4] 'The Oxford Counter-Reformation', 1881.

directions, Froude turned towards Carlyle (imperfectly dramatizing the conflict in his novel *The Nemesis of Faith*), and Tom Arnold eventually towards Newman. But there is ample evidence that in the early 1840's, at Oxford, the two voices were felt to harmonize. In 1841, A. C. Tait, then a tutor at Balliol, noted precisely this double sympathy in a particular 'school of young men' among whom he detected 'the best scholars, metaphysicians and poets of the rising age'[1]—curiously prophetic, for both Clough and Arnold. And in 1840 William Sewell, an eminent Tractarian and White's Professor of Moral Philosophy, became notorious among undergraduates for his habit of diversifying his lectures on Plato with long quotations from Carlyle—delivered with bursting enthusiasm, but always followed by warnings to his young hearers against reading this new author themselves, which was naturally an additional allurement. (Once, it is recorded, he saw the joke, and 'laughed outright at himself, and we all joined him'.)[2] Sewell it was who in 1840 greatly increased Carlyle's fame by a long review in the *Quarterly*, quoting at length, praising his 'earnestness and truth', though a little doubtful whether his writings really contained 'a complete system of church philosophy', and still asserting that, if only by a narrow margin, 'Plato was a wiser man than Mr Carlyle'. Carlyle liked the review and expressed 'a deep sympathy' for Sewell; at this date he found Puseyism 'very cheering in many ways'—one of which, however, was that it presaged the break-up of the Church of England. They had, after all, common enemies. The genuine affinity between Carlyle and Newman lay in their common ground of anti-materialism, which seemed to be reasserted in 1843 by *Past and Present* with its contrast between the age of Faith and modern Mammonism. But the rift was by then rapidly widening; Carlyle privately described *Past and Present* as 'a fiery and questionable Tract for the Times, *not* by a Puseyite',[3] and soon incorporated 'spectral Puseyism' into his large vocabulary of abuse.

[1] Quoted by the editors of *Correspondence of John Henry Newman with John Keble and Others, 1839–45*, 1917, p. 96.

[2] Lionel James, *A Forgotten Genius, William Sewell*, 1945, p. 35.

[3] *Correspondence of Carlyle and Emerson*, ii, 23.

It has seemed worth while indicating these shifts of opinion, to emphasize that there is nothing unusual in Arnold's coupling of the two 'voices', 'forty years ago'.

Arnold probably began to read Carlyle before he went to Oxford; as a boy, indeed a young boy, if he really read the essay on Irving[1] 'in its first freshness' when Irving was 'just dead', which was in 1835. Dr Arnold was one of the early admirers of Carlyle's *French Revolution*; as such he wrote to Carlyle, early in 1840, asking him to join in forming an association to investigate the condition of the poor.[2] No answer survives (but it can be imagined—Carlyle never joined associations); they met at the Prussian embassy in 1842, and a few months after, Dr Arnold, knowing of Carlyle's new work on Cromwell, invited him to visit the battlefield of Naseby. (They visited the wrong place, but Dr Arnold did not live to learn that.) At Rugby, which he called 'a temple of industrious peace', Carlyle met some of the family, including two sons; but Matthew presumably was not one, for it was in Trinity term, and I have as yet found no certain evidence of a meeting between them before 1848.[3] But this early family connection is worth remembering, if only because the Naseby visit arose from a shared interest in the new hero, Cromwell, with whom Matthew Arnold was soon to be particularly concerned.

For Cromwell was the subject of the next Newdigate Prize for English verse, the first to be set by James Garbett, the new Professor of Poetry, who had succeeded John Keble a few months before. The election of this professor followed a long pamphlet war, and had involved many, including Dr Arnold, in painful personal dilemmas; it had indeed exposed the alignment of religious parties in Oxford more clearly than anything since the Martyrs' Memorial. For the new Professor had been nominated with the sole purpose of excluding a follower of

[1] *Fraser's,* 1835. But perhaps he forgot the date of Irving's death and thought of the first appearance of the essay in a volume (1839) as its 'first freshness'.

[2] A. P. Stanley, *Life of Dr Arnold,* ch. ix.

[3] The winter of 1847–8 would seem a likely period for Arnold to meet Carlyle, for several reasons; but the earliest documentary evidence known is Clough's laconic journal entry for 13 June 1848—'Carlyle with Mat'. Clough wrote to Carlyle in 1845, and Tom Arnold met him in 1847 (information from Professor Mulhauser).

Newman and Pusey, and thus foiling their supposed conspiracy to capture a position regarded as one of authority and moral influence. The full story of that election has not yet been told; here I can only say that I suspect that the choice of Cromwell as a Newdigate subject was a sort of cold-war continuation of party warfare. It was a departure from recent precedent (from such subjects as *The Gipsies*, *Granada*, *Salsette and Elephanta*) and possibly aimed especially against the Puseyite cult of King Charles the Martyr. Those who set it may also have had in mind the recent rehabilitation of Cromwell as a 'hero' by Carlyle in *Heroes and Hero-Worship* in 1840. It would be difficult to write that Newdigate in 1842–3 without betraying one's sympathies on a controversial question.

Arnold, as a second-year undergraduate, won the Newdigate, and his *Cromwell* was published in 1843. In his poem may be heard, faintly, the voice of Newman and, more strongly, the 'puissant voice of Carlyle'. Indeed, he could have no other source at that date if he wished to glorify Cromwell. With a hint of the urbanity of his maturer years, Arnold opens non-committally, using a technique of evasion common in prize-poems—what George Gordon described as 'the great No-trick', 'the dodge of Antimachus':

> To twenty verses NO prefixed should be,
> Minutely telling all you *didn't* see.[1]

As Cromwell was born in the fen-country, we have some thirty lines on the mountains and seas beside which he was *not* born which allows the poet to be happily Wordsworthian with only a formal bow to his ostensible theme. Almost to the end he hedges a little, presenting Cromwell's career in the guise of a sketchy vision of his future; but as the heroic purpose dawns, images from Carlyle begin to appear—'shrouded chambers of his heart' and:

> life became
> Threaded and lighten'd by a track of flame
> An inward light, that with its streaming ray....

Carlyle, in exactly the same context, has 'The ray as of pure starlight and fire'. At the close of the poem Arnold dwells, just

[1] 'The Oxford Ars Poetica', 1853, in *Three Oxford Ironies*, ed. G. S. Gordon, 1927.

as Carlyle had done, on Cromwell's 'dying prayer'; and then makes his judgment, almost entirely in Carlylean terms:

> A Life—whose ways no human thought could scan,

('it was not to men's judgment that he appealed')

> A life—that was not as the life of Man;

(a Hero's, in short)

> A life—that wrote its purpose with a sword,
> Moulding itself in action, not in word!

('not used to *speak* the great inorganic thought, but to act it rather!')

> a piercing ken
> Thro' the dark chambers of the hearts of men,

('a man with his whole soul seeing').

Some of these lines should have declaimed well at the Commemoration of June 1843, when the poet was due to read his work in the Sheldonian Theatre. But the date was unfortunate: party feeling in Oxford was now high, Pusey's recent suspension from preaching was in all minds, and, the last straw, an honorary degree was to be conferred upon a Unitarian (the American Ambassador). The undergraduates made such an uproar in the Theatre that the whole ceremony had to be conducted in dumb show, and no prize compositions could be read. On the paper cover of the British Museum copy of *Cromwell*, before the printed words 'Recited in the Theatre, Oxford', a contemporary hand has written 'Not'. Arnold's prize poem is indeed a meeting-point of historical forces.

Cromwell was the one poem of Arnold's published while he was at Oxford, but it alone would be evidence enough that he was already, in his brother's words, 'cultivating his poetic gift'. In the same passage recalling Matthew's time at Oxford, Tom Arnold says 'Goethe displaced Byron in his poetical allegiance';[1] which at once recalls the command in *Sartor Resartus*, in 'The Everlasting Yea': 'Close thy Byron, open thy Goethe'. That it was Carlyle who 'opened Goethe' for him and

[1] *Passages in a Wandering Life*, 1900, p. 57.

most of his generation, Matthew Arnold several times gratefully acknowledged—in the 1863 lecture on Heine, at great length in his article 'A French Critic on Goethe' in 1877:

> We all remember how Mr. Carlyle, 'the old man eloquent', who in his younger days, fifty years ago, betook himself to Goethe for light and help, and declared his gratitude so powerfully and well, and did so much to make Goethe's name a name of might for other Englishmen also, a strong tower into which the doubter and the despairer might run and be safe. . . .

and in the lecture on Emerson:

> The greatest voice of the century came to us in those youthful years through Carlyle: the voice of Goethe. To this day,—such is the force of youthful associations,—I read the Wilhelm Meister with more pleasure in Carlyle's translation than in the original . . . never, surely, was Carlyle's prose so beautiful and pure.

And then he quotes, from that translation, part of the dirge over Mignon. He speaks of 'youthful associations', and *Wilhelm Meister* in Carlyle's translation certainly left its mark on the early poem 'Resignation'; I will venture also to record an impression that the dirge is recalled in the wonderful close of another of his early poems, 'The Church of Brou'. 'Here sleeps she in the marble, undecaying' writes Carlyle; and Arnold, 'So sleep, for ever sleep, O marble Pair!'

The pervasive influence of Goethe, to whom Arnold so constantly recurs both in his poems and his criticism, is no part of my present theme; Carlyle here is simply the vital intermediary. But there are other, and early, signs of his awareness of Carlyle's literary criticism. We too easily forget Carlyle's eminence and influence in that field. (A reviewer of 1849 praised his criticism as 'second to none that our age has produced'.)[1] That awareness is constant in those indispensable critical documents, Arnold's letters to Clough.[2] There is near-quotation from Carlyle's critical essays—Novalis praised for his 'direct communication, insight, and report', Burns for his 'fury', Clough's poems for 'striving to get breast to breast with

[1] *British Quarterly Review*, August 1849, p. 42; an article strikingly representative of the contemporary view of Carlyle. It would be interesting to know its authorship.

[2] *Letters of Matthew Arnold to Arthur Hugh Clough*, ed. H. F. Lowry.

reality'; and Byron is repudiated in Carlyle's manner—'that furiously flaring bethiefed rushlight the vulgar Byron'. There is the raising of the same issues—whether 'to *solve* the Universe' instead of 'dawdling with its painted shell' ('toying with its outside' is Carlyle's phrase); the emphasis on the spirit of the age, '*what you have to say* depends upon your age'; and Arnold's dictum that poets 'must begin with an idea of the world in order not to be prevailed over by the world's multitudinousness' adapts the Fichtean 'divine Idea of the World' underlying 'appearances', a phrase repeatedly quoted by Carlyle. And all this serious discussion exists against a background of Carlylean catchwords bandied about between the two friends as a kind of coterie-speech ('Gig-owning', 'patent Simulators'); and of Carlylean moral admonition ('I desire you should have some occupation—since the Baconian era wisdom is not found in deserts'). The picture is of two young men jointly adopting Carlyle into their private mythology; their intimacy with his writings (and probably also with his conversation) is steeped in the kind of affection, half-reverent and half-irreverent, which the young often accord their pastors and masters. One of the few references which is explicit, and entirely serious, is to Carlyle's article on Louis-Philippe in March 1848:

> how deeply restful it strikes on one amidst the heat and vain words that are everywhere just now—Yet the thoughts abstractly stated are every newspaper's—it is the style and feeling by which the beloved man appears.

The correspondence with Clough was still continuing when Arnold's first volume of poems was published, early in 1849.[1] The discussions also continue inside that volume. Alongside such poems as 'The Strayed Reveller', 'Mycerinus', 'The Forsaken Merman' are several 'occasional' pieces, some of them addressed to Clough, in which Arnold is (to use his own distinction) 'thinking aloud' rather than successfully 'making anything', and thinking in rather the same hortatory, dogmatic

[1] Arnold's later reshuffling of his poems, followed in most modern editions, makes it difficult now to disengage the unity of each separate collection; but the World's Classics edition and Oxford Standard Authors editions up to 1942 give *The Strayed Reveller* volume as a unity, and the 1948 edition in the same series gives the original readings in footnotes.

manner as in the letters. And here too the voice of Carlyle is sometimes unmistakable.[1] The sonnet 'To a Friend' (who is surely Clough) opens with the notorious line:

> Who prop, thou ask'st, in these bad days my mind?

and Arnold could count on Clough, at least, to recognize the quotation from the chapter on 'Hero-worship' in *Past and Present*, where Carlyle says that for 'these bad days' the world of heroes is the 'port and happy haven', in these 'storm-tossed seas' of 'French Revolutions, Chartism, Manchester Insurrections'; a catalogue equally apt to the year 1848. Who then, Arnold asks, are the heroes for *him*? Where lies the 'port and happy haven' now? His choice—Homer, Epictetus, Sophocles—is not Carlyle's, but his main criterion is; he looks, as Carlyle does, for the '*seeing* eye'; 'to the Poet... we say first of all, *See*';

> Who saw life steadily, and saw it whole.

The true *wholeness* of life, man's 'one nature', 'centred in a majestic unity', is the subject of another sonnet, where this unity is contrasted with some men's attempt to rend such unity into 'affections, instincts, principles and powers'; precisely Carlyle's objection in 'The Hero as Poet' and elsewhere. There, Carlyle was speaking of Shakespeare; and notions and even images from the same source are found in Arnold's early sonnet 'Others abide our question'. To Carlyle Shakespeare was 'great, quiet, complete, *self-sufficing*', 'placid', and 'victorious' in his strength (Arnold's 'that victorious brow'), his works growing (according to Carlyle's principle of 'unconsciousness') 'as the mountains and waters shape themselves'; Carlyle emphasized the enigma of his life, 'how much in Shakespeare lies hid',[2] 'we did not account him a god—while he dwelt among us' (Arnold's 'Did'st walk the earth unguessed at').

[1] See also 'To an Independent Preacher, who had preached that we should be in harmony with Nature': 'In harmony with Nature? Restless fool, Who with such heat dost preach what were to thee When true, the last impossibility.' The contortions and impatience of this opening may point to a debt of substance; the argument of the sonnet, 'Nature is cruel', has recalled to Bonnerot (p. 157) the image of Nature as a Sphinx, half beast and half divine, in the second chapter of *Past and Present*.

[2] See also the essay on Goethe: 'who knows, or can figure, what the Man Shakespeare was, in the first, or twentieth, perusal of his works?'

In all these sonnets Carlyle provides the point of departure for Arnold's thinking on the nature and conditions of the poetic vision; and in view of 'The Strayed Reveller' and 'Resignation' this may be accounted a preoccupation of the early poems. A minor one is the search for heroes and true heroism, as seen also in the sonnets 'In Emerson's Essays', 'To the Hungarian nation', and 'To the Duke of Wellington' ('who saw *one* clue to life, and followed it').

In the 1849 volume the Carlylean elements are relatively unimportant and detachable; they figure as part, and a small part, of the contents of the poet's mind, bearing a perhaps accidental relation to the growing points of his poetry. But in his first long poem, *Empedocles on Etna* (also written mainly in 1849, though not published till 1852) the relation is more essential, and I believe completely conscious; and the withdrawal of that poem in 1853 constituted, and may have been partly caused by, Arnold's rejection of an important part of Carlyle's teaching. Soon after the publication of the 1852 volume he said that his poems were 'all wrong'—there were 'clouds massed round' him, he needed 'heat and radiance'. But 'woe was upon me if I analysed not my situation'. In *Empedocles on Etna* he analysed his situation; and put it behind him. That Carlyle was an important part of it is of course generally recognized. In their commentary Professors Tinker and Lowry, though devoting only a few sentences to Carlyle in seventeen pages on the poem, admit the weight of his influence when they say: 'much of Empedocles's talk to Pausanias seems like a résumé of whole pages from *Sartor*'. The 'whole pages' are in the chapters 'The Everlasting No' and 'The Everlasting Yea', the very centre of Carlyle's view of life, and his history of its discovery. Only an analysis of the argument of both writers could exhibit the correspondence adequately; but here are two crucial verses:

> Couldst thou, Pausanias, learn
> How deep a fault is this;
> Couldst thou but once discern
> Thou hast no *right* to bliss,
> No title from the Gods to welfare and repose.

('What act of legislature was there that thou shouldst be

happy?') Or, when man is rebuked for peopling the void air with gods who may fulfil his desire for happiness:

> Fools! That so often here
> Happiness mock'd our prayer,
> I think, might make us fear
> A like event elsewhere:
> Make us, not fly to dreams, but moderate desire.

('lessening your Denominator'). The theme pervades most of the eighty-four stanzas of Empedocles's speech; and even with due allowance for Arnold's other sources, such as Epictetus and Lucretius, it still seems likely that *Sartor Resartus* was the most important.[1] Arnold's manuscript notes for this poem characterize his hero as one who 'sees things as they are . . . in their stern simplicity':

> Once read thy own breast right,
> And thou hast done with fears.
> Man gets no other light,
> Search he a thousand years.
> Sink in thyself: there ask what ails thee, at that shrine.

These lines also capture the exhilarating 'style and feeling' of Carlyle—as do many others (not only by the recurrent apostrophe to 'Fools'). Most clearly, perhaps, the final verse:

> I say: Fear not! life still
> Leaves human effort scope.
> But, since life teems with ill,
> Nurse no extravagant hope.
> Because thou must not dream, thou need'st not then despair.[2]

'Thou need'st not then despair.' It is a notorious flaw in the poem that Empedocles's subsequent despair and the catastrophe seem arbitrarily juxtaposed to, not logically developed from, the statement of his creed. Arnold's omission of much in Carlyles' affirmation, notably all the emphasis on Duty,[3] does not explain

[1] Arnold's preliminary summary of the argument of the poem in the Yale Papers (Tinker and Lowry, *Commentary*, pp. 291–2) strongly suggests this; it could almost be a description of Carlyle.

[2] Compare Carlyle's equal dismissal of fear and hope as 'false shadows' in 'The Everlasting Yea'.

[3] Even the 'gospel of work' appears only in the revised version of 1885, where at l. 269 'work' was substituted for 'fight'.

it. When Arnold said, many years after, that 'if Empedocles throws himself into Etna, his creed can hardly be meant to be one to live by',[1] he stated the difficulty, but the wrong way round. For the creed *is* presented as one 'to live by', and carries conviction to every reader whether or not he accepts it; and the more so to contemporary readers, because it was so recognizable as the creed of *Sartor Resartus*.[2]

Arnold may have written the passage with conviction, and yet outgrown it almost before he finished the poem. Certainly, a few months after publication, he was setting a different value on happiness. The poet, he writes in the 1853 Preface, should 'inspirit and rejoice the reader', and 'add to [men's] happiness', which, he says, *Empedocles* does not do. Here he does not lay the emphasis on his hero's rejection of happiness, but on the whole action of the poem, which he calls (unfairly) morbid, monotonous, and painful. But my belief that this other reason contributed to his motives for suppressing the poem, complicated as these were, is confirmed by a passage in the lecture on Emerson, where the single objection made to Carlyle's teaching is precisely that.

> He fiercely attacks the desire for happiness; his grand point in Sartor . . . is that one shall cease to desire happiness, that one should learn to say to oneself: 'What if thou wert born and predestined not to be happy, but to be unhappy!' He is wrong . . .

and the three following paragraphs develop the argument against Carlyle. The lecture, then, makes explicit one of the objections Arnold had felt to his poem thirty years before.[3]

Letters of 1852 show his mind playing on the subject; he reproaches Clough for not striving after happiness, and even dismisses 'The Scholar Gipsy', because of its 'melancholy', with the stern words 'But this is not what we want'—a key to so much of Arnold's criticism. After 1853 Carlyle also becomes 'not what we want', in common, admittedly, with most other

[1] Letter of 1867, quoted from the Yale Papers by Tinker and Lowry, *Commentary*, pp. 287–8. Arnold's concern there was to disclaim autobiographical intention.

[2] John Crombie Brown, *The Ethics of George Eliot*, 1879, treats it as a corner-stone of the novelist's teaching, and opens with a quotation from *Sartor*.

[3] He recurs to the general objection in a letter to Henry Arthur Jones in 1884 (*Letters*, ii, 267).

living English writers. In Arnold's lectures from the Chair of Poetry at Oxford, and in other critical essays before 1883, he refers to Carlyle some half-dozen times.[1] A fair representative of the tone of all such comments is a passage early in the lecture on Heine. Here Arnold uses a rhetorical device in which he became regrettably expert, which might be called presenting a bunch of snakes tied up with flowers. His line is that though 'Mr. Carlyle' is 'of course a man of genius, and no one recognizes his genius more admiringly than I do', he 'completely mistook the central current of German literature'. 'No one would dream of imputing it as a fault to him'; it might, however, be 'a misfortune, sent as a delicate chastisement' to a critic who lacks 'justness of spirit' and 'has too much of the self-will and eccentricity of a genuine son of Great Britain'. Arnold's controversial method proclaims his divergence from Carlyle ('my sinuous, easy, unpolemical way of proceeding', in contrast to Carlyle's, who once described himself as 'striking red-hot pokers into the vile Pythons of this mud-world'). By example, as well as occasional precept, Arnold's disapproval of the 'self-will and eccentricity' of Carlyle is repeatedly affirmed; indeed, disapproval of 'the eternal enemy, caprice', of the fantastic, of fanaticism in any form, becomes a principle for him. It develops from the dilemma of 1849—'For God's sake let us neither be fanatics nor yet chaff blown by the wind'[2]—and of 'A Summer Night' ('Is there no life, but these alone, Madman or slave, must man be one?'). He had come to see Carlyle as 'part man of genius, part fanatic, and part tomfool'.[3] Yet there is often an affinity with Carlyle's ideas, both in Arnold's literary and social criticism; he surely remembered him, though silently, in his use of the term Philistines, and in his attack, in *Culture and Anarchy*, upon the 'machinery' of modern civilization;[4] and much in Arnold was foreshadowed when Carlyle spoke of

[1] In addition to those referred to in the text, see 'The Incompatibles' (April to June 1881, and *Irish Essays*, 1882).

[2] Letter to Clough; the same letter refers casually to 'moral desperadoes like Carlyle', in a catalogue of contemporary distractions such as 'newspapers' and 'light profligate friends'.

[3] Letter to Tom Arnold in 1857 (see R. L. Lowe, *MP*, lii (1955), p. 264).

[4] 'Signs of the Times' (1829); the parallel is elaborated by William Savage Johnson, *Thomas Carlyle*, 1911, pp. 97–9.

literature as 'a branch of religion . . . the only branch that still shows any greenness'.[1] In 1866 there was a brief *rapprochement*; Arnold was obviously gratified to hear that Carlyle liked 'My Countrymen';[2] but still saw him as typical of Hebraism without Hellenism, because (for example) he found Socrates 'terribly at ease in Zion'.[3] *Friendship's Garland*, Arnold's most characteristic prose work, is also his most Carlylean in its satiric method (imaginary characters like the Rev. Esau Hittall and the Bottles family look back to Bobus Higgins and Plugson of Undershot), but it contains his sharpest shaft—'Avoid Carlylese like the very devil!' The dangers of Carlyle's style as a model were by 1870 alarmingly evident, and Arnold's affirmation a few years later of the ideal of 'regularity, uniformity, precision, balance'[4] was timely, though chilling. In short, Carlyle continued to be to Arnold 'not what we want'. (Of their renewed personal contact, a single anecdote is current, recording their separate comments after one conversation—'Poor Mat!' and 'Poor old Carlyle!')[5] Arnold summed up his radical objection in a letter of 1881, at Carlyle's death:

> He was always 'carrying coals to Newcastle', . . . preaching earnestness to a nation that had it by nature, but was less abundantly supplied with other things.

Such, then, is Arnold's reasoned policy towards Carlyle, from 1853 to 1881. None of his comments suggests that 'the style and feeling' of 'the beloved man' still maintained their hold. But in the poetry, 'airs from the Eden of youth', words, read long before,[6] 'haunt the memory still'. From many examples, I shall mention three, all from *New Poems* (1867): the unusual image of the icebergs in 'Obermann Once More' comes straight from a passage in *The French Revolution*, through an obvious association of context; and the ending of 'Dover Beach' ('where ignorant armies clash by night') recalls the noble close of 'Characteristics': 'Here in earth we are as Soldiers, fighting in a foreign

[1] 'Characteristics' (1831).

[2] *Letters*, i, 317.

[3] *Culture and Anarchy*; see my note in *Notes and Queries*, March 1955, on the probable source.

[4] Introduction to *Six Selected Lives from Johnson's Lives of the Poets*, 1878.

[5] D. A. Wilson, *Carlyle in Old Age*, p. 464.

[6] Arnold's *Notebooks* record no reading of Carlyle during these years.

land; that understand not the plan of campaign. . . .'[1] In my third instance, the 'Stanzas from the Grande Chartreuse', of which I shall speak more fully, the echoes from 'Characteristics'[2] amount almost to conscious quotation; which may be the less surprising, when we find that the conception of this poem goes back to Arnold's Oxford period; its composition appears to have been spread over several years,[3] perhaps to the detriment of its coherence as argument. That argument as a whole I would not claim to interpret; I suggest only that this poem, which is, with 'The Scholar Gipsy', Arnold's most enigmatic and his most widely quoted piece, provides the most striking example of those voices heard at Oxford 'forty years ago', for Newman's voice is as clear as Carlyle's.

Arnold draws most from that section of 'Characteristics' in which Carlyle comments on the vanishing of faith and contrasts the present with the past: 'no Cloister now opens its religious shades; the Thinker must . . . wander homeless'; in the poem Arnold is 'wandering between' the 'two worlds' of the 'dead' cloister and the 'unborn' new world:

> Wandering between two worlds, one dead,
> The other powerless to be born,
> With nowhere yet to rest my head,
> Like these, on earth I wait forlorn.

Carlyle goes on to speak of those 'nobler' men, who 'have dared to say No and cannot yet say Yea'; these, in an age of un-faith, have the task of evoking 'by the strong cry of their soul's agony' the vanished presence of the godlike. 'This miracle has been accomplished', by Goethe; 'but . . . our land knows not of it. Behold a Byron, in melodious tones, cursing his day', a 'Shelley, filling the earth with inarticulate wail' ('What helps it now, that Byron bore . . . What boots it, Shelley, that the breeze Carried

[1] Other parallels have been often noted, including one in *The Bothie*, which is actually nearer to another passage in Carlyle ('The Hero as Priest'); and I do not propose Carlyle as the single 'source' any more than for the images of isolation in 'Yes: in the sea of life'. (See above, pp. 164–6.)

[2] This parallel was first pointed out by Bonnerot (pp. 175–7), though it was doubtless evident to any reader of both the poem and the essay. The other parallels and references in the poem have not been suggested before.

[3] Probably 1849–52; see Tinker and Lowry, *Commentary*, pp. 14, 249, 338. Arnold published it in *Fraser's*, 1855, and revised and collected it in 1867.

thy lovely wail away ...'). Carlyle continues: 'Friedrich Schlegel ... flies back to Catholicism as a child might to its slain mother's bosom and cling there' ('With nowhere yet to rest my head ... Not as their friend or child I speak'). Finally Carlyle defines the modern dilemma in the words, 'The Old has passed away; but alas, the New appears not in its stead; the Time is still in pangs of travail with the new' ('two worlds, one dead, the other powerless to be born'). That figure was a favourite with Carlyle, found also in *Sartor*, and twice in *Past and Present*; and repeated also by Arnold, in 'Obermann Once More'.

In the 'Grande Chartreuse' we may also hear Carlyle's voice from the first lecture of *Heroes*, which especially impressed Arnold, as is seen from his choice of story in *Balder Dead.*[1] A memory of Carlyle's passionate brooding over Norse mythology (then little known to the common reader) may account for Arnold's unexpected comparison of himself to a Greek 'before some fallen Runic stone':

> Not as their friend, or child, I speak!
> But as on some far northern strand,
> Thinking of his own Gods, a Greek
> In pity and mournful awe might stand
> Before some fallen Runic stone—
> For both were faiths, and both are gone.

'Pity and mournful awe' describes the style and feeling of a crucial paragraph in the lecture, a paragraph which hinges on the words 'It was a truth, and is none' ('For both were faiths, and both are gone').

The Carlylean echoes occur in this poem the more naturally since part of it is even *about* Carlyle:

> For rigorous teachers seized my youth,
> And purged its faith, and trimm'd its fire,
> Shew'd me the high white star of Truth,
> There bade me gaze, and there aspire;
> Even now their whispers pierce the gloom:
> *What dost thou in this living tomb?*

[1] Carlyle related the story of Balder's death and Hermod's journey both there and in ch. i of *Oliver Cromwell's Letters and Speeches,* 1854. I have said the less about this matter because of Mr Frederick Page's illuminating study of *Balder* (see above, p. 216, n. 2).

Forgive me, masters of the mind!

The 'rigorous teachers' who seized the poet's youth, 'And purged its faith, and trimm'd its fire' must be Dr Arnold, Carlyle, and perhaps Emerson. (The 1855 version, 'prun'd its faith and quench'd its fire', is less sympathetic.) They are the 'masters of the mind' of whom he asks forgiveness for his truancy in the cloister; and the guilty awareness of 'Ev'n now their whispers pierce the gloom: *What dost thou in this living tomb?*' might well belong to 1850 or 1851, when Carlyle had just declared himself so strongly against the Anglo-Catholic movement, in 'Jesuitism' and the *Life of Sterling*. This brings me to one more reference in the poem: except for writing that *Life*, a short work, Carlyle was in the early 1850's 'clear for *silence*', and was very vocal about his determination—he was also recommending silence to others, and especially (as usual) to poets. Arnold's words in 1855 are topical:

> Achilles ponders in his tent,
> The kings of modern thought are dumb;
> Silent they are, though not content,
> And wait to see the future come. . . .

Finally, I return to 1883 and the Emerson lecture; and first, the exceptionally harassing conditions of its composition.[1] Arnold left England for his 'invasion of America' in October 1883, armed with two of the three lectures which he had announced for delivery; 'Literature and Science', already given as the Rede lecture at Cambridge; 'Numbers', finished only a few days before he sailed, had 'nearly broken his heart'; of 'Emerson' he had 'not written a word'. However, so far he does not seem to have been anxious. He took the newly published *Correspondence of Carlyle and Emerson* to read on the boat, and hoped for further inspiration from the sight of Concord and Boston Bay. He had a little margin, for he was to do several tours with the first two lectures before giving the third. But his plan went wrong, for two reasons—America and Carlyle. Arrived in New York, he wrote to his sister, 'Oh, my

[1] My account is drawn from *Letters*, ii, 217–38, and Charles Eliot Norton's manuscript note on the lecture. (References in Arnold's letters make it clear that some of them were mis-dated by the editor.)

dear Fan, how and when am I to write it? The blaring publicity of this place is beyond all I had any idea of.' His lecturing took him all over New England ('very fatiguing'); he was not well heard, and lessons in elocution (from a 'Professor Churchill') made further inroads on his time. Somehow or other he wrote a first draft of the Emerson lecture, but the date of delivery drew near, there was no time for a fair copy, and the Boston printer would not set it up from his roughly pencilled pages (which indeed look as if they had been written in trains, and possibly dropped into Boston Bay). At the eleventh hour, Charles Eliot Norton and the Harvard University Press came to the rescue, the lecture was set up, revised in type, and delivered.[1] But though the lecture was liked by such people as Norton and W. D. Howells, it aroused 'the provincial ire' of many Bostonians—doubtless for the brevity and coolness of its tribute to Emerson. It is easy to see how this came about. The harsh pressure of time and place and the delights of re-reading Carlyle—Arnold had *Sartor* with him as well as the *Correspondence*—had driven the lecture off its course. Arnold tried to write about Emerson, but Carlyle kept breaking in. Emerson is led up to slowly, as we have seen, through Newman, Carlyle, and Goethe; a few paragraphs are then devoted to a disparaging account of his poetry, after which Arnold returns to Carlyle, who has 'surpassingly powerful qualities of expression, far more powerful than Emerson's, and reminding me of the great poets,—of even Shakespeare himself' (and this although 'he is not a great writer'!). Then Arnold falls back on the letters, and quotes no fewer than six passages from Carlyle's, each with its delighted comment—'What a description! . . . What a portrait! . . . What touches! . . . How inimitable it all is!' We cannot blame him; Carlyle's letters, as Sterling said, 'have the writer's signature in every word, not only at the end'. Arnold tries to remember that they are only letters; that Carlyle is not a great 'literary master', for he cannot 'subdue his materials'; he is 'too

[1] Norton's reward was 'the smudged original', now in the Houghton Library at Harvard, one of the very few prose manuscripts of Arnold's to survive. The proofs are also there, and Arnold's revisions both at this stage and later (when he published the lecture in *Macmillan's Magazine*, 1884) are of great interest, though not affecting the substance of the references to Carlyle. Some were noted by E. K. Brown, *Studies in the text of Matthew Arnold's Prose Works*, 1935, pp. 114–17.

wilful, too turbid, too vehement'. Then Emerson is tried as a philosopher; but Carlyle breaks in again, for it is he who 'perfectly formulates' Emerson's 'defects' (which means two more quotations from Carlyle's letters). After other digressions, and within sight of the close, Arnold begins to produce the rabbit from the hat. It is Emerson's 'hopeful, serene, beautiful temper'; because of this his work is 'much more important' than Carlyle's ('much' was removed in revision). But not in substance: for 'let us be just to Carlyle, provoking as he often is . . . the scope and upshot of his teaching are true' (a major admission); but 'consider Carlyle's temper!' One more quotation, from a letter of Carlyle's, this time gloomy and dyspeptic; so that the comparison comes out in favour of Emerson, who is sanguine, cheerful, hopeful, whereas 'Carlyle's perverse attitude cuts him off from hope'. And then Arnold launches his argument against *Sartor*, remembering, as I have suggested, his rejection of *Empedocles*. This final sleight-of-hand does not redeem the lecture, considered as a tribute to Emerson. We cannot help feeling that though Emerson is the text, Carlyle is the theme; Carlyle, with all his faults ('wilful' and 'vehement'), a man of genius, with powers of expression akin to Shakespeare's, a great moral force, a teacher of the truth—albeit, on one point, mistaken.

The poet has triumphed, in Arnold as well as Carlyle. The whole lecture is framed in a characteristic poetic posture of Arnold's, the retrospective: 'O master of my wandering youth, Though left this many a year.' As in 'Obermann Once More', 'The Terrace at Berne', and 'Thyrsis', he looks back, and hears again the 'puissant voice' which had moved him, forty years ago.

The decorum of the occasion may seem to have suffered; yet the lecture was not wholly inappropriate; Carlyle's writings were even more admired in New England than in England, then as now. In any case, the judgment 'stands'—as Arnold's one attempt at a reconciliation between his early and later views of Carlyle, between his response as a poet, and his sense of 'what we want'; and more than that—between those two levels of apprehension which both he and Carlyle have distinguished. I shall close by quoting each of them once more:

Of our Thinking, we might say, it is but the mere upper surface that we shape into articulate Thoughts;—underneath the region of argument and conscious discourse, lies the region of meditation; here in its quiet mysterious depths, dwells what vital force is in us; here, if aught is to be created, and not merely manufactured and communicated, must the work go on.

Below the surface stream, shallow and light,
Of what we *say* we feel,—below the stream,
As light, of what we *think* we feel—there flows
With noiseless current strong, obscure and deep,
The central stream of what we feel indeed.

XIX

NEWMAN THE WRITER

WHEN A great author writes mainly 'prose of thinking' there is the danger that his writing may come to belong too much to its special field and too little to literature as a whole. Pusey, let us say, was a theologian; his writings are prose of thinking; but the literary critic, for reasons I shall imply later in speaking of Newman, is quite willing to leave both him and his writings to theologians and ecclesiastical historians. With Newman, however, it must always be different. Some of his works are very much read. I recall that when books were scarce in the late war a bookseller in central London told me that, if he had had them, he could have sold two copies of the *Apologia* daily. And there can be few educated people who do not honour *The Idea of a University*.[1] Both those books are of general interest: they

[1] As originally printed the sentence ran '. . . who have not read *The Idea of a University*', but the guess there made has proved to be badly out. Even though the idea of a university has been much in the air of recent years, I have not seen the book much referred to. My present guess is made on p. 272 below, where I say more vaguely that Newman's writings 'speak, and will go on doing so, to the cultivated'. Evidently they do not speak to all the cultivated. When reviewing the selection which my essay introduced Mr Raymond Mortimer contested the truth of my original guess. He thought that if I enquired of my Birkbeck colleagues I should find among them few readers of *The Idea*. For forty years I have been mistaking the implications of what I read as a boy in the excellent pages of Quiller-Couch: in ch. ii of his *Art of Writing* he recommended *The Idea* so warmly to his Cambridge audience that I assumed that his recommendation had been taken by the tens of thousands, Cambridge men and others, who admired his criticism as I did (and still do). Quiller-Couch was wrong in thinking that the lectures that made up *The Idea* are 'fragmentary'. They were designed as a conspectus of knowledge. Most of the 'cultivated' who read them to-day have to make allowances. They find Newman's calm assumption that theology can be shown to be the queen of the sciences a delusion. For most of the cultivated theology is only admissible, if at all, as a part of philosophy, and then mainly because of its historical interest. They see how wrong is the notion that a university exists to teach rather than to teach and research—they will prefer to require university teachers to research so that their research can improve their teaching both in accuracy and brightness. Quiller-Couch was recommending the book for reasons other than the soundness of its schemes of thinking, and those reasons still hold good. To put it briefly, the book is a pleasure to read because of the way it is written and because of its brilliant fragments of truth, whether you are a Catholic or an atheist, a scientist or a humanist, a Russian or an Englishman.

are of as much interest to the secular-minded as to the religious. But if we read much further it is because we are interested in the 'ecclesiastical' matter Newman usually treats of (by 'ecclesiastical' I mean pertaining to the doctrines, character and material being of the Roman and English churches): we go to him as we go to Pusey or his modern equivalent, and should feel equally profited if his writings had been written by Pusey. This sort of reader seeks first his matter and no doubt loves it the more because it comes to him as, say, meaning does in a sung service. Or alternatively we may read on because we like great literature, and know that Newman's writings never cease to deal with the general matters literature likes to deal with. I grant that the reader who mixes these two interests is the best sort of reader for Newman. The perfect reader is one whose mind is as like his as possible—as much that of a sensuous poet as it is that of a thinker and worshipper. The case for meeting an author with what, comparatively speaking, is identity of mind has been much discussed in recent times. It was well urged by Coleridge on behalf of George Herbert:

> G. Herbert is a true poet, but a poet *sui generis*, the merits of whose poems will never be felt without a sympathy with the mind and character of the man. To appreciate this volume [*The Temple*], it is not enough that the reader possesses a cultivated judgment, classical taste, or even poetic sensibility, unless he be likewise a *Christian*, and both a devout and a *devotional* Christian. But even this will not quite suffice. He must be an affectionate and dutiful child of the Church, and from habit, conviction and a constitutional predisposition to ceremoniousness, in piety as in manners, find her forms and ordinances aids of religion, not sources of formality; for religion is the element in which he lives, and the region in which he moves.[1]

This desideratum applies also to readers of Newman. The ideal reader for a writer who is a great writer, and who writes mainly about the ecclesiastical, must be both a literary critic and a believer, and both of them at a high intensity. In practice we find few readers to fill this bill. Writers on Newman tend to be disproportionately one thing or the other. They proceed as by a division of labour, which is the consequence no doubt of a

[1] *Coleridge's Miscellaneous Criticism*, ed. T. M. Raysor, 1936, p. 244.

cleavage of ordinary human minds into species—one sort of mind deals best with a certain thing, another sort with some other thing. Among these species the ecclesiastical exists at a remove from the others. The literary critic can take on historians (say Gibbon) and politicians (say Burke) and art critics (say Ruskin) more comfortably than he can take on Newman. And the reverse is true. The ecclesiastical writer is usually far from being the literary critic. An interesting example of this separation exists in one of the best papers ever written on Newman—the late Father Henry Tristram's 'On Reading Newman',[1] which purports to do nothing more than give the reader a sense of whereabouts amid Newman's many writings, but does a great deal more than that. Tristram was one of the most devoted, learned and wise of Newman scholars—there is no one yet to fill the gap he has left—but I cannot help feeling that his interest in Newman's Catholicism depressed Newman for him as a writer. In that essay he makes one misvaluation, as it seems to me, which strikes at Newman's literary credentials. I shall concern myself with it later on.

2

Everybody agrees that Newman had many dazzling gifts. He was a distinguished holder of several public offices. He was a priest and so looked up to as an example in point of piety, learning, and morality, a preacher, an instructor, a confidant and a counsellor, and his parish—to judge by his postbag—represented the whole of intellectual England. He was Fellow and Tutor of a college, the most intellectually distinguished in the Oxford of his day. He was one of the moving spirits of a great rebellion of thought. He was the centre of at least one informal and one formal fraternity. He founded and directed a school for boys. He edited magazines. He was a fashionable lecturer. He was head of a newly founded university. He became a Cardinal. And while holding all these offices he continued to be a prolific and much-read writer, unmatched for virtuosity: Polonius would have enjoyed listing the kinds—the controversial writings, tracts, poems, dialogues, essays,

[1] Contributed to *John Henry Newman: Centenary Essays*, 1945, pp. 223–41.

histories, open letters, biographies, autobiographies, lectures, treatises, novels, sermons, editorial prefacings, and annotations. In a word he was one of the supreme geniuses of nineteenth-century England. And a supremely literary genius. If we were to take upon ourselves the boldness of arranging his gifts in order of greatness, that for writing would, I think, come out near the top. There will always be a variety of views about his character and personality; as a leader of men he has had his dubious admirers; but to the literary critic he must always appear a writer among those whom it is 'vain to blame and useless to praise'. And so completely did his pen express his self, his affairs and his whole mental life—for so it seems—that his writings survive as a permanent medium for all of them in all their fullness.

He himself did not encourage people to detach his literary gift from what it served and to rank it so high. 'I am hard-hearted', he wrote in 1848, 'towards the mere literary ethos, for there is nothing I despise and detest more.'[1] It was a thing often said in the age of Victoria. He would not have cared to be a poet as Keats had been a poet, or, much as he admired the Waverley novels, a novelist as Scott had been a novelist. He must have despised what he came to see of the movement of 'art for art's sake', which in revolt against the use, or over-use, of literature for the sake of practical matters grew strong in the latter half of the nineteenth century. Few of his writings are created without reference to contemporary affairs—the sort of contemporary affairs to which newspapers like *The Times* and the *Guardian* give their best attention. By the time he had many works to look back on he saw them as so much a part of the big public interests of their time as to fall into the category of things prompted by occasions. In the Advertisement before the *Lectures and Essays on University Subjects*, 1859, he noted (in the third person) that 'It has been the fortune of the author through life, that the Volumes which he has published have grown for the most part out of the duties which lay upon him, or the circumstances of the moment.' And again, in 1874:

> What I have written has been for the most part what may be called official, works done in some office I held or engagement I had made

[1] Quoted by Tristram, op. cit., p. 224.

—all my Sermons are such, my Lectures on the Prophetical Office, on Justification, my Essays in the *British Critic*, and translation of St. Athanasius—or has been from some especial call, or invitation, or necessity, or emergency, as my Arians, Anglican Difficulties, 'Apologia' or Tales. The Essay on Assent is nearly the only exception. And I *cannot* write without such a *stimulus*. I feel to myself going out of the way, or impertinent, and I write neither with spirit nor with point.[1]

Many great works have been prompted by occasions and in the nineteenth century there was a higher proportion of them than in the eighteenth century and perhaps also the seventeenth century; but no nineteenth-century author wrote so high a proportion of them as Newman.

All these self-descriptions are perfectly satisfactory, but on one level only. They ignore what, if I read him rightly, has much importance—the necessity which drove him not only to write so much and to write so clearly but to write so beautifully. To judge by results, if by no other evidence, he was born to be a writer—just as Dickens was, and Thackeray, and the Brontës, and Tennyson, and Ruskin (who believed he was born to be a painter)[2]. Newman began as a born writer should—by copying the styles of the writers he admired: 'At the age of fourteen a sort of passion for writing seems to have possessed him.'[3] And

There are many boyish anticipations or buddings of his after thoughts noted down at about this date [1817]. On reading these later in life, Dr. Newman is severe on his early style:

The unpleasant style in which it is written arises from my habit as a boy, *to compose*. I seldom wrote without an eye to style, and since my taste was bad my style was bad. I wrote in style as another might write in verse, or sing instead of speaking, or dance instead of walking.[4]

And if this is true, we must not take his insistence on occasions for more than it is worth. In the essay I have already named, Tristram drew from the documents the following conclusion:

[1] Wilfrid Ward, *The Life of John Henry Cardinal Newman based on his Private Journals and Correspondence*, 1912, ii, 400.

[2] Augustine Birrell, *Frederick Locker-Lampson*, 1920, p. 109.

[3] *Letters*, i, 19.

[4] *Letters*, i, 25. See also the letter to John Hayes, 13 April 1869, reprinted in *Newman: Prose and Poetry*, Reynard Library, 1957, pp. 802 f.

'whatever [Newman] was . . . he certainly was not a writer, a man of letters, *de son métier*. He only became such incidentally, as it were, in implementing his vocation as a priest, whether in his Anglican or in his Catholic days'.[1] This fails to allow that Newman became a printed author before he became a priest—it was as an undergraduate that he helped produce *St Bartholomew's Eve*. And I shall have something to say later that bears on the word 'incidentally'. Those are small points, but Tristram, I think, soon went wrong more thoroughly: he believed that when Newman had his pen in his hand he was working against the grain, and so gives the impression that in less provoking times he would have written little or nothing. 'He had no joy in writing, as such'—that was Tristram's view, and he based it on the much corrected state of Newman's manuscripts, and on his describing the painful production of the books as 'mental childbearing'.

Of his corrections Newman speaks on several occasions, as, for instance, in a letter of 1838:

> My book on Justification has taken incredible time. I am quite worn out with correcting. I do really think that every correction I make is for the better, and that I am not wasting time in an over-fastidious way, or even making it worse than it was; but I can only say this—openings for correction are inexhaustible.
>
> I write, I write again: I write a third time in the course of six months. Then I take the third: I literally fill the paper with corrections, so that another person could not read it. I then write it out fair for the printer. I put it by; I take it up; I begin to correct again: it will not do. Alterations multiply, pages are re-written, little lines sneak in and crawl about. The whole page is disfigured; I write again; I cannot count how many times this process is repeated.[2]

Nor did the correcting end with the printing of the manuscripts. However satisfactory a manuscript had seemed its printed form always prompted further revisions for the second edition and for each successive one. The remarks I have just quoted are perhaps recalled a quarter of a century later in a letter to W. G. Ward—the most important of all the documents on this matter:

> I suspect your psychological facts [Ward had sent him two of his publications], e.g. you speak at p. 26 of the 'keen and constant

[1] op. cit., pp. 223 f. [2] *Letters*, ii, 250.

pleasure which intellectual processes afford.' I am far from denying there is a pleasure, and one providentially assigned, as pleasant flavour to food; but, if you mean that 'keen and constant pleasure' attends ordinarily on intellectual processes, well, let them say so, who feel it. My own personal experience is the other way. It is one of my sayings, (so continually do I feel it) that the composition of a volume is like gestation and childbirth. I do not think that I ever thought out a question, or wrote my thoughts, without great pain, pain reaching to the body as well as to the mind. It has made me feel practically, that labour '*in sudore vultus sui*,' is the lot of man, and that ignorance is truly one of his four wounds. It has been emphatically a *penance*; and in consequence I have hardly written anything, unless I was *called* to do it, e.g. I had to provide a sermon weekly for the pulpit, &c. I recollect a friend asked me, soon after writing my volume on Justification, whether it was not interesting to write, and my answer was to the effect that 'it was the painful relieving of an irritation,' as a man might go to a dentist, not for 'keen and constant pleasure,' but with the mingled satisfaction and distress of being rid of pain *by* pain. When I wrote the Arians six years earlier, I was so exhausted at length, that for some days as it approached finishing, I could scarce keep from fainting. The exercise which most nearly has approached to pleasure, has been the finding parallel passages to passages in St. Athanasius, or writing verses, processes which have not much of active intellect in them. I might say a great deal more on this subject; but I have said enough as giving the testimony of at least one person.

What I feel, others may feel. Others again may feel *neither* your pleasure *nor* my pain. At all events, I think you must not take for *granted*, what all men do not recognize to be true.

What has been my own motive cause in writing may be that of others,—the sight of a truth, and the desire to show it to others. Juvenal says, 'Facit indignatio versus.' I do not feel this in the case of verse; I do, in the case of prose.

I am far from denying of course, that, if one thinks one has done a thing well, one may be tempted to be pleased at it. But here it is the *work* effected not the *process* that pleases. 'When the shore is won at last, Who will count the billows passed?' Our Lord says, 'When she is delivered of the child, she remembereth not the anguish, *because*, &c.' Of course she may idolize her child, for the very reason that it has cost her pain, but pain never can be 'keen and constant pleasure'; and she never would bear a child for the sake of the childbirth.

Not at all denying, then, that there is a class of minds such as your own, Sir W. Hamilton's, Lord Brougham's, and the Academics, to whom exercises of intellect are simply 'keen and constant pleasure', I cannot think it is more than one class.[1]

It is clear from these accounts that Newman was pleased at least with the results of his labours, as were his readers, even though one of them drew an unacceptable inference as to the 'interestingness' of the process. As to its pleasure Newman was not conclusive: he granted that intellectual processes have a pleasure to them as pleasant as flavours are in food, but he also found in them pain. Not all pain, however, is painful and nothing else, and Newman's must have been qualified into some sort of pleasure by the warmth of his application, and his persisting prospect of success.[2] The labour of writing he might liken to battling with billows, but there are some swimmers who are confident that they can gain the shore. And though it was on the completion of the process that Newman spoke pleasantly of 'little lines [that] sneak in and crawl about', the timing may not be significant, for it is obvious that he enjoyed the use of the pen as a deft instrument. His handwriting had a rapid economy not without elegance,[3] even when modified under stress; and the business of making lines sneak and crawl accommodatingly cannot but please in some sort. We may contrast Shelley. He believed that 'when composition begins, inspiration is already on the decline',[4] and accordingly his manuscripts are without trace of pleasure—Trelawny describes that of 'Ariel to Miranda . . .' as like 'a sketch for a marsh overgrown with bulrushes, and the blots for wild ducks'.[5] Newman is another matter. I cannot but compare him with Pope, whose handwriting was aesthetically similar to his, and who explained his numerous and constant corrections by 'I corrected because

[1] Ward's *Life*, i, 637 f.

[2] Cf. the letter written after the success of the lectures in the University at Dublin: 'I have been prospered here in my lectures beyond my most sanguine expectations . . . my good Lord has never left me, nor failed me in my whole life' (Fr McGrath, *Newman's University*, 1951, p. 161).

[3] Cf. Charles Reding in *Loss and Gain*, Reynard Library *Newman*, p. 321: 'I know persons . . . who believe that handwriting is an indication of calling and character.'

[4] *Defence of Poetry*, para. 10 from the end.

[5] *Recollections of the Last Days of Shelley and Byron*, ed. E. Dowden, 1923, p. 50.

it was as pleasant to me to correct as to write'[1]—an airy account, but airy merely because in accord with Addisonian manners. Only one valid inference can finally, I think, be drawn from the evidence of fact and comment—namely that Newman did not belong to the less common of the two classes of writers distinguished by him, the writers whose words came right straight off, but to the class of inky strugglers. And so the presence or absence of correction has at bottom nothing to do with the presence or absence of joy. For him composition in all its fulness was the only means of making inspiration profitable to great numbers of men—or fully profitable even to himself. Without the aid of words in their concretest and most exacting form, he could not come by his sense as a thing established in the shades of meaning he was so well gifted to discriminate. He had no choice but to *work* at expression, but then he was never one to jib at work.

Nor, finally, do we lack external evidence that pains could sometimes be joyful to the point of hilarity—as they were for Cowper when he wrote 'John Gilpin':

> The author's enjoyment of this task is illustrated by an anecdote told by Mr. Kegan Paul in his 'Biographical Sketches': 'A friend, also a convert, related not long since how, in the winter of 1847, he was a very constant visitor to Dr Newman and was puzzled at finding him so frequently laughing to himself over the manuscript on which he was then engaged, till he said: "You do not know what I have been doing. Poor Burns, the late High Church publisher, a convert like ourselves, has got into difficulties, owing to his change of faith and I am going to give him this manuscript [that of *Loss and Gain*] to see if it may not help him a little out of them". '[2]

Evidently no laughter issued from the writer of *Lectures on Justification*, but I do not think we need go to the other extreme and believe with Tristram that Newman found 'no joy in writing, as such'. Some pleasure must also have come from one of the objects that the corrections had in view. They were not solely intellectual. If they had been only that, the achievement of clarity and order would have been enough. Newman's labours sought also sensuousness, both of music and colour. These are objects of poetical composition and we have Newman's

[1] Preface to *Works* 1717, para. 6. [2] Ward's *Life*, i, 191.

word for it that for him their pursuit 'most nearly ... approached to pleasure'.

3

Nor must we take 'occasions' in too strict a sense. Many were invited. If you take orders you expect to have to deliver sermons. If you become a Fellow of an Oxford college and are also (as you had to be at that time) in orders, you may expect to be asked to preach before the University. If you become eminent in a cause, people on both sides will look to you for guidance or for 'a statement'. Many occasions Newman consciously laid himself open for. Of the rest several were potent only because he allowed them to be. The occasion for his writing *The Tamworth Reading Room* was the report of the speech delivered by a politician in his far-away constituency when opening a library for working men. The occasion for *Who's to Blame?* was less pointed still—Newman wrote it because, like the rest of England, he had read about the conduct of the Crimean War. Even the *Apologia* sprang from a *chosen* occasion—there had been many taunts against him before he chose to reply to Kingsley's. The same is true even of the novel, *Loss and Gain*—there had been many novels about religious converts before Miss Harris's *From Oxford to Rome*. And when he wrote without the sort of stimulus he had in mind, which in varying degrees we can call public, he did not step outside his usual matter—the undergraduate poem is on a religious subject, the *Dream of Gerontius* deals with a theme he had treated in the sermons, the *Grammar of Assent* follows on from the university sermons. In other words, both when he is free and when he is called, he writes on a matter one and the same. He is not a writer who wants to write on one matter but is obliged by duties to write on another. Even if his so-called occasions had not cropped up, we should have had writings, in the main, similar to those we have. Do not therefore let us take his speaking of occasions too seriously.

There was, I think, a psychological reason for his appeal to occasions. Newman subscribed to a then rather old-fashioned conception of the gentleman. We know how charming were his social manners on almost all of the thousands of recorded occasions. In his writings Matthew Arnold found the same 'delicacy' and 'urbanity'. His written words are often beautifully apologetic if he fears that there will be offence or crudity in some point or other he is driven to make. Alternative to this humility and charm there is of course fierceness and sharpness; but that comes from between the cracks. The man and writer when, as almost invariably, he lived up to his ideal for himself, was extremely polite. We can see him as wanting to write under certain conditions, one of which was the psychological or social condition of having an occasion that could be agreed to be public enough to allow him not to seem obtrusive: in the passage quoted above he speaks of his need not to feel 'impertinent'. But again we should note that his required easiness on that score is represented as a literary requirement also. Unless he felt welcome to write, the product would lack the prized literary virtues of 'spirit' and 'point'.

As final reason there was his strong need to feel assured that when he spoke he would be speaking to men. How strong that need was can be illustrated by one of the most remarkable passages he ever wrote, a passage that is one of the additions made from time to time to the manuscript account of his tour in Sicily. The particular addition was made at Littlemore in 1840, when he was taking to his 'deathbed' as an Anglican:[1] 'The thought keeps pressing on me, while I write this, what am I writing it for? . . .'

In any man's life there must be several 'spots of time' when thoughts like these are thought, but few, if any, when they are written down. Newman provided this exception, and a hundred like it, because he was a man who found writing a solace in itself, and also because, for as profound a reason, he longed to have readers—at some near point of time for preference, but if not that, at a later. I think we can discern in much of the writing, public and private, his strong need to achieve communication. This need accounts for the clarity of everything he wrote. Of the millions of his written sentences there can be few which do not convey what they were meant to convey. But along with the need for light went the need for sweetness—or,

[1] I quote the passage below, p. 262.

at times, sharpness. He wished to communicate something definite and to communicate it personally. The motto he chose for his cardinalate was *cor ad cor loquitur*—heart speaks to heart. For many reasons his words had often to be written words, and as means of expression written words have notorious limitations, especially where they are speaking the matters of the heart. Communication of the most piercing kind comes usually by other even more primitive means. 'Voices melt us, looks subdue us, deeds inflame us'[1]—that names three other powerful means. In his sermons he could rely on two of them in addition to words, and he relied on them to some purpose, for we have many accounts of the thrilling experience of hearing and seeing him preach. His lectures, too, availed themselves of the means of words, voice and look. When writings were written only for cold print Newman used many arts to suggest the completer range of medium. His printed words carry as much personal force as any words ever have. They take on as much of tones, looks, and gestures as possible. For us who never heard his voice, the print seems to speak, and the famous face looks out from the page.

4

Newman loved the means of communication and the art of making the most of them. We are fortunate that it was so, for he might not have cared. In the *Apologia* he speaks of his 'mistrust of the reality of material phenomena' and his 'rest[ing] in the thought of two and two only supreme and luminously self-evident beings, myself and my Creator'.[2] The words he designed for his tombstone spoke the same 'fact': 'JOHANNES HENRICUS NEWMAN/ EX UMBRIS ET IMAGINIBUS/ IN VERITATEM/ DIE——A.S. 18[ ]/ REQUIESCAT IN PACE.' Feeling the things of the world to be shadows, he might have been haunted by their insubstantiality to the point of neglecting the material a writer must use. We recall the Scotch-Calvinist gardener in *The Newcomes* who handled the melons and pineapples 'provisionally, and until the end of the world'.[3] In his writings, however

[1] See Reynard Library *Newman*, p. 101.
[2] See id., p. 581 [Ward's edn., p. 108].
[3] Thackeray, *The Newcomes*, ch. iii.

Newman handled earthly things *as if* they were real, as if he were as sure of them as he was of himself and his Creator. In his writings he seems as thoroughly at home among things as Chaucer or Shakespeare or Pope or Dickens. He speaks—if we add his unpublished to his published writings—with complete freedom: in the manuscript text of his account of the Sicilian tour he refers to piles and Epsom salts. There is nothing particularly literary in the mere possessing of this freedom, but it helps to produce the keen effects a piece of writing is the better for. Newman is constantly keen, however, not just because of his free speech but because his mind is sensuous, and therefore ready with the imagery which the sensuous mind contributes freely to thinking and feeling. He was sensitive enough as a physical organism to be sharply aware of the finger-tips of his Sicilian servant when applying vinegar to his nose, and he was agile enough of mind to connect the sensation with one stored in his memory—he writes of them as 'great bullet-tips'. Everywhere in his writings is the proof of this sensitiveness of sense and this prehensile agility of mind. It is the most obvious of the proofs that he is a poet. And it serves him very well as a philosopher. He is often dealing with abstract matter and dealing with it for the benefit of as many readers as he can gather. So that none shall turn aside because of too great an abstraction, he uses much imagery. He 'remembereth that we are dust'. His very account of thinking is as of a physical process.[1]

Finally, it is by virtue of much of his matter that Newman stands square with our great writers. He writes often about what literature most prefers to deal with. His constant attention to the 'scope and nature' of Christianity enfolds an attention as close to quotidian affairs. He is as alert to the trivial round as Wordsworth or Hardy; as alert as Matthew Arnold to those urgent public matters of the day—e.g. cholera, mesmerism, the goldfields—which pitilessly exact from journalists their 'nutshell truths for the breakfast table';[2] as alert as a novelist to the personal characteristics of everybody he met. And since he is often the philosopher, there is much attention to another

[1] See Reynard Library *Newman*, pp. 559 f.

[2] See Reynard Library *Newman*, p. 363.

prime concern of literature—the nature of man. Though his hope is always to shame the nature in man and to divert his natural religion into Christianity, he does not scamp his study of all that we are by unaided nature.

Co-extensive with the consideration of all these things proceeds his untiring introspection. There were several reasons for that activity, one of which was his frank love of particulars. The nearest source of these lay in his own field of body, mind and spirit, each of which seemed to him as important as the others because making an equal contribution to a whole. In *Loss and Gain* we hear that 'a man's moral self . . . is concentrated in each moment of his life; it lives in the tips of his fingers, and the spring of his insteps'.[1] Or there is the mixed account of his leaving Littlemore in 1846: 'I am burning and packing *pari passu* reading and disposing, passing from a metaphysical MS. to a lump of resin or a penwiper.'[2] And in another letter written a little later: 'I quite tore myself away, and could not help kissing my bed, and mantelpiece, and other parts of the house. I have been most happy there, though in a state of suspense.'[3] When in the *Apologia* he recalls how the Anglican Church looked to him after leaving it, he seems to be looking at it with physical as well as mental eyes:

I have been bringing out my mind in this Volume on every subject which has come before me; and therefore I am bound to state plainly what I feel and have felt, since I was a Catholic, about the Anglican Church. I said, in a former page, that on my conversion, I was not conscious of any change in me of thought or feeling, as regards matters of doctrine; this, however, was not the case as regards some matters of fact, and, unwilling as I am to give offence to religious Anglicans, I am bound to confess that I felt a great change in my view of the Church of England. I cannot tell how soon there came on me,—but very soon,—an extreme astonishment that I had ever imagined it to be a portion of the Catholic Church. For the first time, I looked at it from without, and (as I should myself say) saw it as it was. Forthwith I could not get myself to see in it any thing else, than what I had so long fearfully suspected, from as far back as 1836,—a mere national institution. As if my eyes were

[1] See id., pp. 321 f.; cf. the bullet-tips, p. 251, above.
[2] Ward's *Life*, i, 115. For Newman's editing of this passage see below, p. 272.
[3] id., i, 117.

suddenly opened, so I saw it—spontaneously, apart from any definite act of reason or any argument; and so I have seen it ever since. I suppose, the main cause of this lay in the contrast which was presented to me by the Catholic Church. Then I recognized at once a reality which was quite a new thing with me. Then I was sensible that I was not making for myself a Church by an effort of thought; I needed not to make an act of faith in her; I had not painfully to force myself into a position, but my mind fell back upon itself in relaxation and in peace, and I gazed at her almost passively as a great objective fact. I looked at her;—at her rites, her ceremonial, and her precepts; and I said, "This *is* a religion;" and then, when I looked back upon the poor Anglican Church, for which I had laboured so hard, and upon all that appertained to it, and thought of our various attempts to dress it up doctrinally and esthetically, it seemed to me to be the veriest of nonentities. Vanity of vanities, all is vanity! How can I make a record of what passed within me, without seeming to be satirical?[1]

And to take a last random instance from the mass, there is the letter of 1862 which he addressed to the *Globe* newspaper in an attempt to silence once for all the reports that he was returning to the English Church, and in which he seems to be spewing it and all its works out of his mouth:

Therefore, in order to give them full satisfaction, if I can, I do hereby profess 'ex animo' with an absolute internal assent and consent, that Protestantism is the dreariest of possible religions; that the thought of the Anglican service makes me shiver, and the thought of the Thirty-nine Articles makes me shudder. Return to the Church of England! No! 'The net is broken and we are delivered.' I should be a consummate fool (to use a mild term) if in my old age I left 'the land flowing with milk and honey' for the city of confusion and the house of bondage.[2]

He ejects the Anglican Church as if he has it in his system, and his life up to the secession shows us he had. That was why he was so unconscionably long a-dying as an Anglican. He drew all things into himself,[3] so that even an external thing like a logical demonstration or a history issues from him as personal

[1] *Apologia*, Ward's edn., pp. 393 f.
[2] Ward's *Life*, i, 581.
[3] Cf. Leslie Stephen's masterly review of the *Essay in Aid of a Grammar of Assent*, collected in *An Agnostic's Apology*, 1893, pp. 205 ff.

as a love letter. This unusual characteristic was soon seized on by his contemporaries: when the *Quarterly Review* began its sixty-page-long review of that book of his which had so much general interest for its own time and ours[1]—the *Essay on the Development of Christian Doctrine*—it recognized that here was a book that was more than a book:

> Our business is with Mr. Newman's book, not with Mr. Newman himself... It will, however, be impossible altogether to separate the examination of his work from what Mr. Coleridge would have called the psychological study of his mind—so completely is the one the reflexion, dare we use the word, the transfiguration of one into the other.[2]

As we should expect, he does not always rest content with the colouring his mind has given to his matter—he often lingers to describe the pigmentation and how he felt during its process. A frequent effect in his writings is that his thinking is progressing alongside a diary of the experience of the thinking for 'the whole man'.[3] This 'whole man' contained for him the unconscious, or what we should call the subconscious. If he reproduced on paper the light in his mind, he also reproduced the darkness with which it coexisted, and he looked at the darkness as hard as at the light. Instances are everywhere in the correspondence and in the *Apologia*.

Because of all this, Newman is one of the shining demonstrations that the style is the man. His personality exists as clearly in his style as in his choice of matter—or, rather, in his choice of just that shade and aspect of his matter. And since he constantly gives us consideration of the thing as well as the thing itself, it was to be expected that he should offer an account of the personality of style. I quote it at length because it is one of the most luminous things he wrote, confirming his belief that 'simplicity ... is the attribute of genius':[4]

1 See the letter of 1878 from Mark Pattison to Newman, quoted in my *Criticism and the Nineteenth Century*, 1951, p. 200; and A. N. Whitehead's *Adventures of Ideas*, 1933, p. vii, which records a debt to Gibbon's *Decline and Fall* and Newman's *Essay on Development* et al., for his 'general way of looking at [his] historical topic'.

2 *Quarterly Review*, lxxvii (1845–6), p. 405.

3 See Reynard Library *Newman*, p. 704.

4 In the lecture 'Literature' in *Lectures and Essays on University Subjects*, 1859, p. 50.

Here then, in the first place, I observe, Gentlemen, that, Literature, from the derivation of the word, implies writing, not speaking; this, however, arises from the circumstance of the copiousness, variety, and public circulation of the matters of which it consists. What is spoken cannot outrun the range of the speaker's voice, and perishes in the uttering. When words are in demand to express a long course of thought, when they have to be conveyed to the ends of the earth, or perpetuated for the benefit of posterity, they must be written down, that is, reduced to the shape of literature; still, properly speaking, the terms, by which we denote this characteristic gift of man, belong to its exhibition by means of the voice, not of handwriting. It addresses itself, in its primary idea, to the ear, not to the eye. We call it the power of speech, we call it language, that is, the use of the tongue; and, even when we write, we still keep in mind what was its original instrument, for we use freely such terms in our books as saying, speaking, telling, talking, calling; we use the terms phraseology and diction; as if we were still addressing ourselves to the ear.

Now I insist on this, because it shows that speech, and therefore literature, which is its permanent record, is essentially a personal work. It is not some production or result, attained by the partnership of several persons, or by machinery, or by any natural process, but in its very idea it proceeds, and must proceed, from some one given individual. Two persons cannot be the authors of the sounds which strike our ear; and, as they cannot be speaking one and the same speech, neither can they be writing one and the same lecture or discourse—which must certainly belong to some one person or other, and is the expression of that one person's ideas and feelings,—ideas and feelings personal to himself, though others may have parallel and similar ones,—proper to himself, in the same sense as his voice, his air, his countenance, his carriage, and his action, are personal. In other words, Literature expresses, not objective truth, as it is called, but subjective; not things, but thoughts.

. . . Literature is the personal use or exercise of language. That that is so, is further proved from the fact that one author uses it so differently from another. Language itself in its very origination would seem to be traceable to individuals. The peculiarities have given it its character. We are often able in fact to trace particular phrases or idioms to individuals; we know the history of their rise. Slang surely, as it is called, comes of, and breathes of the personal. The connection between the force of words in particular languages and the habits and sentiments of the nations speaking them, has often been pointed out. And, while the many use language, as they find it, the man of genius uses it indeed, but subjects it withal to his own purposes, and moulds it according to his own peculiarities. The throng and succession of ideas, thoughts, feelings, imaginations, aspirations, which pass within him, the abstractions, the juxtapositions, the comparisons, the discriminations, the conceptions, which are so original in him, his views of external things, his judgments upon life, manners, and history, the exercises of his wit, of his humour, of his depth, of his sagacity,—he images forth all these innumerable and incessant creations, the very pulsation and throbbing of his intellect,—he gives utterance to them all,—in a corresponding language, which is as multiform as this inward mental action itself and analogous to it, the faithful expression of his intense personality, attending on his own inward world of thought as its very shadow: so that we might as well say that one man's shadow is another's, as that the style of a really gifted mind can belong to any but himself. It follows him about *as* a shadow. His thought and feeling are personal, and so his language is personal.[1]

Constantly exemplifying this theme, Newman is among the most fascinating writers of English. If the declared aim of his use of English was clarity, the result is not colourless transparency. Art is supposed either to hide or show itself, but there are countless degrees of the concealment and exhibition. The art of Newman's writing is never wholly hidden. It comes near to being so in the 'plain' and 'parochial' sermons, where, as I have said, it was designed to receive the added arts of the voice and general presence of the preacher. Elsewhere in his writings the art is usually less concealed. In the Tracts it is sometimes noticeably abrupt, and deliberately so—Thomas Mozley said that among the Tractarians only Newman 'could write a tract', giving as explanation that only he had read enough of them himself.[2] But, just as the variety of his art is obvious, so, by and large, it is triumphant. And, in accordance with that Newmanian law, he tells us how he made it so. I have already quoted the material evidence of his care and given some of his own accounts of his corrections. The thing written was expression achieved, imperfect at first and then more perfect. What guiding principle was at work is suggested in Newman's definition—one of the

[1] *Lectures and Essays on University Subjects*, 1859, pp. 35 ff.
[2] *Reminiscences chiefly of Oriel College and the Oxford Movement*, 1882, i, 312.

best we have—of style, which he called 'a thinking out into language',[1] a process that was almost palpable for him: 'Besides re-writing, every part has to be worked out and defined as in moulding a statue.'[2] As usual, Newman speaks his difficult matter so clearly because his experience of it has been his own, and being that, has been of extreme vividness.

5

In consequence of all this, the case for regarding Newman as supremely literary as well as supremely 'ecclesiastical' is inescapable. One of the points I wish to make is that Newman is always literary, even, all things considered, when he is most narrowly ecclesiastical. How well he caught himself—all the more truly because from an unusual angle—in a letter of 1850:

> You must undeceive Miss A. B. about me, though I suppose she uses words in a general sense. I have nothing of a saint about me as every one knows, and it is a severe (and salutary) mortification to be thought next door to one. I may have a high view of many things, but it is the consequence of education and a peculiar cast of intellect —but this is very different from *being* what I admire. I have no tendency to be a saint—it is a sad thing to say so. Saints are not literary men, they do not love the classics, they do not write Tales.[3]

In quoting that I feel compunction at taking him when, comparatively, he is off his guard. So strongly does he recoil from the ascribed saintliness that he opposes to it the most secular self-description, imputing to himself the literary ethos he had said he was 'hard-hearted' against. Offered as proof of his weakness, the description is of strength in a different department. And with it goes a remark, which again one feels some compunction in overhearing—it occurs late in those sincerest of sincere documents, the letters he sent to Keble during the long period of his secession: 'My great fault is doing things in a mere literary way from the love of the work, without the thought of God's glory.'[4] It happens that under obedience to

[1] In the lecture 'Literature' in *Lectures and Essays on University Subjects*, 1859, p. 41.

[2] *Correspondence of John Henry Newman with John Keble and Others 1839–45*, p. 382.

[3] Ward's *Life*, i, 229 f.

[4] *Correspondence*, p. 245.

chronology Wilfrid Ward passes directly from the letter repudiating saintliness to the *Lectures on Certain Difficulties felt by Anglicans*, with which, after some hesitation, Newman met the occasion of the Gorham judgment.[1] Merely as a matter of course he describes the lectures as 'brilliantly witty'. Yes, they are accurately that, and the ease with which he can be brilliantly witty seals him of the tribe of the Henry Jameses and Oscar Wildes as certainly as the capacity to write on ecclesiastical matters seals him of the tribe of the Puseys and W. G. Wards. And he had other gifts as literary, like that which made George Eliot find *The Present Position of Catholics* 'full of clever satire and description',[2] or like that which made Pater praise his *Idea of a University* as showing 'the perfect handling of a theory'.[3]

[1] Namely, to use Ward's concise words, the 'celebrated decision of the Privy Council . . . overruling the refusal of the Bishop of Exeter (confirmed by the Court of Arches) to institute Mr. G. C. Gorham to the vicarage of Brampford Speke on the ground that he denied the doctrine of baptismal regeneration' (i, 230).

[2] *George Eliot Letters*, i, 372. Another letter records the stages of her interest in the *Apologia*: 'I have been reading Newman's *Apologia pro Vita Suâ*, with such absorbing interest that I found it impossible to forsake the book until I had finished it. I don't know whether the affair between him and Kingsley has interested you, or whether you have shared at all my view of it. I have been made so indignant by Kingsley's mixture of arrogance, coarse impertinence and unscrupulousness with real intellectual *in*competence, that my first interest in Newman's answer arose from a wish to see what I consider thoroughly vicious writing thoroughly castigated. But the Apology now mainly affects me as the revelation of a life—how different in form from one's own, yet with how close a fellowship in its needs and burthens—I mean spiritual needs and burthens' (iv, 158 f.). Another letter remarks that the *Apologia* has 'breathed much life into her', and that she 'would like to make an expedition to Birmingham for [the] sole end' of 'seeing and hearing Newman' (iv, 160).

[3] *Appreciations*, 1889, p. 14. Father McGrath argues against the unqualified acceptance of this praise, op. cit., p. 292. In 1852 at least Newman was greatly pleased with the work in its first printed form (see Reynard Library *Newman*, p. 354).

XX

NEWMAN: THOUGHT AND ACTION

THE NINETEENTH century, like the seventeenth, was one of those ages in which men of great literary endowment inquired with anxiety whether the inevitable mixing of thought and action could bear the scrutiny of a conscience that had something of the martinet in it. Some in either century may have practised the completest withdrawal—if so we do not hear of them. If any in the nineteenth did, they had the sanction of the ageing Carlyle and his momentous appeal for silence. Hopkins came nearest to obeying him. He partly suppressed his powers of great utterance in obedience to the claims of a more obviously active life. Harriet Martineau, whose *Deerbrook* can stand beside the novels of Jane Austen and those of Mrs Gaskell, Charlotte Brontë and George Eliot, burnt all she had written of her second novel because a publisher refused it as too controversial—incurring a major loss, we must suppose, to nineteenth-century literature.

But in general the choice before the great man at that time was to achieve a balance between two mighty opposites; meditation was no lazy luxury when knowledge was expanding limitlessly, and action took a hundred violent forms. That a book was a form of action, and could be a violent one, we have much evidence—that, for example, of the sharp impact of Carlyle's on individual readers, and of the burning of Froude's *Nemesis of Faith* in an Oxford lecture room. It was an age of 'mental strife' when, if conciliation was attempted, it might earn a remark like that which Newman pinned on an attempt of Pusey's:

> There was one of old time who wreathed his sword in myrtle; excuse me—you discharge your olive-branch as if from a catapult.

There was irony in Mill's discovery that true poetry aspired to the condition of being overheard just when poets were urged to speak at their audience about current problems. If a writer even in a form supposedly devoted to pleasure had nothing to say about those problems, he owned to it. Charlotte Brontë, who generously tried to read a Swift into Thackeray, confessed that she could not attend to the needs of her time as Mrs Gaskell had shown herself able to.

2

For Newman action existed at several degrees of strength, but most of them were crowded together at the lower end of the scale. Much given to meditation, he did not allow it to get ahead of the pen. It is as if he applied literally to himself injunctions that in their context are ironical: 'Let [written] language have the monopoly of thought; and thought go for only so much as it can show itself to be worth in language.' 'A Saint's writings', he said, 'are to me his real "Life".' In the preface to the *Meditations and Devotions* printed from papers left at his death, his friend William Neville wrote:

> That the papers can be presented at all, especially the majority of the Meditations, is owing, it is believed, to the circumstances which accompanied their origin. It was the Cardinal's custom to note down, in the roughest way, any thought that particularly struck him while meditating, that he might reflect upon it during the day or pursue it in the future; and thus he was led on to enlarge such thoughts, and write out notes and re-write them carefully (for he always, he said, could meditate best with a pen in his hand).

Newman's meditation was not more brilliant in one department than another. That he could think is as obvious as that Schubert could write melodies. He could also recall with details as numerous as they were vivid the experiences of the long past, and that this was a gift he liked to exercise is evinced by the strange reason he gave for his Mediterranean tour—he would put up with the sights so as to be able to recall them. Then again, he has no rival as a recorder of experience that is in the act of being experienced; indeed he sometimes seems intent on lifting the charge of improbability from the Clarissas and Pamelas of the epistolary novels. There are even instances of his pen's writing that it cannot go on writing, as if the drowning man were numbering the bubbles he was sending to the surface. The manuscript reliques at the Oratory and elsewhere would be mountainous if Newman and his helpers had not arranged them so tidily. Mr Culler's bibliographical appendix lists the general categories into which Newman sorted those at the Oratory.[1] The letters in the 'Personal Collection' run to 171 volumes, and this, though the biggest collection, is one of seven. From among the 'Miscellaneous Papers' Mr Culler has used four volumes of Memoranda, Personal and Most Private. In the first of these Newman wrote:

> The following reminiscences of my life up to August 1816, were written first in 1820, 1821. Then faithfully transcribed with additions in 1823. Then faithfully transcribed with omissions in the Lent of 1840. Now to be partially and finally re-transcribed, with great omissions and put aside for good. The copies which were superseded were all burned carefully.

The burnings were careful, we may suppose, so that the flames should not spread! What little did get burned without being first printed was burned, on the evidence of what survives, in accordance with nothing more sensational than literary good manners: when he was nearing the age of seventy he wrote: 'How unpleasant it is to read former memoranda—I can't quite tell why. They read affected, unreal, egotistical, petty, fussy. There is much in the above that I should tear out and burn, if I did as I wished'.

If we cannot help wishing we had everything he wrote it is because to have a whole satisfies the imagination—a sentimental satisfaction when the all-but-complete is unmanageably vast for the intellect. One of the most private passages which, like everything else, was meant for publication, in the elastic sense of being seen by others, comes towards the close of his account of the momentous solitary tour of Sicily. It has not yet appeared in its full form in England, but we can now read it whole in the collection of *Écrits Autobiographiques*[2] which has recently appeared in France:

[1] A. Dwight Culler, *The Imperial Intellect.* A Study of Newman's Educational Ideal, 1955.

[2] *Textes Newmaniens.* II: Écrits autobiographiques. Établissement du texte et introduction par Henry Tristram. Traductions par Isabelle Ginot. Révision, notes et avantpropos par Louis Bouyer, 1955. [The desiderated English edition followed in 1956].

The thought keeps pressing on me, while I write this, what am I writing it for? For myself, I may look at it once or twice in my whole life, and what sympathy is there in *my* looking at it? Whom have I, whom can I have, who would take interest in it? I was going to say, I only have found one who ever took that sort of affectionate interest in me as to be pleased with such details—and that is H. W. [Wilberforce] and what shall I ever see of him? This is the sort of interest which a wife takes and none but she—it is a woman's interest—and that interest, so be it, shall never be taken in me. Never, so be it, will I be other than God has found me. All my habits for years, my tendencies, are towards celibacy. I could not take that interest in this world which marriage requires. I am too disgusted with this world—And, above all, call it what one will, I have a repugnance to a clergyman's marrying. I do not say it is not lawful—I cannot deny the right—but, whether a prejudice or not, it shocks me. And therefore I willingly give up the possession of that sympathy, which I feel is not, cannot be, granted to me. Yet, not the less do I feel the need of it. Who will care to be told such details as I have put down above? Shall I ever have in my old age spiritual children who will take an interest such as a wife does? . . .

This passage indicates the conditions of conversation that Newman preferred. He liked it to be with a single person and, when otherwise, with a small number—by preference, a family of 'spiritual children'. *Cor ad cor loquitur* was the motto he chose for his cardinalate: it declared the value he placed on dialogue, whether of looks or of looks and words together. This is why he put heart and soul into his letter writing. He was a profound correspondent because he possessed the gift he saw as lacking in Keble, that 'of entering into the minds of others'. A conversation or a letter of his was a form of action, and often of action in the public sense. Whether he preferred the heart to speak to heart with or without ink we do not know, but ink was much in demand since most of the requests for help came from a distance. The title of Mr Boekraad's book[1] shows the importance he reads into Newman's constant concern with the individual, his belief, to use Mr Boekraad's words, in 'the influence of personality on personality in the acquisition of truth'. That concern is the main reason why he interests present-day philosophers.

[1] A. J. Boekraad, *The Personal Conquest of Truth according to J. H. Newman*, 1955.

Whereas in the eighteenth century it was assumed that reason was the same thing for everybody, and in both the eighteenth and nineteenth that logic carried the same force universally, Newman saw that reason differed from mind to mind, and that logic was, in Mr Boekraad's words, no more than that thin and often barren strip, 'the common measure between minds'. Mr Boekraad quotes a passage from the *Essay in Aid of a Grammar of Assent* that gives the main purpose of an argument in words as 'to stimulate in those to whom we address ourselves a mode of thinking and trains of thought similar to our own, leading them on by their own independent action, not by any syllogistic compulsion'. This being so, the *Essay* and Newman's other close arguments are not his most telling writings, except to 'those to whom we address ourselves', or 'men of good will'. At the hands of men of ill will or no will they might meet the harsh treatment that Fitzjames Stephen, and to some extent Leslie Stephen, gave the *Essay*. A more universally certain means of communication was that adopted on the last page of an earlier essay, the *Essay on the Development of Christian Doctrine*, where the, as it were, secular demonstration is broken off by three rows of dots, on which follows:

> Such were the thoughts concerning the 'Blessed Vision of Peace,' of one whose long-continued petition had been that the Most Merciful would not despise the work of His own Hands, nor leave him to himself;—while yet his eyes were dim, and his breast laden, and he could but employ Reason in the things of Faith. And now, dear Reader, time is short, eternity is long. Put not from you what you have here found; regard it not as mere matter of present controversy; set not out resolved to refute it, and looking about for the best way of doing so; seduce not yourself with the imagination that it comes of disappointment, or disgust, or restlessness, or wounded feeling, or undue sensibility, or other weakness. Wrap not yourself round in the associations of years past; nor determine that to be truth which you wish to be so, nor make an idol of cherished anticipations. Time is short, eternity is long.
>
> NUNC DIMITTIS SERVUM TUUM, DOMINE,
> SECUNDUM VERBUM TUUM IN PACE:
> QUIA VIDERUNT OCULI MEI SALUTARE TUUM.

It is as if a voice ceased speaking in a lecture room and began to whisper from a pillow in the small hours.

Preferring action to the completest solitude, Newman preferred action that remained as private as possible, and therefore when it could not but be public affected the few rather than the many, the 'set' rather than the crowd. He shrank from action on too broad a scale, though in the age in which he lived some of his actions had far-reachingness thrust upon them. Of one of his most decisive acts, the writing and publication of *Tract Ninety*, Frederick Oakeley said: 'It is a fact, though almost an incredible one, that Mr. Newman was totally unprepared for the reception which this most remarkable essay encountered both in the university and throughout the country'. His voice would not fill a large church, nor did he really want it to. When he did touch masses of people it was not from deliberate choice. His gift as man of action lay first of all with those of like mind, of like educated or educable mind. In the *Present Difficulties of Anglicans* he contrasted the Sicilian beggar and the typical English gentleman and preferred the social outcast because she was religious; but as Mr Culler rightly remarks: 'Happily these were not the only alternatives—one could be both [religious and a gentleman]'.

Like George Herbert, Newman was fastidious as well as saintly. The field he felt most at home in was that of the college: at one time his first wish was 'to live and die a Fellow of Oriel', and after his secession his place was in the bosom of a small oratory, to which he soon attached a small school. When preparing his lectures on that select matter, university education, he felt he was working *con amore*:

> no position whatever, in the whole range of administrations which are open to the ambition of those who wish to serve God in their generation, and to do some great work before they die, would have had more attractions for me, than that of being at the head of a University like this. When I became a Catholic, one of my first questions was, 'Why have not Catholics a University?' and Ireland, and the metropolis of Ireland, was obviously the proper seat of such an institution.

He drew satisfaction from the small scale of his operation—the room in the Rotunda at Dublin where his show lectures were held could only seat 400: 'The room is very good for my purpose being very small. It is just the room I like, barring want of light; I cannot make myself heard to many, and few care to hear me; paucorum hominum sum'. And again, of ordinary lectures: 'That attendance is satisfactory—not which is numerous, but—which is steady and persevering'.

The aim that he had most at heart, he tells us, was 'that of doing definite good to definite persons'. Definite persons and therefore known persons: 'I commonly have failed when I addressed strangers'.

3

Mr Culler is to be congratulated on choosing his theme—Newman's life as student and teacher. The credit for distinguishing its existence goes to Fr Henry Tristram, keeper of the Newman archives at the Oratory till his death some two years ago.[1] Mr Culler expresses his deep indebtedness to Tristram, and no one would have loved this book more than he, a book which, like Newman himself, 'he could, any day have sat down and written almost out of his head'. 'Indeed', Mr Culler adds, 'he had all but done so many years before, and one day he showed me, and allowed me to read, an incompleted (*sic*) manuscript of his own, begun on somewhat the same plan as I had adopted myself'. Mr Culler's plan can be gathered from the following:

> I have tried to make my study dependent as much as possible on manuscript materials. Thus, even where the story that it tells is already familiar in its main outlines to Newman scholars, the details of that story, and the quotations by which it is illustrated, will often be fresh. It should, of course, be clear that I am not writing a general biography of Newman. The story that I tell is simply that of Newman's education, of his work as an educator of others, and of his educational thinking as expressed in the *Idea of a University*. But it also happens that one effect of this restriction is to reveal aspects of Newman's life which the general biographies have missed. For these works, following the line laid down in the *Apologia*, have concentrated upon the development of Newman's religious opinions, narrowing his life to the compass of the Tractarian movement and measuring his opinions by their approximation to Rome. What they forget is that all this while Newman was living in a university and was professionally engaged in the work of education. 'Now from first to

[1] This was written in 1956.

last', he wrote in 1863, 'education, in this large sense of the word, has been my line', and by following out this line one discovers an interaction betweeen Newman's educational and his religious interests which provides the central pattern of his entire life. That pattern is not the steady, ineluctable march toward Rome, but an oscillation between an intellectual liberalism and a religious submissiveness which revealed itself most dramatically in the five crushing illnesses of Newman's adolescence and early manhood. From most biographies one would hardly know that these illnesses had occurred. Even where they are mentioned they are not related to each other nor is their significance emphasized. And yet, in my opinion, these illnesses provide an essential key to the understanding of Newman's intellectual and religious development.

Mr Culler has a great and new story to tell, and tells it worthily. He traces the course of Newman's education and his long and sometimes 'fierce' career as a reforming organizer of the education of others. The surprises of the story are many—which of us knew beforehand that Newman took part in the revival of mathematical studies at Oxford? While we acknowledge that his educational career was led as consciously as possible in the light of his religion, we cannot but call much of it secular. James Anthony Froude has left a fine account of the mind he cared to show in commonrooms:

> Newman's mind was world-wide. He was interested in everything which was going on in science, in politics, in literature. Nothing was too large for him, nothing too trivial, if it threw light upon the central question, what man really was, and what was his destiny. . . . Keble had looked into no lines of thought but his own. Newman had read omnivorously; he had studied modern thought and modern life in all its forms, and with all its many-coloured passions. . . .
>
> He seemed always to be better informed on common topics of conversation than any one else who was present. He was never condescending with us, never didactic or authoritative; but what he said carried conviction along with it. When we were wrong he knew why we were wrong, and excused our mistakes to ourselves while he set us right. Perhaps his supreme merit as a talker was that he never tried to be witty or to say striking things. Ironical he could be, but not ill-natured. Not a malicious anecdote was ever heard from him. Prosy he could not be. He was lightness itself—the lightness of elastic strength—and he was interesting because . . . he had something real to say. . . . He seemed to be addressing the

most secret consciousness of each of us—as the eyes of a portrait appear to look at every person in a room.

This is the Newman who in the midst of the Crimean War wrote *Who's to Blame?*; who was as much at home when considering the contribution of science and classical literature to a university curriculum, as in considering the relation of philosophy to religion; who could assure a Catholic audience that Milton and Gibbon could not be neglected if only because, as he often said, 'we must take things as they are, if we take them at all', if only because 'there they are, an integral portion of English Literature; we cannot extinguish them; we cannot deny their power; we cannot write a new Milton or a new Gibbon; we cannot expurgate what needs to be exorcised'.

Everybody who is interested in education—and who is not?—and in Newman, and in the nineteenth century, will delight in Mr Culler's work: and Newman would have approved it warmly—not least for its readability. It is one of those books where there is not too big a bump as one passes from a quoted passage of Newman's to the surrounding letterpress. To end with a point small but significant: Mr Culler writes the sentence 'Newman was in on it from the very first'. Newman might have considered that to have over-passed the bound between the colloquial and the slangy, but would have counted it an error in the right direction—we recall his counsel to an aspiring contributor to a magazine, not to begin his essay with 'Of all the virtues that adorn the human breast'.

4

Among Newman's surviving manuscripts, the nearest to pure meditation exists in the *Meditations and Devotions*. There is much of it in the autobiographical papers. It is from these papers that the *Écrits Autobiographiques* are drawn. This volume belongs to a series of *Textes Newmaniens* which is to comprise a translation of the main works with editorial apparatus. The first volume contained a translation of the *University Sermons*, and the present volume departs from the plan by giving the English text in addition to the translation. Englishmen cannot but be roused to jealousy here. The 'personality and work' of Newman, the preface claims, is more appreciated in France than in England by English Catholics. But surely not if we consider Englishmen as a whole. It is beyond question that English readers would welcome a complete edition of Newman's autobiographical remains. But they must be edited as well as possible.

The establishment of the text of the present volume is said to be Tristram's, and the claim is made that it is *complète* and the editing *fidèle*. The claim that a printed text is faithful to a manuscript, especially to a manuscript in a current hand, would seem a hubristic one. One cannot help wondering how far from faithful this printed text is. The present writer, as it happens, possesses his own transcript of the corrections Tristram made in a copy of Anne Mozley's *Letters and Correspondence* of 1891, the incomplete source on which we have hitherto had to rely for Newman's autobiographical manuscripts about his years as an Anglican. That transcript does not agree with the text here given. There are a host of small discrepancies between the two and also between both of them and that part of the material which Mr Culler happens to reproduce. Sometimes there are differences in wording. At one point Anne Mozley, the transcript and Mr Culler all read: 'And at one time I had a most consoling overpowering thought of God's electing love, and seemed to think I was His', for which the French edition reads '. . . God's abiding love. . . .' One is loth to think this theological variant due to anything other than careless or silently doubtful transcription on the part of one or more transcribers. That the Oratory itself is willing to leave the readings of the manuscript exactly as Newman left them is beautifully clear from their having allowed Yale University, from which Mr Culler hails, to photograph them whole.

All told, we must follow up our plea for an English edition of these documents with the plea that the text should be prepared by a scholar well skilled in textual work. How complicated some part at least of this task will be there is one manuscript in particular to show—the manuscript of the account of Newman's illness in Sicily. It is mainly autograph, and was worked over from time to time as Newman returned to it in order to urge himself to retrieve as much as possible from his memory. He retrieved a great deal in the end, and the additions made to the manuscript trace the sporadic course of the archaeological process. As a psychological document it is surely unique—it shows a great man searching his memory of three weeks' experience at odd points over more than forty years, a short stretch of a memory that was usually well and clearly stocked but which during this particular run of experience was stocked during physical sickness. The French editors use the term 'proustien' about Newman's autobiographical documents in general, but of this document the principle is a part of the scientific principle—Newman is searching for the fact, for all the facts, of whatever sort, not to do anything with them except gaze at them as a record of what happened on a mysterious occasion to one of God's creatures. That the effort results in a document of aesthetic as well as other values is merely accidental. Of all the documents Newman left, we may suspect that it is the trickiest to represent faithfully in print, but it is the one for which it is most worth while to try.

5

Something has already been indicated about Mr Boekraad's book. It takes the whole of Newman's printed writings, and also some manuscripts, in order to demonstrate the unity of Newman's ideas. Of the most unified of his books, *An Essay in Aid of a Grammar of Assent,* Newman wrote to a friend, and the letter, it seems, is here printed for the first time:

> Unless it had already grown so fat, and I was desperately tired of the whole subject, I had intended to sum up in a last chapter. You see, I called it an *Essay,* as it really is, because it is an analytical inquiry. A *Grammar* ought to be synthetical. But to put it in synthetical form, had I after all attempted it, would have been to write a new book. And it would, to my own feelings, have been bumptious.

In doing for Newman what he did not do for himself, Mr Boekraad may be wholly cleared of the charge of bumptiousness. He has shown himself to possess what Newman lacked, or what Newman did not evince that he possessed, the power to assemble his tens of thousands of brilliant thoughts into a single line of thought. It was surely enough to have had thoughts of such brilliance in their tens of thousands, to have had them on matters hidden for most of us though our everyday lives imply their existence somewhere in that 'Africa' (to use Sir Thomas Browne's image) of our sub- or semi-consciousness, and also to have grouped so many of them into runs, more or less long, of argument. For all their thinking, Newman's writings, like Shakespeare's plays, are for most of us a world of experience, as they were first of all for their author, a second Creation, as it were. Mr Boekraad may be said to have completed the diagram of the vast maze which its author built glittering stone by stone, and only partly built according to a plan. Tristram saw enough of the book before his death to know that it would 'redound to Newman's honour'. Newman himself would have read it with gratitude as a book doing him a service. He would also have appreciated Mr Boekraad's interest in relating his thinking to that of the twentieth century, to which he consciously looked forward. Newman's instrument was the pen, which he used on all possible occasions. Fascinated as a young man by the accounts of Wellington and Napoleon, he had longed to be a great soldier; but for him the pen proved as mighty as any sword.

XXI

NEWMAN IN HIS LETTERS

READERS OF Newman fall into several categories; Fr Dessain[1] enumerates:

> The students of literature; the historians, both secular and ecclesiastical; the educationalists, the psychologists, the social scientists, those interested in the theory or the practice of politics; the philosophers and theologians, the men of religion and those concerned for the spiritual life and perfection; the controversialists; and, although the list is not exhausted, not least the 'general readers', the ordinary men whose rights and needs Newman had always so much at heart.

Yes, all these sorts of person will be interested in these letters, as in everything that Newman published, but we must not think the aggregate will be legion. Newman will always have readers, but the devotion burning in the few has to do instead of numerosity. Apart from 'Lead, Kindly Light . . .', his writings can never be popular. Fr Dessain speaks of his interest in the ordinary man, and when he went among the victims of cholera at Bilston, and when the Oratory was at Deritend (Birmingham), he did much for them at their most oppressed. But that interest was never overmastering. On more than one occasion in the letters before us Newman discriminates his proper milieu: 'As yet my influence has lain among educated people, and therefore London seemed more suited to me, where the higher classes, the learned professions, &c., congregated, than Birmingham'. He could have done anything he set his mind to, and would have accepted any 'clear call', though he admits that it is hard to tell when a call *is* clear; but he was grateful that his lines did not fall in East London. The letters in this volume are all to his social equals or superiors, except for one or two business letters. There is evidence of his kindness to the poor, but social scientists will find the almost total absence of a

[1] *The Letters and Diaries of John Henry Newman*, ed. C. S. Dessain, vol. xi.

pressing sense of the other of the 'two nations' as interesting as anything he has to say about the rich. His writings, and also perhaps his life, speak, and will go on doing so, to the cultivated.

In drawing up his list of classes Fr Dessain was thinking of the letters as a whole. This volume contains only a small proportion of them, those covering the fifteen months after his secession, when he was becoming acquainted with his new friends among the members of the Catholic hierarchy, travelling about England on a sort of tour of inspection, settling in to the temporary menage at Maryvale (near Oscott) and later at Milan and Rome, and carrying on ample correspondence with former Anglican friends who were 'moving' into the other church or thinking of doing so—or coming to see that they would not do so. (It is a great thing to read the letters against the chapter in Ward's biography, which makes the life of these months into a convenient picture.) We see how strong was the reason for beginning with Volume XI—the letters of the Anglican period have been available in some sort in Anne Mozley's two volumes, and in the volume edited at the Oratory in 1917, while only a small fraction of the later letters is available (mainly in Ward's *Life*), and then in much edited shape—some of which editing Newman himself had done in anticipation (in the following passage, for instance: 'Your packing, Charissime, is nothing to mine. I am burning and packing pari passu—reading and folding—passing from a metaphysical MS to a lump of resin or an inkglass' he had changed 'folding' to 'disposing', and 'an inkglass' to 'a penwiper'.)

In the letters of these first months in the Roman church some of the categories of reader will not find much, as it happens, for their special interests, though 'social scientists' may like to know what 'the true sense' of 'gentleman' was for Newman in 1845, and educationists to note his comparison of the Catholic public schools and the rest—'I suspect [they are] much rougher places.... The terms show this—the College expenses at Stonyhurst are not, I *suppose*, £40 a year....' What 'controversialists' will note is a snub to their subject:

You may fancy I am not in cue for controversy . . . for controversy is a means to an end—and when one has raised a building, why keep up the scaffolding? and when one enjoys the shore, why count the billows which preceded the landing [he is adapting a favourite couplet from the *Christian Year*] ? I do not say this to defend selfishness, but to account for what, for a time at least, is an incapacity. Would that all others had what I have—and many in time, I trust, will have it—though of some I despair, if it is right to say or feel such a thing.

(It may be noted that Newman is deeply happy in his new church.)

Theologians get little—but they will expect little from him—and so do philosophers. But most of the others get a great deal. And not least the psychologists. For Newman has much to say of the mental process (if mental is understood in its widest possible sense) of conversion, and of its varieties. The most searching and comprehensive remarks come in the letters preceding Mrs J. W. Bowden's secession, of which this is part:

There are persons who must be taken at a moment or they will not act—and whose minds are so variable and who go so little by reason that they are incapable of going through a *process* of change. But you, I suppose, are very different . . . among the anticipations you must entertain, I think must be this—that you *cannot* have 'certainty', to use your words. The class of minds to which I have just now referred *have* certainty—that is, they have no doubt at all. But calmer and more sober minds from the nature of the case see difficulties on all sides of them, in every course of action—and must in a certain sense act in the dark . . . what would I have given for a clearer view at the time of acting, and for a year before!

This letter and so many more are also for the 'general reader'. As so often in the sermons and other writings, Newman, in speaking of religious matters, is speaking of life. What he says of the act of conversion applies to all acts of any consequence—of marriage, for instance.

It is already clear that the 'men of religion' will find much in these letters, and the student of literature no less. Newman's writing of English is unsurpassed. In his letters there is almost as wide a variety of styles as in his published writings. When occasion calls for it he rises to a formality that shines consciously right in every particular of rhythm and diction—'delicate yet rich' is the phrase we might borrow from his description of the Milan churches. (And the classical scholar will note that

Cardinal Fransoni admired the 'Latinity' of a formal letter in Latin.)

But mainly his style, like that of the annotations to the translation of Saint Athanasius, is 'in what may be called an undress conversational style'; and of course the informal has its own sort of perfection. One favoured ingredient is university slang—'a prose' (a boring preachment), a 'scrape', 'fidgets me', 'to row a person', and there is the odd sentence: 'Dr. W[iseman] floors the yellow wax', where the sense of *floors* might be clearer if one knew what 'the yellow wax' could possibly mean in a context concerning passports. (There is an absence from the edition of notes on obsolete details, which are not numerous fortunately, but which do ask for explanation.) The best instance of Newman's descriptive powers, displayed at length and very happily in the 'foreign travel' letters, comes in the sentence: 'And now good night, for it is 11 p.m. and this gas twirls my eyes into my brain'.

Whatever the particular interest of readers they will all be drawn in fascination to Newman himself. These letters are the biography of their writer, since, when the series is complete, it will run from his early days right to the end—and for the last seventy years with great amplitude. Newman held that a man's letters were his best biography, perhaps by analogy with the principle enunciated by Gray when he advised a young traveller to take a note on the spot, such a note being worth 'a cartload of recollection'. Nor with Newman is there any disproportion in the quantity, for Fr Dessain has assembled some 20,000 items. It is amusing to find Newman saying 'I am a poor letter writer'. He meant that he could not hope to rival the descriptive letters—he has just reached Milan—which travellers write as if for print. Newman's letters are remarkable for being practical. He writes because he has something that needs to be said, and his letters are so numerous because there was much to be said to many. Occasionally he tells his correspondents that he writes because, for the moment, he is idle, and then the correspondent is lucky to be chosen for a long letter, which if idleness had been lacking would still have been written, only at briefer length.

Each letter is written vis-à-vis its addressee. This is even true of the score he wrote on October 8 or 9, 1845, for dispatch when 'all is over' and Father Dominic had received him. And true again when he feels he has so many people to tell of his physically trying journey to see the ailing Pusey at Tenby—'a long way off, coach, road and water [from Bristol] taking the place of steam', 'I was sadly tossed and seasick going, and got drenched to the skin coming back travelling 140 miles outside a mail'. And all fruitless: 'It is a simple "mystery" to him still, that I have made a move'; and to another: 'I have never had so bootless, or rather so sorrowful a toil. . . . And such a stupid waste of money, when one thinks of the number of books which could have been bought instead'. (When in Rome, he hopes he won't be directed or 'called' to join an Order that proscribes personal property.)

Newman faces each correspondent in turn. We can feel the power of his spell, for not only 'cor ad cor loquitur' but always to a particular heart. Some of his correspondents must have half-dreaded to receive a letter from him, knowing that some phrase or other of it would press on their sore place. He appreciated the invincible individuality of men in their hundreds. Evidence of his power for the retentive grasp of detail is everywhere. There is the long letter of reprimand sent to J. B. Morris, a member for a time of Newman's community at Maryvale. It begins with three paragraphs beating (though it is rather breathing) about the bush—he was always afraid of being 'abrupt'—but the body of it amounts to a long *catalogue raisonné* of Morris's major and minor acts of selfishness. It is like a reading from the neatly kept ledger of a recording angel. In this instance Newman did not know his man. His delicacy was in vain, for Morris's note on the letter in question shows him to be puzzled by its charges. (It is a feature of the edition that helpful commentary is drawn from the manuscripts of Newman's friends.)

It was like Newman to do as much towards editing his letters as possible. He began by dating them, and so saved his editor endless trouble. He arranged that many should be returned to him, and annotated them himself. It was part of his love for his own past in all its easily recoverable fullness, what with his powers of memory and the evidences before him. To have done a thing was always more pleasant for him than the doing of it, however pleasant. He disliked moving about, and looked on the years at Littlemore as likely to be the most peaceful he could hope to experience, because the quietest. One of the last Littlemore letters Ward has already given us; here is part of it in its original form:

Part of us are gone—part going—I shall, I suppose remain the last, as I came in first. A happy time indeed have I had here, happy to look back on, though suspense and waiting are dreary in themselves:—happy, because it is the only place perhaps I ever lived in, which I can look back on, without an evil conscience. In Oxford indeed, where I have been near 30 years from first to last, I trust I have all along served God from the day I went there—but in those many years, amid the waywardness and weakness of youth and the turmoil of business, of course many things must have occurred to leave sad thoughts on the memory. Nay even my responsibilities at St. Mary's, as one who had the care of souls, have always all along weighed most oppressively on me and do still. Alas, I will not speak against my circumstances, when my own personal fault is so great—Yet how dreadful is a *cure of souls* in the English Church, an engagement, with no *means* to carry it into effect—a jewish yoke! . . . Doubtless if my life here for these last years were placed in the light of God's countenance, it would be like a room when a sunbeam comes into it, full of hidden unknown impurities—but still I look back to it as a very soothing happy period. I came into this house by myself, and for nights was the sole person here, except Almighty God Himself, my Judge; and St. Francis's 'Deus meus et omnia' was ever and spontaneously on my lips. And now, so be it, I shall go out of it by myself, having found rest.

But that is no more exclusively the real Newman than a letter written ten days earlier, which opens as follows:

I am going to try your patience if you kindly let me; and as I write in a hurry, I hope I shall not be unintelligible, as well as troublesome.

1. St. John and perhaps Penny propose to make their appearance at the *New* College on Tuesday or Wednesday.

2. The books are to arrive at the Old College on Wednesday—please to order two rooms, viz the boy's play room (the large square room with a brick floor) and the Refectory, to be carefully swept out for the purpose of receiving them. They will be unpacked all in

one day, viz Thursday, as the boxes are to go back forthwith for a second load, and the books will be deposited on the floor of the two rooms, *on* the paper in which they are packed. . . .

One thing Newman must have liked about the Roundheads —they trusted in God, and kept their powder dry.

XXII

DONNE'S POETRY IN THE NINETEENTH CENTURY (1800-72)[1]

No serious student is deceived by statements frequently encountered in literary journals that Donne's poetry was 'discovered' forty or fifty years ago; such statements generally signify no more than the writer's emotionally possessive attitude to Donne, with perhaps a vague recollection of the dates of Mr Eliot's essays of 1921, or Grierson's edition of 1912. But the latter, indeed a landmark in Donne scholarship, was a culmination as well as an initiator of interest in his poetry; publishers cannot afford to be philanthropists, and the edition would not have been undertaken without some assurance of existing demand. The period really notable for a rapid quickening and extension of interest in Donne is the 1890's; the evidence has been well assembled by Joseph E. Duncan in 'The Revival of Metaphysical Poetry, 1872–1912',[2] and some of it will be readily remembered by those who grew up in days when Saintsbury, Dowden, and Gosse were still obvious critics to consult.

Mr Duncan chose 1872 as the date of the Rev. Alexander Grosart's edition, from which existing demand is not a necessary inference as it was printed for private circulation and Grosart's choice of poets was nearly as undiscriminating as his editorial methods. Nevertheless the interest was there,[3] and it is a mistake

[1] Since the publication of this essay in 1959 I have found a few other relevant references to Donne; Godwin's and Scott's have been added to the text, and Kipling's parallel between Browning and Donne has been added in a footnote.

[2] *PMLA*, LXVIII (1953), p. 658.

[3] Interest in Donne's text is evident in *Notes and Queries* from the 1860's. In 1868 W. C. Hazlitt wishes that 'some competent person could be found to undertake [an edition] *con amore*'; a correspondent calling himself 'CPL' (doubtless the Rev. T. R. O'Flaherty, vicar of *Capel*, Surrey, and owner of important Donne manuscripts) agrees, and says that he has made large collections but 'cannot find time or courage to carry out my intention' (pp. 483, 614).

to dismiss the forty years before Grosart as a period of neglect or misunderstanding, and to regard Browning's known admiration as merely another instance of his oddity and independence in his time. No doubt what has blocked inquiry is the notorious omission of any poem of Donne's from the most popular and influential of Victorian anthologies, Palgrave's *Golden Treasury of Songs and Lyrics* (1861); but Palgrave, as I hope to show, had some excuse, and is not in this respect representative of nineteenth-century anthologists. The forty years before Grosart have their own contribution to the establishment of Donne's poetic reputation, and the true picture is rather one of a gradual (though not steady) recovery than of a revolutionary discovery; so gradual that any starting-point much later than Johnson's *Lives of the Poets* would be arbitrary, and it has seemed best to include the early nineteenth century[1] in this inquiry, although this means recalling some familiar material.

2

There is some apparent set-back after that first and best-known phase associated with the 'romantics'. This is understandable; while to the modern reader the evidence of appreciation and insight in Lamb, Coleridge, Hazlitt, Landor, and De Quincey is clear enough to constitute a body of enlightened opinion, their references to Donne are in fact mostly casual, fugitive, or oblique. Lamb seems to have been the first of them to record his appreciation in print and was probably the instigator of Coleridge's interest,[2] certainly of Hazlitt's; but all he has left us is in the long note to *Philaster* in his *Specimens of English Dramatic Poets* (1808), where he quotes the whole of Elegy xvi and commends its sense, wit, and pathos, and a 'fragment of criticism' countering the common antithesis of wit and feeling and defending Donne and Cowley: 'in the very

[1] A. H. Nethercot, 'The Reputation of the "Metaphysical Poets" during the age of Johnson and the Romantic Revival', *SP*, XXII (1925), p. 81, deals mainly with the eighteenth century; see also the same author's 'The Reputation of John Donne as Metrist', *Sewanee Review*, XXX, (1922), p. 463.

[2] His earliest known reference is in the 'Memoranda for a History of English Poetry' which Dr Coburn (*Inquiring Spirit*, 1951, p. 120) thinks may be 1796–8. See also the notebook quotations of 1800 and 1803–4 (*Notebooks*, ed. K. Coburn, 1957, i, nos. 698, 1786–7, 1789).

thickest of their conceits,—in the bewildering mazes of tropes and figures,—a warmth of soul and generous feeling shines through'. Most of the other evidence of Lamb's reading of Donne comes from Hazlitt, who in 1820 remembered from twelve years before his reading of that same Elegy 'with suffused features and a faltering tongue' and the 'gusto' with which he quoted Donne's 'most crabbed passages'.[1] Hazlitt, whose remarks on Donne are the nearest approach to formal criticism in the period, never really assimilated his poetry, which he seems not to have read until 1818. Early in that year, in his *Lectures on the English Poets,* he says he 'know[s] nothing' except Lamb's favourite Elegy and 'some quaint riddles in verse which the sphinx could not unravel'. Some months later, in the third of the lectures on *English Comic Writers,* he quotes from three of the *Songs and Sonets,* with comments emphasizing Donne's unevenness: the second verse of 'The Blossom', for example, is 'but a lame and impotent conclusion from so delightful a beginning'.[2] Coleridge, who had already in 1811 begun annotating volumes borrowed from Lamb, referred to Donne in the *Biographia Literaria* (chs. i and xviii), and in 1818 projected a lecture on 'Dante, Donne, and Milton' ('the middle name will perhaps puzzle you', he wrote to Cary);[3] but no report survives, and Crabb Robinson's diary records it simply as a lecture on Dante and Milton. Some of Coleridge's comments and marginalia were published in *Table Talk* and *Literary Remains,* but the best of his criticism—the marginalia in Lamb's copy of the *Poems*—not until 1853, in *Notes Theological, Literary, and Miscellaneous,* and (more completely) in the American *Literary World.* De Quincey's reading of Donne is known only from a few penetrating sentences on the 'metaphysical' poets (whom he prefers to call 'Rhetorical') in a review of Whately's *Rhetoric* in *Blackwood's* (1828): 'Few writers have shown a more extraordinary compass of powers than Donne; for he combined —what no other man has ever done—the last sublimation of dialectical subtlety and address with the most impassioned majesty'; and Landor's reading, probably extensive, is known

[1] 'Of Persons one would Wish to have Seen' and 'The Conversation of Authors'.

[2] He included no Donne in his *Select Poets of Great Britain,* 1824.

[3] It would not have done so, for Cary's journal shows him reading Donne's satires in 1800.

only from the 'Imaginary Conversation'[1] of Walton, Cotton, and Oldways (1829) where the several imaginary quotations indicate what struck him most in Donne; these lines are a comment in themselves:

She was so beautiful, had God but died
  For her, and none beside,
Reeling with holy joy from east to west
  Earth would have sunk down blest;
And, burning with bright zeal, the buoyant Sun
  Cried thro' his worlds *well done*!

Leigh Hunt shows some knowledge of Donne in his later writings, and in a review of Tennyson's 1830 poems[2] notes, of 'Love and Sorrow', that 'the author must have been reading Donne. . . . This is the very Analogical Doctor come back again.' The poem is one of those that Tennyson never reprinted; it exemplifies an interest which was evidently current among his undergraduate contemporaries, and which we shall meet again, with a difference, in Henry Alford. Hartley Coleridge has some verses on Donne which quote and expand his father's line on iron pokers; and two more sympathetic notes, buried among his marginalia on Carew in Anderson's *British Poets*:

Men may joke or quibble till they cannot do otherwise, and yet not have joked away all feeling. . . . Is there any difference in style between Donne's Sacred Poems and his wildest love riddles?

Carew is far smoother [than Donne]; but where is the strength, the boundless wealth of thought, the heart beating beneath its twisted mail?[3]

An unexpected enthusiast from an older generation was William Godwin, who in *Thoughts on Man*, 1831, a volume of essays published in his old age,[4] calls Donne 'one of the most

[1] There is also a brief and conventional reference to Donne's 'hobbling' verse in 'A Satire on Satirists', 1836.

[2] *Leigh Hunt's Literary Criticism*, ed. L. H. and C. W. Houtchens, 1956, p. 358; see also pp. 498, 526, 561, and for the reference in *The Book of the Sonnet*, p. 318 below. Hunt also annotated a copy of Donne's poems which was borrowed by G. H. Lewes; see below, p. 319.

[3] *Essays and Marginalia*, 2 vols., 1851, ii, 7, 10.

[4] According to Kegan Paul, *William Godwin, his Friends and Contemporaries*, 2 vols., 1876, they were essays 'written during many previous years', probably in 1817–18 (ii, 248, 290). Godwin's reading in Elizabethan literature began in 1799, perhaps under the influence of his friends Lamb and Coleridge.

deep-thinking and philosophical poets', and praises his 'originality, energy, and vigour . . . every sentence . . . whether in verse or prose, is exclusively his own . . . his thoughts are often in the noblest sense of the word poetical; and passages may be quoted from him that no English poet may attempt to rival, unless it be Milton and Shakespeare'; the present neglect of Donne is attributed to his obscurity (Jonson's 'Donne, for not being understood, would perish' is quoted as 'prophetic') and his 'crabbed and repulsive' phraseology and versification.

Thomas Phillips in a lecture at the Royal Academy in 1827 (published 1833) compares Giotto with Donne; the student of art should forget his 'gothic imperfections' which resemble Donne's 'uncouth phraseology' in being nevertheless 'full of sentiment'—a stock distinction, but an unexpected application. The extent of Wordsworth's knowledge is doubtful; the sermons and poems were in his library, and in the winter of 1830 he was reading the sermons aloud to his wife, but he refers only once to any poem, when urging Dyce to include 'Death be not proud' in his *Specimens of English Sonnets*; Dyce did so, and recorded Wordsworth's plea in his copy of the 1633 poems.[1] Scott's references in the 'Life of John Dryden' in his edition of 1808 are perfunctory, and unfavourable. Southey was unconverted in 1807, when he collected his *Specimens of the later English Poets*: 'Nothing indeed could have made Donne a Poet, unless as great a change had been worked in the structure of his ears, as was wrought in elongating those of Midas';[2] which possibly provoked Coleridge to his masterly defence of Donne's verse.

Coleridge's notes, our most valued legacy of Donne criticism from this period, seem not to have been well known save for the line 'wreathes iron pokers into true-love knots'. Nothing came of Barron Field's project of a Percy Society edition incorporating these marginalia[3]—though their publication in the *Literary*

[1] *Letters of William and Dorothy Wordsworth, The Later Years*, ed. E. de Selincourt, 3 vols, 1939, i, 469, ii, 652; cf. *Divine Poems*, ed. Helen Gardner, 1952, p. 69.

[2] Compare Nathan Drake, *Literary Hours*, 1798, p. 452, and *Shakespeare and his Times*, 2 vols., 1817, i, 615.

[3] Field's comments are quoted from the manuscript in the Houghton Library at Harvard, by Roberta Florence Brinkley in *Coleridge and the Seventeenth Century*, 1955, p. 519 n. This book includes some previously unpublished notes on Donne (pp. 527–8).

World may have stimulated Lowell's interest and his encouragement of the Boston edition of Donne in 1855,[1] the only near-complete and separate collection of Donne's poetry between Tonson's and Grosart's. But American interest goes farther back and Emerson's, as shown in his letters and journals, has a more obvious source. A letter written in 1815, at the age of fifteen, shows him reading Johnson's life of Cowley, and struck (like Ayrton at the evening party of 1808, in 'Of Persons one would Wish to have Seen') by the stanza beginning 'Here lies a he-sun and a she-moon here'. His comment is 'I should like to see the poem it was taken from.'[2]

For many readers meeting Donne for the first time in Johnson's dozen or so of ample quotations, this would be a natural response. We need not go to Johnson to account for Lamb, who had his own 'midnight darlings, [his] folios'; but there is other evidence, some of it on lower levels,[3] that Donne was increasingly read after about 1790, and this almost certainly reflects the popularity of the life of Cowley.[4] Boswell thought it the best of the *Lives*, because Johnson had 'exhibited' the metaphysical poets 'at large, with such happy illustrations from their writings, and in so luminous a manner, that indeed he may be allowed the full merit of novelty, and to have discovered to us, as it were, a new planet in the poetical hemisphere'. This is a tribute often overlooked.

The curious could not pursue their interest in Johnson's edition, which started with Cowley; but Donne's poems were available in Bell's edition (1781), and after 1793 in Robert Anderson's *British Poets*, which adds a 'life' based on Granger's in his *Biographical History*, and quotes Johnson. Any Victorian

[1] Lowell's annotated copy of this was used in the Grolier Club edition of 1895.

[2] *Letters*, ed. R. L. Rusk, 6 vols., 1939, i, 10. On Emerson's interest in the metaphysical poets generally see Norman Brittin, *American Literature*, 1936, pp. 1–21, J. Russell Roberts, id., 1949, pp. 298–310, and Emerson's anthology *Parnassus*, 1875.

[3] Such as an otherwise negligible article on Cowley, Donne, and 'Clieveland' [*sic*] by 'M. M. D.' in the *European Magazine*, August 1822, pp. 108–12.

[4] Johnson knew Donne's poetry very well, and quoted from it constantly throughout his Dictionary, 'for instance, ninety-seven times under Q, R, S' (W. B. C. Watkins, *Johnson and English Poetry before 1660*, 1936, p. 80) and as the Dictionary long remained a standard work, this may have had considerable influence in familiarizing readers with Donne's poetry.

gentleman's library would be likely to include Bell or Anderson or Chalmers (1810), and though the text of Donne is unsatisfactory the collection is reasonably complete,[1] and the lack of any further edition in England until Grosart's is not necessarily an indication of neglect. After the turn of the century, Donne also begins to be represented in anthologies and selections: George Ellis's *Specimens* (1801)[2] has 'Go and catch a falling star' and the first stanza of 'Negative Love', and Capel Lofft's *Laura; or an Anthology of Sonnets* (1814) has three sonnets. Thomas Campbell's *Specimens* (1819) has four poems (two incomplete), Ezekiel Sanford's *Works of the British Poets* (Philadelphia, 1819) has fourteen of the *Songs and Sonets* and twenty-three other poems or parts of poems, James Montgomery's *The Christian Poet* (1827)[3] has two Holy Sonnets and the 'Hymn to Christ', Southey's *Select Works of the British Poets* (1831) has five *Songs and Sonets*, all the Holy Sonnets, and sixteen others, Robert F. Housman's *Collection of English Sonnets* [1835] has two sonnets, Richard Cattermole's *Sacred Poetry of the Seventeenth Century* (1836) has seven Holy Sonnets, the First Anniversary, 'Hymn to Christ', and a few others, and Samuel C. Hall's *Book of Gems* (1836) has ten *Songs and Sonets*. The choices rarely coincide; each editor has read Donne for himself, and made his own selection. In the same period, casual quotations from Donne turn up in odd places; the 'Biographical Notice' of Jane Austen by her brother Henry (1818) says that 'her eloquent blood spoke through her modest cheek' (this is in all periods the most frequently quoted passage); Scott quotes from Carew's elegy on Donne in his introduction to *The Black Dwarf*, and has a chapter-motto wrongly attributed to Donne in ch. iii of *The Legend of Montrose*; Julius and Augustus Hare, *Guesses at Truth* (1827), quote from the third satire (and in the 1838 edition also from a sermon); Hood quotes both the 'he-sun'

[1] All follow 1719 (which follows 1669), each adding its own misprints. (The 1719 life, in accidental anticipation of the late Professor F. P. Wilson has 1572 as the date of Donne's birth.) Elegy xx was first printed from manuscript in Francis G. Waldron's *Collection of Miscellaneous Poetry*, 1802.

[2] 2nd edition, 3 vols.; these poems were also in the one-volume edition of 1790, and in all later ones (1803, 1811, 1845, 1851).

[3] The Rev. John Mitford's *Sacred Specimens*, 1827, has only the wrongly attributed Psalm 137.

lines (perhaps caught from Hazlitt or Lamb) and another favourite pun from 'old Donne';[1] Edmund H. Barker, the ill-starred classical scholar, quotes two 'Specimens' from *Paradoxes and Problems* (1652) in the *Constitutional Magazine* of September 1835 (p. 156); two lines (53–4) of Elegy xvi appear as motto to a story in the annual *Friendship's Offering* (1835); and No. 76 (by Newman) of *Tracts for the Times* (1836) quotes a passage from Sermon xxxi. A different kind of knowledge is suggested by Anna Jameson's *The Loves of the Poets* (1829), who quotes 'The Message' as 'long popular, and I can remember when a child, hearing it sung to very beautiful music'.

Most of the selections mentioned also include some criticism, some but not all in stock phrases about harsh versification, obscurity, and cold conceits. 'His ruggedness and whim', says Campbell, 'are almost proverbially known'—testimony at least to common knowledge; 'yet there is a beauty of thought which at intervals rises from his chaotic imagination, like Venus smiling on the waters'. Cattermole thinks that modern readers find Donne obscure only because they prefer 'voluptuous sweetness' to 'depth of sentiment and originality of thought'. S. C. Hall, while taking the usual line about 'beauties and deformities', tilts the balance decisively; his specimens, he says, show that Donne was often 'smooth even to elegance'.

> He was absolutely saturated with learning—his intellect was large and searching . . . his wit playful yet caustic. At times he is full of tenderness; and in spite of himself submits to the mastery of nature.

He believes that Donne's 'name as a poet is largely known and esteemed'—in contrast both to Anna Jameson seven years earlier, who had thought him 'little read, except by those who make our old poetry their study', and probably chiefly known 'from the lines at the bottom of the page in Pope's version'; and also to the egregious Nathan Drake, who in 1817 writes that 'A more refined age, and a more chastized taste, have very justly consigned his poetical labours to the shelf of the philologer.'

[1] *Atlas*, 25 June and 9 July 1826, and *Whims and Oddities*, 'The Marriage Procession', November 1827 (I owe the Hood and Barker references to Mr P. F. Morgan) Another wit, Douglas Jerrold, was also, according to his son's 'Memoir', a reader of Donne.

'Those who make our old poetry their study' are best represented by an unknown, independent, and at times strikingly perceptive writer in the *Retrospective 'Review* of 1823.[1] Here indeed are the accents of discovery; if the progress of Donne's reputation is ever to be fully charted, 1823 should be as important a date as 1921.

This essay I propose to describe in some detail. Though headed with the title of the 1669 *Poems*, it is almost entirely concerned with the *Songs and Sonets*, seventeen of which are quoted, either whole or in part. It begins by mocking at Theobald's phrase 'nothing but a continued heap of riddles' but makes no other reference to earlier criticism, and never uses the term 'metaphysical'. At the outset Donne is placed 'at the head of the minor poets of his day', for his learning, his

> active and piercing intellect . . . imagination, if not grasping and comprehensive, most subtle and far-darting—a fancy rich, vivid, and picturesque, and at the same time, highly *fantastical* . . . a mode of expression singularly terse, simple, and condensed . . . a wit, admirable as well for its caustic severity as its playful quickness.[2]

Far from objecting to his verse, the critic finds in Donne 'an exquisite ear'; his only deficiencies are in 'sensibility and taste', and the former is interestingly qualified:

> His sensibility was by nature strong, but sluggish and deep-seated. It required to be roused and awakened by the imagination, before it would act; and this process seldom failed to communicate to the action which it created an appearance of affectation (for it was nothing more than the appearance).

His 'scholastic habits . . . without weakening his sensibility', contributed greatly 'to deform and denaturalize its outward

[1] Vol. viii, pt. i, pp. 31–55. The essay is cited by Allibone, and was known to Grosart (*Notes and Queries*, 1870, p. 505), but the only modern critic who speaks of having read it is Wightman F. Melton, *The Rhetoric of Donne's Verse*, 1906, and no attempt has ever been made to identify the writer. The editor of the *Retrospective*, Henry Southern (who also edited the *London Magazine* in 1825–8), wrote some articles, and so did Charles Wentworth Dilke, P. G. Patmore, W. J. Fox, and Thomas Noon Talfourd. On present evidence Talfourd seems a possible conjecture. (Since this article was sent to press I have seen the third edition of Keynes's *Bibliography of John Donne*, 1958, where the review is attributed to 'J. Spence'.)

[2] S. C. Hall borrowed from this passage; see p. 285 above. It is also recalled in some anonymous *Lectures on the English Poets*, 1847, pp. 27–8.

manifestations'; feelings and thoughts were heightened and illustrated by a 'host of images and associations', supplied by 'quick-eyed wit' and 'subtle ingenuity'. This is seen as a fault, but a fault of his age and school, springing from a disregard of the principle 'that an idea or a sentiment may be poetical *per se*':

> They considered that *man* was the creator of poetry, not Nature; and that any thing might be made poetical, by connecting it, in a certain manner, with something else. A thought or a feeling was, to them, not a thing *to express*, but a theme to write *variations* upon—a nucleus, about which other thoughts and feelings were to be made to crystallize.

Donne's 'school' is then compared with, but distinguished from, the Della Cruscans: superior, because the latter 'tried to make things poetical, by means of words alone', the former, by 'a vast fund of thoughts and images'.

Having thus cleared the ground, the critic announces his main intention: 'to bring to light some of the exquisite beauties which have hitherto lain concealed from the present age'—beauties of every kind, though unaccountably mixed with 'deformities', which perhaps explains the 'total neglect', remarkable in 'an age which boasts that it has revived a knowledge of, and a love for its great predecessor'. The reader of Donne should not judge hastily from transient irritation; he will soon find 'great exercise for his *thinking* faculties (if nothing else) even in the objectionable parts of Donne'. Some pieces are entirely free from this 'mixed character': notably the 'Valediction: forbidding mourning' (quoted complete), which 'for clearness and smoothness of construction, and a passionate sweetness and softness in the music of the versification, might have been written in the present day'—if indeed any modern poet is capable of it. 'The simile of the compasses, notwithstanding its quaintness, is more perfect in its kind, and more beautiful, than anything we are acquainted with.' On other poems, the critic is often felicitous, finding in 'The Good-Morrow' 'an air of serious gaiety . . . as if composed in the very bosom of bliss', and in 'The Message' 'a certain wayward simplicity of thought peculiarly appropriate to such compositions'; in 'The Prohibition' Donne 'bandies a thought about (like a shuttlecock) from one hand to the other, only to let it fall to the ground at last'. No other poet could have made the comparison of the nerves and the braid of hair in 'The Funeral' *tell* as he had done; 'The Will'[1] illustrates 'his infinite fullness of meaning . . . almost every line would furnish matter for a whole treatise in modern times'; 'Negative Love' shows 'a love for the passion excited, rather than the object exciting it . . . that lives by "*chewing the cud* of sweet and bitter fancy" . . . that broods, like the stock-dove, over its own voice, and listens for no other'. Later, this comparison with Wordsworth is made explicit, and his style is called a return to that of the first stanza of 'The Blossom'. Many more poems and passages are quoted and praised, and the divergence from traditional views is evident in the repudiation of Pope's 'brilliant and refined' version of the satires: nearly a hundred lines from the fourth Satire[2] (from 'Towards me did run') are quoted, with the simple comment, 'It strikes us as being nearly the perfection of this kind of writing.' And although the essay concludes with some concessions to the common view of Donne's faults, this enthusiasm is the note of the whole; indeed, the specific comments seem slightly at variance with the general framework, as if the writer were captivated in the act of quoting. His judicious assessment of faults and beauties crumbles before the conviction of Donne's uniqueness—his poems 'bear a mark that we cannot very well expound, even to ourselves, but which we know no one could have placed on them but him'.

3

In the Victorian period, 'official' opinion, as represented in histories of literature, encyclopedias, and biographical collections,[3] represents a hardening and simplification of the views of

[1] This poem later became a favourite; it is in the selections of Southey, Hall, Alford, and in *Chambers's Cyclopaedia*, and is the only poem chosen from Donne in Dyce's *Early English Poems, Chaucer to Pope*, 1863.

[2] Almost the only previous discussion of the satires is in John Payne Collier's *The Poetical Decameron*, 2 vols., 1820, and he is mainly concerned with questions of date.

[3] Such as G. G. Cunningham, *Lives of the Most Eminent and Illustrious Englishmen*, 4 vols., 1837, iii, 240–2; Robert Bell, *Lives of the Most Eminent Literary and Scientific Men of Great Britain*, 2 vols., 1839, i, 50–3.

Johnson and of Hazlitt; the term 'metaphysical' is generally objected to,[1] but Donne is associated with his 'school', and the same phrases recur parrot-wise—'remote analogies', 'far-fetched images'—and usually with emphasis on his inequalities—'He mixed up with what was beautiful and true much that was fantastical and false'. But the merely contemptuous tone of Henry Hallam in his *Introduction to the Literature of Europe*[2] is exceptional:

> Donne is the most inharmonious of our versifiers, if he can be said to have deserved such a name by lines too rugged to seem metre. Of his earlier poems many are very licentious. The later are chiefly devout. Few are good for much; the conceits have not even the merit of being intelligible, and it would perhaps be difficult to select three passages that we should care to read again.

To parallel that we must go back to Southey or Theobald. But in the same year, 1839, Henry Alford allows Donne 'a fine musical ear' (with three examples cited in a footnote) and attributes his harshness to that 'laborious condensation' typical of the juvenile poems of great men. The anonymous editor of the *Book of the Poets* (1841 ?), who includes 'His Picture', part of 'The Dissolution', and one sonnet, finds, despite harshness and pedantry, 'an innate vigour and freshness which will always ensure [his poems] a high rank in English poetry'. The writer of the article on Donne in *Chambers's Cyclopædia of English Literature* (1844) trims his course; this poet's reputation has 'latterly in some degree revived', and whereas earlier critics spoke of his 'harsh and rugged versification, and his leaving nature for conceit', it is now acknowledged that 'amidst much rubbish, there is much real poetry, and that of a high order'. To show his merits four quotations are given, including the first verse of the 'Valentine' *Epithalamion*,[3] a passage from the fourth satire, the 'Valediction: forbidding mourning', and 'The Will'. (The later fortunes of this entry are not without interest; the 1858

[1] The sense in which Johnson used the word (see A. H. Nethercot, 'The term "Metaphysical Poets" before Johnson', *MLN*, xxxvii (1922), p. 11) is not understood, which is itself an interesting comment on its altered associations.

[2] 4 vols., 1837–9; iii, ch. v.

[3] This is probably the reason for its becoming a common quotation; I find it, for instance, in a paper by G. A. Sala in Dickens's *Household Words*, 19 June 1852, and in the Causton edition of Walton's *Life*, 1855.

edition merely added a little more information on editions and manuscripts, but the 1876 edition was revised, and 'rubbish' was altered to 'bad taste'.)[1] G. L. Craik in his *Sketches of the History of Literature* (1845) quotes 'Sweetest Love' to illustrate Donne's ear for melody, and thinks the verse of the satires was 'adopted by choice and on system' and is 'not without a deep and subtle music'.

'Why are Donne's sermons not reprinted at Oxford?' Coleridge had asked, and the question was repeated by his nephew, the editor of *Table Talk*, and by the *Quarterly*'s reviewer of *Literary Remains* in July 1837. The result was the six-volume edition by the Rev. Henry Alford[2] in 1839, miscalled *Works of Dr John Donne*; the new interest in Donne's prose was also reflected in *Selections from the Works of John Donne D.D.* (Talboys, 1840), two editions of the *Devotions* (Talboys and Pickering, both 1840), Richard Cattermole, *Literature of the Church of England* (2 vols., 1849), James Brogden, *Illustrations of Liturgy and Ritual* (3 vols., 1842), and Robert Aris Willmott, *Precious Stones, Aids to Reflection* (1850). All this helped to draw further attention to the divine poems. Alford included them all, the 1840 selection had several, and so did another Oxford collection, *Gems of Sacred Poetry* (2 vols., 1841), with an introductory essay which notes 'a great, though gradual revolution' in the taste of the last thirty years, for both the poetry and the theology of Elizabethan and Jacobean writers. Cambridge followed in 1847 with *Select Poetry Chiefly Sacred of the Reign of James the First*, edited by Edward Farr, which has a fuller selection. There are similar later examples (including a very Gothic-looking volume, W. H. Rogers's *Spiritual Conceits, extracted from the Writings of the Fathers, the old English Poets, etc.*, 1862), and one interesting omission; Leigh Hunt's posthumous *Book of the Sonnet* (1867), though praising 'La Corona', refrains from including it because 'Donne's piety, though sincere, was unhealthy'. No extended criticism of the divine poems is found until 1868 when George Macdonald, recently Professor of English Literature at Bedford

[1] In 1892 the entry shows no change except a reference to Grosart's edition; it was entirely rewritten, with the help of Edmund Gosse, in 1901.

[2] The edition was prepared in 1838 at the request of the publisher, J. W. Parker; but Alford had been interested in Donne since his undergraduate days at Cambridge (*Life, Letters, and Journals*, edited by his widow, 1873, pp. 75, 112).

College, included a chapter on them in *England's Antiphon*, a popular account of English religious poetry. He is perplexed by their 'incongruities', on which he at least is specific, commenting in some detail on 'Hymn to God in my Sickness', which he regards as typical of Donne's 'best and worst'. The 'best' is contained in the first and in the last two stanzas: he explains, and praises, the music image:

> To recognize its beauty . . . we must recall the custom of those days to send out for 'a noise of musicians'. Hence he imagines that he has been summoned as one of a band already gone in to play before the king of 'The High Countries': he is now at the door, where he is listening to catch the tone, that he may have his instrument tuned and ready before he enters. But with what a jar the next stanza breaks on heart, mind, and ear!

The sudden shift of comparison of himself from map to navigator is thought 'grotesque and absurd'; still worse is the next stanza, where 'he is alternately a map and a man sailing on the map of himself'. These strictures must have influenced Emerson, who gives only Macdonald's three preferred stanzas, without notice of omission, in his anthology *Parnassus* (1875). In the same year as Macdonald's book, the Archbishop of Dublin (R. C. Trench) brought out his *Household Book of English Poetry*, which included the 'Lecture on the Shadow' and two Holy Sonnets, 'Death, be not proud' and 'As due by many titles', the last of which he describes as 'rough and rugged' but 'the genuine cry of one engaged in that most terrible of all struggles'; he goes on to compare Donne with St Augustine, 'the same tumultuous youth . . . and then the same passionate and personal grasp of the central truths of Christianity'.

But sometimes the new interest in Donne as divine encouraged the playing-down of his secular poems. Alford apologized for having 'pruned' so 'unsparingly' from them, but 'it seemed to me that the character of this work being theological, the Poems which were to be inserted should be of the same stamp'. He accordingly gave no satires, only three of the *Songs and Sonets*, one elegy, and one epithalamion. The Rev. Augustus Jessopp in his edition of *Essays in Divinity* (1855) regarded Donne as 'the greatest preacher England has ever produced' but thought his powers 'comparatively trifled away' up to 1613—a remark which prepares one for his article on Donne in the *Dictionary of National Biography* (1888), twenty columns long but with only a cursory reference to the poems. To accept Donne whole has been difficult for critics ever since Walton.

That is one reason why there are few attempts at comprehensive criticism, though it is not quite fair to call Donne 'yet unappreciated', as De Quincey did in 1851.[1] In 1838 the youthful G. H. Lewes[2] apostrophizes the poet as 'Honest John Donne —rough—hearty—pointed and sincere' and observes in 'The Good-Morrow' 'the true language of passion, which will appear unnatural only to those who never felt *une grande passion*'. There is true appreciation in an essay in *Lowe's Edinburgh Magazine* of February 1846, the first of a series of three including Herbert and Herrick. Grosart quoted it as 'by Dr. Samuel Brown of Edinburgh, I believe'; it has since been attributed to Coventry Patmore.[3] Whoever the author, his approach is independent and unusual (though there are signs that he has read the *Retrospective* essay), and he has strongly marked views on poetry in general. Some of his preferences in Donne are surprising at that date. The satires are ranked highest, 'the best in the language', and Pope's sophistications exposed by parallel quotations from the fourth satire (this passage is quoted by Grosart). Donne's verse may be rough, 'But who . . . would not . . . prefer climbing, with Donne, these crags where all the air is fresh and wholesome, to gliding, with Thomas Moore, over flats, from beneath the rank verdure of which arises malaria and invisible disease?' Those who submit his poems to 'affectionate reflection' will pardon his worst versification: 'since no sacrifice of meaning is ever made to it,—it thus being so much more palatable to the

[1] *Works*, ed. Masson, 1897, xi, 110.

[2] 'Retrospective Reviews—No. VII' in the *National Magazine and Monthly Critic*, April 1838, pp. 373–8. Lewes's name is given at the head of No. 1 of the series, which is unknown to his biographers. He had borrowed a copy of Donne from 'L. H.' and quotes some of the owner's marginalia: this must be Leigh Hunt, whom Lewes knew well by 1837.

[3] See Frederick Page, *Courage in Politics*, 1921, appendix ii, and J. C. Reid, *The Mind and Art of Coventry Patmore*, 1957. Patmore was writing for periodicals in 1845–6, but the evidence here is of the dubious sort called 'internal'. Dr Samuel Brown contributed an essay on Herbert to *McPhail's Journal* in 1848, which has a slight resemblance to the Herbert article in *Lowe's*; Grosart's recollection probably confused the two.

truly cultivated taste than the expensive melody of some modern versifiers'. The unfavourable contrast with modern poetry is pursued in a rather obscure statement that in Donne's day poets acted unconsciously on their 'instinctive immediate perception ... without limits imposed by the logical faculty, or the hyperbole-hating decencies of flat conventionality', whereas 'our modern carpet-poets tread their way upon hyperbole, as nicely as they would do over ice of an uncertain strength, dreading every moment to be drowned in ridicule'. Donne was also fortunate in living in an age 'when English intellect was at its height' and when religion had 'enhanced poetic liberty' and 'extinguished that false shame which Romanism had attached to the contemplation of the sexual relations'. But his poetry is never likely to be popular, because of its ruggedness and its difficulty; the meaning demands constant attention, and only to the 'most faithful and disciplined lovers of the muse' will he be 'a peculiar favourite'. This aristocratic, rather truculent tone is certainly not unlike that of Patmore's later criticism.

He has not much to say of particular poems. The love-poems show 'the love of love' rather than the passion for its object, and their conceits make them inferior to the satires; but the 'Valediction' is an exception, a 'noble poem', 'exquisite' in versification. It is quoted entire, and there are also short quotations from 'The Ecstasy', 'The Good-Morrow', 'The Blossom', and the first Epithalamion, but the quality of the last is impossible to show in extracts—it has an 'inexplicable, incommunicable aura'. There are quotations from the First Anniversary, but the divine poems as a whole are slighted.

His next essay, on Herbert, contrasts Donne's rough strength with Herbert's smooth sweetness, and reveals the writer as an admirer of Tennyson, who is compared with Herbert in his combination of 'activity of thought' with 'native sweetness of feeling and ... expression'. But he adds, disputing Coleridge's view, that the highest genius is 'masculine', and Herbert's and Tennyson's 'feminine'; which again is reminiscent of Patmore. If he is the writer, we may guess that this early interest was stimulated by Coleridge, and by his father P. G. Patmore, the friend of Lamb and Hazlitt. It may have affected his poetry. Mario Praz (who is unaware of the essay in *Lowe's*) makes a case for Donne's influence,[1] citing similar images ('as turning spirals draw the eyes'), verbal echoes ('some say, "It lightens", some say "No" '), and the movement of the quatrains. Dowden had noted this too, with more moderation: 'The metre of the *Extasie* is the same as that of the *Angel in the House*, and the manner in which meaning and metre move together closely resembles that of Mr Patmore's *Preludes*.'[2] But if Patmore really was inspired by Donne, the effect is counteracted by his firm narrative line and the deliberate surface simplicity of his style; his contemporaries were not so obtuse as Praz thinks in emphasizing the influence of Tennyson.

Tennyson's only known comment on Donne is on the 'Valediction: forbidding mourning'. But as this poem is quoted in full in Walton's *Life*[3]—which, as the *Lowe's* essay says, had 'a hundred readers' for every one of Donne's poetry—this is not necessarily evidence of wider knowledge of Donne. Such wider knowledge is, however, shown by some of Tennyson's friends and contemporaries, besides Browning: for example, Sir Henry Taylor, who quotes not only the 'Valediction' but twice from the *Elegies* in his *Autobiography*;[4] by Edward FitzGerald;[5] John Forster, who praised Landor for catching the style of the poet so happily, 'not only its extravagance, but its genius';[6] and George Eliot, who quotes 'The Undertaking' and 'The Good-Morrow' in two chapter-mottoes[7] of *Middlemarch*—chosen, significantly, for chapters concerning Ladislaw and Dorothea, and the latter (ll. 8–11) touchingly forecasting Dorothea's admission of her love.

Palgrave's knowledge of Donne is not in doubt. He quotes him in *The Passionate Pilgrim* (1858); in preparation for the *Golden Treasury* (1861) he went through Chalmers's *English*

[1] *The Hero in Eclipse in Victorian Fiction* (translated 1956, first published 1952), pp. 431–9.

[2] *Fortnightly Review*, June 1890, p. 805.

[3] The *Lives* were constantly reprinted, and the edition of 1855 is very fully annotated (by Thomas Edlyne Tomkins) with many additional quotations from Donne's poetry.

[4] Published 1885, but begun in the 1860's; see i, 183, 273, 288.

[5] *Letters* [ed. W. A. Wright], 2 vols., 1894, ii, 26 (letter of 1861).

[6] *Life of Landor*, 1869, ii, 183 n. Forster owned a copy of the 1633 Poems which had been in the Drury family.

[7] chs. xxxix, lxxxiii.

Poets twice; and he shows his knowledge and his opinion of Donne in a review[1] published in the same year, where he contrasts the 'imaginative conceits' of Ralegh's 'Come live with me' with the 'frostwork ingenuities of the intellect' in 'The Bait', and notes that 'far-sought conceits and allusions' and 'strange contorted phraseology' are not peculiar to Donne and Cowley 'but more or less mark English poetry from Surrey to Herbert and Crashaw'. In his *Treasury of Sacred Song* (1889) he included three Holy Sonnets and one hymn, noting in Donne's poetry generally a 'strange originality almost equally fascinating and repellent', and a 'strange solemn passionate earnestness' underlying the 'fanciful conceits'.

It was Palgrave who recorded Tennyson's moving recitation of the last four stanzas of the 'Valediction' and his praise of their 'wonderful ingenuity'.[2] We do not know whether this was before or after 1860, or whether 'all that stood near admission' to the *Golden Treasury* and was submitted to Tennyson for final decision included any of Donne. The manuscript, Tennyson's notes, and several marked volumes, survive, but provide no answer, Chalmers's *Poets* unfortunately not being among them. But it is interesting to see from notes on the manuscript that Tennyson, who was an enthusiast for Marvell and introduced the 'Horatian Ode' to Palgrave, not only approved for inclusion 'The Garden' and 'The Emigrants' Song' but 'greatly pleaded for the *Lover*' ['To his Coy Mistress']—'but', adds Palgrave, 'I thought one or two lines too *strong* for this age'. We know too that Palgrave omitted Spenser's *Epithalamion* 'with great reluctance as not in harmony with modern manners', and other love-poems which he privately described as 'too high-kilted', and that he thought of a separate collection of the more 'decidedly amorous'. The original standard for inclusion was evidently strict; one of the advisers wrote 'too coarse' against 'It was a lover and his Lass',[3] which was, however, included. This fear of the 'young person' is one possible reason for omitting

[1] *Quarterly Review*, October 1861, pp. 449–50, 456. His authorship is known from his copy of the article in the British Museum (*Opuscula*, I, press-mark 012274 ee. 1).

[2] 'Personal Recollections', contributed to Hallam Tennyson's *Memoir*, ii, 503.

[3] Note in Palgrave's copy of Bell's *Songs of the Dramatists*, in the present writer's possession.

many of the *Songs and Sonets*;[1] as Grosart says, 'it needs courage to print the poetry of Dr. John Donne in our day', and even he hesitated long over Elegy xix. But a nearly contemporary anthologist, J. C. M. Bellew, who says in the Preface to his *Poets' Corner* (1868) that he had a 'black list' of authors 'whose works it would be impossible to put into the hands of a youth or a schoolgirl', nevertheless managed to find seven poems which could safely represent Donne, mostly divine poems, but one of them 'The Anniversary' from *Songs and Sonets.* Palgrave, however, had narrowed his choice at the outset by explicitly excluding religious lyrics; and some of the other criteria given in his notes and Preface would tend, on his view, to keep Donne out:

> a comparative absence of extreme or temporary phases in style . . . will be found throughout.
>
> That a poem shall . . . reach a perfection commensurate with its aim—that we should require finish in proportion to brevity—that passion, colour and originality cannot atone for serious imperfections in clearness, unity or truth . . . above all, that excellence should be looked for in the whole rather than in the parts,—such and other such canons have been always strictly regarded.
>
> If no verses by certain writers who show . . . more thought than mastery of expression are printed in this volume, it should not be imagined that they have been excluded without much hesitation and regret.

Palgrave made many later additions to Books I and II,[2] but he did not take the opportunity to add any of Donne; by 1891, the last revised edition, there could be no doubt of Donne's recovery of fame, and his continued exclusion shows rather Palgrave's firmness in holding to his original principles. But I have found some interesting new evidence of a momentary wavering. He acquired Grosart's edition, and his copy is in the

[1] Palgrave included two verses of 'Absence' (from Davison's *Poetical Rhapsody*) which was approved by all the selectors, but did not attribute it to Donne until the edition of 1891, on Grosart's authority. In the edition of 1912 the name was removed.

[2] Over thirty poems in all were added; some are mentioned in Colin J. Horne, 'Palgrave's *Golden Treasury*', *English Studies*, N.S. II (1949), pp. 54–63, the best account of the work.

British Museum, with a few markings.[1] He used this for his *Treasury of Sacred Song*, marking with approval five Holy Sonnets (two more than he finally included) and also writing 'fine and pathetic' against the 'Hymn to Christ' and 'spoiled by its own cleverness' against 'The Cross'; but he was evidently also thinking of the revised *Golden Treasury*, for he set a mark of approval on 'Sweetest Love', and also on the first verse of 'The Anniversary', with the words 'Si sic omnia!' That might be taken as his final word on the love-lyrics.

'More *thought* than mastery of expression' was a disqualification for the *Golden Treasury*. But Grosart dedicated his edition of Donne 'to Robert Browning, the poet of the century for *thinkers* . . . knowing how much his poetry, with every abatement, is valued and assimilated by him'. As Browning's poetry gained in fame and influence in the last quarter of the century, the way was prepared for a wider and truer appreciation of Donne. The extent of the 'assimilation' is less important than the increasing notice taken of the likeness between them, not only by Grosart but by Dowden, Gosse, Schelling, and many others;[2] it is clear from these critics that the movement of their reputation was partly interdependent, like Tennyson's and Keats's in the 1840's, or Mr Eliot's and Donne's in the 1920's.

At the date of Grosart's dedication, Browning had known Donne's work for over forty years. He was reading it in 1826–8 (fired, perhaps, by the *Retrospective Review*?) and is said by Griffin to have set 'Go and catch a falling star' to music. When writing *Paracelsus*, as he afterwards recalled, he was once light-headed and fancied he had to go through a complete version of the Psalms by Donne. In 1844 he and Miss Barrett, as yet unknown to each other, were applied to by R. H. Horne for mottoes to suit individual writers in *A New Spirit of the Age*, and one for

[1] Press-mark 2326 d. 3. It is not catalogued as Palgrave's, and his signature has disappeared in recent rebinding, but the marks are unmistakably his.

[2] See Joseph E. Duncan, 'The Intellectual Kinship of Browning and Donne', *SP*, l, (1953), p. 81; and Edward Dowden, *Fortnightly Review*, 1890. A writer in *Putnam's Monthly Magazine*, April 1856 (quoted in L. N. Broughton, *Robert Browning. A Bibliography 1830–1950*, 1953, p. 99) may be the first to draw the parallel. Kipling, who was interested in Donne's poems 'many years before they became a literary fashion', said that 'Donne was Browning's great-grandfather . . . with Browning's temperament for turning his mind upside-down and letting the ideas get out as they could'. (Charles Carrington, *Rudyard Kipling*, 1955, p. 477).

Henry Taylor was an aptly-chosen quotation from Elegy iv.[1] The quotations in his letters to Elizabeth Barrett in 1845–6 show a close familiarity with Donne, and are lightly interwoven with his courtship; he quotes (from memory and inaccurately, but very aptly in the context) from the third stanza of the 'Valentine' *Epithalamion*; in another letter he asks her why she should 'lean and hearken' after Italy. The line 'as an amber drop enwraps the bee', from 'Honour is so sublime perfection', is applied to Carlyle's view of poetry. (It has not previously been noticed, however, that another quotation, from 'Donne's pretty lines about seals', is really from Herbert's 'In Sacram Anchoram Piscatoris'.)[2] Elizabeth Barrett quotes in her turn from 'The Will' and the second satire, calling the author 'your Donne'. When Browning writes 'Soule-hydroptique with a sacred thirst' in 'The Grammarian's Funeral' he is again virtually quoting Donne; not, as Mr Duncan suggests, the Second Anniversary, but 'an hydroptique immoderate desire of human learning and languages', in the well-known letter given by Walton. In 1869 William Rossetti[3] recorded Browning's enthusiasm for 'a poem by Donne named *Metempsychosis*'; by then he had written the poem in which he quotes it, *The Two Poets of Croisic*:

> *He's greatest now and to de-struct-i-on*
>   *Nearest.* Attend the solemn word I quote,
> O Paul! *There's no pause at perfect-i-on*
>   Thus knolls thy knell the Doctor's bronzed throat!
> *Greatness a period hath, no sta-ti-on*!
>   Better and truer verse none ever wrote

[1] *Letters of E. B. Browning to R. H. Horne*, 2 vols., 1877, i, 136. But the quotation is not in Browning's letter to Horne (*New Letters*, ed. De Vane and Knickerbocker, 1950) and may have come from Miss Barrett, whose quotations from the Holy Sonnets in *The Seraphim*, 1838, and reference to Donne in *The Book of the Poets* (*Athenæum*, 1842) show that she had some knowledge of Donne before she met Browning.

[2] Printed in editions of Donne (1650–1719), and also in Alford, but not in Anderson or Chalmers; this fact, taken with the early date of Browning's reading of Donne, and the presentation to him of a copy of 1719 in 1842, suggests that he used an early edition. (The particular lines are not in Walton's *Life*.)

[3] D. G. Rossetti was reading Donne, evidently for the first time, in 1880 (*Family Letters*, ii, 356); Swinburne discovered the *Anniversaries* in 1876 (letter to Theodore Watts-Dunton, printed in T. J. Wise, *Autobiographical Notes by A. C. Swinburne*, 1920) and has several interesting references to Donne in his *Study of Ben Jonson*, 1889, e.g. pp. 99, 129, 142.

(Despite the antique outstretched *a-i-on*)
Than thou, revered and magisterial Donne!

Finally, in a late uncollected poem, 'Epps', he called Donne 'brave' and 'rare', and drew on the supposed sixth satire and Grosart's note on it.

Whether Browning did more than read, quote, and praise is impossible to establish. Readers of both poets—fewer now than fifty years ago—must often be haunted by a fleeting sense of likeness, especially in Donne's satires and *Metempsychosis*, but it is doubtful whether this amounts to influence. Mr Duncan has collected possible parallels, and also considers the 'kinship' of the two poets under the four general headings of philosophical ideas; casuistical logic, metaphor, and wit; development of the dramatic monologue; and experiments with a conversational metric and idiom. The first seems to me the weakest, the last the strongest part of his case. But, as he justly says in conclusion, the influence was such as 'to supplement and reinforce . . . natural talents and predilections'; and therefore, we might add, virtually impossible to distinguish from them. Both poets were eccentrically learned, restless in thought and fancy, proud, reserved, and independent; free of 'all the four corners' of 'grammar'; and both sometimes harsh and unconciliating in their attitude to readers—'this sullen writ Which just as much courts thee as thou dost it'. But the danger of emphasizing the 'kinship' is that it may blind us to some of the special virtues of each poet: on the one hand, to Donne's control and scrupulosity, the habitual leanness of his style, as opposed to Browning's comparatively slapdash and sprawling exuberance; and on the other, to Browning's dramatic power of penetrating into a great variety of other characters and situations, where Donne is almost wholly confined to his own various but single self. Consider each at his best: though the verse and style of 'My Last Duchess' carry echoes for the reader of Donne, the character and situation lie outside his range; and Browning could never have attained the intensity and formality of the *Holy Sonnets*. It might be hazarded that no later poet has come nearer to Donne than Browning, though the nearness is the measure of an impassable distance.

But this is doubtful ground, and what I have wished to

establish is rather the nature of the whole nineteenth-century context of Browning's interest in his 'revered and magisterial Donne'. Unenlightened as many Victorian critics and readers of Donne may appear to our own far more fortunate age, they were not so benighted as it has been the fashion to suppose.

XXIII

THE VICTORIAN FRAME OF MIND

MR HOUGHTON is to be congratulated on his new book,[1] so much wider in scope than his former good book, *The Art of Newman's 'Apologia'*. Of its kind *The Victorian Frame of Mind* is not, chronologically speaking, the first in the field, nor perhaps the last. We have had several good books that have attempted the same difficult task, though not of the length of this, nor, since Mr Houghton does not waste words, of its substance. It goes without saying that there is ample room for all these books—past, present, and future. For though I have called the task of making them a difficult one, it should rather be called impossible, and the fittest name for one and all is *The Victorian Frame of Mind as it strikes one bright particular scholar*. Even if we can imagine—and even the scholarly imagination has been known to soar pretentiously—that something so incommensurable as half a century did in fact achieve something so orderly as a frame of mind, we are left with the practical impossibility that anybody can gain more than an impression of it—as Mr G. M. Young suggested when he called his book *Portrait of an Age*. Some features will persist, no doubt, in all the portraits. Before we open Mr Houghton's book, we know that he will have found the Victorians, say, earnest, much-thinking, hero-worshipping. So far, so expected. If, however, the fresh artist is worth his salt, the portrait he sketches will also include the unexpected.

By that test Mr Houghton comes off well—witness in particular his chapters on 'Anxiety', 'Anti-intellectualism', 'Enthusiasm'. As we read these chapters we have the pleasant sense that things we know as scattered are being drawn into a unity: at one point, for instance, we are shown a common element in 'Ulysses' and 'The Scholar Gipsy.' A further originality exists in Mr Houghton's individual quality of mind, which shows in the quiet responsibility of the book; if there is a resemblance between

[1] Walter E. Houghton, *The Victorian Frame of Mind, 1830–70*, 1957.

him and any of the men and women of genius he is dealing with it is with Arthur Hugh Clough—the Clough of *Ambarvalia*—that we should compare him. 'Honest labour wears a lovely face.' He has found everything, expected and unexpected, for himself. His book is an account of his own sensitive, neatly placed footsteps proceeding through hundreds of Victorian books great and less than great. Through these he has found his own way, and brought back his trove in actual pieces. For his book belongs to the sort that is generously laden with quotations. That principle of presentation is, surely, the best possible—what made Mr Young's brilliant book difficult for most readers was that it was laden, almost snobbishly, with *allusions*: reading and re-reading it, we seem to remain in the same frustrate state of climbing after knowledge infinite. Mr Houghton has worked under the sound principle that any one age that is abundantly articulate is its own best exponent, and usually its own best critic; and under the companion principle that no later age can improve on the expression accorded an age by its own writers. It is easy to imagine a book on Mr Houghton's theme consisting solely of the right quotations linked together by an anthologist who limited his further function to the use of 'and' and 'but.' Mr Houghton seems aware of the possibility of such a book: he aspires to be a sound organizer—*hoc opus, hic labor est*—of vivid passages, short or longer, of a hundred years ago. Here and there any reader of the result—his own reading being his own—will recall what seem more striking passages that have been overlooked or rejected, or of an earlier passage that seems the source of the one chosen. Meanwhile here are those Mr Houghton has found, and interpreted both by his choice of them and by his quiet showmanship.

Despite the help afforded by Mr Houghton's preface, I am not sure how much of the sum of things is to be included in a 'frame of mind'. I rather think that what I should see as a deeper book lies behind this one. For I cannot discern enough connection between the 'frame' here offered and the teeming literature and art and music of the age. Setting aside the art (which, at its best, was that of Cruikshank, Stevens, Keene, and Morris) and the music (which, at its best, was Sullivan's, who was not to be despised when guided by Gilbert)—setting aside all this, there remain all the poems and novels. It is usually assumed—and Mr Houghton quotes Whitehead to this effect—that the whole literature of an age preserves the fullest record of its 'inmost thoughts'. Mr Houghton has tried to read that record mainly as it survives, consciously spoken, in the 'literature of thinking'. Does not the 'pure' literature of the age, the literature unconcerned with current thought, witness powerfully to its frame of mind? Is it not part and parcel of that frame that the Victorian age—not to mention its infatuation with 'stagy' drama—was the golden age of the novel? and of the comic? Think of the range of the Victorian comic—it stretches from *Pickwick* and *Jorrocks* to the learned high-spirits of Carroll, from the musical nonsense of Lear to the Shakespearean 'humour' of Trollope's and George Eliot's rustics, from the half-jaded hilariousness of Thackeray to the heady academic irony of Arnold. And what of the vigorous and yet 'snail-horn' sense of beauty that flourished in so many of the Victorians? Even Carlyle and Reade are the poets of a thousand volcanic fragments of poetry, and no author can match Tennyson and Ruskin on this point, unless it is Keats. The works that embody the narratives, the laughter, the sense of beauty of the Victorians come squarely out of its frame of mind, if only because those works were all best sellers. On the whole Mr Houghton's book is too darkly coloured, and lacks liveliness. After all it was towards the end of his period that Arnold saw everybody as likely to go into drab—and even then the gay warning was ignored. If Lytton Strachey were still alive and still persisting in his delusions, I do not think that Mr Houghton would shake him out of them.

XXIV

WRITERS AND READERS IN 1851

[This lecture was contributed to a series of six public lectures entitled '1851', given in the summer of 1951 to a general audience at Bedford College, University of London, by members of the teaching staff with particular interests in nineteenth-century history, literature, philosophy, or science. The year marked the centenary of the Great Exhibition and was the year also of the Festival of Britain. In now preparing my lecture for publication I have removed only a few of the allusions that were topical in 1951 and I have retained the discursive method, frequent quotation, and informal style, which arose from the subject and the occasion. But I have removed a few illustrations which I afterwards used elsewhere, and for the same reason I have also omitted one section, on the different forms in which fiction reached the reading public.]

WRITERS IN 1851 seem in one respect to have resembled other people in Exhibition summers. The anxiety of Londoners to get out of London was only equalled by the anxiety of provincials and exiles to get there.

> This strange disease of modern life
> With its sick hurry, its divided aims. . . .

(Arnold's lines were written about this time). I propose first to look at some of the superficial symptoms of this disease.

Carlyle had no patience with the Exhibition: it interrupted his study of Danish. His first thought was to go to Denmark from May to October. When proof-correcting detained him till August, we hear that he complained bitterly at 'the Sawneys assembling from all parts of the world till you can't get along Piccadilly'. He was (reports the same witness) 'worn to death with bores all summer who present themselves by twos and threes in his study, saying Here we are!' At last he escaped to Malvern to take the new water-cure (as did also Macaulay); and later to Paris. Three other writers living in London went abroad for a great part of the year: Ruskin to Venice, to continue his study of its stones: Matthew Arnold to Switzerland

and Italy, on his wedding journey; likewise Tennyson—who recorded his travels in a poem of which one stanza is an exquisite mosaic of Italian place names and the word 'rain' five times repeated. Thackeray got to Germany in July, by chance crossing the channel with another writer, a man, he says, 'with narrow eyes' but 'extraordinarily brave blue and honest'. This was Charles Kingsley, on whom the previous six months had pressed hard; besides the usual work of his country parish—and it was Kingsley's habit to visit sick parishioners with a Bible in one hand and an auger in the other (to bore a hole in the bedroom for ventilation), there had been the savage reviews in the Church press of his novel *Yeast*, his visits to the Exhibition (over which he shed tears of joy), and his course of sermons to working-men in London; after one of which the incumbent arose and denounced him for dangerous doctrine which nearly caused a riot (in Kingsley's favour): 'Divided aims', indeed. After all this he had to go abroad to avert a breakdown.

Dickens's wish to escape from London this summer was equally strong. He speaks in letters of this year of his 'hatred of London' and his 'natural horror of *sights*'. But he did not go so far afield: he made his headquarters from May to October at his favourite Broadstairs, then 'a fishing village and small watering-place': the longest and last of many such visits—the last, because even there, street musicians were becoming intolerable.

Meanwhile in the other direction came the Brownings, on their first return visit to England—meeting the Tennysons midway in Paris, and leaving England again in September in time to accompany Carlyle, who was helpless about his luggage and tickets. From the north came Mrs Gaskell and Charlotte Brontë—who had shot into fame with their first published novels—and that old war-horse Harriet Martineau, indefatigable journalist and recently proclaimed atheist, in a work of which one contemporary said it should have on its title-page 'There is no God, and Harriet Martineau is his prophet'. All these three authoresses were 'literary lionesses'; it was a red-letter summer for Mrs Leo Hunter, who was by no means extinct. A famous writer was then on exhibition himself. For readers, then as now, included a fair proportion of those whose interest in literature was other than literary. Macaulay was at the Zoo in 1850 when two young ladies were going in and spotted him. They went no further. 'Mr Macaulay!' cried the lovely pair. 'Is that Mr Macaulay? Never mind about the hippopotamus.' When Charlotte Brontë went to literary parties 'groups cluster round the charming Currer Bell, all the ugly men giving themselves Rochester airs'.

In this conspectus of the comings and goings of writers I have recalled the names of most of those best known to readers of 1851. But not quite all. Some were professionally occupied: Newman was at the Oratory in Birmingham, having left London the vivid memory of his lectures on *Difficulties of Anglicans* in 1850. And the name of Arthur Hugh Clough (poet of *The Bothie*, and amateur of European revolutions) appears in print in 1851 only when a new term is announced at University College; for this was the last year of his brief tenure as Principal of University Hall, Dean of the Faculty of Arts and Laws, and Professor of English Literature. He was not however earning enough to marry on and was contemplating the exchange of 'Doubting Castle' (Arnold's name for University Hall) for Australia or America. Lastly, to mention two names known in 1951 but not in 1851: Trollope was busy establishing rural posts in the West Country—rather discouraged by the failure of his first three novels (one historical and two Irish) but pausing in his duties to muse over the cathedral close at Salisbury as a possible scene for a new one. (It was four more years before *The Warden*.) And the future George Eliot was still plain Mary Ann Evans, preparing to be Assistant Editor of the new *Westminster Review*, and attending a course of lectures in geometry at the Ladies' College in Bedford Square.

This roll of names is impressive; and indeed the twenty years from 1845 to 1865 are, I suppose, unparalleled in English literature for their production of masterpieces from the press (I say 'the press' to evade the difficult comparison with the last twenty years of the sixteenth century.) When, for example, a single year produced *The Prelude*, and *In Memoriam*, and *David Copperfield* and *Pendennis* and *Christmas Eve and Easter Day* and *Sonnets from the Portuguese*, one sees why a modern historian has said that 'a wise man would choose the 1850's to be young in'. All such fanciful projects need some qualification; your wise man had better make careful choice of his class—and not land himself in the East End of Henry Mayhew's *London Labour and the London Poor* (1851); and he had better also make careful choice of sex. The situation of the young woman of the 1850's is perhaps most conveniently summed up in the title of a popular work of the day: *The Pursuit of Knowledge under Difficulties illustrated by Female Examples.*

The year whose publications I cited just now was 1850; 1851 has nothing equal to show as far as mere publication goes, and is probably only specially remembered by students of Carlyle and Ruskin. For this comparative pause the Exhibition itself may be partly to blame. (As we shall see, in Exhibition years writers tend not to write books but to give lectures.) And there are other reasons too. 'All trade is at a stand', complains Carlyle when his proofs are held up; and a review of his book opens with this revealing sentence, 'As soon as the closing of the Great Exhibition afforded a reasonable hope that there would once more be a reading public, the *Life of Sterling* appeared' (the anonymous review was Mary Ann Evans's in the *Westminster*). Printers were busy with Exhibition literature and guides to London. For whatever reason, there was scarcely one important poetical work published; only Mrs Browning's poem of revolutionary Florence, *Casa Guidi Windows*, and an almost neglected first volume by a new poet, George Meredith. (It was sent to Tennyson, who thought it promising, especially a piece called 'Love in the Valley'.) But Tennyson himself, and Browning, published nothing and wrote nothing. And there was no great new novel—neither in 'monthly numbers', in the greeny-blue paper covers long sacred to Dickens, nor the more recent yellow associated with Thackeray—nor in three volumes from Mr Mudie's library. Readers had to look for Dickens in his new twopenny weekly *Household Words* (where they might also recognize Mrs Gaskell), or on the amateur stage; they had to look for Thackeray in *Punch* or *The Times* or in the lecture-hall. But I doubt if most readers in 1851 were conscious of this vacuum in publication. In the reading of poetry especially there is always a time-lag; it takes time to sink in; and people were still reading *In Memoriam*, the first work to extend Tennyson's reputation to a wide circle of readers, although he had been writing for thirty-six years and publishing for twenty-three. His recent laureateship carried no obligation to write poems on public events: when Elie Halévy puts 'Boadicea' in 1851 he has got his Exhibitions mixed. The May-Day Ode in *The Times* on the opening of the Exhibition was by Thackeray; it took him five days to write ('the hardest work I ever did in my life. I don't wonder at poets being selfish, such as Wordsworth and Alfred'—'clearing a primaeval forest is nothing to it'). Readers would not miss their Browning in 1851; he was, to the general reading public, only the man Miss Barrett had so romantically married. 'I find that *Mr* Browning also writes verses' is an actual quotation from a private letter of one reader, even later than 1851. Mrs Browning's claim to the laureateship had been canvassed by one periodical: an appointment equally satisfying to feminism and economy—helping two poets at the price of one. And as for novels: Dickens and Thackeray perhaps would be missed more; for great novelists were also popular novelists in the mid-nineteenth century, to an extent inconceivable today. But there were also other popular novelists. There were new novels in 1851 from Harrison Ainsworth and G. P. R. James; and from Mrs Marsh and Geraldine Jewsbury and Dinah Mulock and Mrs Oliphant and Eliza Lynn, for we have now a new phenomenon: the successful woman (as distinct from *lady*) novelist, who was, G. H. Lewes complained, driving the men from the field. 'It will never do', he writes in *The Leader*, 'we are overrun. Women carry all before them.' He had decided he said, to quit London and wed some savage woman. . . . This was a year or two before he met George Eliot. There were other novels by authors quite unknown (but probably female) whose titles sound enticing: *The Wife's Sister, or the Forbidden Marriage*; *The Lady and The Priest.* There were imports from America, ranging from *The Wide, Wide World* to a 'mad, frantic novel' called *The Whale.*

We know too little now of minor Victorian novels, except where their life was prolonged in Edwardian nurseries and schoolrooms (as with Ainsworth and Marryat and Captain Mayne Reid—all publishing in 1851). More regrettably perhaps, we know little directly of the opinions of ordinary readers: not much more than can be inferred from reviews, from sales, and from authors' references to their fan mail. This was very extensive; writers then received the embarrassing attentions now concentrated on stage and film actors; but sometimes not unwelcome, as when an admirer of Carlyle sent Mrs Carlyle a shawl, or the firm of Brookes of Sheffield sent Dickens a case of plate, because he had unconsciously mentioned them in *David Copperfield.* Of course there are records of reading in contemporary letters and diaries: but where these are preserved and printed it argues a more than ordinary reader. For example, I could adduce evidence that Cambridge undergraduates in 1851 were reading Kingsley and Arnold; but it would be based on the letters of exceptional undergraduates like Henry Bradshaw and Frederick Hort.

We know however a good deal of the reading of those not so ordinary readers, the writers themselves. At no time perhaps have great writers so freely read each other and registered their views. Dickens is the only one who either read little (save editorially) or else commented little; in his numerous letters of 1851 I find only one literary reference, and that is to 'a wonderful book' he 'has just read for the 500th time'—Carlyle's *French Revolution.* He is perhaps chiefly a re-reader—going back and back to that shelf of boyhood favourites lovingly enumerated in *David Copperfield.* One thinks of Dickens as rarely keeping still long enough to read poetry. (It was, however, when on the beach at Broadstairs that he read most: and in a paper published this year on the charms of that resort he quotes twice from Tennyson and once from *The Tempest.*)

Many were of course reading in the past as much as the present: or even more—

> Edith reads aloud Wordsworth in the evening in order that I may not hear any of the newer productions, which I do not love or admire as I do their predecessors.

Thus Sara Coleridge in 1851. Macaulay read fourteen books of the *Odyssey* while he walked from Malvern to Worcester and back:

> I was afraid to be seen crying by the parties of walkers. Crying for

Achilles . . . crying for Priam . . . mere imaginary beings, creatures of an old ballad maker who died near 3,000 years ago.

Early in 1851 Matthew Arnold ('though young, intolerably severe') was reading Pindar, Sophocles, Milton, Thomas à Kempis, and Ecclesiasticus.

I retire more and more from the modern world and modern literature, which is all only what has been before and what will be again, and not bracing or edifying in the least.

There you see the foundation of the *Essays in Criticism*; and, nearer at hand, the 1853 Preface:

amid the bewildering confusion of our times . . . I seemed to myself to find the only sure guidance, the only solid footing, among the Ancients.

In short:

> The world but feels the present's spell:
> The poet feels the past as well.

Nevertheless it is Arnold, of the new generation of writers—as Carlyle of the old—who most clearly voices the spirit of the age for readers of about 1851. (Arnold was twenty-nine and had published one anonymous volume. Carlyle was fifty-six, with only *Frederick* still to come.) If anyone remains who thinks of that as an age of tranquil security, the Carlylean phrase must answer him—'Not so; quite otherwise, in fact!' In his *Life of Sterling* Carlyle characterized the age as 'this confused and revolutionary epoch, which now lasts above 60 years', and spoke of the 'diseased self-listenings, self-questionings, impotently painful dubitations . . . so rife in our day'. Arnold found 'the dialogue of the mind with itself' characteristic of modern literature. And Arnold also wrote, looking back to 'tranquil years' of the eighteenth century (as foolishly perhaps as some people now look back to the tranquil years of the nineteenth):

> But we, brought forth and rear'd in hours
> Of change, alarm, surprise—
> What shelter to grow ripe is ours?
> What leisure to grow wise?

Those who, like Arnold, were young in the 1840's had to be

tough if they were to stand four-square to all the winds that blew: winds from the Continent; from Chelsea; from Oxford; from Concord, Massachusetts. Arnold had written to Clough in 1849:

These are damned times—everything is against one—the height to which knowledge is come, the spread of luxury, our spiritual enervation, the absence of great natures . . . newspapers, cities . . . the sickening consciousness of our difficulties—but for God's sake let us neither be fanatics nor yet chaff blown by the wind.

In 1851 Arnold visited the the Grande Chartreuse and perhaps wrote the poem containing the famous lines:

Wandering between two worlds, one dead,
The other powerless to be born.

The world that is dead is represented for Arnold by the monastery. But he writes of it wistfully, as if with apologies.

And what am I, that I am here?

For rigorous teachers seized my youth,
And purged its faith, and trimm'd its fire,
Shew'd me the high white star of Truth,
There bade me gaze, and there aspire;
Even now their whispers pierce the gloom:
What dost thou in this living tomb?

Forgive me, masters of the mind!

Arnold's 'rigorous teachers' and 'masters of the mind' included Carlyle; Carlyle, who, Clough had said, 'had led us all out into the wilderness and left us there'. And Clough, in 1851, is writing, in his bleaker manner, to the same effect:

'Old things need not be therefore true'?
O brother men, nor yet the new:
Ah! still awhile the old thought retain
And yet consider it again!

To return to Arnold, still in 1851: the poem is Arnold on holiday; here is Arnold at work—in a letter from Birmingham:

I have had a hard day. 30 pupil teachers to examine in an inconvenient room and nothing to eat except a biscuit which some charitable lady gave me.

For it was his first year as a School Inspector: the first of thirty years. At this time he had half England as his district and 104 schools to report on. The usual comment is

> Not here, O Apollo
> Are haunts meet for thee.

But is it a just one? As Newman said, 'Birmingham people have souls'. The poem is characteristic, with its sense of the past (all that is represented in the monastery) impinging on the changeful present and the doubtful future. The letter also shows his hopes for that future:

> I think I shall get interested in the schools after a little time; their effects on the children are so immense, and their future effects in civilising the next generation of the lower classes, who will have most of the political power in their hands, may be so important.

That he did 'get interested', all his work in poetry and prose from then on is eloquent. It affected his view of his own poetry. He writes in 1853: '"The Gipsy Scholar" at best awakens a pleasing melancholy. But this is not what we want'.

> The complaining millions of men
> Darken in labour and pain.

Here is the other side of the Grande Chartreuse:

> The millions suffer still, and grieve;
> And what can helpers heal
> With old world cures men half believe
> For woes they wholly feel?
> And yet they have such need of joy!
> But joy whose grounds are true.

That was in the sixties when Arnold is earnestly in search of those true grounds.

To return to 1851. Another verse in this poem of Arnold's may be a more immediate comment on that year:—

> Silent—the best are silent now.
>
> Achilles ponders in his tent,
> The kings of modern thought are dumb;
> Silent they are, though not content,
> And wait to see the future come . . .

There I seem to catch another echo, from Carlyle; who was this year expressing his disgust with the Exhibition in a letter to Emerson in the following characteristically vituperative terms (it had, as I said, held up his proofs):

Such a sanhedrin of windy fools was surely never gathered in one city before. But they will go their ways again. . . . One sits quiet in that faith, nay, looks abroad with a kind of pathetic grandfatherly feeling over this Universal Children's Ball which the British Nation in these extraordinary circumstances is giving itself. Silence above all, silence is very behoveful.

But Carlyle's plea for silence followed the writing of his *Life of Sterling*, a work in which he speaks out clearly, pointedly, and personally, and through which he recovered some of the reputation lost by *Latter-Day Pamphlets*. (Crabb Robinson writes 'it all but made me forgive his brutal paper on *Slavery*'.) 'The kings of modern thought are dumb.' The brief biography of a friend who had died almost unknown seven years before, might seem unlikely to contribute to modern thought in 1851. To the question 'What has Sterling done to have a life of him written?', Jane Carlyle gave the 'arch and airy reply': '*Induced* Carlyle somehow to write him one!' But the serious reply is Carlyle's closing chapter, where he says that Sterling was 'a man of infinite susceptivity; who caught everywhere, more than others, the colour of the element he lived in . . . whose history therefore is, beyond others, emblematic of that of his Time'. Carlyle's impulse to write came (and it is a traditional motive for biography) from the desire to defend Sterling against the misrepresentation of another biographer; because he had been a curate for eight months and then had resigned, he had been shown as 'a pale sickly shadow in torn surplice . . . Who in this miserable figure would recognize the brilliant, beautiful and cheerful John Sterling?' Sterling is seen as 'emblematic' partly *because* he withdrew from the Church; but not therefore as a failure, nor simply as a sceptic; but as typical of the best in modern man and yet able to find no place in his age. Sterling is the text; the age is the theme.

It is in the history of such vehement, trenchant, far-shining and yet intrinsically light and volatile souls, missioned into this epoch to seek their way there, that we see best what a confused epoch it is.

Without open controversy, but simply in the natural course of tracing his ten years' friendship with Sterling and the subjects they discussed, Carlyle reaffirms his own position; his view of the 'flaming core' of the age in the 'battle between Radicalism and the Church' and of the 'heroic worth' that 'lies on each side of the quarrel' (that was Clough's and Arnold's difficulty too); his view of his own work, especially *Sartor*, whose style Sterling had criticized and, most interestingly, his view of literature as an activity. Sterling is seen as potentially the Artist, the Poet. But in that unfortunate—for this was, Carlyle thought, no age for poetry (compare Arnold again—'how deeply *unpoetical* . . .' and '*arid*—that is what the times are'). Many poets were Carlyle's friends; he talked to them, smoked with them—Alfred Tennyson was his best 'companion over a pipe'—he even read their poetry—but always begged them to write prose. (He was especially urgent with Browning, who perhaps recalled this in the poem which begins 'Stop playing, Poet! May a brother speak?') To Sterling he wrote:

> Why *sing* your bits of thoughts, if you *can* contrive to speak them? . . . As to song so-called, and your fiddling talent,—we will talk of that a couple of centuries hence, when things are calmer again. Homer shall be thrice welcome; but only when Troy is *taken*: alas, while the siege lasts, and battle's fury rages everywhere, what can I do with the Homer? I want Achilles and Odysseus, and am enraged to see them trying to be Homers!

Carlyle's own wish was to be an Achilles: to make history, rather than write it; or to make it by writing it. The passage is suggestive. For it may be to Carlyle—or to the germ of truth in his exaggeration—that we owe the preponderance of speech over song in much contemporary poetry. In Clough, for instance; in Browning; in Arnold, whose characteristic poems another contemporary critic described as 'recitative'.

2

I have spoken of Carlyle's complaints. For one at least he had solid grounds. He had finished writing the *Life of Sterling* in May, when the Exhibition opened; but it was not published till October, when it was anonymously reviewed by Thackeray in *The Times*, and by George Eliot in the *Westminster Review*. He complains of this in that same letter to Emerson, written in July; and blames the Exhibition, that 'inane tornado' of the 'Wind-dust-ry of All Nations' for this quite abnormal and unprecedented delay. A book written in May, and not published till October! The passage of literature from writer to reader, it is important to emphasize, was a great deal more rapid a hundred years ago than now; like much railway travel. The manuscript even of a long work would be normally accepted, printed, and on sale all in a matter of weeks; a serial part of a novel would be *written*, printed, and read in a matter of days.

We cannot undervalue this quick communication: it gave a warmth, vitality, and immediacy to the writer–reader relationship: a sense of contact with an audience from whom the writer has been receding steadily since the invention of printing. Consider the great serial novels of Dickens and Thackeray: not only published, but written, from month to month; and written therefore with a finger on the readers' pulse....

If the serial was not published independently, but in a monthly or weekly periodical, the problem was more complicated; for that meant an editor (Dickens of course was often his own) and a certain submission to editorial wishes. Kingsley had had to curtail *Yeast* as a serial in *Fraser's* in 1848 (the country squires protested): he published it in full and even augmented in 1851. Mrs Gaskell eventually broke with Dickens because she could not submit to his views on serial division: for Dickens, democratic in sentiment, was very dictatorial in his private and professional life. In 1851, however, relations are still happy. When Dickens started *Household Words* in 1850 he said there was no one he would prefer as a contributor to the author of *Mary Barton*; and the 1851 numbers contain several of her short stories, which raised few problems except that he thought that she was too much given to deathbeds ('I wish her people would stand a little firmer on their legs'!). But for the issue of 13 December 1851, she wrote a new kind of story, one which indeed concluded with a death, but which nonetheless Dickens and other readers urged her to make the first of a series. It was called 'Our Society at Cranford' and was intended to be complete in itself. 'I never meant to write any more', she wrote to Ruskin, 'and so killed Captain Brown, very much against my will.' To the co-operation of editor and readers, therefore, we owe the book by which Mrs Gaskell is popularly remembered. It was a new vein for her, this half-mocking, wholly-loving recollection of the past: hardly anticipated by the grim tales of Manchester life which had won her reputation. And a vein which at this time appealed to Dickens. He had been looking over the recent numbers of his periodical and finding them too factual and 'documentary'—'a dreary arithmetical dustyness which is powerfully depressing'. (And further, the chronological study of *Household Words* proves that two of his own sketches had given Mrs Gaskell her lead to *Cranford*: for there is the same loving and tenderly comic touch on the remembered and vanishing past in his articles, 'Our School' and 'Our Watering-place', which had appeared in June and October.)

I turn now to the other activities of Dickens (and also Thackeray) in 1851: both were in one sense resting from the high-pressure creative agonies of 1850, for *David Copperfield* and *Pendennis* in monthly numbers had run almost neck and neck to their final numbers at the close of that year. The relation thus established with their readers is part of the background of their doings in 1851; for both were now seeking an even more intimate relation—that of the personal appearance, perhaps not innocent of the wish to cash in on the Exhibition crowds. In May there appeared two adjoining announcements in the press: two special performances of Bulwer Lytton's play *Not so Bad as we Seem* at Devonshire House, under the direction of Mr Charles Dickens; and a course of six lectures on 'The English Humourists' at Willis's rooms by Mr Thackeray. Dickens is frank about his timing: 'We conceive', he writes to the Duke of Devonshire in March, 'that the changing current of people probably setting into London . . . might afford us an audience at high prices'. But the economic motives of Dickens and Thackeray showed one significant difference. Dickens's dramatic exhibition was in aid of 'The Guild of Literature and Art', a project for assisting needy authors; while Thackeray was (by his own standards) a needy author himself, desiring to lay by an independent fortune for his daughters. He was not yet so successful a serialist as Dickens; he was slaying his thousands and Dickens his tens of thousands. Jane Carlyle said Dickens wrote for the 'greatest happiness of the greatest number (of Cockneys)'. One can understand the difference: Thackeray would have little to say to the charwoman in Albany Street who read *Dombey*.

Preparations for play and lectures occupied them both in the early spring; Dickens had the management, casting, production, and rehearsals; his team, all gentleman-amateurs, included journalists and novelists, from Douglas Jerrold of *Punch* and John Forster of the *Examiner* down to Wilkie Collins in a servant's part. 'But the word *difficulty* does not exist in my dramatic vocabulary'. The editing of *Household Words* went on concurrently, and in one small respect, usefully; for Dickens was writing a series of articles on London's detective police, and his investigations enabled him to provide a plain-clothes policeman for the royal performance (advisable, because Bulwer Lytton's estranged wife had threatened to gate-crash, disguised as an orange girl). And this same Police Inspector was also to turn up in Dickens's next novel, *Bleak House*, as Mr Bucket: the first detective in English fiction. Thackeray meanwhile had his lectures to write, which he had as usual left to the eleventh hour; but by the end of April he too is rehearsing: 'I tried the great room at Willis's yesterday and recited a part of the multiplication table to a waiter at the opposite end . . .' The day before the opening lecture he writes to his friend Dicky Doyle, who is coming to hear him

> When I touch my neck-cloth, clap with all your might. When I use my pocket handkerchief, burst into tears. When I pause, say Bravo. God save the Queen. No money returned. Babies in arms not admitted.

That shows how nervous he was. And one source of nervousness is hinted in a letter to the Carlyles the day after the opening lecture, signed 'W.M.T. Tight-rope dancer to the nobility' and illustrated with a comic drawing. Was he losing dignity by lecturing? Did the social brilliance of the audience make it better, or worse? At any rate he would laugh at himself to be on the safe side.

Both Dickens and Thackeray did have very grand audiences:

Dickens succeeded in getting the Queen for the first performance; Thackeray had 'the cream of London society'. So writes an attender at his second lecture, a visitor from the country. She goes on: 'I did not at all expect that he would know *me* or notice *me* . . . with admiring Duchesses and Countesses seated in rows before him'. But he was perhaps prouder to see there the young lady who had lectured him on his frivolity the year before; far from not noticing her, he introduced her to his grand friends, as 'Jane Eyre'. However, a fortnight later it was the noble ladies' convenience and not Charlotte Brontë's that was consulted. She writes: 'he was to have delivered another this week but the Duchesses . . . have petitioned him to put it off because of Ascot races—wearisome selfish seraphim that they are'.

These two sideshows to the Exhibition—Dickens's acting and Thackeray's lecturing—show also a curious parallel in content. Both are concerned with the past. Lytton's play, written for the occasion, was a comedy of eighteenth-century life—'a very striking picture of the time of George I'; and the plot hinges on the romantic virtue of a Grub Street author who is rewarded by noble patronage. And Thackeray's lectures were on the English humorists—from Congreve to Goldsmith; on 'the men and their lives, rather than their books'. He defines the 'humorist', at the outset, as 'the weekday preacher'; and 'yesterday's preacher becomes the text for to-day's sermon'. The underlying theme of Thackeray's 'sermon' is the place of the author in society. He was fully aware of all the ironies latent in the situation: he, an author, in the doubtfully dignified position of lecturer, with an audience who had come less to hear about the eighteenth century than, as his readers, to see how he would acquit himself: he, an author who had exposed society to itself, so that one of his aristocratic readers wrote in horror to her more tolerant daughter-in-law: 'How can you tolerate Thackeray? . . . Really he should be banished from the society he has so wonderfully found his way into!' and he, an author who had been involved in controversy (arising from certain chapters in *Pendennis*) on this very topic of 'the dignity of literature'; and now here he is, in Willis's Rooms, telling the audience about the lives of past authors. These lectures are always misjudged by modern critics, as if they were offered as a solemn contribution to eighteenth-century biography and criticism. So judged, they are outdated, and were so even then. No, they are, as he said, a tight-rope act, a display of technique; a more exquisite example than even his novels afford of the interplay between Thackeray, his subject, and his audience; in which he uses the past as a stalking-horse for the present. Constantly he trails his coat, draws sly parallels and contrasts between conditions then and now:

What man of note . . . would *now* think of writing a congratulatory ode on the birth of the heir to a dukedom?

Or on Congreve, who got a place in the Pipe Office for writing a comedy:

Men of letters there still be: but I doubt if there are any Pipe Offices left.

And this was Thackeray speaking; the man who, as some of that noble audience must have known, was at this time place-hunting himself. At the conclusion to the course he tells them, with diplomatic gracefulness, that their kind reception of his lectures proves that the literary profession is no more despised than in the eighteenth century—an effective lecturer's exit. But this half-concealed parallelism between patronage past and present is only one instance of his serious playfulness. Constantly in the lectures he is teasing the whole notion of 'progress': as, on the changed face of London:

Over yonder road, by which Dick Turpin fled to Windsor, and Squire Weston journeyed to town . . . what a rush of civilisation and order flows now.

A very appropriate sentiment for Exhibition year. But wait.

What armies of gentlemen with umbrellas march to banks, and chambers, and counting-houses! What regiments of nursery-maids and pretty infantry; what peaceful processions of policemen . . . what swarms of busy apprentices and artificers, riding on omnibus-roofs, pass daily and hourly!

He is constantly hinting that changes in manners are not quite what they appear. Especially changes in refinement.

We can't tell—you would not bear to be told—the whole truth

regarding those men and manners. You could no more suffer in a British drawing-room, under the reign of Queen Victoria, a fine gentleman or fine lady of Queen Anne's time or hear what they heard and said, than you would receive an ancient Briton.

After which he gives an instance. We have to remember that the whole subject of the literature of Restoration and early eighteenth century was in 1851 nominally on the danger line. If 'ladies had protested' at the temptations of Arthur Pendennis, how would they receive Sterne's Eliza and the creator of Tom Jones and Sophia Western? And receive them from the very novelist for whom conventions were no restrictions, but a stimulus to subtleties of evasion? Here Thackeray (relieved of the fiction-writer's responsibility) puts on another act—figure-skating on thin ice. He enjoys provoking a sense of pleasurable alarm, only to allay it—and then perhaps to smile at the audience's disappointment.

Things were done in that society, and names were named, that would make *you* shudder now.

(What is he going to say next?)

What would be the sensation of a polite youth of the present day, if at a ball he saw the young object of his affections taking a box out of her pocket and a pinch of snuff, or if at dinner she deliberately put her knife into her mouth?

Fashionably and financially, these lectures were a success: a success which Thackeray half-despised. 'The lectures won't do. They were all friends, and a packed house.' But despite private reservation, he took the lectures on tour, in the following winter, to Cambridge, Oxford, Edinburgh, and Glasgow, and afterwards to America; and repeated his success; everywhere except Glasgow.

To satisfy himself, and perhaps to revenge himself, he also in this year wrote his third novel; the only novel which he did *not* serialize, and in which he deliberately recedes from his audience; a novel also of the past, and superficially related to the lectures: but wrote it from the melancholy sense of mystery which lay at the deepest level of his mind—*Henry Esmond*.

3

That is one of the hidden interests of the year 1851; the great novels that were not then published but being slowly quarried out of the thought and experience of three writers—*Esmond*, and *Bleak House*, and *Villette*. They form a corrective, if any is needed, to any easy generalization about the spirit of the age. Where is progress, where complacency, in these grand gloomy novels—two of them about the past, though with private and present heart-hungers thinly concealed? And *Bleak House* is almost like *Latter-Day Pamphlets*, a 'red hot poker' stabbed into the 'vile pythons' of 'this mud-world'. How could the self-satisfaction of those 'at ease in Zion' survive the picture of Chancery, and Tom-all-alone's, and Chadband, and Mrs Jellyby—who could see nothing nearer than Africa?

Everyone recognizes that *Bleak House* is partly a 'tract for the times'; in the twelfth chapter Dickens explicitly challenges those 'elegant readers' who will not allow the arts 'to be in earnest or to receive any impress from the moving age'. Less commonly seen is that 'impress' in *Villette* and *Esmond*. I will select one illustration. On her visit to London, the rector of Haworth's daughter saw more than the Crystal Palace and Mr Thackeray. She also went to hear Cardinal Wiseman, and reported on him to her father as 'a sleek hypocrite surrounded by a bevy of inferior priests . . . very dark looking and sinister men. The whole scene was impiously theatrical'. What she saw sharpened her memories as a teacher in Brussels; and this queer combination of disapproval and fascination (including Lucy's despairing visit to the confessional) runs through *Villette*.

Now this springs not only from Charlotte Brontë's particular experience; it is in fact also of the time. There are very few writers in 1851 whose work is not coloured (or discoloured) by the strong contemporary feelings awakened by the so-called 'Papal Aggression' and the establishment of a Catholic hierarchy in England. Everyone knows how strong those feelings were. The ironic coincidence of this supposed menace with the Great Exhibition was noted by more than one writer. Englishmen, says one, 'had made up their minds to have an invasion of foreigners from all parts of the world, but it appears they have first to reconcile themselves to an invasion of Roman bishops'.

In the pages of *Punch* for 1851 the Crystal Palace is hardly even the most prominent feature; in every number are cartoons and quips and sketches aimed at the two targets of Popery and Puseyism—Puseyism being regarded by the majority as simple fellow-travelling. These were not casual jokes, but settled policy (which lost *Punch* its best artist, Dicky Doyle, because he was a Catholic); and the satire was bitter and violent beyond the imagination of our more polite (or mealy-mouthed) age. Newman hardly exaggerated when he said 'the rack and pulley are still affirmed to be busy in the dungeons of Edgbaston'. Indeed the provision of a new drain for the Oratory *was* mistaken by passers-by for underground torture-chambers. He did not exaggerate when he said, speaking of the feeling of this year:

> The atmosphere is tremulous with agitation, and discharges its vibration far and wide. . . . Spontaneously the bells of the steeples begin to sound . . . off they set, swinging and booming, tolling and chiming, with nervous intenseness, and thickening emotion, and deepening volume, the old ding-dong which has scared town and country this weary time . . . all about the *Popish aggression*, *insolent* and *insidious*, *insidious* and *insolent*, *insolent* and *atrocious*, *atrocious* and *insolent* . . . bobs (I think the ringers call them) bobs and bobs royal and triple-bob-majors and grandsires. . . .

I quote from Newman's brilliant one-man Exhibition of 1851: in his course of nine lectures on the *Present Position of Catholics*, given at the Birmingham Corn Exchange in June, he plays on the phrase 'insidious and insolent' used by Lord John Russell in his published letter to the Bishop of Durham. The lectures show Newman's serious but exuberant wit at its best: the modern reader can understand the shouts of laughter heard by passers-by in the street outside. And whatever his beliefs, he can share that laughter, for Newman in these lectures is not simply counter-attacking the Protestants. He is laughing at their beliefs and the bogeys they have set up or inherited: laughing at the credulity that saw in every female convert a nun liable to be bricked up alive; laughing at the witch-hunting mentality, at the irresponsible power of press and pulpit; things we ought all to laugh at, in order not to weep.

This 'bogey' view affected the reigning popular taste in fiction and quasi-factual narratives. Not only *Maria Monk*, the escaped nun of the 1830's (whom Newman makes great play with), whose revelations were still selling in their thousands; but stories advertised in large type in literary weeklies like the *Athenaeum*: *The Perverter in High Life*; *The Female Jesuit: or the Spy in the Family. A true narrative of recent intrigues in a Protestant household.* 'Works of fiction are all now connected in some way with the condition of society', wrote a reviewer in 1850; and the Papal Aggression seemed an even direr threat than the slums and the bad drains. Of respectable novels published in 1851, easily the most aggressively anti-Roman is *Lavengro: the Scholar, the Gypsy, and the Priest*, Borrow's fictionalized autobiography. Though ostensibly concerned with the 1820's, and written before 1843, its appearance was obviously timed for 1851, and a Preface written in that year draws out its implications. 'Since the Reformation Popery has kept her emissaries here, individuals, contemptible in intellect, but catlike and gliding.' Newman would have enjoyed that. He would also have appreciated the attribution by Borrow's priest of the new religious movement to the 'rage of the middle-classes for grandeur and gentility'. Their religion, they find, 'is not the religion . . . used by the grand personages of whom they have read in their novels and romances, their Ivanhoes, their Marmions, and their Ladies of the Lake'. Borrow was not alone in his suspicions of Scott; Newman sees Scott as 'ashamed of his own Catholic tendencies', but has no doubt that they are there. Thus again the past is enlisted in the feuds of the present. As also by Carlyle, when at the climax of his chapter on Coleridge in the *Life of Sterling* he calls him the procreator of the 'spectral Puseyisms . . . and ecclesiastical chimæras which now roam the Earth in a very lamentable manner'. And the present is insinuated into the past. Thackeray makes his subtler and more oblique comment on the 'dark looking sinister men', the 'catlike and gliding' individuals, in Father Holt, the Jesuit priest in *Esmond*. Kingsley in 1851 was writing *Hypatia*, to be serialized in 1852; the subtitle of this romance of the fifth century is pointed—'New Foes with an Old Face'—and it almost certainly stimulated Newman to write his novel of the third century, *Callista*. Kingsley also revised and augmented his novel *Yeast* in this year; and among his additions are the hero's correspondence with the young curate Luke, who is in process of a long-drawn 'secession'—the worst symptom is that he is losing sympathy with that 'superstitious reverence for mere verbal truth so common among Protestants'—and a clear portrait of Newman in the fourteenth chapter. Thus early began the antagonism that was to issue in the *Apologia*.

The principles and prejudices of 1851 had also one curious negative literary result; I will call it 'The Strange Case of Oliver Weld'. They deprived us of the second novel of Harriet Martineau. The facts are instructive. Here was a famous authoress, whose reputation, won with the *Political Economy* tales of the thirties (the only literature that would sell in the Reform Bill years), had been extended to more literary circles by *Deerbrook*, the first serious novel of middle-class provincial life since Jane Austen: who had set up a stir with her American journey and her recovery from an apparently mortal illness through mesmerism; and whose recent *Letters on Man's Social Nature and Development*, published early in 1851, were much discussed reading. Under Charlotte Brontë's persuasions, and the stimulus of reading and hearing Thackeray, she wrote, in the autumn of 1851, another novel; and it was submitted through Charlotte Brontë to her publisher George Smith, an exceptionally enlightened man. It should have been a publisher's dream: *Oliver Weld*, by the author of *Deerbrook*. But the publisher felt bound to reject it. You might think, because it was atheistic; but no: 'He dared not publish it, on account of some favourable representations and auguries on behalf of the Catholics'. So the novel was abandoned and destroyed, and Miss Martineau turned back to the translation of Comte's *Positive Philosophy* and articles on factory life for *Household Words*. Until later she quarrelled with Dickens, on that same religious issue. She was one of the few writers who raised a disinterested voice for religious tolerance and freedom of opinion.

It was clear enough where Dickens stood, if easier, as with Carlyle, to see what he was against than what he was for. Already in 1849 he had made his sly commentary on the High Church fuss over the bicentenary of Charles I's execution: King Charles's head is the obsession of the imbecile Mr Dick. In 1851 he was writing history, serializing in *Household Words* the first part of his *Child's History of England*, in which the Pope is the villain throughout. It supports all that Newman says about Protestant history. In his next novel Dickens made one other contribution to religious party controversy: the small but sharp sketch of Mrs Pardiggle in *Bleak House*, the more noticeable for her unimportance in the story—a mere superfluous little gargoyle. She is a Puseyite 'visiting lady', whose hapless children, named according to the new cult, Egbert, Oswald, and Felix, have their pocket money anticipated for good causes and whose day begins, winter and summer, with 'matins, very prettily done, at half-past six'.

Dickens also attacked the new Pre-Raphaelite paintings in an article in *Household Words*. The relevance of this may not be clear; his 'Protestant' motive is not betrayed, and may have been unconscious. But there is plenty of evidence that at this time the name of the Pre-Raphaelite Brotherhood (unfortunate word) suffered from its supposed connection with Romanism. *The Times* spoke of 'these monkish follies' in its Academy criticism of May; and when Ruskin wrote his famous letters in defence of Hunt and Millais he was at pains to discriminate; he 'did *not* wish to encourage their Romanist and Tractarian tendencies'—this defence first brought him into touch with the painters, with effects on his personal life only too well known. Ruskin should have been secure from the suspicion of such tendencies; for in March he had published, as a kind of appendix to the first volume of *Stones of Venice*, a shilling pamphlet called *Notes on the Construction of Sheepfolds*. The title is said to have misled some Scottish farmers; but the work is a plea for the reunion of the evangelical and high-church parties, and a clear affirmation of Ruskin's position. Though pro-Gothic, he was nevertheless Protestant. The distinction, in 1851, was necessary: one's admiration for anything remotely connected with Roman Catholicism must be safeguarded with apology. As Arnold felt, at the Grande Chartreuse—

> And what am I, that I am here?
> What dost thou in this living tomb?
> Forgive me, masters of the mind . . .
> Not as their friend or child I speak.

4

I have traced only a very few of the crossing threads that set the writings of 1851 in their contemporary context. I could, for example, still without leaving this particular year, have considered the 'Condition-of-England question' as reflected in literature. 'What a yet unspoken poetry', says Carlyle, 'is that Sanitary Reform! It is the great *fact* of the age!' Or I could have considered the reflection in literature of the new science; for as Tennyson said, two new Muses had been added to the Nine —'Astronomy and Geology, terrible Muses!' Perhaps anyhow I have over-emphasized the contemporary relations of literature; but that I think is inevitable whenever one looks closely at a single year. And it may sometimes be useful to turn from the difficult exactions of true literary criticism, and the large-scale map-making of literary history (I do not pretend that there has been much of either in this discourse) to writers and readers living in a given time and place, concerned with other things besides their writing and reading. When we look back, as we generally do, at past literature as something fixed and stable and serene, we overlook, unless they are forced on our notice, the strains and stresses that surround it: 'the sick hurry, the divided aims': the 'atmosphere tremulous with agitation'. We overlook also the contemporary divisions between writers, arising from the moral, religious, social, and aesthetic issues of the time. Looking at the past is always, as Thackeray found, a tight-rope act. We want to be detached and objective, to see great works of literature existing in their own right, timelessly out of context; but we ought not to smudge distinctions; to become what Carlyle called Lord Houghton 'Perpetual President of the Heaven-and-Hell Amalgamation Society'.

But we may both see the differences and see what transcends them. And if we choose rather to minimize differences, we have the great Victorians with us there too. They have their own Amalgamation Society. More magnanimously then than now, writers and readers were prepared to forget differences of opinion, to recognize greatness. 'Identity of sentiment, difference of opinion: these are the elements of a pleasant dialogue', says Carlyle in his *Life of Sterling*. And George Eliot, reviewing that work, was 'gladdened with a perception of the affinity that exists between noble souls, in spite of diversity of ideas'. Carlyle again wrote of his long friendship with John Stuart Mill 'agreeing in everything (save only in opinion)'. There is a moral in this for modern readers; too many conceive themselves exempt from reading Carlyle, chiefly on the grounds of presumed difference of opinion; that past is brought into our present, and Carlyle is seen as the ancestor of ideas which he would have hated. The modern reader's verdict might at least be subsequent to the act of reading. Or do his non-readers recall what Harriet Martineau said of Robert Owen 'He was not the man to think differently of a book for having read it'?

As I remarked at the beginning, the great writers sank differences of opinion, and read and admired each other. May I conclude with a few instances? Within the one year, 1851, George Eliot admired the sceptic Francis Newman (and she approved when he left the Ladies' College—as he did in May—as a protest against their dismissal of a Geography Professor of unorthodox religion); but she also admired the Birmingham lectures of his Roman Catholic brother, John Henry Newman. Again: one does not think of that Newman as a novel-reader. He said that he read no novels of which the general tendency did not make for righteousness. But he read and delighted in all Thackeray's novels. *Cor ad cor loquitur*. Again, Arnold called the Carlyle of *Latter-Day Pamphlets* a 'moral desperado'; but, looking back thirty years later, he remembered 'what moved us most (in Carlyle) was that which will always move the young most—the poetry, the eloquence . . .' Or, finally, one of the things that Charlotte Brontë disapproved of in Thackeray was his admiration for Fielding; she repudiated the supposed likeness between them ('he resembles Fielding as an eagle does a vulture'); but she prolonged her visit to London in 1851 especially to hear that particular lecture—'Nor was I disappointed . . . he put forth his great strength—and though I could not *agree*, I was forced to admire'. In those lectures Thackeray was not only searching the past for means of teasing the present. When he came to quote the closing lines of Pope's *Dunciad* he forgot his mischief, and became serious; he saw that this was something beyond satire on Grub Street; he recognized his ally:

It is Truth, the champion, shining and intrepid, and fronting the great world-tyrant with armies of slaves at his back. It is a wonderful and victorious single combat, in that great battle which has always been waging since society began.

Across differences and across time reach these gestures of essential recognition. Nor are we disqualified from them. I shall end by quoting Thackeray's advice in his 1851 lectures:

Might I give counsel to any young hearer, I would say to him, Try to frequent the company of your betters. In books and life that is the most wholesome society; learn to admire rightly; the great pleasure of life is that.

INDEX